Sustainable Development Goals Series

The **Sustainable Development Goals Series** is Springer Nature's inaugural cross-imprint book series that addresses and supports the United Nations' seventeen Sustainable Development Goals. The series fosters comprehensive research focused on these global targets and endeavours to address some of society's greatest grand challenges. The SDGs are inherently multidisciplinary, and they bring people working across different fields together and working towards a common goal. In this spirit, the Sustainable Development Goals series is the first at Springer Nature to publish books under both the Springer and Palgrave Macmillan imprints, bringing the strengths of our imprints together.

The Sustainable Development Goals Series is organized into eighteen subseries: one subseries based around each of the seventeen respective Sustainable Development Goals, and an eighteenth subseries, "Connecting the Goals", which serves as a home for volumes addressing multiple goals or studying the SDGs as a whole. Each subseries is guided by an expert Subseries Advisor with years or decades of experience studying and addressing core components of their respective Goal.

The SDG Series has a remit as broad as the SDGs themselves, and contributions are welcome from scientists, academics, policymakers, and researchers working in fields related to any of the seventeen goals. If you are interested in contributing a monograph or curated volume to the series, please contact the Publishers: Zachary Romano [Springer; zachary.romano@springer.com] and Rachael Ballard [Palgrave Macmillan; rachael.ballard@palgrave.com].

S. Mohammed Irshad

Economics of Disasters and Climate Change

Risk and Uncertainties

palgrave
macmillan

S. Mohammed Irshad
Jamsetji Tata School of Disaster Studies
Tata Institute of Social Sciences
Mumbai, Maharashtra, India

ISSN 2523-3084 ISSN 2523-3092 (electronic)
Sustainable Development Goals Series
ISBN 978-981-97-9414-0 ISBN 978-981-97-9415-7 (eBook)
https://doi.org/10.1007/978-981-97-9415-7

This Palgrave Macmillan imprint is published by the registered company Springer Nature Singapore Pte Ltd.
The registered company address is: 152 Beach Road, #21-01/04 Gateway East, Singapore 189721, Singapore

Preface

A book on risk economics arises out of my more than a decade of teaching disaster economics to postgraduate students. Risk has multiple manifestations globally; hence, each region experiences risk differently. Applying economic logic to risk is a need of time as climate and disaster risks increase over time. Disaster and climate risks are increasingly pushing a large section of the population into risks and uncertainty and also making public institutions into a crisis of governance. Disaster and climate risks are increasingly becoming an everyday reality now. No region or country is free from disaster and climate-induced risks; hence, every economic institution is subject to theoretical and policy-level interventions. This book offers a theoretical discussion on contextualizing the risk concerning risk sharing, governance, and applying economic tools in interpreting the impact of disaster and climate risk on the economy and society. Disaster and climate risks are further manifest on collective and individual economic behaviour. It could result in permanent changes in consumption patterns and also a shift in the priorities of development. Every natural calamity creates linkages effects, both forward and backward; hence, externalities of risk manifest according to the existing socio-economic structure of the economy.

Natural and climate-induced disasters are increasingly displacing a large section of the vulnerable population in the Global South. The International Displacement Monitoring Centre data shows that about 25.3

million people have been displaced since 2008 by sudden-onset disasters alone. Climate change also displaces communities, especially the ecosystem communities, from livelihood and existence. An *at-risk* society is increasingly emerging worldwide, and they are interfacing with risk society and class society in the Global South. Forming an at-risk population is the most significant political economy issue, as this at-risk population serves as an agent of economic transactions. Economists try to understand and capture the complexities of disaster and climate-induced risk in the Global South and North; however, these attempts are primarily confined to economic governance. For instance, Kahn (2005) and Keefer et al. (2011) discuss the relationship between income, fatality, and the democratic process of governing disasters. Disaster risk changes economic function and relations, including production, supply, capital mobility, and accumulation. Higher-income countries experience higher financial loss and low fatalities; however, low- and middle-income countries experience a low macro-economic loss with high fatalities. The economic analysis of disaster hardly moves beyond this empirical discourse. Evidence or incident-based theorization of disaster often fails to theorize the root causes of disaster risk creation in backward regions and countries.

The core and critical objectives of the book are to engage with the concept of risk and utility. So, the chapters reflect the theory and policy-level discussions on engaging and interfacing economic theories with emerging climate and disaster risks. This book starts with a detailed discussion of utility and risks, including expected utility. Changes in relative and absolute capital values due to disaster risk provide the scope for in-depth analysis of economic troubles. This chapter proposes to review and analyse the contemporary theories of financial risks and offers new critical insight into the linkages between economic risk to disaster and climate risks. The Chapter 1 focuses more on the Global South's experience of financial risks regarding development and social inequalities. So, this chapter carries a critical review of risk economic theories and connects it with the economic impact of natural and climate risks in the Global South. Sharing risk burden is an integral part of economics of disaster and climate risks. The Chapter 2 of the book offers a theoretical and conceptual debate on risk sharing and risk transfer mechanism. What makes this chapter important is that its discus the economic rationale of risk sharing by government investments in relief and responses. The government spends money to replace the capital from tax income; however, such replacement may not lead to capital mobility in developing countries like India. Disaster insurance is being emerged as a global platform to govern, manage and responds to disaster risks, however, there is huge gap in the capital which insurance firms accumulate the actual disbursements. There is huge gap in the ratio of insured losses and uninsured losses in developed and underdeveloped economies, so the causes of poor institutional growth of insurance firms in developing country like India are being discussed in Chapter 2 of the book. Risk sharing is indeed a project of governing risks as well; the chapter on risk governance offers a theoretical review of the economics of risk governance. The emerging and unprecedented impact of climate and disaster risks challenges the government and market's institutional capability to adapt to the risk and govern the crisis. The chapter discusses various conceptual and theoretical positions explaining risk and the institutional focus of adaptations.

There exists a general perception of the economics of disaster and climate risks and its economic implications in terms of asset loss. Chapters 4 and 5 discuss the economics of disaster and climate change in detail with reference to Global North to South. Chapter 4 discussed the theoretical base of disaster economics, its practices, and methods. The interface and impact of the disaster on production, supply shock, public expenditures, loss assessment method, economic inequalities, and capital assets of vulnerable communities are elaborated on in the chapter. The economic impact of the disaster in developing and underdeveloped countries is never equal to that in developed economies. The unequal distribution of risks and the differential impact of the disaster on the community and region is an important aspect that needs to be discussed, and the chapter on disaster economics has done justice to this critical question and elaborated on the essential interface of disaster and its economic costs. The economics of climate risk is a timely debate, and it is a global discourse as well. Assessing the economics of climate change is a complex process as it includes its causes, effects, and possible solutions. The economics of climate change is intricate and diverse. This area of study combines knowledge from public policy and environmental science. There is economics to reduce the impact of climate change risks in terms of loss of capital assets, infrastructure, and the general decline of economic productivity. Chapter 5 discusses the economics of carbon emission reduction and the political economy of carbon trade. The colonial method of carbon trade is a reality, and the chapter discusses it in detail. The effects of climate change are felt differently in different parts of the world, with certain places being more vulnerable than others because of their location, economy, and climate. Economically disadvantaged populations are frequently more susceptible to the consequences of climate change, which can worsen inequality. Climate change also necessitates climate action as well. Climate action is being given priority in the sustainable development goals; the core arguments of this book emphasize the critical importance of Goal 13 of sustainable development, i.e., climate action. Goal 13 has five major components, each requiring institutional and financial support to implement climate action. Increasing climate-induced disaster risk and its unequal economic impacts make risk mitigation inevitable. Building resilience and adaptive capability of the economy is possible through assessing and managing utilities and expectations. The developing economies are indeed forced to integrate climate action; however, they are often confronted by the expansion policies of capitalism. Chapters IV and V of the book discuss the importance and challenges of climate action in the context of disasters and climate change. The increasing economic impact of disaster and climate change also reflects the lack of proper climate action and integration of development with climate mitigation. Green funds, loss, capital funds, etc., are part of climate action and Goal 13 of the Sustainable Development Goal. Increasing risk and capitalization make climate action an institutional challenge, so any discussion on climate action should be located in a broader context.

The book offers a comprehensive and critical interface of economic theories with disaster and climate risks in the global context with reference to the Global South.

Mumbai, India S. Mohammed Irshad

Acknowledgement

The idea of this book evolved from my postgraduate level teaching of disaster economics and risk economics. I thank my students for asking questions and commenting while delivering lectures; those interactions helped me conceptualize this book's chapter. I thank Prof Jacquleen Joseph, dean, Jamsetji Tata School of Disaster Studies, Tata Institute of Social Sciences to enable an environment for debate and our short conversations on various issues, and I thank my colleagues, Prof Janki Andharia, Prof Nirmalya Choudhary, Mr. Mahesh Kamble, Dr. Vineet Kumar, Dr. Lavanya Aravind, Ms. Niti Mishra, Dr. Rameesh Veerapan, Ms. Saumya Kumar and Dr. Ravinder Dhimman for creating a vibrant academic environment for debate and discussions. I am incredibly thankful to Ms. Aparajita Singh, editor of Palgrave Macmillan, for suggesting chapter scheme changes in the book in this format. I thank my colleague, Dr. Luthufi M, Prof Sunil D Santha, Dr. Devisha Dr. Yahiya for their patient listening. It is also the moment to thank my teacher and PhD guide Prof G Karunakaran Pillai and Prof N C Narayanan for all support to pursue my academic life.

I am continually thankful to the late Prof M. Kunhaman for encouraging me to think critically and question the dominant discourse of the time. I thank my wife, Sajitha, for her support, love, and care and my children, Amaan and Aaima, for their warm and loving support. I thank my father, Sharafudeen, my mother, Ozeela, and my sister Jaseetha, Shamnad, Nizam and, my nieces and in-laws for their support during this journey.

Contents

List of Figures

List of Tables

List of Boxes

CHAPTER 1

Theorizing Risk Economics

Risk economics is a theoretical inquiry of expected utility theory (EU), and the EU is closely associated with probabilities. The history of the EU traces back to the concept of the St. Petersburg Paradox. It talks about the people's willingness to make small sacrifices for higher expected benefits. It is a game in which the person desires a probability of outcome from each attempt. It is about tossing a coin and expecting the value. To resolve the St. Petersburg conundrum, Bernoulli proposed in "Specimen theoriae novae de mensura sortis" that individuals should maximize the expected value of a utility function as opposed to the expected value of financial outcomes (Bernoulli, 1954). The expected utility theory's tenets are frequently broken by people's decisions, as demonstrated by the Allais paradox, which raises the possibility that the theory falls short of accurately describing people's actual decision-making behaviour (Allais, 1953). The normative process for designing an experiment involves determining a utility function, evaluating the likelihoods, and selecting the design with the highest expected utility. A problem with this perspective is that a scientist usually has no notion, nor should one be expected to have, precisely the practical implications of his findings (Bernardo, 1979). The relevance of expected utility theory in economics is emphasized by highlighting it as a critical theory for risk-averse decision-making when the probability distribution of events is known (Takemura, 2021). People who

S. M. Irshad, *Economics of Disasters and Climate Change*, Sustainable Development Goals Series,
https://doi.org/10.1007/978-981-97-9415-7_1

participate in this game expect higher utility value by paying less. Sharpe's (2007) study argues that the utility function may be more complex than that of mean–variance analysis, and the objective of asset allocation is to maximize predicted utility. Based on the supposition that a single representative investor wants to maximize expected returns, the analysis's inputs are. Scholars have attempted to understand the complexities associated with decision-making and utility expectations. Gul and Pesendorfer (2006), in their study, observed that a decision made at random rule maximizes a random utility function only if it is a mixture of continuous, monotone (i.e., when more lotteries are added to the decision problem, the probability of a lottery being chosen does not increase), extreme (i.e., the probability of choosing a lottery is 0 for those that are not the decision problem's extreme points), and linear.

Decisions to participate in the match arise from linear or complex expectations. Time also influences the decision to participate in gambling (Cowen & High, 1988). Here, time could be the temporal context as well. What is needed to have an epistemology to define risk economics rather than move around utility theories? Still, one cannot give up the importance of utility theory and approach in theorizing expectations. An evolutionary epistemology needs to be applied to understand the complexities of risk economics. Campbell (1974) developed the evolutionary epistemology, and one could connect it to Darwin's theory of evolution. Evolutionary epistemology is a method to understand the evolution of ideas, norms, and concepts. Evolutionary epistemology offers an in-depth theoretical inquiry into risk economics. It also enables a scholarly assessment of expected utility as the base of evolving risk economics and moves around risk and uncertainty. Some scholars attempt to understand the basic ideas that underpin rational decision-making processes are crucial, as seen by the emphasis on interpreting axioms in decision-making under ambiguity (Grant & Van Zandt, 2007).

The complexities associated with decision-making indeed reflect the expected effectiveness of decision-making. Strategic decision-makers more influenced by the effect of framing a decision (Sebora & Cornwall, 1995). In the prospects theory, decision-makers, like Simon (1955), prefer to satisfy rather than maximize when making decisions by cognitively simplifying them.

Davis et al. (1998) argue that decision-makers choose between risk and uncertainty in comparing expected utility values. Uncertainty can be associated with an information state in which a choice may have various outcomes, the likelihood of which may not be known (Mathieu-Nicot, 1986). Expected utility is a game based on a binary of results. The "expected utility" is considered as a method to mathematically assess the expectations of the variable $U(x)$ (the individual's "utility of wealth") if wealth x has distribution $P = (\times 1,\ p1, \ldots,\ xm,\ pm)$ (Machina, 2003). The expected utility of action also relates to the marginal utility of wealth (Rabin, 1999). Expecting higher marginal utility also drives individual actions in gambling and lotteries. Theories of expected utility broadly use statistical probability techniques to assess the chance of getting a utility that is quite appropriate for the person who participates in the decision-making. The decision on utility depends on a comparative assessment of the loss of a small amount with a chance to win a significant amount. People choose uncertainty in preference to certainty (Friedman & Savage, 1948). Decisions about expected utility are connected with the certainty effect and the probability of distortion effect (Munier, 1986). Expected utility theories assume that there is consistency in decision-making; however, it may not be true that there would be errors in computing expected utility (Blavatskyy, 2007). Individuals have a specific reason to participate in choosing multiple attempts to satisfy their expectations; however, the ability to interpret the utility or benefit plays an important role. Decision-making on expected utility function is close to guaranteeing expected utility interpretation (Snow, 1987). An agent's desire and choice play an essential role in maximizing the minimum expected utility (Karni, 2014).

The expectation of utility is closer to the awareness of risk and uncertainties. Expected utility theory is based on anticipation, asset integration, and risk aversion (Kahneman & Tversky, 1979). Decision-makers often mentally construct a state-space to organize their thoughts and influence the expectations' probabilities (Karni, 2006). Making a mental space or state is the process of preparing to avoid risks or manage the risks. Yaari (1987) proposes a dual approach to expected utility theory. Yarris argues that in the expected utility approach, an agent's preference towards wealth is forward bonded together. Yarris proposed the idea of a decumulative distribution function to define expected utility theory. Some scholars argue that non-additive measures should be considered in utility maximization in the context of Rawlsian social utility function (Hougaard & Keiding, 2005). Rawls (1971) argues, *'greatest net balance of satisfaction summed over all the individuals belonging to it'*. Rawls (1971) discusses utility as the satisfaction of desire as the satisfaction of rational selfishness.

The Rawlsian concept is that expecting utility is rational desire. It could be otherwise read as the rationale for the welfare of worst-off individuals in society.

The initial non-stochastic wealth of the decision-maker may challenge the usual interpretations of expected utility (Fukuba & Ito, 1984). A theoretical inquiry into risk economics is critically connected with utility maximization and risk aversion. It is also about a consumer behaviour approach as well. In an uncertain context, an economic agent assesses the expected utility of each action (Bryant, 2014). Econometric models of expected utility also consider secretive expansion of choice (Zellner & Zilberman, 2011). An individual has all the right to be rational while engaging with market-led choices. In a rational choice approach, a consumer has specific strong preferences; however, such strong preferences are seldom possible to practice in an uncertain situation. The utility is nonlinear in probabilities, and the expected projective utility is also nonlinear regarding risk. It is often linear concerning subject-specific uncertainty (La Mura, 2009). A rational agent expects a linear process to maximize the return. It is a conscious effort to seek utility; however, linearity in expecting favourable results in every action is hardly possible.

The epistemology of risk economics is the rationality of expecting utility from economic decision-making. The lottery method has been used to define the expected utility theory in general; however, a rational decision-maker does have a reason to imagine a diverse set of expected utilities. The epistemic base of utility theories is agents' decision, and any decision-making crisis influences utility expectations. It is imperative to see that decision-makers inability to assess the exact value of probabilities has some crucial economic relevance. It is otherwise called imprecise probabilities (Segal, 1987). Some scholars argue that expected utility cannot be measured based on intervals. However, it should depend on risk-taking behaviour (Van der Hoek & Sherris, 2001). A decision-maker's ability to forecast utility is associated with preference over commodities and being averse to risks. Decision-making is a rational process and expects the maximum possible fortune from actions. In a decision-theoretic framework, success is measured based on an arbitrary preference for outcomes (Haddawy & Hanks, 1998).

Decision-making in gambling is to avoid the risks that lead to loss, and the probability is a decisive factor. The risk and probability of getting an expected utility determine the maximum return for participating in gambling. Every decision-maker attempts to avoid the risk of unexpected returns. Riskiness is based on the uncertainty of outcomes resulting from the uncertainty of state occurrence, and the decision-makers expected utility. A higher state of uncertainty results in higher risks and vice versa (Yang & Qiu, 2005). Risk-taking is an organised behaviour it needs the skill and capability to understand utility. It assumes that the decision-makers are conscious of their activities while choosing a utility. The hypothesis on expected utility determines and influences the decision-making criteria (Pötzsch, 1972). One could see the rational relationship between decisions and expectations of utility. Economic decision-making is based on the expectation of a higher return on values.

The Code of Hammurabi, The Babylonian text of 2250 BC could be read as the first authentic method of modulating risk behaviour. This document proposed a risk premium on the travel of commodities to regulate risk-taking behaviour. A risk premium on a voyage to ensure loss, and the risk premium was proportional to the risk of the journey (Harper, 1904). Risk-taking behaviour represents the individual perception of ability and willingness to engage with risks. Personal capability often interfaces with the institutions and builds risk-taking behaviour. The capability approach is a well-discussed concept in development economics. Risk and capability are correlated regarding the ability to choose, measure utility, and perceive uncertainties.

Sen (1985: 129) explained capability as a function to achieve or to reach out to what they manage to do or be. It is about an individual's ability to have an active state of being, such as good health, shelter, mobility, and education. Risk tolerance itself is a capability; however, it does not exist in itself. Capability is a relative process, and one must consider its institutional process to ensure risk tolerance. Institutional intervention in society is essential here in defining capability. In a developmental discourse, inequality and risk are mutually correlated and determine utility expectations. Poverty traps influence risk-taking behaviour (Lybbert & Barrett, 2010). Poverty affects economic behaviour and causes a negative state of affairs, leading to risk-averse (Haushofer & Fehr, 2014). People's exposure to disaster and ability to withstand the risk is an example to prove this relationship. Figure 1.1 gives a general overview of the correlation between vulnerability and hazard exposure. A vicious circle exists between poverty and disaster losses (Hallegatte et al., 2020). The ability to withstand a natural disaster risk is closely associated with vicious cycles of poverty and inequality. Proper benefit–cost analysis is essential for DRR (Hochrainer-Stigler et al., 2019).

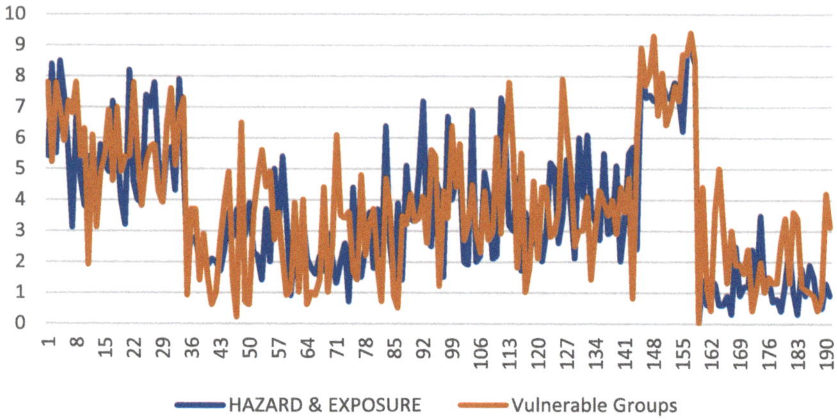

Fig. 1.1 Hazard and vulnerable population (*Source* www.ourworldindata.org)

The economic system plays a vital role in determining risk tolerance. Macro-level empirical research proved that higher GDP tends to reduce disaster mortalities. Disaster risk increases with poverty (Kellenberg & Mobarak, 2008). GDP cannot be an indicator to assess the disaster damage; the best option is to determine the loss of stock of durable goods, housing, and productive capital or the reduced aggregate investment expenditure (Strulik & Trimborn, 2019). Governments prefer to look into aggregate economic loss due to natural disasters. Aggregate loss due to a natural catastrophe explains the total capital stock from a micro or macro perspective. The financial analysis of capital stock is about destroying the use value of capital, and the risk is the replacement cost of capital. The risk of capital replacement is an un-economic process in any economy. The theory of money is about exchange, production, and capitalization (Montesano, 2008). The study of capital is about seeing how an economy develops over time, and capital is about the means of production and consumption (Usher, 1965).

Capital is money, and it is not just an object alone. Rather, it is the system of rules that connect empirical individuals triadically and not dyadic (Cartelier, 2007). Capital is the circulation of money from one form to another. Marx defined it as C–M–C. Commodities transform into money and again into commodities. This cycle of operations M–C–M creates surplus value, so capital is the surplus value of the means of production. So, capital has value. Capital is subject to depreciation, and all investment decisions consider depreciation while preparing the investment. Depreciation-induced capital replacement is critical to assessing diminishing returns and declining marginal productivity. The existing method and ideas of capital replacement are driven by different business models that operate with diverse economic interests. Capital replacement is also associated with taxation (Moore, 1987). The application of replacement of capital depends on the circumstances (Scarf, 2002). Time plays a vital role in capital replacement. The capital replacement in the normative system is driven by the motive to earn profits and sustain the business model. Natural calamities displace the normative practices of capital replacement.

Approaching disaster as an event of 'destruction' necessitates immediate capital replacement to continue the business. The business continuity process (BCP) theorizes it as a project to prevent market disruption and retain the market. BCP models always look for an active market-driven agent to take the lead in overcoming the crisis of capital replacement. However, the mounting climate and slow onset risks push the capital value into a crisis. The economic cost of replacement could be visible; however, the climate risk and natural disasters make the marginal utility reduction also assessed to see the increasing cost of replacement. Capital replacement is an investment, too, so one could expect an incentive to put capital into replacing the lost money. The destructive impact of natural disasters pushes the value of capital down, and climate-induced hazards slowly decrease the value of capital. Economic decision-making on replacement capital is a complex process. It depends on the macro–micro economic characteristics and the economy's institutional structure. The fundamental question is who will invest in replacement capital. Any such investment decision should be able to assess both the externality and accelerating effect of investments. Disasters replace the economic process, including the production and distribution process; hence, a standard return to capital is impossible for investments. Regional economic disparities and the mounting income gap of disaster-affected communities explain this crisis. Economic recovery answers these questions; however, recovery from a natural disaster depends on output recovery in a given spatial and temporal context. Proper economic recovery depends on estimating spatial disaster loss (Wu et al., 2014). Disasters in a local region may not create any macroeconomic impact or make other impacts due to recovery (Albala-Bertrand, 2007). The post-disaster period should be considered context to recognize the need to reduce vulnerability (Jouannic et al., 2016). Capital replacement is driven by the time taken to recover from a disaster. Economic recovery is also often measured in time (as in "years to recover") (Chang & Rose, 2012). Time is a financial cost, and it influences the expectations of utility as well. Utility also has a temporal dimension and influences society's perception.

Economic recovery is an integral part of capital replacement. Financial recovery from a natural disaster depends on proper procedures and direction (Sardana & Dasanayaka, 2013). An economic system in which the disaster occurred influences the behaviour of the capital to increase its value. Replacing lost capital is possible through the divers' use of capital. Flexible use of variable capital is among them, and labour is one of the most flexible variable capital. Flexibility in labour and market determines economic resilience (Van De Klundert, 1986). Flexible use of labour is a capitalist project to enhance production in a given time; however, the command economies like China also apply labour flexibility with state control. One needs to define resilience with the specific context here. Resilience is theorized as the ability to bounce back; otherwise, it is the process of expecting maximum utility.

Economic decision-making to increase efficiency and productivity becomes reactive and causes a loss of resilience (Admiraal et al., 2013). The market can define resilience with specific reference to market risks, i.e., challenges of running a commodity market. The market often dominates the resilience concepts in emerging market economies. Perrings (2006) defines resilience as "*the ability of the system to withstand either market or environmental shocks without losing the capacity to allocate resources efficiently or to deliver essential services*". Perrings' idea of resilience explains the complexities of focusing on resilience as an extension of the economic system. Economic resilience needs to be specifically discussed and has differential impacts on the economy and communities. Economic resilience is about the policy-induced ability of an economy to recover from the negative effects of adverse exogenous shocks and to benefit from positive shocks (Briguglio et al., 2009). Economic resilience is essential for replacing capital since it carries forward the existing economic production and distribution process. A positive correlation exists between economic resilience, capital replacement, and utility maximization. Developed economies with high capital bases and practical use value could replace capital faster. Economic resilience is about the ability of the system to recover its growth path or otherwise throw it off the growth path (Hill et al., 2008: 4). It is about the capacity of an economy to reconfigure its structure and to maintain an acceptable growth path in output and employment (Martin, 2012: 10).

The institutional capability of the economy determines economic resilience. The market plays a vital role in replacing the values and continuing the business process. Financial resilience is about the ability of a system to maintain its function (Rose, 2007). An economist talks about the risk of investing in emerging market economies. Those risks are primarily volatile credit markets, governance, legal protection, and commodity market constraints. Such risks are being assessed based on the volume of capital investment and sources of the investments. Capital expects state protection as well. There are risks other than the market, which displaces the devalued volume of investment and often makes it idle for the short run. From a practical perspective, resilience is about the rate at which capital accumulates its replacement value. Resilience increases the speed of recovery from a shock (Rose & Krausmann, 2013). Resilience is about the system's elasticity to rebound after a shock (Seeliger & Turok, 2013: 2119). Disasters and climate risks often make one look at the elasticity of the production and distribution debates. The contextual meaning of economic resilience is about ensuring the utility value of the resources, primarily capital.

Economic resilience is also about the system's ability to absorb shocks without any catastrophic changes in the basic structure of the institutions (Reggiani et al., 2002). Economic resilience could be captured as sustaining the utility of the capital. The long-run process of resilience building does not offer a better result, so some scholars argue that the short-run process focusing on business behaviour would be effective (Rose & Krausmann, 2013). Economic resilience is meant to analyse the speed with which a system returns to pre-disaster conditions or the capacity of the system to reach new possible equilibria (Modica & Reggiani, 2014). Resilience as returning to a pre-disaster state is a minimalist definition, which is quite acceptable worldwide as a convenient concept. It could also be called a reductionist approach to resilience. Pre-disaster vulnerability and the cumulative effect of hazards that lead to disaster exposure are often neglected in articulating resilience.

The differential impact of vulnerability on resilience determines the long-term impact of a disaster. It could also be economic; however, economic resilience does not have a linear flow. As Duval et al. (2007) argue, economic resilience may be loosely defined as maintaining output close to potential in the aftermath of shocks. Externalities also matter in practising economic resilience. The ability of the financial system to consider risk as a reduction of the capital value and increase the replacement value of capital is determined by the economic policies of the country or the region. There is a specific definition of resilience; hence, opportunity cost is tough to define (Regibeau & Rockett, 2013). The opportunity cost of the disaster is very critical, and it is true that in developing countries, disaster results in negative externalities. Opportunity cost is otherwise called changes in utility preferences. Often, the risk of externalities is unequally distributed and accumulates in vulnerable communities. The institutional understanding of resilience must capture the risk accumulation in vulnerable communities. Capturing economic resilience is a complex process that needs to be incorporated into the loos assessment (Rose, 2004). Financial resilience is generally a linear process because it has specific institutional methods to follow, such as income, capital replacement, livelihood restoration. Economic resilience refers to an equilibrium point in which the economy reaches at least a break-even point. Pimm (1984) defines resilience as a process in which an ecosystem returns to its former equilibrium state. The issue at which equilibrium is fixed is zero loss or retaining the break-even, so this break-even is different across economies and societies.

The economy's size and growth path matter at break-even points. Here, one needs to refer to the stages of theory. W. W. Rostow explained his economic development concepts in the book 'The Stages of Economic Growth: A Non-Communist Manifesto.' Capitalist economists consider this classical book as an alternative to the communist manifesto of Marx and Lenin. The political importance of this work is that it has tried to develop a counter-narrative of the Marxian theory of historical materialism. He developed an approach to trace society's development through five stages. His model began with the idea of a traditional society. Rostow (1991) explained that a traditional society develops its structure within limited production functions, which is based on the pre-Neo-Newtonian perspective of science and technology and pre-Neot Newtonian attitudes towards the physical world. The traditional society that Rostow explained still exists in backward economies. The socio-economic conditions of both rural India and the African regions justify Rostow's theory. The theory also critiques the evolutionary model of development. Apart from rural India and African regions, disaster-affected areas and disaster-prone areas also justify Rostow's perception of a traditional society. Disaster and climate risk forcefully introduce specific changes in economic behaviour, and hence, society often moves back to the pre-capitalist nature of production and distribution.

The sudden loss of capital base and production structure in vulnerable regions leaves the community without resources. Modern science is embraced for economic progress. However, it would not be an immediate requirement for a disaster-affected community. Their goal, instead, is to survive or to regain the loss. The survivors hardly demand speedy economic progress.

Moreover, the dilapidated infrastructure in affected areas barely allows for such a growth rate. Applying stages of growth theory in a disaster context does not endorse the theories and politics around this model. However, the concept of stages of growth is critical since disasters deviate the economy's growth path. Deviating from the economy's existing growth path slows economic recovery after disasters. Also, the stages of the growth model remind us that disaster loss is different across the community and region. Regional developmental disparities are important in determining the nature and impact of disaster risks. Say's (Baptiste Say, 1821) law defines the market as a space where demands are demonstrated, goods are exchanged, and money is only facilitated. Say's law argues that all products would reach where they are demanded. The evolution of the law of market traces back to the European system of massive production in the later part of the eighteenth and early nineteenth centuries (Rassekh, 2017: 126). Keynesian revolution questioned this massive European production and proposed the concept of practical demands. The nature of the market has considerably evolved, and it has become a decisive force in determining the risks and uncertainties as well. The theories of market perfection imperfections try to homogenize the production process towards surplus. The perfectly competitive market idea is being prioritized in the modern economic strategy, which is why competitive market economies consider disaster as a force to disrupt the market. It deviates from the growth path of the economy. It is pretty visible in the present context of climate risks. Capital growth depends on the economic utility expected. The following section discusses the interface between risk and expected utilities.

1.1 Risk and Expected Utility

The utility was first conceived as quantitatively measurable satisfaction, and there are criteria for comparing the preferences (Von Neumann & Morgenstern, 1953). In decision-making, risk and expected utility theory are closely related ideas. As several writers have explained, expected utility theory offers a framework for assessing decisions involving uncertainty by taking into account the probabilities of various events and the corresponding benefits. However, this hypothesis has come under fire for failing to take into account the changing stages of knowledge and attitudes about risk. It is fact that people can either be attracted to or averse to risk, which calls into question the conventional expected utility paradigm. Furthermore, especially when dealing with big stakes, the concavity of utility functions in expected-utility theory may result in excessively high levels of risk aversion. Ultimately, even if expected utility theory is a key idea in making decisions under uncertainty, in order to give a more thorough understanding of risk in decision-making, it is crucial to take into account changing knowledge, attitudes towards risk, and the constraints of utility functions. As explained before, utilitarianism is an instinct that drives economic production. In decision-making, risk and expected utility theory are closely related ideas. As described by a number of authors, expected utility theory offers a framework for assessing decisions with uncertainty by taking into account the benefits that correspond with distinct events and their probabilities. However, this hypothesis has come under fire for failing to take into account how knowledge and attitudes towards risk evolve over time (Pope & Selten, 2009; Mathew, 2000). Expecting a specific utility from a product is associated with normative choices and decision-making. Statistically expected utility is assessed based on the weighted average of the expected utilities of each outcome, and this outcome is preferred in comparison with the other alternatives. Expected utilities depend on independent decision-making (Luce & Krantz, 1971). Decisions could be subjective and objective in terms of expectations. All rational decision-making is to expect to get maximum utilities and wants to avoid interfacing with risks. Axioms of decision theories prefer to put expected value with certainty effects; however, risk displaces the certainty effects on expectations. If the risk is embedded in decision-making, then the choice would not be rational. Risk dictates the choices. Preference over utility is encoded with the sensitivity of risks (Pettigrew, 2015). Buchak (2013) theorizes the risk-weighted expected utility theory in the context of choices. Buchak argues that risk is a function of neither belief nor desire; instead, it measures how to structure the potential realization of aims. It is a subjective probability function. Rudra (1966) explains that probability is a numerical method to measure the relationship between a hypothesis and an event. The event may not determine the hypothesis, so it is a question of subjectivity, and often, the probability is also a generalization. Choosing if a formal theory is feasible is the challenge of probability theory. Such a theory would be impersonal in the same sense as common logic: if various individuals starting with the same evidence followed the rule, they would all arrive at the same conclusions (Jeffreys, 1955).

Probability could be an expectation of defined values. Nagel (1939) argues that coins bearing distinct marks (such as the position of the centre of gravity) fall roughly equally frequently on either side when tossed in particular ways. The interpretation of the chance that heads will come up depends on the style of argument used to derive the assertion. Negal's statement is situated in the context of the Second World War, and hence, it was a period of crisis and recovery. Probability and risk have a complex relationship, and in a crisis, its agent expects probability with certainty effects. Rottenstreich and Hsee (2001) observed that putting more weight on the worst-case scenario with fear and putting more weight on the best-case scenario with hope. For an economist, putting differential weightage to decision-making is subject to prediction and loss of capital/asset/market value. The recurring effects and externalities of assets are important in determining utility expectations as Hagen (1979) identifies a preference for positive skewness with hope and a preference for negative skewness with anxiety. The economic conditions of society influence the skewness; a vulnerable economy always expects positive skewness.

Keynes (1921) argues that the terms 'certain and probable' define the various degrees of rational belief and expectations. Keynes's theory of probability is a neoclassical approach to uncertainty, as demonstrated by indifferences. Keynes (1921: 45) argues that '*The Principle of Indifference asserts that if there is no known reason for predicating of our subject one rather than another of several alternatives, then relatively to such knowledge the assertions of each of these alternatives have an equal probability. Thus, equal probabilities must be assigned to each of several arguments if there is an absence of positive ground for assigning unequal ones*'. The

Keynesian concept evolved from a historical context in which the global economy was subject to a market crisis. Keynesian theory of short-run introduces a new set of economic approaches that expect equal probability in each of actions. The short-run economy runs on maximum probability expectations. The Keynesian theory introduces various propositions to engage with risk and probability. Cate and Johnson (1998) observe that given specific empirical facts, Keynes proposed an objective degree of belief theory of probability based on the objective degree of belief in an expected event. This idea offers an alternate approach to determining the prerequisites for a stable society. Keynes also looked at the factors influencing the speculative demand for money using his subjective degree of belief hypothesis. Keynesian approach to stable economic value and output offers a more comprehensive theoretical inquiry into the risk and uncertainty in post-war economies. Investment and demand are the two core concerns of Keynesian economics, subject to risk and uncertainties. Positive probability or certainty over outcomes is the expectation of every investment; however, such linearity is hardly possible in an environment where the probability of risk exists. Uncertainty refers to situations in which probabilities are neither known nor can be deduced, calculated, or estimated objectively (Gilboa et al., 2008).

Risk is known probabilities, and their effects may vary from situation to situation. Some scholars attempt to study the changing risk preference nature of human beings, and they argue that two-thirds are genetically and one-third are environmentally determined (Zyphur et al., 2009). This theory may not be appropriate in the present context of risk embedded in decision-making and investments. Knight (1921), in the study, made the critical observation that "risk" designates situations in which probabilities are known or knowable in the sense that they can be estimated from past data and calculated using the laws of probability (Knight, 1921). Economists use the method of forecasting profitability and return, using multiple indicators to arrive at a decision or prediction. For instance, inflation forecasting is based on money supply, interest rate, community price, disposable income, macroeconomic variables, etc. The forecaster may give different weights to each variable and attempt to provide perfect results. There is another taker for the prediction. However, the critical question is how the agent assigns risk-weighted expectations on each variable. James (1896) points out that we must choose between two competing goals: avoiding error and believing the truth. William's theorization of assuming risk as fact is the issue of risk governance. So, decision-making under risk includes the probabilities of different possibilities, and the weight assigned to each outcome is the probability of the result (Pettigrew, 2022). Economic risk is certainty on value loss or gain; hence, the agent should understand utilities critically. A rational financial agent would assess the outcome. It also considers the weighted average of the utilities of each possible product (Fishburn, 1982).

The economic risk is highly correlated to the flow of capital in developed market economies; however, it affects the investment in stock capital in developing economies. Economists mainly consider the market risks regarding capital market loss and interest rate fluctuations. Liquidity crisis and market risk are given priority in risk analysis (Holmström & Tirole, 2000; Jorion, 2010). Analysis of economic risks primarily focuses on liquidity and capital market risks, and the economic risk assessment framework is quite effective in evaluating financial market risks. Economic risk assessments focus on (i) capital adequacy ratio, (ii) return on assets, (iii) bank credit over bank deposits, (iv) cumulative 3-year growth in credit to GDP, and (v) foreign liabilities assessed as foreign loans and deposits over domestic credit (Ahuja et al., 2017). The market economist applies this method to frame and evaluate the risk to find solutions. Economic risk assessment is used to make decisions. Real-world subjectivity, ambiguity, and vagueness are the primary causes of risks being challenging to manage. Consequently, risk analysis, mitigation, and control guide wise decisions (Abdel-Basseta et al., 2019). The probability theory has changed and still governs risk (Bernstein, 1998). Economists see the probability of risk and loss along with the benefits options. The trouble is the likelihood that a hazard will materialize and the extent of that occurrence (Tummala & Schoenherr, 2011). Each variable of the general economic risk assessment is subject to risk regarding hazards and vulnerabilities.

1.2 Risk and Utility Are Mutually Correlated

Risk changes the utility of economic action. A vague definition of risk includes the potential for a negative consequence (Moskowitz & Bunn, 1987). Its negative return on investment is the most critical aspect of risk and utility. Utility could be an individual's choice over returns of economic decision-making. Risk is related to the probability of an event occurring. These two are volatile. Risk presents uncertainty and pushes the marginal utility down, so the risk determines the utility level. Fear of failure and loss determines the risk-taking behaviour (Hancock & Teevan,

1964). Risk is not an independent event and has no forward or backward linkages. Economic risk is having forward and backward linkages and may change from the context of context. The probability of risk is associated with the changes in financial decision-making and dependent variables in economics. Behavioural, technological, and natural factors affect the risks. Individual strategies only sometimes meet collective challenges (Hausken, 2002). So, risk in economics often acts as an independent and dependent variable, too. Risk as an independent variable is related to macroeconomic variables such as interest rate, market volatility, and consumption behaviour of the economy and society. Risk is determined by the general social and economic vulnerability of an economy/society. A financial agent assesses risk concerning utility.

The defining risk is determined by the consequences it should include (Fischhoff et al., 1984).

The utility is an independent factor that determines the acceptability of risk. Economic utility has a demonstration effect, and it influences risk perceptions. Changing marginal utility is the driving force that determines the utility and dangers. Maximizing expected utility is similar to avoiding risks and minimizing the probability of loss or gain (Weirich, 1986)—economic definition of marginal and instrument of changing value. Macvane (1893), in the eighteenth century, argues that marginal utility is an exchange value, too. Macvane's theory is derived from classical mercantilist history. Still, in economic discourse, marginal utility is correlated to exchange. The risk could become an agent that fixes the utility's exchange value over one commodity over another. Gossen ([1854] 1983) developed a concept called Gossen's First Law, which says that more of one good consumed in each unit provided less addition. This theory has indeed influenced the understanding of the marginal utility in consumption. It is an empirical fact based on a specific pattern of consumption, and it largely depends on an individual's ability to consume. Vickrey (1945) argues that only the quantity of one other commodity y, but not necessarily all the other commodities, determines the marginal utility of one commodity x.

Disaster risk is widely recognized as the diminishing return or risk return. The belief is that independent risk is substituted for independent risk rather than being complementary when one danger is avoided (Quiggin, 2003). Disaster risk is dependent on the amount of diminishing utility. It could be ecological risks, vulnerability, and climate change. As said before, economists consider risk a loss of value, including negative externalities. Any increase in uncertainty would increase the expected long-run capital stock (Abel, 1984). The value of capital and growth in a normative economic system depends on a lack of delays; hence, risk has a demonstrated impact. It determines the flow and stock of capital. Flow capital is assumed to be proportional to the level of stock capital (Shashua et al., 1974). In a capitalist concept, risk has broader definitions and implications. The capitalist production process follows the idea of fully utilizing capital; hence, user or opportunity cost becomes a serious concern. Keynes's (1936) theory of user cost explains that it is the link between the present and the future. It is a choice to use up the resources for the present and keep them for future use. There is a positive correlation between capital utilization and economic development (Chatterjee, 2005). Therefore, risk and utility have equal weightage in a financial analysis of capitalism. Non-capitalist and command economies always prefer to supplement the diminishing marginal utility with public support.

A significant issue with loss aversion is determining the reference point around which gains and losses are defined. Kahneman and Tversky (1979) assume that the reference point is prior wealth. Risk reduction in this specific context is capitalization. Koszegi and Rabin (2006, 2007, 2009) create a loss aversion model with endogenous reference points, where one's expectations choose the reference point for the future, and one's choice determines those expectations. Asset volatility is a critical concern (Nwogugu, 2006). Risk and asset value often dictate the economic assessment of risks. Every investment expects an amount of depreciation, and such values are assessed as part of investments. Risk and utility could be otherwise called value at risks. The risk of natural disasters, climate change, and war puts the utility at risk, hence capital loss and its recurring value. Some assess utility by compatible risk measures to see the possibility of risk return (Bell, 1995). The value-at-risk (VaR) analysis is the worst loss over a target horizon with a given confidence level (Gençay et al., 2003). It affects the business prospects; hence, value at risk makes investment decisions at risk. This has to be discussed from the significant perspective of climate change and disaster risks.

1.3 Utility and Disaster Loss

Utility loss is the term used to describe the reduction in benefit or level of pleasure that an individual or entity feels as a result of a specific action, event, or choice. This idea is frequently applied in decision theory, economics, and other disciplines that deal with risk management and optimization. The term "utility loss" in economics refers to a decline in customer satisfaction brought on by adjustments in prices, income, or spending habits. In the context of finance, it could allude to the decline in investor utility brought on by investment losses. Utility loss is closely related to expectations of utility in a normative context. Effective risk management and opportunity evaluation depends on an understanding of the role that uncertainty plays in decision-making processes (Briggs et al., 2012). Although risk is frequently associated with the possibility of unfavourable outcomes, it is closely related to the ambiguity around possible occurrences (Vilko et al., 2014). The possibility that uncertainty may give rise to both hazards and opportunities further complicates the relationship between risk management and uncertainty (Qazi et al., 2021). While reducing variability has been a common emphasis of traditional risk management techniques, it is also crucial to take into account ambiguity and lack of clarity in project contexts (Rabechini & Carvalho, 2013). Utility loss is the term used to describe how changes in remuneration, such as lower benefits or higher taxes, affect a person's general well-being or happiness (Melese et al., 1992). As said before, utility is an expectation of return from economic decisions and choices—the interface of utility and disaster results in differential impacts. Disaster and disaster risk push utility into a volatile condition. The asset values are subject to change during disasters. It is indeed the most critical aspect of disaster management that changes the economy's general structure. The value assigned to capital assets varies both naturally and humanely. Figure 1.2 gives a general overview of disaster loss at the global level.

General economic growth and disaster loss are correlated. Higher per capita income reduces the fatalities; however, a higher income level results in a higher loss. A close relationship exists between economic impact and economic conditions (Padli et al., 2010). The asset at risk is high as the GDP grows, and so does the risk of volatile utility. The critical concern is the capital asset pricing model (CAPM) and its applications in disaster contexts. CAPM is based on firm expectations about the economy and the preferences of investors. A speculator focuses on outperforming the market, while an investor attempts to balance risk and return to balance current and future consumption (Vovk & Shafer, 2008). CAPM model looks for an expected rate of a rerun on investment, and risk is integrated into this framework. The risk could be a market risk or anything that disrupts capital growth. It is being used in assessing financial risks.

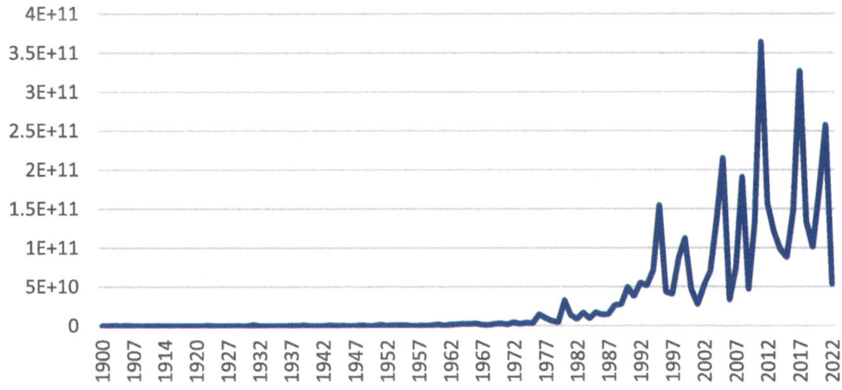

Fig. 1.2 Total economic damage from natural disasters (*Source* www.ourworldindata.org)

The CAPM model accepts that investors are risk-averse and demand extra return as compensation for bearing risk (Chen, 2021). CAPM model evolved to understand the complexities of investment behaviour in a market economy, aiming at a higher return on investments. It may be odd to connect CAPM with disaster; however, it is the best framework to see the disaster loss assessment risks. Nations with higher per capita income see less fatality in catastrophe. However, it is subject to heavy income loss. So, the higher GDP of a country does not necessarily ensure a higher return on investments in disaster contexts. The CAPM model assumes that

$$Ra = R_{\mathrm{r}}f + (B_{\mathrm{a}} \times (R_{\mathrm{m}} - R_{\mathrm{r}}f))$$

Ra = expected return on a security, $R_{\mathrm{r}}f$ = risk-free rate, B_{a} = beta of the security, R_{m} = expected return of the market.

The beta of the security in CAPM has specific effects in disaster situations. Climate change also poses a massive risk to the value of capital. Disaster and climate risk are becoming agents of the beta security. The Reserve Bank of India (2022) assessed that the value of assets held by bank customers might be lowered by increasing the frequency and severity of extreme weather events. Supply chains may impact client operations, profitability, and viability. Reserve Bank of India's assessment of climate risk finance is bankers' perspective on the impact of climate risk on the

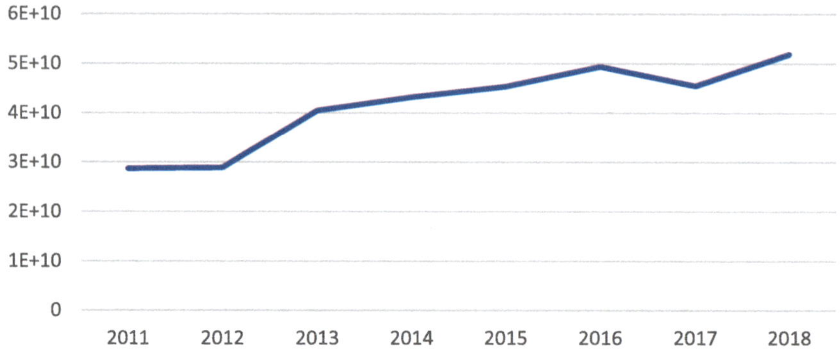

Fig. 1.3 Total financial support provided (Billions of current United States dollars)—DC_FIN_TOT (*Source* https://ourworldindata.org/grapher/green-climate-gcf-fund-pledges?country=~OWID_WRL)

financial sector. Figure 1.3 gives the details of total financial support under green fund support.

Figure 1.2 also shows the general trend in the last couple of decades and Fig. 1.4 shows the GDP loss due to disasters. These two figures need to be considered along with the climate action fund support and the global disaster mitigation finances. Macroeconomic stability and the tax base of the economy matter in determining the impact of disaster and climate change risks.

The price of capital assets and the externalities of the resource are linked with the risk factors. Some scholars assessed that climate risk affects manufacturing companies' financial performance (Giang et al., 2021). Some studies prove that financial performance is better for companies with lower exposure to climate transition risks (Reboredo & Ugolini, 2022). Economic loss due to climate and disaster risk should be treated along with mitigation costs. The cost of mitigation often obstructs higher financial returns from investments. Still, climate action or risk mitigation is prioritized in the sustainable development goals (SDGs). The SGD Goal 13, i.e., climate action, is an institutional intervention that promotes climate action as part of sustainable development goals. Climate action is a multi-prong project, and it includes institutional intervention and financing. Goal 13 of the SDGs could be read as the project of ensuring maximum utility expectations. However, the expectations on economic return and utility make climate action a complex project and

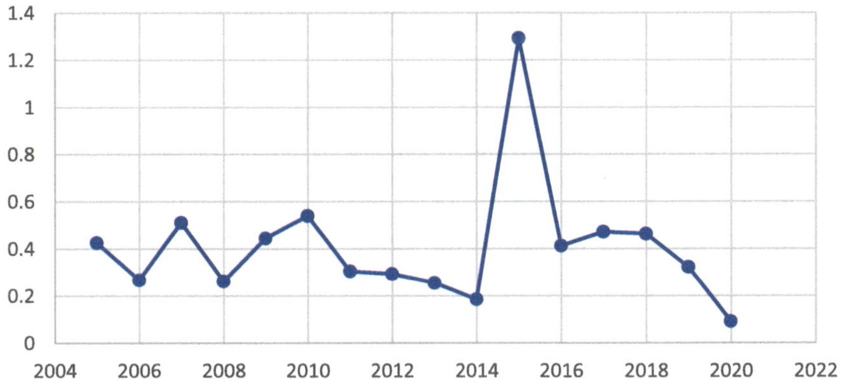

Fig. 1.4 Direct economic loss attributed to disasters relative to GDP (%) (*Source* https://ourworldindata.org)

are often set aside in the decision-making. Climate action should be given priority in economic decision-making, as it ensures higher utilities; however, the trade-off between climate action and expected utility needs to be elaborated with reference to capital investment, market economy, and increasing disaster and climate risks. The disaster loss assessment should add the trade-off between the mitigation cost and financial return. The cost of averting risk is also capital investment, and the value of this investment increases the capital's value in general. Economically backward countries and societies have to pay much for these losses. So, risk aversion and reduction become an inevitable economic process in countries experiencing climate and disaster risks. In life cycle models, risk aversion is crucial since people are exposed to risk in their work, income, asset return, health, and other factors (O'Donoghue & Somerville, 2018). The resources that ensure higher utility alone make a considerable loss; however, the utility varies according to the economy and society. The utility is also influenced by vulnerability, and consequences are determined by the decision-making (Cox, 2009). Risk-vulnerable people act more risk-averse when unjustified risk is added to wealth, which raises the competitive price of risk in the economy (Gollier & Pratt, 1996). Disaster and climate-induced losses are indeed utility losses, too. It could also be marginal utility and associated with economic return.

1.4 Risk and Economic Return

Risk and economic return are popular concepts and terminology in modern market analysis. The market economy uses this term to assess a method to generate equal returns from each economic agent. The asset pricing models assume that all random variables have symmetric stable distributions. Such expectations determine the optimal consumption-investment decisions (Fama, 1971). Risk return is often treated as a firm's ability to manage it to save the shareholders (Feigenbaum & Thomas, 1988). The theory of the firm is the central theme of managerial economics. Managerial economists consider firm-level capability to be a process that coordinates production and distribution. Managerial economics discusses the theory of the firm and the optimization of input cost, profit output, and input profit. Holmstrom and Tirole (1987) argue that the theory of a firm is a more extensive theoretical analysis that talks about decision-making and capitalization. They further say that always-evolving institutions are essential to the expansion and development of the economy. Some scholars argue that firms in neoclassical theory discuss the importance of price systems; if the price system works well, resources are well allocated (Demsetz, 1997). A firm is viewed as a contract between numerous people. The primary premise is that implicit and explicit contractual arrangements are made to reduce the costs of transactions between specialized production factors (Holmstrom & Tirole, 1989). It operates on multiple expectations and assumptions. The principle theory of firms talks about coordinating various aspects of production and resources to make an output. Every rational economic agent expects and trusts the firm's ability to withstand risk and uncertainty. The famous Coase theorem puts forward the social cost issue and introduces the idea that a firm is a relationship system. Coase (1960) argues that ' *the gain from preventing the harm is greater than the loss which would be suffered elsewhere as a result of stopping the action which produces the harm.'* One could use the Coase theorem to explain the idea of economic return and risk. Governing risk to ensure economic return needs a system of relationship approach to firms.

Risk return is closely associated with the ability of the firms to manage the assets. Also, individual choices and expectations of return do not match the firm's choice of recovery. A firm's level of capability is the critical core of economic return; however, the firm capability is also subject to multiple levels of institutional linkages. Firm capability evolves through various kinds of engagement with actors' connections with firms. Richardson (1972) expanded on the concept by positioning capabilities as the firm's knowledge, expertise, and skills as the force behind and a restriction on its operations. The organization's beliefs, culture, and collective capacity to quickly implement a new business model or other changes are called dynamic capabilities (Teece, 2010). Dynamic capability is considered a complex set of routines that ensure the ability of firms to resolve the crisis. It could be otherwise called the competitive advantage of firms to ensure return. The capacities approach aims to explain organizational longevity, business evolution, and interfirm heterogeneity (Teece, 2019). Dynamic capacities must be established through investment in discovery, knowledge development, and learning (Teece, 2019).

The internal and managerial ability of the firm matters in risk management; however, the location of the firm or an economic entity is also equally important. A market economy with private capital is always volatile to risks. The financial market in these countries responds to the dangers if a disaster leads to capital replacement. Here is the significance of firm capability, which puts firm capability on economic institutions to engage with emerging disaster and climate risks and utility.

Economic loss and return are dependent on firms' capability. It could otherwise be defined as institutional capability. Macroeconomic understanding of economic return is the institutional ability to ensure the multiplication and acceleration of capital assets. Institutions are the rules of the game in a society, which govern how its members interact and influence society's economic behaviour. Integrated financial institutions ensure better GDP per capita (Demetriades & Hook Law, 2006). An institutional approach to risk and return offers a broader discourse on disaster and climate change context. An institutional approach to disaster and climate risks considers risks within the capability of the institutions to define and govern. Institutional norms of disaster and climate risk reduction exist, but risk economics governs transaction costs to ensure economic return. Transaction cost is coordinated between buyers and sellers. Economic understanding of transaction cost determines the economic activity, i.e., no activity is possible with high transaction costs. Opting for the optimum transaction cost is associated with the institutions' ability.

Transaction costs are the expenses associated with negotiating, overseeing, and enforcing an exchange between two parties (Jones & Hill, 1988). Institutions have to engage with other agencies to optimize transaction costs. Transaction cost is also about how firms choose governance

(Chiles & McMackin, 1996). Selecting the proper method to govern the institution decides the sustainability of institutions. The lower transaction has a dual association with risk and return. Lowering the transaction cost is likely to ensure high returns from investments; however, the factors determining the transaction cost are multiple and may not be identified. Some scholars argue that transaction costs are the expenses incurred when transacting with another agent (Axelsson & Easton, 1992). Transaction cost is not an independent phenomenon; instead, it is connected with multiple agents and entities. Bounded rationality of transaction costs is a critical factor influencing decision-making under uncertainties.

The second important feature of behavioural decision-making is related to bounded rationality. It follows that an individual is incompetent to make allowance for every possibility that a particular transaction or decision would have (Williamson, 1981). According to Williamson (1975), organizations and individuals have limited capacity to process and understand information. This is because a certain amount of uncertainty always exists associated with a transaction, and it is costly to design all possible effects the transaction would have (Williamson, 1987). Institutions make decisions based on expecting a rational outcome or an impact. Every institution prefers not to make a decision in uncertainty, which leads to chaos. Investment decisions will be significantly affected if uncertainty rises to a particular level. Firms and institutions prefer not to make decisions that lead to uncertainties; however, in some contexts, firms and institutions have to decide under uncertainty. Uncertainty could be a loss of income or high capital replacement in the case of natural calamities. Institutions in a market economy never let uncertainty determine the economic values.

Disasters often act as a catalyst to change economic certainty into uncertainty and risks. The impact of climate risk on financial loss proves this issue. Climate change influences the ecosystem and human mortality, which results from economic losses (Auffhammer, 2018). There is a correlation between climate risk and GDP at different levels in different economies (Estrada et al., 2015). It is a significant issue for developing economies to withstand natural disaster risks and climate change. Climate change costs the economy in different socio-economic systems (Rizzati et al., 2023). Institutional capability plays a critical role in engaging with this crisis. There is an institutional challenge between developing and developed economies in this regard. Developing countries and societies have broader institutional structures performing economic and non-economic responsibilities. For instance, India's grassroots bureaucracy is often the source of income and facilitator. Climate action projects in India are implemented through the bureaucracy and act as agents themselves. Though developing countries like India have adopted a market economy, risk management is still the domain of bureaucracy. It is a combination of economic and non-economic interventions. It could be called ‘social technologies’ to produce productive economic activities (Nelson & Sampat, 2001).

Natural disasters and climate change always demand institutional support and interventions. It could be otherwise called the need for the dynamic capability of public, private, and market institutions. There are differential expectations of institutions by society and the economy. It could be capital saving, increased use value, and high resource rent. Disaster and climate risk change the use value of the resource, and hence, the net present value also varies. A financial calculation known as Net Present Value (NPV) estimates the current value of future cash flows. It is a technique for determining if an investment or project will be profitable. Estimating a project’s financial inflows and outflows over a long period, usually several years, is required for the NPV calculation. Then, using a discount rate that considers both the investment’s risk and the time value of money, the future cash flows are discounted back to their present value. Scholars have engaged with these issues in detail. Using concise and convincing financial language, the decoupling net present value (DNPV) method includes risk and risk reduction strategies in project estimates. DNPV recasts the economic impact of risk reduction initiatives by assessing the risk exposures of assets to hazards and decreasing such exposure through upfront investments (Espinoza et al., 2023). The economy’s size and prospects matter when putting in an NPV assessment. The market economy is more volatile to climate and natural disasters due to colossal market borrowing for reconstruction and capital replacement. In addition, countries largely dependent on public funding for disaster and climate risk reduction get the more comprehensive option to apply DNPV.

Public and private capital would follow different DNPVs in disaster and climate change contexts. It helps decision-making regarding investments in the volatile nature of climate risks. Average economic forecasting is market and demand forecasting; however, the application of NPV helps assess the use value and cost of capital replacements. Climate risks demand a higher capital value, which is not expected to increase output in a normative form. This allows the investors to assess the financial impact of decisions to invest in resilience and adaptation measures and value the possible exposure of physical assets to climate-related hazards (Espinoza et al., 2019). DNPV proposes to save the net benefits from investments; however, some scholars argue that the distribution of net benefits among various groups of people is not taken into account by NPV, nor is it taken into account whether the stream of net benefits is stable or turbulent (Knoke et al., 2020). This question is significant for marginal economies and societies. A fully employed market economy accommodates DNPV in determining investment decisions. The use value and asset value vary across economies. The Reserve Bank of India (2022) assesses that there are credit, market, liquidity, and operation risks due to climate change. Still, RBI-like entities cannot propose a financial model to reduce the impact of climate change on investments. Green finance is being proposed; however, it still evolves in developing economies. The economic agents know this crisis still needs to become a strategy. The World Economic Forum assessed that climate change will reduce four percent of global annual economic output by 2050.[1] IPCC reports warn the international community about the probable economic loss due to climate risks. It affects global financial capital movements and investments. Higher emission productivity results in higher FDI inflows and fewer FDI outflows following extreme weather events (Gu & Hale, 2022). The capital market is sensitive to climate risks; those investments need DNPV analysis before investments. Economists do environmental cost accounting to assess output-related pollution and emissions costs. It concerns the cost of prevention, detection, and internal and external losses. This is a standard method of environmental cost–benefit analysis; however, extreme weather, disasters, and climate risks pose different challenges per capita.

Compared to local businesses (companies that are not international or multinationals operating in their headquarters country), which naturally have fewer options for where to place their facilities, foreign companies tend to avoid locations with greater degrees of physical and climatic risks (Li & Gallagher, 2022). It is not simply a cost accounting that saves output value; it is a process to protect capital from replacement cost and value reduction. Profitable resource management depends on skills like asset orchestration and market generation (or co-creation) (Pitelis &

[1] https://www.weforum.org/agenda/2022/04/climate-change-global-gdp-risk/ (accessed on 29th March 2023).

Teece, 2010). Natural disasters have a regional impact, leading to regional developmental imbalances; hence, risk-return is an economic risk.

Return of risk or uncertainty over risk influences the economic system, and it has been explained under the risk-return trade-off theory. This concept is mainly applied in assessing stock market volatilities (Bali & Peng, 2006). Applying this concept to natural calamity and climate risk scenarios helps theorize the debate from a broader perspective. Economists see the risk return as a reduction in capital assets, and for vulnerable communities, risk return is the total loss of support and livelihoods. The frequency of disasters is one example of risk-return; later on, climate change has extended the impacts and increased economic costs.

Risk return has another meaning in a country like India, where state funding is essential for capital replacements. Though a country like India has adopted the market economy model, private capital support for disasters and climate action must still be included. It is through some charity support and not part of any major initiatives. The state has to maintain total control over disaster and climate actions. So, the state institutions always keep the market economy from defining India's disaster and climate risks. Also, the disaster and climate risks impact many vulnerable populations in India, so the state has to raise capital to replace capital. This is why economists are not trying to develop theories about disaster economics in India. There are differential perceptions of the economic aspects. The widespread assumption is the rent-seeking of resources. Rent-seeking is the idea that transfers are converted into social costs when individuals expend natural resources and efforts to capture them (Tollison, 2012). Climate and disaster risks affect the capital value of the resources and rents.

One of the challenges of theorizing risk concerning disasters and climate risk is the different approach to the natural value of capital and opportunity cost for 'replacing capital.' Capital is not a free commodity and can potentially increase value in a normative economic system. Alternative measures might influence the economic system's decision-making (Reneke, 2009). The present global economic system is supposed to be resilient to shocks, including climate risks; however, the differential impact of these risks proves that the modern economic system is equally vulnerable to risks. An evolutionary approach is needed to theorize the risks and risk economics. Normative approaches to economic theory hardly help theorize economic risks; a discursive approach is necessary for theorizing risk economics. The following chapters of this book discuss this in detail.

One of the challenges of theorizing risk concerning disasters and climate risk is the different approach to the natural value of capital and opportunity cost for 'replacing capital.' Capital is not a free commodity and can potentially increase value in a normative economic system. Alternative measures might influence the economic system's decision-making (Reneke, 2009). The present global economic system is supposed to be resilient to shocks, including climate risks; however, the differential impact of these risks proves that the modern economic system is equally vulnerable to risks. An evolutionary approach is needed to theorize the risks and risk economics. Normative approaches to economic theory hardly help theorize economic risks; a discursive approach is necessary for theorizing risk economics. The following chapters of this book discuss this in detail.

References

Abdel-Basseta, M. M., Gunasekaranb, M. M., & Naveen, C. (2019). A framework for risk assessment, management and evaluation: Economic tool for quantifying risks in supply chain. *Future Generation Computer Systems, 90*(2019), 489–502.

Abel, A. B. (1984). The effects of uncertainty on investment and the expected long-run capital stock. *Journal of Economic Dynamics and Control, 7*(1), 39–53.

Admiraal, J. F., Ada, W., de Wouter, T. G., & de Geert, R. S. (2013). More than total economic value: How to combine economic valuation of biodiversity with ecological resilience. *Ecological Economics, 89*, 115–122.

Ahuja, A., Murtaza, S., & Wiseman, K. (2017). *Assessing country risk—Selected approaches—Reference note*. Strategy, Policy, and Review Department. IMF.

Albala-Bertrand, J. M. (2007). Globalization and localization: An economic approach. In H. Rodriguez, E. L. Quarantelli, & R. R. Dynes (Eds.), *Handbook of disaster research* (pp. 147–167). New York: Springer.

Allais, M. (1953). Le Comportement de l'Homme Rationnel devant le Risque: Critique des Postulats et Axiomes de l'Ecole Americaine. *Econometrica, 21*(4), 503–546. https://doi.org/10.2307/1907921

Auffhammer, M. (2018). Quantifying economic damages from climate change. *Journal of Economic Perspectives, 32*(4), 33–52.

Axelsson, B., & Easton, G. (1992). *Industrial networks: A new view of reality*. Routledge.

Bali, T. G., & Peng, L. (2006). Is there a risk-return trade-off? Evidence from high-frequency data. *Journal of Applied Econometrics, 21*(8), 1169–1198. https://doi.org/10.1002/jae.911

Baptiste Say, J. (1821) (1971 Reprint). *A treatise on political economy or the production, distribution and consumption of wealth*. Augustus M. Kelley.

Bell, D. E. (1995). Risk, return, and utility. *Management Science, 41*(1), 23–30.

Bernardo, J. M. (1979). Expected information as expected utility. *The Annals of Statistics, 7*(3), 686–690.

Bernoulli, D. (1954). Exposition of a new theory on the measurement of risk. *Econometrica, 22*(1), 23–36. https://doi.org/10.2307/1909829

Bernstein, P. L. (1998). *Against the gods: The remarkable story of risk*. Wiley.

Blavatskyy, P. R. (2007). Stochastic expected utility theory. *J Risk Uncertainty, 34*, 259–286.

Briggs, A. H., Weinstein, M. C., Fenwick, E. A., Karnon, J., Sculpher, M. J., Paltiel, A. D., ISPOR-SMDM Modeling Good Research Practices Task Force. (2012). Model parameter estimation and uncertainty analysis: a report of the ISPOR-SMDM Modeling Good Research Practices Task Force Working Group-6. *Medical Decision Making, 32*(5), 722–732. https://doi.org/10.1177/0272989X12458348

Briguglio, L., Cordina, G., Farrugia, N., & Vella, S. (2009). Economic vulnerability and resilience: Concepts and measurements. *Oxford Development Studies, 37*(3), 229–247.

Bryant, W. D. A. (2014). The microeconomics of choice under risk and uncertainty: Where are we? *Vikalpa, 39*(1), 1.

Buchak, L. (2013). *Risk and rationality*. OUP.

Campbell, D. T. (1974). Evolutionary epistemology. In P. A. Schilpp (Ed.), *The philosophy of Karl R. Popper* (pp. 412–463). Open Court.

Cartelier, J. (2007). The hypostasis of money: An economic point of view. *Cambridge Journal of Economics, 2007*(31), 217–233.

Cate, T., & Johnson, L. E. (1998). The theory of probability: A key element in Keynes' revolution. *International Advances in Economic Research, 4*(4), 324–334.

Chang, S. E., & Rose, A. Z. (2012). Towards a theory of economic recovery from disasters. *International Journal of Mass Emergencies and Disasters, 32*(2), 171–181.

Chatterjee, S. (2005). Capital utilization, economic growth and convergence. *Journal of Economic Dynamics and Control, 29*(12), 2093–2124.

Chen, J. M. (2021). The capital asset pricing model. *Encyclopedia, 1*, 915–933. https://doi.org/10.3390/encyclopedia1030070

Chiles, T. H., & McMackin, J. F. (1996). Integrating variable risk preferences, trust, and transaction cost economics. *The Academy of Management Review, 21*(1), 73–99.

Coase, R. H. (1960). The problem of social cost. *The Journal of Law and Economics, 3*, 1–44.

Cowen, T., & High, J. (1988). Time, bounded utility, and the St. Petersburg paradox. *Theory and Decision, 25*(3), 219–223.

Cox, L. A., Jr. (2009). Game theory and risk analysis. *Risk Analysis, 29*(8), 1062–1068.

Davis, J. B., Hands, D. W., & Miiki, U. (Eds.). (1998). *The handbook of economic methodology*. Edward Elgar Publishing.

Demetriades, P., & Hook Law, S. (2006). Finance, institutions and economic development. *International Journal of Finance and Economics, 11*(3), 245–260. https://doi.org/10.1002/ijfe.296

Demsetz, H. (1997). The firm in economic theory: A quiet revolution. *The American Economic Review, 87*(2), 426–429. Papers and proceedings of the hundred and fourth annual meeting of the American economic association.

Duval, R., Elmeskov, J., & Vogel, L. (2007). *Structural policies and economic resilience to shocks*. OECD Economics Department Working Papers No. 567.

Espinoza, D., Morris, J., Baroud, H., Bisogno, M., Cifuentes, A., Gentzoglanis, A., & Vahedifard, F. (2019). The role of traditional discounted cash flows in the tragedy of the horizon: another inconvenient truth. *Mitigation and Adaptation Strategies for Global Change*. https://doi.org/10.1007/s11027-019-09884-3

Espinoza, D., Rojo, J., Phillips, W., & Eil, A. (2023). Decoupled net present value: Protecting assets against climate change risk by consistently capturing the value of resilient and adaptable investments. *Sustainable and Resilient Infrastructure, 8*(supl), 323–336. https://doi.org/10.1080/23789689.2022.2148453

Estrada, F., Tol, R. S. J., & Gay-García, C. (2015). The persistence of shocks in GDP and the estimation of the potential economic costs of climate change. *Environmental Modelling and Software, 69*, 155–165.

Fama, E. F. (1971). Risk, return, and equilibrium. *Journal of Political Economy, 79*(1), 30–55.

Fiegenbaum, A., & Thomas, H. (1988). Attitudes toward Risk and the Risk-Return Paradox: Prospect Theory Explanations. *The Academy of Management Journal, 31*(1), 85–106. https://doi.org/10.2307/256499

Fischhoff, B., Watson, S. R., & Hope, C. (1984). Defining risk. *Policy Sciences, 17*(2), 123–139. https://doi.org/10.1007/bf00146924

Fishburn, P. C. (1982). *The foundations of expected utility*. Springer.

Friedman, M., & Savage, L. J. (1948). The utility analysis of choices involving risk. *Journal of Political Economy, 56*, 279–304.

Fukuba, Y., & Ito, K. (1984). The so-called expected utility theory is inadequate. *Mathematical Social Sciences, 7*(1984), 1–12.

Gençay, R., Selçuk, F., & Ulugülyağci, A. (2003). High volatility, thick tails and extreme value theory in value-at-risk estimation. *Insurance: Mathematics and Economics, 33*(2), 337–356. https://doi.org/10.1016/j.insmatheco.2003.07.004

Giang, N. T. H., Hanh, T. M., Hien, P. T., Trinh, N. T., Huyen, N. T. K., & Trang, V. H. (2021). The impacts of climate change risks on financial performance: Evidence from listed manufacturing firms in Vietnam. In *Proceedings of the international conference on emerging challenges: Business transformation and circular economy (ICECH 2021).*

Gilboa, I., Postlewaite, A. W., & Schmeidler, D. (2008). Probability and uncertainty in economic modeling. *Journal of Economic Perspectives, 22*(3), 173–188.

Gollier, C., & Pratt, J. W. (1996). Risk vulnerability and the tempering effect of background risk. *Econometrica, 64*(5), 1109–1123.

Gossen, H. ([1854] 1983). *The laws of human relations and the rules of human action derived there from.* MIT Press.

Grant, S., & Van Zandt, T. (2007). *Expected utility theory*. INSEAD working paper series.

Gu, W., & Hale, G. (2022). *Climate risks and FDI grace*. National Bureau of Economic Research. Working Paper Series-30452. https://www.nber.org/papers/w30452

Gul, F., & Pesendorfer, W. (2006). Random expected utility. *Econometrica, 74*(1), 121–146.

Haddawy, P., & Hanks, S. (1998). Utility models for goal-directed, decision-theoretic planners. *Computational Intelligence, 14*(3), 392–429.

Hagen, O. (1979). Towards a positive theory of preference under risk. In M. Allais & O. Hagen (Eds.), *Expected utility hypothesis and the allais paradox* (pp. 271–302). Reidel.

Hallegatte, S., Vogt-Schilb, A., Rozenberg, J., Bangalore, M., & Beaudet, C. (2020). From Poverty to disaster and back: A review of the literature. *Economics of Disasters and Climate Change, 4*, 223–247.

Hancock, J. G., & Teevan, R. C. (1964). Fear of failure and risk-taking behavior. *Journal of Personality, 32*(2), 200–209.

Harper, R. F. (1904). *The code of hammurabi king of babylon: About 2250 B.C.* The University Of Chicago Press Callaghan & Company London.

Haushofer, J., & Fehr, E. (2014). On the psychology of poverty. *Science, 344*(6), 186.

Hausken, K. (2002). Probabilistic risk analysis and game theory. *Risk Analysis, 22*(1), 17–27. https://doi.org/10.1111/0272-4332.t01-1-0000

Hill, E. W., Wial, H., & Wolman, H. (2008). *Exploring regional economic resilience*. Working paper 2008-04. Institute of Urban and Regional Development, University of California, Berkeley.

Hochrainer-Stigler, S., Linnerooth-Bayer, JoAnne, & Mochizuki, J. (2019). Flood proofing low-income houses in India: An application of climate-sensitive probabilistic benefit–cost analysis. *Economics of Disasters and Climate Change, 2019*(3), 23–38.
Holmstrom, B. R., & Tirole, J. (1987). *The theory of firm*. Massachusetts institute of technology (chrome-extension://efaidnbmnnnibpcajpcglclefindmkaj/https://core.ac.uk/download/pdf/4431147.pdf. Accessed on 27th February, 2023).
Holmstrom, B. R., & Tirole, J. (1989). Chapter 2 The theory of the firm. In *Handbook of industrial organization* (Vol. 1, pp. 61–133). Elsevier.
Holmström, B., & Tirole, J. (2000). Liquidity and risk management. *Journal of Money, Credit and Banking, 32*(3, Part 1), 295–319.
Hougaard, J. L., & Keiding, H. (2005). Rawlsian maximin, Dutch books, and non-additive expected utility. *Mathematical Social Sciences, 50*(2005), 239–251.
James, W. (1896). *The will to believe*. Reprinted (excerpt) in Reason and Responsibility, J. Feinberg, & R. Shafer-Landau (Eds.). Wadsworth/Thomson (2005) (pp. 101–9).
Jeffreys, H. (1955). The present position in probability theory. *The British Journal for the Philosophy of Science, 5*(20), 275–289.
Jones, G. R., & Hill, C. W. L. (1988). Transaction cost analysis of strategy-structure choice. *Strategic Management Journal, 9*(2), 159–172. https://doi.org/10.1002/smj.4250090206
Jorion, P. (2010). Risk management. *Annual Review of Financial Economics, 2*, 347–365.
Jouannic, G., Crozier, D., Chloé, T. D. M., Kolli, Z., Arki, F., Matagne, E., & Omperin, L. (2016). Post-disaster recovery: How to encourage the emergency of economic and social dynamics to improve resilience? *E3S Web of Conferences, 7*, 17004. https://doi.org/10.1051/e3sconf/20160717004
Kahneman, D., & Tversky, A. (1979). Prospect theory: An analysis of decision under risk. *Econometrica, 47*(2), 263–292.
Karni, E. (2006). Subjective expected utility theory without states of the world. *Journal of Mathematical Economics, 42*(2006), 325–342.
Karni, E. (2014). Axiomatic foundations of expected utility and subjective probability. In M. J. Machina & W. K. Viscusi (Eds.), *Handbook of the economics of risk and uncertainty*. London: Elsevier.
Kellenberg, D. K., & Mobarak, A. M. (2008). Does rising income increase or decrease damage risk from natural disasters? *Journal of Urban Economics, 63*(3), 788–802.
Keynes, J. M. (1921). *A treatise on probability*. London: Macmillan and Co., Limited St. Martin's Street.

Keynes, J. (1936). *The general theory of employment, interest and money*. London: Macmillan.

Knight, F. H. (1921). *Risk uncertainty and profit*. https://oll-resources.s3.us-east-2.amazonaws.com/oll3/store/titles/306/Knight_0192.html

Knoke, T., Gosling, E., & Paul, C. (2020). Use and misuse of the net present value in environmental studies. *Ecological Economics., 174*, 106664.

Koszegi, B., & Rabin, M. (2006). A model of reference-dependent preferences. *Quarterly Journal of Economics, 121*(4), 1133–1165.

Koszegi, B., & Rabin, M. (2007). Reference-dependent risk attitudes. *American Economic Review, 97*(4), 1047–1073.

Koszegi, B., & Rabin, M. (2009). Reference-dependent consumption plans. *American Economic Review, 99*(3), 909–936.

La Mura, P. (2009). Projective expected utility. *Journal of Mathematical Psychology, 53*(2009), 408–414.

Li, X., & Gallagher, K. P. (2022). Assessing the climate change exposure of foreign direct investment. *Nature Communications, 13*, 1451. https://doi.org/10.1038/s41467-022-28975-5

Luce, R. D., & Krantz, D. H. (1971). Conditional expected utility. *Econometrica, 39*(2), 253–271.

Lybbert, T. J., & Barrett, C. B. (2010). Risk-taking behavior in the presence of nonconvex asset dynamics. *Economic Inquiry, 49*(4), 982–988.

Machina, M. J. (2003). States of the world and the state of decision theory. In D. J. Meyer (Ed.), *The economics of risk*. Michigan: W.E. Upjohn Institute for Employment Research.

Macvane, S. M. (1893). Marginal utility and value. *The Quarterly Journal of Economics, 7*(3), 255–285.

Martin, R. L. (2012). Regional economic resilience, hysteresis and recessionary shocks. *J Econ Geogr, 12*, 1–32.

Mathieu-Nicot, B. (1986). Fuzzy expected utility. *Fuzzy Sets and Systems, 20*(2), 163–173. https://doi.org/10.1016/0165-0114(86)90075-8

Matthew, R. A. (2000). The environment as a national security issue. *Journal of Policy History, 12*(1), 101–122.

Melese, F., Blandin, J., & Fanchon, P. (1992). Benefits and pay: The economics of military compensation. *Defence and Peace Economics, 3*(3), 243–253.

Modica, M., & Reggiani, A. (2014). Spatial economic resilience: Overview and perspectives. *Networks and Spatial Economics*. https://doi.org/10.1007/s11067-014-9261-7

Montesano, A. (2008). A restatement of walras' theories of capitalisation and money. *History of Economics Review, 47*(1), 86–109. https://doi.org/10.1080/18386318.2008.1168212

Moore, G. (1987). Depreciation, inflation and capital replacement. *Contemporary Accounting Research, 3*(2), 375–383.

Moskowitz, H., & Bunn, D. (1987). Decision and risk analysis. *European Journal of Operational Research, 28*, 247–260.
Munier, B. R. (1986). *Risk, decision and rationality*. D. Reidel Publishing Company.
Nagel, E. (1939). *Principles of the Theory of Probability*. University of Chicago Press.
Nelson, R. R., & Sampat, B. N. (2001). Making sense of institutions as a factor shaping economic performance. *Journal of Economic Behavior and Organization, 44*, 31–54.
Nwogugu, M. (2006). Volatility, risk modeling and utility. *Applied Mathematics and Computation, 182*(2), 1749–1754. https://doi.org/10.1016/j.amc.2006.01.079
O'Donoghue, T., & Somerville, J. (2018). Modeling risk aversion in economics. *The Journal of Economic Perspectives, 32*(2), 91–114.
Padli, J., Shah Habibullah, M., & Baharom, A. H. (2010). Economic impact of natural disasters' fatalities. *International Journal of Social Economics, 37*(6), 429–441.
Perrings, C. (2006). Resilience and sustainable development. *Environment and Development Economics, 11*, 417–442.
Pettigrew, R. (2015). Risk, rationality and expected utility theory. *Canadian Journal of Philosophy, 45*(5/6, Special Issue: Belief, Action, and Rationality over Time (October_December 2015)), 798–826.
Pettigrew, R. (2022). *Epistemic risk and the demands of rationality*. OUP.
Pimm, S. L. (1984). The complexity and stability of ecosystems. *Nature, 307*, 321–326.
Pitelis, C. N., & Teece, D. J. (2010). Cross-border market co-creation, dynamic capabilities and the entrepreneurial the-ory of the multinational enterprise. *Industrial and Corporate Change, 19*(4), 1247–1270.
Pope, R., & Selten, R. (2009). *Risk and expected utility theory*. Bonn Econ Discussion Papers 5/2009, University of Bonn, Bonn Graduate School of Economics (BGSE).
Pötzsch, R. (1972). Decision-theoretic aspects of risk-taking behaviour. *Theory and Decision, 3*(2), 107–125.
Qazi, A., Daghfous, A., & Khan, M. S. (2021). Impact of risk attitude on risk, opportunity, and performance assessment of construction projects. *Project Management Journal*. https://doi.org/10.1177/8756972820985673
Quiggin, J. (2003). Background risk in generalized expected utility theory. *Economic Theory, 22*(3), 607–611.
Rabin, M. (1999). *Risk aversion and expected-utility theory: A calibration theorem*. https://escholarship.org
Rassekh, F. (2017). *Four central theories of the market economy conception, evolution and application*. Routledge.

Rawls, J. (1971). *A theory of justice*. Harvard University Press.

Reboredo, J. C., & Ugolini, A. (2022). Climate transition risk, profitability and stock prices. *International Review of Financial Analysis, 83*, 102271.

Reggiani, A., De Graaff, T., & Nijkamp, P. (2002). Resilience: An evolutionary approach to spatial economic systems. *Networks and Spatial Economics, 2*(2002), 211–229.

Regibeau, P., & Rockett, K. (2013). Economic analysis of resilience: A framework for local policy response based on new case studies. *Journal of Innovation Economics and Management, 1*(11), 107–147. https://doi.org/10.3917/jie.011.0107

Reneke, J. A. (2009). A game theory formulation of decision making under conditions of uncertainty and risk. *Nonlinear Analysis: Theory, Methods and Applications, 71*(12), e1239–e1246.

Reserve Bank of India. (2022). *Discussion paper on climate risk and sustainable finance*. RBI

Richardson, G. (1972). The organisation of industry. *Economic Journal, 82*(326), 883–889.

Rizzati, M., Standardi, G., Guastella, G., Parrado, R., Bosello, F., & Pareglio, S. (2023). The local costs of global climate change: Spatial GDP downscaling under different climate scenarios. *Spatial Economic Analysis, 18*(1), 23–43. https://doi.org/10.1080/17421772.2022.2096917

Rose, A. (2004). Defining and measuring economic resilience to disasters. *Disaster Prevention and Management, 13*(4), 307–314.

Rose, A. Z. (2007). Economic resilience to natural and man-made disasters: Multidisciplinary origins and contextual dimensions. *Environmental Hazards, 7*, 383–398.

Rose, A. Z., & Krausmann, E. (2013). An economic framework for the development of a resilience index for business recovery. *International Journal of Disaster Risk Reduction, 2013*, 1.

Rottenstreich, Y., & Hsee, C. K. (2001). Money, kisses, and electric shocks: On the aff ective psychology of risk. *Psychological Science, 12*(3), 185–190.

Rudra, A. (1966). Use of probability in economics. *Economic and Political Weekly, 1*(8), 317–322.

Sardana, G. D., & Dasanayaka, W. S. B. (2013). Economic recovery from natural disaster Spotlight on interventions in Tsunami affected micro and SMEs in Sri Lanka's Galle district. *Competitiveness Review: an International Business Journal, 23*(4/5), 384–397.

Scarf, P. A. (2002). Characterization of optimal policy for capital replacement models. *IMA Journal of Management Mathematics, 13*(4), 261–271. https://doi.org/10.1093/imaman/13.4.261

Sebora, T. C., & Cornwall, J. R. (1995). Expected utility theory vs. prospect theory: Implications for strategic decision makers. *Journal of Managerial Issues, 7*(1), 41–61.

Sen, A. 1985. *Commodities and Capabilities*. Amsterdam.

Seeliger, L., & Turok, I. (2013). Towards sustainable cities: Extending resilience with insights from vulnerability and transition theory. *Sustainability, 5*, 2108–2128.

Segal, U. (1987). The ellsberg paradox and risk aversion: An anticipated utility approach. *International Economic Review, 28*(1), 175202.

Sharpe, W. F. (2007). Expected utility asset allocation. *Financial Analysts Journal, 63*(5), 18–30.

Shashua, L., Melnik, A., & Goldschmidt, Y. (1974). A note on stock and flow capital inputs in the production function of multi-product firms. *Applied Economics, 6*(3), 229–233. https://doi.org/10.1080/00036847400000021

Simon, H. A. (1955). A behavioral model of rational choice. *The Quarterly Journal of Economics, 69*(1), 99–118.

Snow, P. (1987). Maximizing expected utility is a survival criterion. *Theory and Decision, 22*(1987), 143–154.

Strulik, H., & Trimborn, T. (2019). Natural disasters and macroeconomic performance. *Environmental and Resource Economics, 2019*(72), 1069–1098.

Takemura, K. (2021). Expected utility theory and psychology. In *Behavioral decision theory*. Springer. https://doi.org/10.1007/978-981-16-5453

Teece, D. J. (2010). Business models, business strategy and innovation. *Long Range Planning, 43*(2), 172–194.

Teece, D. J. (2019). A capability theory of the firm: An economics and (strategic)management perspective. *New Zealand Economic Papers, 53*(1), 1–43.

Tollison, R. D. (2012). The economic theory of rent seeking. *Public Choice, 152*(1–2), 73–82.

Tummala, R., & Schoenherr, T. (2011). Assessing and managing risks using the supply chain risk management process (SCRMP). *Supply Chain Management: an International Journal, 16*(2011), 474–483.

Usher, D. (1965). Traditional capital theory. *The Review of Economic Studies, 32*(2), 169–186.

Van De Klundert, T. (1986). Economic resilience: A two-country analysis. *De Economist, 134*(1), 25–41.

Van der Hoek, J., & Sherris, M. (2001). A class of non-expected utility risk measures and implications for asset allocations. *Insurance: Mathematics and Economics, 28*(1), 69–82. https://doi.org/10.1016/s0167-6687(00)00067-6

Vickrey, W. (1945). Measuring marginal utility by reactions to risk. *Econometrica, 13*(4), 319–333.

Vilko, J., Ritala, P., & Edelmann, J. (2014). On uncertainty in supply chain risk management. *The International Journal of Logistics Management, 25*(1), 3–19.

Von Neumann, J., & Morgenstern, O. (1953). *The theory of games and economic behavior*. Princeton University Press.

Vovk, V., & Shafer, G. (2008). The game-theoretic capital asset pricing model. *International Journal of Approximate Reasoning, 49*(1), 175–197.

Weirich, P. (1986). Expected utility and risk. *The British Journal for the Philosophy of Science, 37*(4), 419–442.

Williamson, O. E. (1975). *Markets and hierarchies: Analysis and antitrust implications*. Free Press.

Williamson, O. E. (1981). The economics of organization: The transaction cost approach. *American Journal of Sociology, 87*(3), 548–577.

Williamson, O. E. (1987). *Antitrust economics: Mergers, contracting, and strategic behavior*. Basil Blackwell.

Wu, J., Li, N., Xie, W., Zhou, Y., Ji, Z., & Shi, P. (2014). Post-disaster recovery and economic impact of catastrophes in China. *Earthquake Spectra, 30*(4), 1825–1846.

Yang, J., & Qiu, W. (2005). A measure of risk and a decision-making model based on expected utility and entropy. *European Journal of Operational Research, 164*(3), 792–799.

Yaari, M. E. 1987. The dual theory of choice under risk. Econometrica. *Journal of the Econometric Society*, pp.95–115.

Zellner, A., & Zilberman, D. (2011). The economics and econometrics of risk: An introduction to the special issue. *Journal of Econometrics, 162*(1), 1–5.

Zyphur, M. J., Narayanan, J., Arvey, R. D., & Alexander, G. J. (2009). The genetics of economic risk preferences. *Journal of Behavioral Decision Making, 22*(4), 367–377.

CHAPTER 2

Economics of Risk-Sharing

In principle, risk sharing divides the stakeholders' economic and financial risk burden. The method of risk sharing varies across economies and countries; modern capitalism has evolved different frameworks and approaches to sharing risks. Risk sharing is a global debate due to the influence of gain and loss of capital on contemporary capitalism. Steady growth of capital assets is the fundamental principle of modern capitalism, so any risk that disrupts the growth path is a risk. So, sharing risk means saving capital from further depreciation. In the global discourse, studies argue that the amount of risk sharing offered by capital gains is consistent across national samples and periods, and the amount of risk sharing through measured factor income flows is highly variable (Balli et al., 2012). Risk sharing is essential for many areas of the economy, including financial stability, monetary policy effects, innovation, and entrepreneurship. It can influence the number of people pursuing entrepreneurship and the work entrepreneurs put in, affecting entrepreneurship-driven innovation Kilström & Roth, 2024). Studie emphasizes that economic systems are inherently uncertain and that limitations in human understanding cannot be the only reason why it is impossible to forecast the future· (Maghrebi et al., 2023). Chen and Xie (2020) observe risk sharing among agents facing uncertain costs, where the joint distribution of these costs is not entirely known due to distributional ambiguity. Compared

S. M. Irshad, *Economics of Disasters and Climate Change*, Sustainable Development Goals Series,
https://doi.org/10.1007/978-981-97-9415-7_2

to an equilibrium without risk sharing, the equilibrium with full diversification has lower growth rates across the board and potentially lower welfare levels for each nation (Devereux et al., 1994). Also, globalization may worsen domestic risk sharing and lower welfare. We show how these effects depend on various characteristics of tradable goods and explore the roles of borrowing limits, debt renegotiations, and trade policy (Broner & Ventura, 2011).

Risk sharing aims to combine hazards and distribute them among participants based on their ability to take on risk (Mirakhor & Hamid, 2011). Uncertainty and risk are there to test and try man to facilitate his growth and development (Iqbal and Mirakhor, 2011). Risk sharing as a business project theoretically emerged in early Islamic societies in the Middle East. It was an approach to share the profit and loss. For instance, in Islamic finance, the mudarabah is a type of partnership in which one party contributes capital (Rab al-Maal) while the other party provides management and knowledge (Mudarib). If there is demonstrated negligence or malfeasance on the part of Mudarib, losses are exclusively borne by the capital provider, while profits are divided according to a pre-arranged ratio (Askari et al., 2015). Mudarabah is a type of fiduciary partnership that handles agreements between businesses that involve profit-sharing and loss-bearing (Hassan & Saleem, 2017). It was based on the philosophy of wealth distribution and ethical way of capital mobilsation. One could read it as an economic practice of pre-modern community who had no exposure to the rest of the world. It was practice of the Arabs, who then known for trade across the world, so this practice was connected with uncertainty of business and trade of the time. These contracts are made between two parties: mudarib, who provides the managerial abilities needed to run the company, and Rab-al-mal, who contributes the capital (goods of financial capital). When the economic cycle ends, each party is entitled to split the business's earnings and losses (Islam & Ahmad, 2020). It was contract between two parties: mudarib, who provides managerial abilities to run the firm, and rab-al-mal, who supplies capital (goods of financial capital). Both parties have the right to split any profit or loss the business makes at the end of the cycle (Islam & Ahmad, 2019).

They practised a different method of joint venture company Musharakah, in which two or more people pool their capital for a project or venture. Profits are then divided based on a predetermined ratio and losses, however, are split according to each party's investment (Siddiqi,

2006). Musharakah was financing system as well. Musharakah does not anticipate a set rate of return, and in Musharakah, return is determined by the joint venture's real profit (Usmani, 1999). Under this system, interest rate charges on capital were prohibited and treated as a sin, so Musharakah offers a mechanism to overcome interest-bearing financial transactions. It was the belief system of the early Islamic system. However, Islamic countries often follow this system. The Islamic banking system is primarily based on the Musharakah method and has a global presence. It evolved in the early ninth-century Middle Eastern countries. The principle of Musharakah is base of the banking system under the Islamic system. Studies prove that Musharakah is an economically viable financial system as it shares the risks and profits (Al-Harran, 1999). This idea evolved in a historical context in which pre-modern capitalist systems were in operation and values were not based on surplus. Rather, it was assessed based on sustainability. Profit or surplus is essential for growing capital and is the primary source of modern economic systems. Knight (1921) argues that profit is the reward for bearing uncertainties. Hawley (1907), in the classical text, observed that '.the profit of an undertaking, or the residue of the product after the claims of land, capital, and labor (furnished by others or by the undertaker himself) are satisfied, is not the reward of management or coordination, but of the risks and responsibilities that the undertaker... subjects himself to'. Profit is one of the driving forces behind production and, as such, one of the key "endogenous" drivers of productivity. While profit is the most significant incentive for starting new businesses, it also pushes people to risk their cash and invest it in profitable ventures (Magni, 2019). Adam Smith (1776) defines profit as compensation due from capitalist entrepreneur, linking it to the capitalist accumulation process and highlighting the financial gains from pursuing one's interests. Smith defined profit is the result of workers' labour producing more value than what is required to pay their salary. Smith highlighted how the division of labour and competition drives profits. Hirsch (2020) argues that Smith saw profit as a necessary, justifiable, and acceptable compensation for the "risk and trouble" that came with being the capital employer. Profit must continue to be sufficient to ensure capital accumulation and the largely risk-free use of it. Since the turn of the twentieth century, an entrepreneur's personal risk-taking has been a major justification for earnings (Hawley, 1893). Classical economists emphasize profit as an essential part of capital accumulation, and hence, the capitalist economy must continue in production. So the classical theories consider risk as a challenge in accumulating profits. Ricardo (1817) explains profit that profits result in from surplus value created by the difference between the cost of labour (wages) and the value of the output produced by labour. Classical economists connected profit with labour and surplus value; for instance, Marx (1887) who had defined profit as "the rate of surplus-value, all other circumstances remaining the same, will rise with the rising productivity of labor; it will fall with the falling productivity of labor. Now, given the working day's length, the surplus value rate is determined by two factors: the rate of surplus labor and the real wage". Marxian method of profits is well articulated in the context of surplus value and wage rate. So classical economics defined profit as a surplus arising out of entrepreneurship and the division of labour. Neoclassical economist suggests, on the other hand, that profit be viewed as mere income, representing the capital productive factor's compensation according to its marginal productivity (Magni, 2019). The definition of profit in neoclassical economics is the difference between total revenue and total costs. Total revenue is the money a business makes from selling its products. In contrast, total costs include all the expenditures associated with creating a product, such as labour, rent, raw materials, and capital depreciation.

Profit (π) can be represented as:

$$\pi = TR - TC$$

where TR = total revenue, TC = total costs.

Profit is the instrument for capitalist development and it is an engine of capitalism all economic models indeed ensure profits for capital to accumulate. Profit is the surplus and surplus is capital so defining risk sharing under this simple logic of economics is complex since it needs to establish an economic rationale for sharing risk among the actors. Capitalist and socialist economies need surplus and profits to survive. Hence, risk sharing does mean the sharing of negative externalities. Marxian theory's primary focus is the surplus value created. He defined it as "*the value of the product is exactly equal to the value of the capital advanced. The value so advanced has not expanded, no surplus value has been created, and consequently, money has not been converted into capital*[1]". It explains that

[1] Karl Marx. *Capital Volume I*. p. 131.

if the value of advanced capital is increased and distributed, it is called surplus value. It is the most critical part of advanced capitalist economies. In simple terms, it can be defined as profits or undistributed profits. The capital accumulation of every capitalist economy depends on the profits to survive; hence, the production process primarily ensures profits. Risk sharing is not about sharing profit alone. Instead, it is about sharing the program of making profits. From a Ricardian perspective, profits are solely the outcome of society's ability to work with nature to produce an excess of a good or service that exceeds what is needed to support the people (Obrinsky, 1983). Profit maximization is considered as the efficiency of the economy and economic system. Alfred Marshall (1890) defines profit sharing as, '*thus under the scheme of Profit-Sharing, a private firm while retaining the unfettered management of its business, pays its employees the full market rate of wages, whether by Time or Piece-work, and agrees in addition to divide among them a certain share of any profits that may be made above a fixed minimum; it being hoped that the firm will find a material as well as a moral reward in the diminution of friction, in the increased willingness of its employees to go out of their way to do little things that may be of great benefit comparatively to the firm, and lastly in attracting to itself workers of more than average ability and industry*'. Marshall refers to profit maximization as paying market wage and ensuring maximum labour participation, this could be otherwise called profit maximization. In microeconomics, a company functioning in a competitive market can maximize its profits by comparing its marginal revenue (MR) to its marginal cost (MC), i.e., MR = MC.

Profit maximization has been an important economic theory in neoclassical economics; Baumol (1959) explained profit maximization in the context of a competitive economy. Baumol argues that firms want to maximize profits by the optimum utilization of their resource and decisions are aimed at maximization of profits. The theory of profit maximization by Baumol offers a thorough framework for comprehending how businesses behave and strive for profit in constantly changing market conditions. It draws attention to how managerial choices, market rivalry, and long-term growth goals interact to influence the profitability and behaviour of businesses. Dierker and Grodal (1996), in their study, argue that utility maximization increases price competition whereas profit maximization does not. Profit maximization may be seen as advantageous for the owners overall because it typically results in higher prices. As said before profit maximization is associated with x-efficiency as Leibenstein

(1969) argues the degree to which businesses use their inputs to generate outputs at their highest possible efficiency level. He contends that organizational culture, reward systems, managerial conduct, and other factors can all contribute to X-inefficiency. X-inefficiency comes from both external and internal factors. Internal issues could be the root of it, such as resistance to change, rent-seeking behaviour, or poor management. External factors like market domination, a lack of competition, or regulatory restrictions can lead to X-inefficiency. The financial prospect and shareholder rights play a role in enabling risk sharing, highlighting the importance of sophisticated financial systems and a supportive regulatory framework (Kalemli-Ozcan et al., 2003). Profit maximization is a complex yet integral part of capital accumulation and capitalist development. Williamson (1962) proposes a managerial theory of profit maximization that emphasizes the importance of managerial decision-making in producing maximum profits.

The managerial theory of profit maximization emphasizes the role of managerial decision-making in maximizing profits. Managers are seen as agents who may pursue goals other than profit maximization, such as personal utility or job security. Managerial theory explores how managerial discretion influences firm behaviour and profitability. The firms seek to increase efficiency and the stakeholders' wealth and share (Baye & Prince, 2017). Sustaining a firm's competitive advantage is a critical tool for profit maximization (Boyes, 2003). Collaborative approaches that enable risk sharing and reduce uncertainty have emerged as a promising solution to the challenges faced by organizations during this crisis (Sopha et al., 2022). A firm could also be an institution, and every firm intends to ensure that it has the inherent institutional capability to enhance its competitive ability to make profits. Risk sharing is a critical path to profit maximization since it needs an internal change in the production process. Studies argue that businesses can optimize earnings in the short term by producing at a level where marginal revenue equals marginal cost (MR = MC). In the long run, businesses modify their inputs to reach the most profitable production level, where marginal revenue equals marginal cost and average total cost (MR = MC = ATC) (Mankiw, 2014). Decisions on maximizing profits are frequently made in unpredictable and risky situations. It is also well known that limited liability contracts' provision to reinvest losses in the economy distorts risk decisions and encourages higher volatility (Gollier et al., 1997). When deciding how much to produce and how much to charge, businesses must take into account variables, including demand volatility, input price swings, and competitive dynamics (Thomas & Maurice, 2019).

2.1 Profit, Risk, and Capital Accumulation

The expansion of capital is closely associated with profit, however, profit is connected with various kinds of risks and uncertainties. Individual firms to macro economies are susceptible to profit maximization risks. The classical economic theories were more concerned about risk as they were restricted to the idea of a stagnation theory. Classical economists were aware of the potential stagnation of the economy and its results on profit maximization. Adam Smith indicates the possibility of a stagnant stage in the economy in which an economy reaches poor economic growth due to resource constraints. The idea of division of labour is one of the methods to overcome the stagnation of the economy.

Smith's perception of wealth creation depends mainly on the idea of effective utilization of resources. The consumption of resources is limited to the current needs. According to him, *though the whole annual produce of the land and labour of every country is no doubt ultimately destined for supplying the consumption of its inhabitants, and for procuring revenue to them; yet when it first comes either from the ground, or from the hands of the productive labourers, it naturally divides itself into two parts. One of them, and frequently the largest, is, in the first place, destined for replacing a capital, or for renewing the provisions, materials, and finished work, which had been withdrawn from a capital; the other for constituting a revenue either to the owner of this capital, as the profit of his stock, or to some other person, as the rent of his land.*

Stagnation is a risk as well and classical and neoclassical economic literature have extensively discussed this critical concern. Alvin Hansen (1939), one the economist who has studied the question of the stagnation theory, argues that the challenge of sustaining full employment in a capitalist economy in the absence of dynamic investment expansion sufficient to absorb labour force growth and to provide for the capital replacement required to offset depreciation and obsolescence is known as economic stagnation or secular stagnation.

Keynes's (1937) theory of demand also reflects Hansen's thesis of secular stagnation; Keynes argued that demand for capital should come from the demand of a growing population and also from the demand for inventions and improvement to increase the output. Classical and neoclassical economists connect stagnation with the crisis of capitalism since it undervalues capital and disrupts capital growth. Classical economists discussed it with great emphasis, and the risk of stagnation is still haunting the global economy. Ricardo (1817) focuses on the law of diminishing returns and his idea of the differential fertility of land, Ricardo predicted that natural profit rates would decline. According to him, "*The natural tendency of profits, then is to fall; for, in the progress of society and wealth, the additional quantity of food required is obtained by the sacrifice of more and more labor. This tendency, this gravitation as it were of profits, is happily checked at repeated intervals by the improvements in machinery connected with the production of necessities, as well as by the discoveries in the sciences, which enables us to relinquish a portion of labor before required, and therefore to lower the price of the prime necessities of the laborer. The rise of labor is, however, limited; for as soon as wages should be equal to 720 pounds, the whole receipts of the farmer, there must be an end to accumulation, for no capital can yield any profit whatever, and no additional labor can be demanded, and consequently, population will have reached its highest point*". Ricardo's theory of stagnation primarily evolved from the theory of diminishing returns in agriculture. A key idea in economics is known as the rule of diminishing returns, which holds that when one input factor is raised while other factors remain constant, the resulting output will eventually decrease while keeping everything else constant. Chapter 1 refers this concept in the context of disasters. Decreasing marginal returns has been extensively analysed with different historical and economic contexts. Smith assessed it in the context of commodity and the level of satisfaction. Smith (1776) connected the diminishing returns with the increase of revenue and capital stock of the nation, according to him demand for wages would necessarily increase with the increase in national wealth. Smith never expected a stationary stage in which income and wealth move down; he defined this situation as an increase in labour costs inevitably driving up the price of many goods by raising the portion that becomes wages, which reduces both domestic and international consumption of those goods. Smith's problem was the cost of labour input; hence, it was population and consumption. It was a different kind of stagnation associated with consumption, as reducing capital surplus leads to poor investment and decreased economic activity. Their idea of stagnation is the threat of a stationary state. Classical economics theory of stagnation is the threat of underinvestment or a lack of funds to fund profitable investment might cause stagnation, which would slow down capital development and economic activity. Classical theory connects labour cost and population in a complex relationship in which labour is required at a lower price with the slow growth of the population. The classical economist is primarily influenced by the Malthusian trap, in which population increase would exceed the economy's ability to provide food, resulting in a stagnation of living standards. According to this theory, unrestrained population expansion may result in declining labour and resource returns. The iron law of population, which Malthus proposed, was another risk sharing concept of the classical period. Classical economists' concept of risk sharing is reducing the labour population. A higher labour population was equated with a lower surplus. By distinguishing between marginal and average surplus, declining returns enable hiring to respond forcefully to productivity shocks while retaining the ability to quantify unemployment's reaction to benefit changes (Dao & Delacroix, 2018). Some studies provide the notion of tolerable risks, which is expressed as a positive expectation following distribution function distortion. This results in a definition of capital requirements that only serves to justify the risks taken (Madan, 2009).

Classical economist proposes risk sharing at the cost of several labour populations and it was a period of slave labour in which mercantilists' understanding of labour was associated with slave labour. Beckert (2015) gives a detailed account of the connection between slavery and mercantilism. Beckert explains that European colonial powers established cotton farming in the Americas by exploiting slave labours. Slavery was a source of cheap labour for agricultural production, including, sugar, tobacco, and cotton. These products were the major source of income for mercantile capitalism. The profits were accumulated by Mercantilism and risks were transferred to slave labour. Another study by Williams (1943) explains the relationship between capitalism and slavery, in 1815 a bill was presented in the parliament to proscribe slave trade as an investment for British capital. According to him, the rise of capitalism did depend on slavery. His study discusses that European traders and investors were able to obtain a substantial amount of wealth from the profits made from the slave trade and goods made by slaves, which supported economic expansion and industrialization. Slave labour was controlled labour, and classical economists were in favour of controlled labour to protect the capital and share the risks. Slaver labour was indeed a method to overcome trade stagnation. Slave trade and exploitation in backward regions were one of the methods of preventing stagnation in terms of production and markets. Also trade stagnation under mercantile capitalism is associated with political empires, hence, the territorial expansion for slave labour and trade was part of empire-building. A detailed inquiry into production and stagnation is essential to understand risk sharing and transfer complexities.

Marxian analysis connected economic crisis with overproduction as a result of the pursuit of profit leads to overproduction. Marx defines *over-accumulation of capital and underconsumption as real barriers to capitalist production. Marx in Capital Vol, III part III, argues that 'it is that capital and its self-expansion appear as the starting and the closing point, the motive and the purpose of production; that production is only production for capital and not* vice versa, *the means of production are not mere means for a constant expansion of the living process of the society of producers*'. Marxian interpretation of stagnation is the overproduction through overaccumulation of capital, and hence risk of crisis is embedded in the system. $R = \delta \cdot (P - C)$, where, δ is economic risk sensitivity, P is production and C is consumption. So, the idea of stagnation in the Marxian approach is the result of underconsumption and a falling rate of profits. Clarke (1990) explains this critical issue of surplus value question and observes that this 'productivism' has implications for the theory of crisis, namely that the conditions necessary for the generation of surplus value had to be the source of the crisis rather than issues about the realization of surplus value. In the classical Marxian perspective falling profits lower the surplus and stagnation is inevitable. Classical Marxian theory proposes stagnation as the permanent crisis of monopoly capitalism. Monopoly capital is indeed susceptible to consumption crisis and risk-sharing is inevitable for survival. Paul and Sweezy (1966), explain that powerful businesses agencies control several economic sectors which result concentrations of political and economic power. Baran and Sweezy contend that under-employment, overproduction, stagnant wages, and a propensity towards economic instability are some of the main outcomes of this concentration of power in contemporary capitalism. Paul and Sweezy (1966: 336) explain that '*it is of the essence of capitalism that goods and labor power are typically bought and sold on the market. In such a society relations among individuals are dominated by the principles of exchange of equivalents of quid pro quo, not only in economic matters but in all other life as well*'. Monopoly capitalism operates at an underemployment level, and unlike other competitive economies, the tendency of stagnation is increasingly high in monopoly capitalism. Studies show that the rise of industrial concentration, increasing profit margins and profits, adverse effects on aggregate demand from the shift towards profits (and rising inequality), and the adverse effects of oligopoly on innovation and investment are just a few of the factors that the monopoly capital perspective identifies as contributing to slower growth (Sawyer, 2023). Monopoly capitalism developed a critical path for dealing with stagnation, however, distribution and consumption inequality makes stagnation inevitable.

The falling profit maximization and rate were economists' major points of inquiry for a longer period. For instance, Foster and McChesney (2012), defined stagnation as '*an economy in which decisions on savings and investment are made privately tends to fall into a stagnation trap: existing demand is insufficient to absorb all of the actual and potential savings (or surplus) available, output falls, and there is no automatic mechanism that generates full recovery*'. Foster and McChesney's theorization of stagnation is that it is the outcome of an economic decision-making process in which economic decisions are made at the private, i.e., within the monopoly capital. It is the result of monopoly capital and hence the growth rate is determined by the capability of the firms. Risk sharing, which is essentially the combination of two procees such as public risk sharing, which is the reduction in income risk resulting from the progressivity of income taxes, and, second private risk sharing, which is the reduction of consumption risk below after-tax income risk originating from private financial markets (Krueger & Perri, 2011). Monopoly capitalism does not ensure distribution and hence accumulation of capital may not result in investment to meet the demand. They further argue that '*stagnation also did not necessarily mean deep downturns with negative growth, but rather a slowing down of the trend-rate of growth due to overaccumulation. Net investment (i.e., investment beyond that covered by depreciation funds) atrophied, since with rising productivity what little investment was called for could be met through depreciation funds alone*'. The classical economists perceived stagnation as a situation in which the economy reaches a negative growth rate and surplus becomes zero. Overaccumulation of capital is possible through controlling production and also reducing variable costs. Valuation, or the expansion of value, is the fundamental logic of capitalist production; to be more precise, production is oriented towards an ongoing increase in profit. Production is directed towards rising profits, which suggests that capital is always being forced to exert more control, lowering costs per unit of physical output and accelerating the profit rate (Reuten, 1991). Reducing issues with risk selection is another justification for risk sharing, which can also be a handy tool for compensating health plans for unpriced risk heterogeneity. However, there are trade-offs associated with risk sharing, chiefly the dilution of plan incentives to contain costs (McGuire & Van Kleef, 2017). Theories of stagnation explain that capital accumulation itself is the reason for stagnation. Accumulation is otherwise defined as profit maximization and hence risk of profit maximization could be defined as accumulation. The risk of profit maximization could be the reason for stagnation.

2.2 Risk and Profit Maximization

Classical and neoclassical economics equally emphasize the depletion of the value of capital, which results in a situation in which capital becomes idle. This is the beginning of risk sharing as a project to save capital assets and asset value. Classical economists found the reasons for the idle capital stage, such as labour population and poor consumption. As explained above, mercantile capitalism was run on overaccumulation capital, so harsh measures were recommended to make capital safe. Risk on profit maximization is the empirical effect of the law of diminishing returns on firms. Firms expect higher expected utility as a method to risk aversion, so investment decisions determine the risk on profitability. Averting firm-level stagnation to secular stagnation at the macro-level is part of this critical process. For a firm, risk is anything that affects its profits. It could be operational strategies, finance, and competition. Neo-classical economists emphasize the importance of firm, as institutions that improve the efficiency of economic decision-making.

Marshall (1890) definition of the firm is the interface of the principle of organization arising from the division of labour and the principle of substitution. Marshall conceptualizes industry and firm as organization to maximize profit and efficiency. Marshall (1890: Chapter XIII of the Principles of Economics) explains that, '*and lastly we saw how every increase of wealth and every increase in the numbers and intelligence of the people increased the facilities for a highly developed industrial organization, which in its turn adds much to the collective efficiency of capital and labour. Looking more closely at the economies arising from an increase in the scale of production of any kind of goods, we found that they fell into two classes—those dependent on the general development of the industry, and those dependent on the resources of the individual houses of business engaged in it and the efficiency of their management; that is, into external and internal economies*'. The capability of the firm to operate an efficient economy was the critical focus of Marshall. Though Marshall did not discuss the firms explicitly, it led to many inquiries on the theory of firm and organization. Hague (1958), in the study, argues that Marshall's idea of a firm supports the principles of monopolistic competition based on product differentiation. Marshall's theory of firms operates on sharing knowledge across firms, for him, "it has many forms, *e.g.* that of a single business, that of various businesses in the same trade, that of various trades relatively to one another, and that of the State providing security for all and help for many" (Marshall, 1890). A firm's nature, profitability, and market vary across the economies and systems. Among them, Marshall prefers state security as an instrument that influences the structure of the firm. A firm is a fundamental institution of an economy, and it is a basic unit of economic risk management as well. Risk management at the firm level is indeed an effective method to identify the stakeholders and share the risks. As said before, a firm's critical ability with reference to risk sharing is to innovate and strategize the falling profit and loss of market access. Strategies of risk sharing are rooted in firms' capability to manage profitability.

Coase (1937) elaborates that a firm consists of a system of relationships that comes into existence when the direction of resources depends on an entrepreneur. Coordination and decision-making within the company can occur more profitably, reducing transaction expenses. Coase's research cast doubt on the idea of perfect competition and offered an alternative viewpoint on the function of businesses in the economy. His findings stimulated more investigation into organizational economics and established the groundwork for transaction cost economics. Williamson (1985a, 1985b) defined the costs of carrying out an economic exchange, such as those associated with information gathering, bargaining, and enforcement, as transaction costs. These expenses may differ based on the transaction's complexity, uncertainty level, and participant communication frequency. An interdisciplinary method for studying organizations, transaction cost analysis combines elements of contract law, organization theory, and economics. It comprehensively explains various organizational phenomena (Williamson, 1981). Transaction cost economics argues that the economic agents plan their operations to minimize transaction costs (Lowe & Teece, 2000). Transaction cost economics explains why businesses outsource or use markets rather than internally developing every aspect of their operations (Tate and Ellram, 2022).Transaction cost economics is a framework for comprehending transaction costs between economic agents—such as firms—and how these costs affect the decision between market and hierarchical governance structures, provided by transaction cost economics (Zajac & Olsen, 1992). Transaction cost studies help to predict the governance structure, such as market, hybrid, or hierarchy, as a function of the attributes of the transaction process (Chiles & McMackin, 1996a, 1996b). Transaction cost economics gives a theoretical framework to discuss the idea of risk sharing. Opportunism hazards, limited rationality, uncertainty, and small-number bargaining lead to transaction costs (Foss, 1996). Williamson (1998: 393) defined that '*transaction cost economics acknowledges that technology and ownership of assets are both important, but it maintains that neither is determinative of the economic organization nor are both together. Rather, the study of economic organization has to go beyond technology and ownership to examine incentives and governance. Transaction cost economics maintains that the transaction is the basic unit of analysis and gives special emphasis to the study of governance*'. Williamson emphasizes the need for the institutional ability to measure incentives and risk in economic decision-making. It is pretty critical for governing policies to ensure incentives in decision-making. The rationale for selecting the right decision when the crisis of losses is embedded in economic institutions requires a practical assessment of the far-reaching implications of the crisis on assets and value. Considering the human and institutional constraints in assessing the probabilities of risk in the changing context of environment and market risks. These discussions and theories concern capitalism's sustainability; market, cost, and variable inputs affect the risks. Risk influences the decision-making of capitalism, and capitalism will always try to build its adaptive method to overcome the risks. Risk is often interpreted within the institutional rationality of the capitalist firm. Williamson (1998) has initiated this discussion on risk neutrality. Risk neutrality is embedded in the fact that human agents are intended to be rational but only limitedly so. Human and institutional agencies prefer to make risk-neutral decisions on the assumption that the firm would adopt or share the risks with other stakeholders. Williamson (1998) further elaborates that risk neutrality facilitates analysis and captures central decision-making tendencies. If the expected average of the potential fluctuating profits is equal to a certain profit, then an assumption of risk neutrality implies that a risk-neutral party is unaffected by the possibility of uncertain profits or a certain profit (Aoki, 1984: 15). Risk sharing evolves out of the deep concern of risk aversion. This assumption can be compared to the risk aversion assumption of neoclassical economics, which postulates that a risk-averse party will always favour a fixed profit over the possibility of fluctuating profits—as long as the fixed profit's expected value is greater than some positive value than the expected average of the prospective profits (Chiles & McMackin, 1996a, 1996b). Risk aversion is essential for finance capital, so institutions in finance capital propose risk diversification as a strategy. Markowitz (1952) demonstrated that an investor can obtain a higher expected return for a given level of risk, or conversely, a lower level of risk for a given expected return, by maintaining a diverse portfolio of assets whose returns are not completely correlated. This results in the Capital Asset Pricing Model (CAPM) and the Efficient Market Hypothesis (EMH) model being used to assess the risks. Risk aversion is associated with asset value; when neither opportunism nor transaction-specific investments are present, risk aversion incentivizes the acquisition of assets—so long as the assets in issue can fluctuate in value throughout use (Martynov & Schepker, 2017).

Risk aversion is an institutional process itself and a theory, too. Pricing of economic uncertainty occurs only in times of significant aggregate risk aversion. The risk aversion-related component contributes most of the uncertainty premium in financial uncertainty. While the remaining component swings with market mood, this portion varies with the real economy (Ren et al., 2023). Risk aversion is connected with economic policy uncertainties (Zhang et al., 2021), and as a theory, it challenges the capability and rationality of financial decision-making. One needs to refer to the bounded rationality approach in risk aversion and transaction cost to understand the complexities of risk sharing. Contends that cognitive limitations and information-processing capacities are intrinsic constraints on decision-making processes (Simon, 1955). Scholar argues that collective risk-taking, in contrast, is a social malaise, fuelled by a malicious profit motive (Nacol, 2016). Risk sharing could be consider as the method to meet the impact of consumption shocks (Holzmann et al., 2000; Townsend, 1994). Risk sharing as an economic concept primarily assesses the utility of assets and expected returns.

Studies highlight the importance of Net Profit Margin and Company Size in shaping Risk Disclosure. It has been discovered that company size significantly affects risk disclosure in the companies under analysis (Fatmawatie et al., 2021). Risk sharing, in principle, is the loss and profit sharing, i.e., an agency expected to take the risk of loss of expected value and net present value of assets. The Islamic models perceive risk as an integral part of asset pricing. The extent of risk sharing determines the expected outcome disparities between sharing partners; the more significant the predicted inequality, the less risk shared. When there is full risk sharing, the results are precisely equal (Cettolin & Tausch, 2015). It is also a fact that increased risk-taking creates an increased need for risk sharing (Belhaj et al., 2014). People who prefer risk aversion prefer risk sharing, i.e., insuring against exposure (Biais et al., 2016). Cherry et al. (2015) examine the social dilemma associated with risk pooling and sharing. Arrow (1971) presents the idea of risk aversion; it refers to people's propensity to favour known outcomes over uncertain ones, even when the uncertain events have higher expected values. He contends that many people are experiencing risk aversion due to things like the declining marginal value of money. Expectations on fluctuating utility are the driving force of risk sharing; however, risk sharing is an institutional process in which the individual and systems need a contract and an assuring economic system capable of ensuring value later. The mutuality principle highlights that risk can be properly dispersed among individuals depending on their preferences and baseline endowments (Aase, 2021). Risk-sharing agreements lessen people's susceptibility to unforeseen circumstances that could negatively impact their financial status. This is because sharing risks entails redistribution, with fortunate people and communities supporting the vulnerable (Cettolin & Tausch, 2015). Risk sharing is a contract with an agency in which the agency's economic capability plays a critical role in ensuring risk aversion. Risk aversion is meant to save the value of assets and capital; hence, risk sharing, in principle, is a contract to ensure a higher asset price. The critical aspect of this contract is that it needs a differential assessment of risks vis a via asset value. Risk sharing and contracts are indeed an economic process meant to generate surplus. It is not about saving and interest generation alone; rather, it is an economic process to ensure a productive return on capital. Risk sharing is a contact, too; contracts are essential to economic interactions because they give people and businesses a framework for risk management and efficient resource allocation. A contract is an agreement between two parties that requires them to reciprocate behaviour obligations; it is a bilateral coordination framework (Brousseau & Glachant, 2004). Insurance is a critical institution in risk sharing, and it has become an institution over time. Stiglitz (1974) studied risk sharing in an agricultural system, and he found that a landowner and his tenant engage in risk sharing through sharecropping, which may be seen as a type of insurance. The nature of that insurance contract is significantly impacted by the landlord's challenges in keeping an eye on the tenant's contributions. Insurance is a contract, too; hence, the parties in the contract should better understand the risks and benefits. Insurance contract design must strike a balance between risk and incentive effects; the more risk-averse an individual is and the more hazards they encounter, the more crucial it is to reduce those risks (Stiglitz, 1983). The pre-modern Arabian system's risk sharing was in demand of moral and collective responsibility in asset management, and win and loss needed to be shared. They were not apprehensive about the stagnation stage of the economy, which was a period in which trade was the major source of capital. Later, Mercantile capitalism demonstrated the importance of the stagnation stage due to poor demand. Keynesian and neoclassical economics emerged from the stagnation stage crisis and the Great Depression of the 1930s. There are different explanations for the causes of the great depression; some scholars argue that industrial production increased dramatically throughout the 1920s, but wages did not rise in line with productivity increases. As a result, there was an excess of items compared to the demand from consumers, which lowered prices and reduced earnings (Temin, 1976). Another explanation is the role of income inequality at the time. There was a growing disparity in the nation's wealth distribution as the wealthy accumulated a disproportionate amount. This income disparity intensified the economic downturn and led to a drop in consumer expenditure (Shiller, 2005). The Depression of 1930 taught the lesson of the risk of capital accumulation and distribution, and it also taught the need for risk sharing. Keynesian and neoclassical discourses attempted to engage with the causes of depression and find methods to overcome it. It has become an integral part of the modern economy to have safety measures to survive. Monopoly, marketization, cartel economy, etc., evolved over some time to survive the crisis. The insurance sector is one of modern capitalism's most effective risk sharing institutions.

2.3 Insurance as Risk Sharing

Insurance is a capital formation, as Allan H. Willett (1901), defined insurance, *the essential features of economic insurance as we have defined it are the accumulation of capital to meet uncertain losses and the transfer and combination of risks.* Accumulating capital for future risk prevention is possible only when there is certainty on the future value of capital and also higher expectations than the present consumption value. Risk insurance is an outcome of an organized economic project to secure asset value and price. This is a theoretical and institutional rationale for insurance as a separate economic system. Insurance is indeed a process when future income or return from an investment is unknown; there is a risk that needs to be assessed by the economic agent taking on the risk. Every discussion on risk sharing begins with the story of a Chinese merchant's idea of sharing their merchandise among different small boats while crossing a river, so if a boat sinks, only a tiny portion of merchandise is lost. Another narration was about caravans travelling across the Babylonia deserts, distributing their merchandise among camels and several caravans to reduce the risk of loss due to extreme weather risks (Outreville, 1998). This narration tells us how the economic decision on loss and future return is assessed. The willingness to take risks is the driving force of insurance, and the willingness is nothing but the trade-off of future returns. Over time, insurance has become an institution of risk-taking and sharing. Lowry et al. (2011) define insurance as a contract wherein one party undertakes to compensate the other for potential financial loss if certain defined events occur in exchange for a sum of money known as the premium. An insurance contract is an agreement whereby one party, the insurer, agrees to pay another party, the policyholder or a third party, a premium or assessment if an event that is the subject of a risk materializes. It is frequently described as an indemnification contract (Outreville, 1998).

Scholars also observed that insurance is not a mitigation tool, so a carefully designed insurance scheme could encourage the adoption of loss reduction based on economic incentives such as low premium (Petak, 1998). Insurance strengthens people's and communities' resilience by offering a financial safety net. Reconstruction and rehabilitation depend heavily on this financial assistance (Botzen and Van Den Bergh, 2008). The insurance sector faces enormous challenges due to the frequency and severity of natural disasters increasing due to climate change. Better risk assessment models and innovative insurance products are needed (Averchenkova et al., 2016). Furthermore, insurance can be viewed as a tool for both recovery and preparedness for enhanced resilience to create a resilient society and adapt to long-term hazards (Faure & Heldt, 2016).

It is a contract to protect the utility value of capital in a given period with specific expectations. Actuarial science has developed a method to combine economics and mathematics to assess the premium and investment strategies. Klugman et al. (2012) observe that actuaries analyse historical data, forecast future claims, and estimate the costs of providing coverage, all of which are critical in determining insurance rates. To calculate the proper rate, they consider various aspects, including age, gender, health status, and experience with losses. The growth of actuarial science is part of the transformation of risk sharing as an economic and business entity.

2.3.1 Insurance as 'Risk Industry'

Islamic finance proposed a model of risk sharing in which both the losses and profit are shared among the stakeholders. The cornerstone of the risk sharing paradigm in Islamic finance is the ban on interest rate-based contracts. Islam forbids interest-bearing because all transactions involve the counterparties moving or transferring risk (Swastika & Mirakhor, 2021). Sharing is possible only when all the stakeholders are equally aware of the probability of loss due to external causes. The transformation of the modern economic system, especially finance capitalism, changed the risk sharing and insurance sectors. Risk insurance has become a ' priced commodity', and that indeed makes governing risk a comparatively easy task. Risk premiums and claims become the tools for governing risk sharing. Estimating expected claims to be paid and costs associated with taking on the risk of a defined loss exposure can be pricing an insurance contract. Only when the risk is correctly identified, and a significant number of comparable loss exposures (i.e., traits of an ideally insurable risk) are available to compute the expected frequency and severity of the losses can the prediction of claims be considered reliable (Outreville, 1998). Insurance depends on expected utilities, so insurance growth could be read as the growth of uncertain capitalism. Arrow Debreu (1954) defines risk sharing in a general equilibrium framework based on households, producers, and the market. Risk sharing is possible through hedging unexpected incidents by exchanging claims. More comprehensive definitions and possibilities have expanded the market for risk industries; here, one needs to clearly understand the linkages between the risk industry and at-risk capitalism. The risk industry is an integral part of the current global market economy. Thus, 'capitalism' and 'risk' worked in tandem, with the former providing ideas for generating the latter by pointing out dangers that might be valued economically and legally, packaged in marketable forms, and exchanged freely for gain (Purcell Jr, 2016). The crisis of capitalism and at-risk capitalism should be assessed explicitly since the capitalist crisis has its history. Studies on risk and capital observed that capital shields and mitigates a corporation from bankruptcy or catastrophe brought on by significant unforeseen losses. Such "risk capital" must be held at a cost since investors want a sufficient return on their investment. Some studies attempt to distinguish between risk capital and risk-based capital (RBC), risk capital is the overall amount of money available to support risk, whereas risk-based capital is the capital allotted to support a particular risk or risks (Kull, 2009). From the Great Depression to the neoliberal market economy, capitalism experienced a crisis and overcame it with adaptation measures. Capitalism at risk has to be looked at from its institutional nature and adaptive ability to run a business with multiple risks. Bower et al., (2011: 186) have discussed this critical question concerning the business process; according to them, rather than being seen as exogenous to the enterprises that we study and that our forum members lead, the global economy and its social, political, and physical conditions should be seen as profoundly impacted by the actions of these firms. Consequently, it is impossible to consider these external conditions outside the proper management jurisdiction. Also, firms need to improve their abilities to mitigate the disruptive factors that could otherwise affect market capitalism for the sustainability and well-being of the system they rely on. Business firms are increasingly becoming aware and capable of engaging with the social, economic, political, and environmental factors that push business prospects down. Capitalism makes everybody believe it is capable enough to withstand any external threats, however, finance and market capitalism are equally vulnerable to external risks. Kindleberger and Aliber (2011: 12, 25) discuss risk in the context of bubbles in the asset price market, and they argue that when the economy is expanding, lenders become less risk-averse, and investors become more upbeat and eager to seize profitable possibilities that will pay off in the far future. It is a complex process of asset price and investments. Investors updated their estimations of the profitability of a wide range of assets throughout the growth phase, increasing their optimism about the future and their willingness to borrow. Lenders became more willing to give loans, even for investments that had previously seemed too dangerous, due to a drop in their risk aversion and estimates of the risk of particular assets.

Global capitalism has experienced the rise of asset price speculations and collapse, so investors and firms seek risk sharing, however, the higher expected return on an asset hardly ensures any risk sharing. The collapse of the bubbles results in a loss of assets and capital, so insurance-based risk sharing becomes another loss of capital loss and not accumulation. Excessive debt is another risk that market capitalism cannot share; Reinhart and Rogoff (2009) underline how debt accumulation frequently occurs before financial disasters. Through their analysis of public and private debt dynamics throughout several historical events, they demonstrate how excessive borrowing and leverage can result in economic downturns and financial instability. The debt is otherwise a process of capital accumulation; however, increasing debt without a higher return on value leads to a debt trap. The debt trap puts the economy and business at risk; hence, no insurance institutions or firms would be willing to share the risks. Country-level debt is another macroeconomic crisis often resulting in risk accumulation rather than sharing. See Fig. 2.1

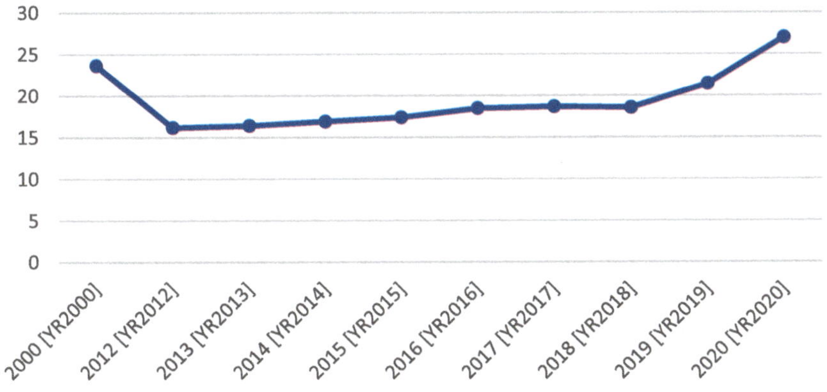

Fig. 2.1 Average growth of insurance companies assets to GDP (*Source* https://databank.worldbank.org/source/global-financial-development/Series/GFDD.DI.11#)

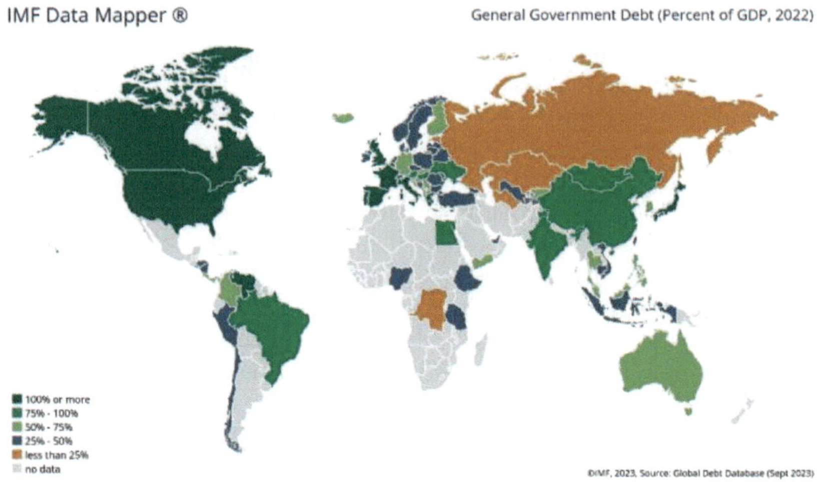

Higher debt is a developmental risk that limits the risk sharing. A significant factor in impeding risk sharing during the sovereign debt crisis was fiscal austerity programs (Kalemli-Ozcan et al., 2013). Both developed and developing economies have problems with debt as a limiting factor, often leading to debt overhangs. It is a situation in which an entity's current debt load prevents it from making profitable investments or operations because of worries about its financial health and borrowing capacity restrictions. The indebtedness of an economy raises the risk premium and interest rate, so higher interest rates push lower capital accumulation (Hwang et al., 2010). Increasing debt is also a risk; it will affect the natural growth of capital. The International Monitory Funds debt relief to highly indebted poor countries indicates the global risk sharing mechanism. About 7.6 billion dollars is spent to relieve these countries from paying their debt relief.[2] It was global risk sharing and meant to save these economies. Such risk sharing is possible through international financial institutions' interventions. Also, developing countries like India offer debt relief to poor farmers to save the sector from debt overhang. An assessment by the government source proved that in

[2] https://www.imf.org/en/About/Factsheets/Sheets/2023/Debt-relief-under-the-heavily-indebted-poor-countries-initiative-HIPC.

India, 50.2% of agricultural households are in debt,[3] and India is known for the highest number of farmer suicides as well. India's National Crime Records Bureau (NCRB) data released on December 4, 2023, at least one farmer is committing suicide every single hour in India. The number of farmers' suicides in India shows the critical linkages between debt and risk sharing. Still, the Indian agricultural insurance sector is emerging, and substantial private capital and government subsidies play a crucial role in promoting insurance. So, it is critical to understand the evolution of the insurance industry and risk sharing.

2.4 Insurance as 'Risk Sharing Industry'

It may sound odd to call risk sharing an industry since this financial sector is meant to pool risk and share. Insurance is a critical sector in risk sharing that pools the risks that are expected to ensure better utility. Individual demand for insurance contracts is straightforward, and insurance is purchased on expected returns (Rothschild & Stiglitz, 1976). Risk sharing is a demand-driven sector in which individuals demand an institution to share the risk while keeping their expectations on utility high. It is anticipated that every person will operate in a way that maximizes their expected utility of money, avoids risk, acknowledges the possibility of financial loss, and can influence the probability distribution of loss by careful consideration (Shavell, 1979). Kahneman and Tversky (1979) propose a theory of prospects in which they argue that people assess results in terms of deviations from a reference point rather than net asset levels, and determining this reference point is a crucial factor. They also tend to place greater weight on losses than on comparable gains, and they are generally risk-averse when it comes to gains and risk-acceptant when it comes to losses. The insurance sector depends on this prospect theory of loss, which is possible through institutions. Prospects theory involves identifying the various options, the potential results or ramifications, and the values associated with each outcome (Levy, 1992). Prospects theory is the theory of decision-making at risk, as Kononovych and Myasoid (2020) observe personal qualities that impact decision-making processes, including emotional intelligence, intolerance for uncertainty, and rationality. Prospects theory has been the theme for many academic

[3] National Sample Survey Office's (NSSO) 'Situation Assessment of Agricultural Households and Land and Livestock Holding, 2019.

inquiries; Sawa (2021) discusses how prospect theory-abiding participants' bargaining games are affected by stochastically stable division, demonstrating persistent deviations from the Nash bargaining solution under expected utility theory. Every rational human choice expects higher expected utility, so the evolution of insurance institutions and demand for risk sharing is the most critical realization of human choice out of risks.

2.5 Institutions of Insurance and Risk Sharing

Uncertainty is the rational outcome of social process, and profit could be otherwise the result of governing uncertainties. Knight (1921), in the classical work, defined uncertainty, develops when probabilities cannot be assigned, but the risk is associated with circumstances in which the likelihood of various events is known. Knight maintained that uncertainty could not be minimized by computation or analysis since it is essentially unknown. Uncertainty is part of every economic system, and capitalism seems to be more susceptible to risk and uncertainty. Insurance as a sector of governing risks evolved out of this critical juncture of development and finance capitalism, which meant to be averse to any risk on profitability. With insurance, people, and companies can provide an insurer with the risk of possible losses in return for a payment. This risk transfer may result from financial stability and a sense of security (Harrington and Niehaus, 2016). Insurance is otherwise called risk pooling and sharing; however, studies prove that risk pooling alone cannot justify insurance activities because issued policies have familiar risk drivers that are difficult to diversify. Insurers can transfer these risks to reinsurers (Bernard, 2013). Risk sharing through insurance is possible only when both firms/individuals have strong preferences over higher utility. Risk sharing through insurance is primarily a project to ensure effective risk aversion and depends on the institutional capability of the firm. Borch (1974) explains this concept with a critical insight: 'the focal point in the theory of risk, has been the probability of ruin for almost a century. *It has been assumed that at least a partial objective of the insurance company is to ensure that the probability of ruin does not exceed a given number, say a sum. The theory is usually vague or utterly silent about how the number should be determined. The model seems to make the most sense if a value of a is imposed from outside, for instance, by a government inspector*'. Borch's analysis of the probability of ruin tells that risk sharing is associated with institutions, strategies, and contracts. The unique risk associated with life insurance is the likelihood of future unfavourable development in factors critical to the business's ability to remain solvent, such as inflation, interest rates, mortality, and invalidity (Beard et al., 1969). The probability of ruin is otherwise defined as the probability of loss of assets and future capital accumulation. It could be otherwise called a moral hazard economic operation. Moral hazards in insurance are the idea that people may change their behaviour in reaction to having insurance, which could result in increased risk-taking or neglect. This is known as the theory of moral hazard in insurance. Stated differently, individuals with insurance coverage against specific risks could be less likely to act responsibly or take preventative measures since they are sure of their financial security in the event of a loss.

There is an economics in moral hazards and it is dependent on the capability of the institutions to assess the risk value of assets. Pauly (1968) proposed two partial solutions to the moral hazard problem, first is insufficient loss coverage and, the second is "observation" by the insurer of the precautions taken to avert loss. Firm-level capability also matters in engaging with moral hazard problems; it is primarily a process of assessing the risk of capital loss and ensuring gain. Moral hazard is subject to multiple levels of academic and policy studies. The history of moral hazard is indeed the history of Insurance. Insurance is a manifestation of governing moral hazards with an economic logic of gain and loss. Preceding the Common (or Christian) Era by several thousand years are the earliest documented instances of insurance. Chinese traders, or the entrepreneurs of the day, came up with a way to safeguard themselves against cargo losses that could occur at sea from storms, pirate attacks, or other mishaps (Vaughan, 1997). The origins of insurance can also be found in Babylon, where merchants were incentivized to take on the transportation risks associated with the caravan trade using loans that were only paid back (with interest) once the products had arrived without incident (Franklin, 2001: 259; Buckham et al., 2010: 2). The first instances of risk transfer may be discovered in ancient civilizations like Egypt, China, and Babylon, demonstrating the long history of the insurance idea. Mutual aid agreements were a part of these early customs, in which people combined their resources to guard against shared threats (Scott, 2011). In fact, insurers are likely to refrain from underwriting catastrophic or systemic risks, sometimes called "uninsurable risks" (Jaffee and Thomas Russell, 1997). It illustrates how insurance works with other risk reduction tactics, including socio-economic policy and construction regulations, demonstrating how insurance may help achieve more general social objectives than just providing financial compensation for losses (Franco, 2021). Insurance is an economic enterprise that requires profit for risk management to survive.

2.6 Risk Sharing and 'Risk Profit'

Over time, insurance has become an industry with profits. One needs to distinguish between risk and uncertainty in insurance. Studies argue that insurance covers risk but not uncertainty (Masci, 2011). Insurance as an industry is run on the idea of mutual gain. As said before, premiums and claims are the two prominent mechanisms that regulate this sector and ensure the 'profits' to the firms to provide insurance products and retain the risk sharing business. The general narrative of risk is that Risk = Probability × Impact, here for an insurance firm probability of risk occurring and the expected value of loss is the main concern for an insurance firm. The profitability and the firm-level sustainability of insurance as risk sharing depends on the predicted value capital loss confronting the probabilities of occurrences. Insurancdepends on the predicted value capital loss confronting the probabilities of occurrences. Among the various factors, the expected value of loss and gain is the critical factors that run the insurance firm.

$$EV = \sum_{i-1}^{n} P(X_i) * V(X_i)$$

EV = Expected Value, $P(Xi)$ = Probability of the ith outcome occurring, $V(Xi)$ = Value (or payout) associated with the ith outcome, n = Total number of possible outcomes.

The amount and volume of asset loss vary over time, and classical economists referred to the station of the economy as a risk. Capitalist enterprises' business and expansion have increasingly changed the determinants of expected values. In the study of probability and statistics, especially in the context of insurance, the idea of anticipated value is crucial. It shows the mean result of a random variable over numerous trials, each result being weighted according to its likelihood. Expected value is a tool used in insurance to help calculate the appropriate premium an insurer should charge to cover possible losses. There is an economic logic that works in insurance which is about accumulating capital for averting risks at the same time increasing the value of assets. So, this risk sharing itself is more susceptible to uncertainties and risks. Risk-sharing industries have evolved along with the uncertainties of economic development, finance capitalism, and natural calamities. Risk profit is dependent on how risk shifts the value of assets and their future growth prospects. Insurance profit is otherwise an investment to overcome uncertainties and risks, so the value of premium plays a critical role in ensuring the institutional sustainability of risk sharing. As an economic institution dependent on capital, the insurance sector has evolved multiple methods to ensure profits and govern the risk to arrive at a win–win situation. Raviv (1979) observed that insurance is about the probability of losses, hence the institutional interventions of risk sharing effectively developed a method to ensure risks. Actuarial value is an important instrument in the insurance business. The field of actuarial science uses statistical and mathematical techniques to evaluate risk in the insurance, financial, and other sectors of the economy. When calculating insurance premiums using complex calculations that include expected values, actuaries are essential. For instance, premium rates and actuarial values are determinants of risk sharing profits.

$$AV = \frac{\text{Total value of covered benefits}}{\text{Total allowed charges for covered benefits}} \times 100$$

Premium and actuarial value assessment enables the insurance sector to establish itself as an industry and control risk sharing as a business. This is a critical juncture to discuss the growth of insurance, and the following part discusses it in detail.

Figure 2.1 shows the average growth of insurance companies' assets from 2000 to 2020; it shows the development of capital accumulated by the insurance firms. What does it indicate? It otherwise shows the stability of capital and risk aversion. The information in Fig. 2.1 needs to be compared with Table 2.1. The figures in Table 2.1 indicate the importance of insurance capital in countries' Gross Domestic Products. There are countries whose insurance share is even higher than the total GDP. It is a complex economic relationship since, theoretically, the entire risk of financial collapse should have the institutional capability to withstand the moral hazards. Studies proved the positive correlation between insurance and GDP growth (Apergis & Poufinas, 2020; Peleckienė, et al., 2019). Cristea et al. (2014) also establish the contribution of insurance to the growth rate of the Netherlands, the UK, and Finland. Another study also established that life insurance positively impacts economic growth in 15 European countries. The specific nature of these studies is that the economies that benefitted from insurance are the high-income and economically forward countries and not economically backward or underdeveloped economies.

Insurance becomes a decisive factor in economic decision-making, and one of the core reasons for this increasing growth rate of insurance is the expansion of finance capital. For instance, Fig. 2.2 gives information on the share of insurance and financial services in the balance of payment for global exports.

Insurance spending has also increased over some time as a source to ensure capital security. Figure 2.3 shows the percentage of insurance growth in GDO in OECD economies. It shows a consistent increase in insurance spending as a percentage of GDP, so it also indicates the presence of uncertainty over the business process. The insurance industry itself is subject to an increasing growth rate; Fig. 2.4 shows the asset growth of insurance companies at the global level from 2002 to 2022. It indicates the rising firm-level capacity of the firms along with the risk aversion practice of capitalism.

The growth rate of insurance companies' assets, the share of insurance in GDP, and insurance spending are signs of an economy that expects future certainty and accumulating capital. Technically, insurance is primarily a decision of the firms, as Mayers and Smith (1982) argue insurance purchases are part of a firm's financing decision. Wealth accumulation by insurance firms is a risk as it carries assurance against uncertainties in the growth of assets. It is otherwise defined as capital accumulated to save the capital. As said before, the project of capital accumulation for insurance needs a scientific method to predict the actual loss and set the limit of risk sharing. Terms like actuarial and indemnity value (i.e., Actual Cash Value (ACV) – Deductible) resolve the issue of capital loss and gain of both the insurer and insured. This process is often linear in general risk sharing; however, such general conditions of win–win or win–loss confront massive shocks when they are subject to disaster and climate risks. It is imperative to see the critical institutional, financial, and policy-level risk sharing crisis under disaster and climate risks. Disasters pose theoretical and policy challenges to insurance firms and prove the institutional vulnerability of insurance as risk sharing in natural calamities.

Table 2.1 Insurance company assets to GDP by country, in%

Country	*In %*	*Country*	*In %*	*Country*	*In %*	*Country*	*In %*	*Country*	*In %*	*Country*	*In %*
Angola	1.26	Botswana	10.55	Estonia	6.66	Jamaica	23.42	Malaysia	22.22	Russia	3.17
Albania	2.4	Canada	83.68	Finland	33.25	Japan	80.2	Namibia	38.42	Saudi Arabia	2.58
United Arab Emirates	7.28	Switzerland	101	Fiji	19.76	Kazakhstan	2.1	Niger	0.6716	Sudan	0.6653
Argentina	4.98	Chile	27.26	France	132	Kenya	6.64	Nigeria	1.05	Senegal	3.32
Armenia	1.1	China	22.74	United Kingdom	112	Kyrgyzstan	0.8235	Nicaragua	3.14	Singapore	63.73
Australia	12.59	Ivory Coast	2.5	Georgia	1.85	South Korea	73.61	Netherlands	69.04	El Salvador	3.94
Austria	30.55	Cameroon	1.88	Gambia	0.7326	Laos	0.8537	Norway	53.21	Serbia	5.71
Belgium	81.87	Republic Of The Congo	0.7661	Greece	11.82	Lebanon	9.44	Nepal	10.02	Slovakia	8.26
Benin	1.69	Colombia	9.12	Guatemala	1.96	Sri Lanka	4.65	New Zealand	6.8	Slovenia	17.2
Burkina Faso	2.9	Cape Verde	4.87	Guyana	7.58	Lithuania	4.7	Oman	4.57	Sweden	113
Bulgaria	5.75	Costa Rica	7.1	Honduras	4.3	Latvia	5.05	Panama	6.67	Chad	0.2382
Bahrain	17.35	Cyprus	17.33	Croatia	12.56	Moldova	1.47	Peru	8.43	Togo	4.24
Bahamas	15.79	Czech Republic	8.66	Hungary	6.84	Mexico	7.65	Philippines	10.76	Thailand	23.72

(continued)

Table 2.1 (continued)

Country	*In %*	*Country*	*In %*	*Country*	*In %*	*Country*	*In %*	*Country*	*In %*	*Country*	*In %*
Bosnia and Herze-govina	5.58	Germany	67.87	Indonesia	4.61	Macedonia	3.87	Papua New Guinea	1.32	Trinidad and Tobago	24.22
Belarus	2.88	Denmark	128	Ireland	91.42	Mali	0.617	Poland	8.8	Turkey	5.66
Bolivia	2.74	Dominican Republic	2	Iran	3.08	Mongolia	1.04	Portugal	27.04	Tanzania	0.8248
Brazil	17.21	Ecuador	1.99	Iceland	5.69	Mozambique	4.9	Paraguay	1.82	Uganda	1.36
Barbados	35.03	Egypt	1.92	Israel	44.42	Mauritius	25.33	Qatar	5.3	Uruguay	10.47
Uzbekistan	0.6232	Venezuela	6.29	Vietnam	7.66	South Africa	60.14	Zambia	1.47	United States	58.75
Brunei	6.46	Spain	32.62	Italy	61.71	Malawi	9.97	Romania	2.17		

Source /tradingeconomics.com/

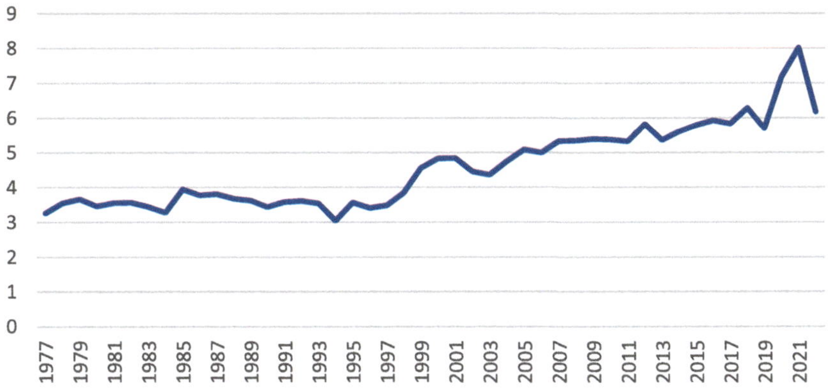

Fig. 2.2 Insurance and financial services (% of service exports, BoP) (*Source* https://data.worldbank.org/)

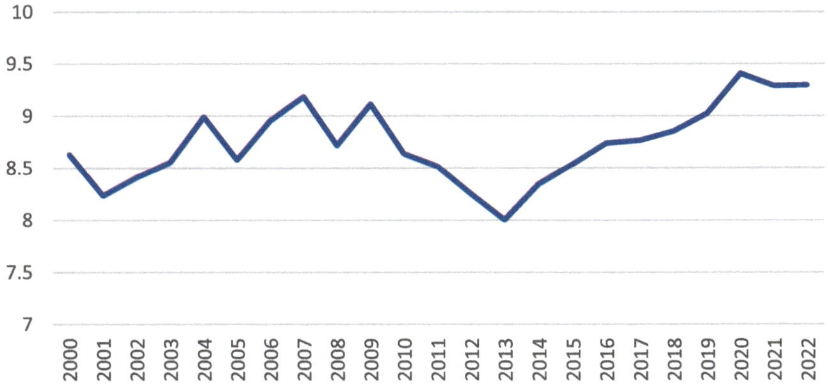

Fig. 2.3 Insurance spending. Total, % of GDP, 2000–2022 in OECD (*Source* https://data.oecd.org/insurance/national-insurance-market-share.htm#indicator-chart)

2.7 Disaster and Risk Sharing

In India, the 9th Finance Commission of India in 1987 decided to constitute disaster insurance, however, the Finance Commission found that '*the concept of an insurance fund for disaster relief was neither viable nor practicable on the ground that the process of assessing loss by an external*

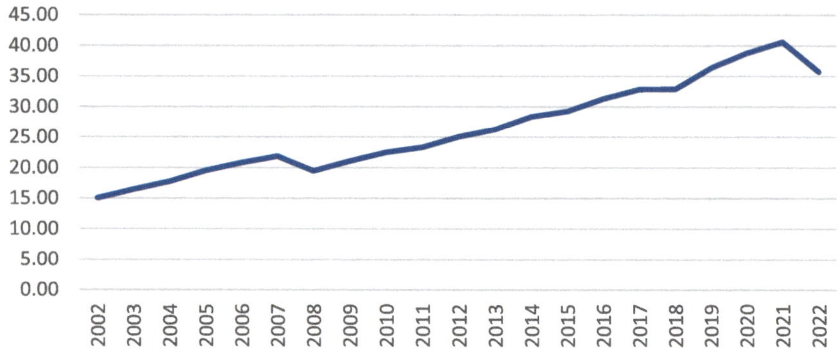

Fig. 2.4 Total assets of insurance companies worldwide from 2002 to 2022 (in trillion U.S. dollars) (*Source* https://www.statista.com/statistics/421217/assets-of-global-insurance-companies/)

agency was bound to be complicated and time-consuming, which would defeat the very purpose, that is, of providing timely succor to the affected people'. The 9th Finance Commission's observation on assessing disaster loss is indeed the theoretical and policy-level discourse. Following this, the 13th Finance Commission (2010–2015) assessed that pooling disaster risk at the individual level is a big challenge in India. It endorses the 9th FC view on disaster insurance in India. One of the critical observations of 13th FC is that disasters primarily impact the poor, who have minimal capacity to pay for an insurance premium. The finance commission of various working committees takes up this insurance-based disaster finance in India, however, these government-led initiatives are unable to come up with a proper insurance tool. This policy dilemma needs to be discussed regarding the changing insurance policy and privatization of the insurance business. Also, in India, one of the significant challenges in implementing disaster insurance is the poor creditworthiness of affected people, as disasters impact poor and marginal communities the most. Some studies established that natural disasters could strengthen informal risk sharing networks (Islam et al., 2020).

Studies prove the vicious circle of poverty and disaster losses and poverty pushes people into disaster risks and disaster further pushes them into poverty (Hallegatte et al.,). Chapter 4 of this book explains this in detail. Another study also found that the land markets perform poorly and land scarcity can be more acute in developing nations with informal markets, the availability of land with suitable access to jobs and services may force the poorer population into dangerous areas (Durand-Lasserve et al., 2013). The Emergency Event Database EM-DAT one of the sources of the global database on disasters shows that 387 natural hazards and disasters worldwide resulted in the loss of 30,704 lives and affected 185 million individuals in 2022.

Figure 2.5 is a general indication of the disaster and fatality data for the last century, and it indicates the success of disaster mitigation. This success needs to be corroborated by the exposure to hazards. The INFORM risk index gives an index of hazard and risk exposure, so over some time the number of fatalities reduced, however, the exposure to hazard has increased along with capital growth. Exposure to hazards is indeed a market for insurance firms as it puts future capital at risk, and investors aspire to protect future asset prices. Figure 2.6 explains the market for risk financing and it also has to cross-refer with the development and deprivation index mentioned in Fig. 2.7.

Figures 2.6 and 2.7 also indicate the relationship between hazard exposure and developmental deprivation. So, the economies that are exposed to hazards are equally vulnerable to disaster losses, and chances are high that these economies and societies will fall into poverty. See Box 2.1.

Economic losses due to disaster should be calculated along with the replacement cost and also cost of mitigation. Insurance is one of the most prevalent risk financing systems, and its effectiveness is related to the assets/capital that are insured for recapitalization. Though the insurance industry is expanding its capital base, disaster insurance still has yet to progress. Figure 2.8 gives the details of economic losses and insured

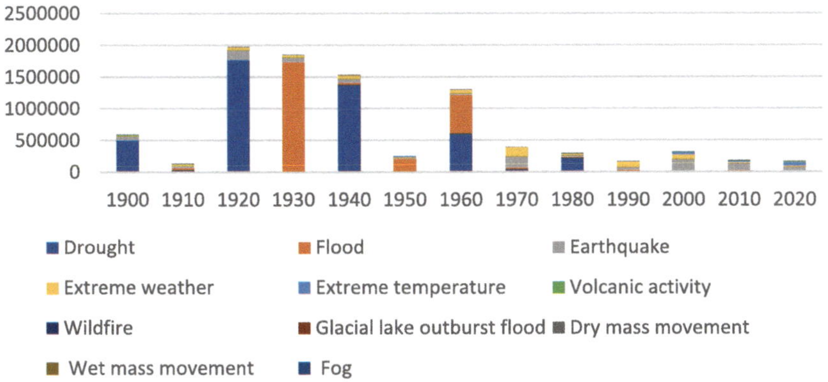

Fig. 2.5 Death due to disasters from 1900 to 2020 (*Source* ourworlddata.org)

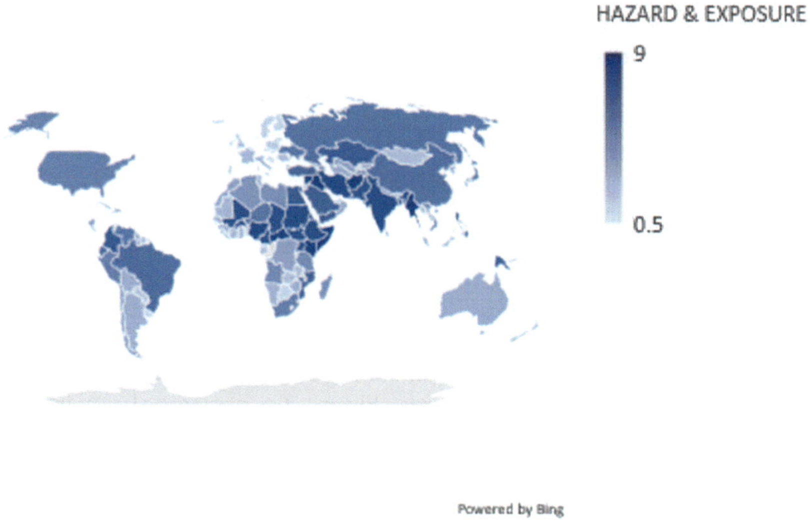

Fig. 2.6 Harzard exposure (*Source* INFORM Risk 2024)

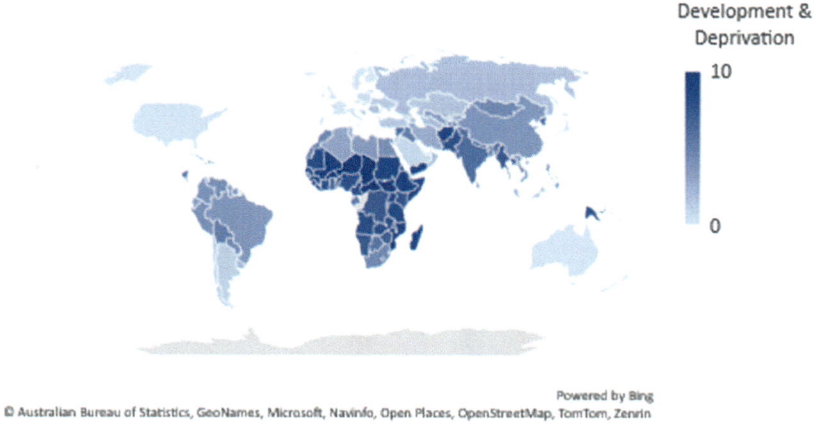

Fig. 2.7 Development and deprivation index (*Source* INFORM Risk 2024)

Box 2.1 Risk and poverty

In addition to frequent landslides, droughts, cyclones, floods, and lightning strikes, the nation also faces environmental pollution, increasing sea levels, and coastline erosion. Natural calamities that cause the most damage include floods and droughts. Floods typically coincide with the monsoon; during the southwest monsoon (May–September), which occurs in Sri Lanka's south and west, and during the northeast monsoon (December–February), which occurs in the north and east, floods are possible. The nation's most vulnerable areas to drought include the northwest, north-central, and south-eastern regions. The leading cause of this is the little rainfall. There are increasingly more and more severe droughts than there used to be. Serious droughts used to happen every 3.4–5 years, and a catastrophic drought of national significance every 10 years or so. According to the study on household vulnerability, 27% of poor households and roughly 17% of non-poor households are vulnerable. Non-poor households can recover financial losses in 3 months, but not poor households; it can take up to ten months

Source De Silva, M and Kawasaki, A. 2018. Socioeconomic Vulnerability to Disaster Risk: A Case Study of Flood and Drought Impact in a Rural Sri Lankan Community. *Ecological Economics*, *152*, 131–140. https://doi.org/10.1016/j.ecolecon.2018.05.010

losses. Uninsured losses are higher than insured losses, and this higher rate of uninsured losses is a critical challenge to disaster recovery.

Theoretically, insured loss is a capital secured for rehabilitation and the reduction of the economic impact of disasters. Studies have argued that disaster insurance reduces the final financial impact of the disaster.

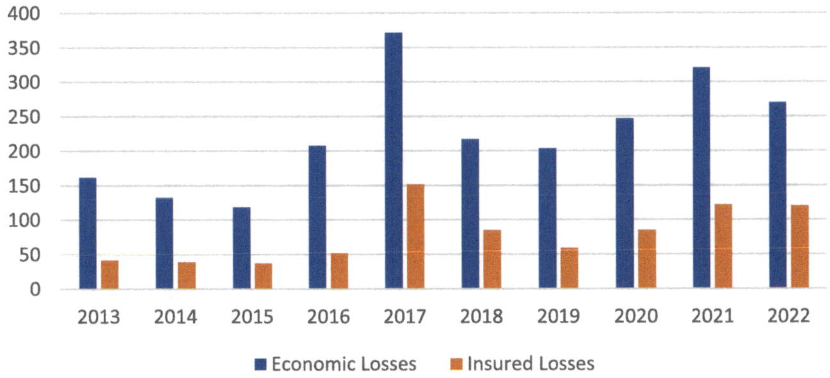

Fig. 2.8 Global losses from natural disasters 2013–2022 (US$ bn, inflation-adjusted) [*Source* https://www.munichre.com/en/risks/natural-disasters.html (accessed on 21/04/2024)]

Hunter (1994) observes that insurance firms' profits relate to insurance's effect in reducing losses. Purchasing insurance is less common when the cost of the policy is high, the predicted loss is slight, and the policyholder is wealthy (Ganderton et al., 2000). The cost of disaster insurance is close to the expectations of the loss. One of the critical constraints is that prices and cost of insurance depend on risk reduction and mitigation of losses as economic investments. This could be why the developed capitalist economies are far ahead in implementing risk insurance. Some studies proved that about 30% of disaster losses are insured in rich countries, whereas in low-income countries, only 1% of losses are insured (Linnerooth-Bayer et al., 2011). Less than 1% of people in Bangladesh, India, Vietnam, the Philippines, Indonesia, Egypt, and Nigeria have access to insurance. They are also some of the least equipped to finance recovery efforts and among the most vulnerable nations to hazards like climate change.[4] The literature on disaster insurance gives a broader understanding that there is a correlation between gross income, asset base, and disaster insurance. Some studies refer to the flood risks and observed that flood insurance helps to cope with the risk of flooding, but take-up rates are relatively low in many places, mainly in developing countries (Achtnicht & Osberghaus, 2017). Interestingly, flood insurance densities in Austria, Germany, Italy, and Poland are less than 50% (Lamond & Penning-Rowsell, 2014). In Germany, market penetration of flood insurance is about 37% (GDV, 2016). The higher-order preference for insurance among high-income countries otherwise proves the influence of the financial market as well—for instance, the stock market impact of disasters differently. Studies have indicated that the effects of natural disasters on global stock markets vary depending on the event and region. Europe is more vulnerable to climate, biological, and disaster-related changes that affect stock indices (Pagnottoni et al., 2022). Large-scale natural disasters in the United States, including hurricanes, floods, and winter storms, can cause unusual returns and volatility for businesses situated in affected areas (Bourdeau-Brien & Kryzanowski, 2017). In Hong Kong's stock market, extreme weather events have the potential to cause greater volatility than other kinds of events (Nguyen and Chaiechi, 2021). Similarly, empirical research conducted in China has demonstrated that, while the importance of these swings differs by industry, domestic shocks

[4] https://www.assets.lloyds.com/assets/pdf-lloyds-underinsurance-report-final/1/pdf-lloyds-underinsurance-report-final.pdf (accessed on 28/04/2024).

have a noticeable effect on the Shenzhen Stock Exchange (Cao et al., 2015). In India, the recurring landslide in Uttarakhand also significantly impacted the Indian stock market (Mishra, Vyas, and Meena, 2021). If we compare India and the US stock market, the volatility is different; the US market is more volatile to disasters than the Indian market. This different volatility is primarily due to the other financial sources for disaster risk management. As an advanced capitalist economy, the capital market has to respond to disaster relief in the United States, and hence, the market has to be volatile; however, for India, disaster management is still a public funding process. So, a broader theoretical framework is required to understand and explain the lower uninsured economic rationale of poor insured losses in developing and poor economies that face recurring disasters.

Economies have adopted insurance against natural calamities and built institutions to practice it. Disaster Risk Insurance Facility for Southeast Asia (SEADRIF) In December 2018, SEADRIF, a trust established to own a general insurance firm in Singapore, was agreed upon by Cambodia, Indonesia, Lao PDR, Myanmar, Singapore, and Japan. A regional disaster risk pool, specifically for flood risks, created by and for Cambodia, Lao PDR, and Myanmar is the first financial solution created by SEADRIF. To calculate the food print of the event, the product employs data from remote sensing, modelled gauge stations, and river gauge stations. The total number of individuals impacted over 21 days is used to evaluate the parametric trigger. Additionally, SEADRIF intends to offer financial assistance to other middle-class ASEAN nations like Indonesia, which are already creating or improving public insurance arrangements.[5]

The CCRIF, or Caribbean Catastrophe Risk Insurance Facility as a virtual organization supported by a network of service providers, was established as a segregated portfolio company (SPC), registered in the Cayman Islands, and is presently owned by its 19 member countries in the Caribbean. Since 2007, CCRIF has provided member nations with parametric insurance policies that guard against losses resulting from earthquakes and hurricanes (tropical cyclones). An extra rainfall cover has been part of the service since 2013. In 2019, CCRIF expanded its coverage to include the fishing industry in two member nations, thanks to funding from the US State Department and the World Bank. Coverage

[5] https://www.seadrif.org/wp-content/uploads/2024/01/ToR_SEADRIF-Initiative-Director_final.pdf (accessed on 30/04/2024).

for power grid and transformation stations—generally regarded as uninsurable risks—was added by CCRIF in October 2020.[6] An organization under the African Union called African Risk Capacity works with African governments to strengthen their ability to anticipate, prepare for, and handle risks associated with climate change and natural disasters. It has an insurance fund that pays participating nations in the event of certain weather calamities like floods and droughts.[7]

The Pacific Catastrophe Risk Assessment and Financing Initiative aims to increase the financial resilience of Pacific Island nations to natural catastrophes and climate change. It is a collaborative effort between the Asian Development Bank (ADB), the World Bank, and the Secretariat of the Pacific Community (SPC). It consists of a regional catastrophe risk insurance facility and a component for risk assessment.[8] These global initiatives indeed explain that governments and financial institutions make efforts to ensure capital for risk reductions. All these initiatives are part of specific institutional interventions to ensure the uninterpreted economic activities with the help of capital.

2.8 Insurance as Risk Mitigation

As Kelly and Kleffner's (2003) theoretical framework demonstrates, government assistance reduces the amount spent on mitigation and insurance. So, the biggest challenge associated with disaster insurance is public spending for disaster rehabilitation in countries like India. It is considered an order to make uncertain futures amenable to intervention, manipulation, and control; risk is conceptualized as a dispositif for governing social problems (Aradau & Van Munster, 2007). Risk mitigation in developing countries is part of practising development. In India, disaster response and rehabilitation are institutional projects, and all developmental institutions contribute to disaster intervention, including recapitalization. Insurance could be an option to support institutions, for instance, the Caribbean Catastrophic Risk Insurance Facility strengthens the state's ability to sustain its vital infrastructure in an emergency by

[6] https://www.ccrif.org/about-us?language_content_entity=en (accessed on 30/04/2024).

[7] https://www.arc.int/.

[8] https://www.gfdrr.org/en/pacific-catastrophe-risk-assessment-and-financing-initiative-phase-3.

linking preparedness to proactive financial strategies that take advantage of environmental vulnerabilities (Grove, 2012). Additionally, insurance secures the necessary resources ahead of time and reduces dependency on ex-post resources. It transfers the onus of loss from the society or state to the insurer (Sakshi, 2009). The insurer or institution of insurance is ideally the partner of risk sharing. So, insurance programs and institutions are relevant, as Lobo-Guerrero (2010: 79) claims that states can fulfil their sovereign duty to protect the growth and well-being of their citizens against disasters by securitizing catastrophic risk through parametric insurance programs. Economically weaker sections in developing countries identify adverse weather, crop failure, animal diseases, illness, and unemployment as income shocks, so insurance is treated as a safety measure against income shocks (Irac & Minoiu, 2006).

Choosing insurance as an instrument for financial risk reduction is a complex economic decision, and it is close to the economy's capital asset replacement projects. Choosing disaster insurance is not a voluntary process (Kunreuther, 2006). Chen et al. (2012) observed that under normal circumstances, the disaster risk premium would probably be modest and smooth, but when the optimists' ability to share risk is diminished, it will rise sharply. The effect of insurance on mitigation is associated with premiums (Kleindorfer & Kunreuther, 1999). Risk insurance is associated with a risk reduction plan (Carmichael & Gartell, 1994), so in developing economies, insurance is an economic initiative coupled with risk reduction. For instance, to reduce flood risks and promote the implementation of floodplain management rules, the National Flood Insurance Program (NFIP) in the United States offers flood insurance to property owners in participating towns (Michel-Kerjan, 2010). For the government, it is part of larger disaster mitigation projects, and for communities and firms, disaster insurance prevents risks. As Paradine (1995) defines it, there are two methods to manage a disaster's financial risk: choose to take on the risk yourself, retain it, or transfer it to the insurance company. Only when a risk is insurable do insurers choose to cover it and carry out governance and compensation tasks to reduce long-term hazards (He & Faure, 2023). Higher disaster events, including loss, theoretically, a chance for higher demand for disaster insurance. The demand for financial instruments to mitigate the disaster risk at the governmental level is possible through public funding sources. The National Disaster Mitigation Fund (NDMF) is an example of government-level risk reduction; however, it is not risk sharing here. Instead, it is a risk-taking behaviour. Still, the National Disaster Mitigation Fund (NDMF) acts as a preventive investment to promote environment-friendly settlement and livelihood practices and also encourages large-scale construction of resilience measures. The National Disaster Mitigation Fund (NDMF) is an example of government-level risk mitigation, however, it is not an answer to the question of risk sharing. Mitigation as a fund-driven program needs a proper assessment and forecasting of risks and uncertainties. When one can expect financial support from the government in a natural disaster, it makes perfect sense to forgo insurance coverage against probable losses (Coate, 1995). Accurate weather forecasts assist in navigating the uncertainties brought on by environmental change, from organizing daily activities to making wise decisions in catastrophe management (Grislan-Letremy, 2018). Some studies argue that choosing disaster insurance related to governmental and private aid lowers the aid and increases the tendency to have insurance (Raschky & Weckhannemann, 2007). In India, disaster risk sharing is the sharing of mitigation costs and, hence, managing the risk under administrative control. See Fig. 2.9 to understand the difference between insured and uninsured losses in India.

Figure 2.9 indicates the challenges of ensuring disaster risk insurance, theoretically and institutionally it is possible in an environment that enables a competitive insurance products supply. Studies prove that the

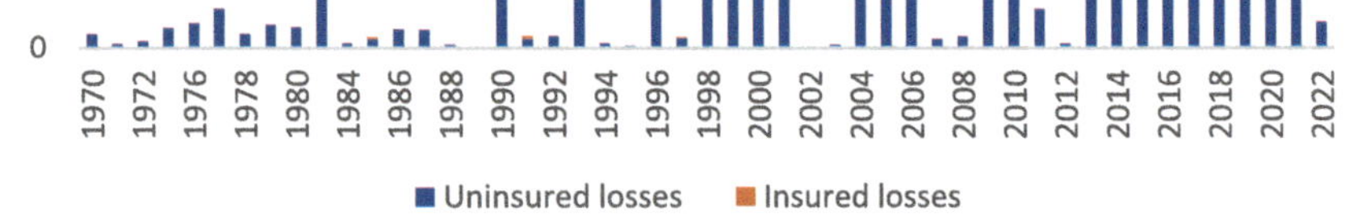

Fig. 2.9 Economic losses from natural catastrophes in India (US$ Bn, 2023 price) for period 1970–2022 [*Source* https://www.swissre.com/institute/research/topics-and-risk-dialogues/economy-and-insurance-outlook/india-insurance-market-growing-fast-build-resilience/main/06~index~.html?1705335248660 (accessed on 21/04/2024)]

tendency to take prevention insurance is high with competitive insurance (Picard, 2008). Investors' disapproval of an insurer's massive disaster-related liability exposures could cause availability issues unless the insurer can reduce its asset value losses in the financial market (Chen & Hamwi, 2012). Asset value losses are a big economic challenge in a country like India, which is evident in the recurring disaster risk in some parts. Table 2.2 gives a detailed account of insured losses. This data concerning recurring disaster losses and insurance in India needs to be discussed.

There is a strong empirical observation that insurance is not extended to any frequent disaster-prone area of the country (Kaushalya et al., 2014). The disaster insurance fund is an extra asset that has a perfect correlation with capital (Boulatov & Dieckmann, 2013). These critical aspects need to be empirically proven with the help of a case study on Prime Minister Fasal Bima Yojana and its operation among marginal and small farmers in India.

2.8.1 Prime Minister Fasal Bima Yojana

PM Fasal Bima Yojana is one of the crop insurance schemes in India and is now one of India's most famous crop insurance. The Pradhan Mantri Fasal Bima Yojana (PMFBY) offers reasonably priced crop insurance that covers farmers' crops against all non-preventable natural risks from the pre-sowing to the post-harvest stage, using an Area Approach Basis. It was started in 2016. Crop insurance is an essential support to farmers in India as 60% of the country's net sown area is rain-fed, and 65% of Indian farmers depend on rain-fed irrigation.[9] Drought and floods are the two major recurring disasters in India, and about 68% of the cultivable land is vulnerable to drought risks. The two states of India, Maharashtra and Assam, are known for recurring drought and flood risks, and almost 80–84% of agriculture in Maharashtra is in the rain-fed area, i.e., dependent on rainfall[6]. Furthermore, numerous scholarly and policy studies have demonstrated a connection between Maharashtra's high rate of farmer suicides and the state of agrarian distress and debt[7]. Another state that frequently experiences flooding is Assam. Approximately 39.58%, or 31.05 lakh hectares, of Assam's total land area, out of the state's total area

[9] No. 30/RN/Ref./October/2015. Lok Sabha Secretariat.

Table 2.2 Extent of insured losses in recent natural disasters in India

Year	*Disaster type*	*Location*	*Economic Loss ($ Bn)*	*Insured Loss ($ Bn)*	*Insured as % of total losses Total (%)*
1991	Flood	Mumbai, Kerala, Gujarat	0.1	0	48
1997	Flood	Himachal Pradesh	0.1	0	9
1998	Storm	Gujarat, Maharashtra	0.5	0.2	46
1999	Storm	Orissa, Andhra Pradesh, West Bengal	2.5	0.1	4
2001	Earthquake	Gujarat	2.6	0.1	4
2004	Earthquake	Tamil Nadu, Andhra Pradesh, Kerala	1	0	0
2005	Flood	Multiple States	3.3	0.8	25
2005	Flood	Gujarat	2.3	0.2	7
2006	Flood	Multiple States	3.4	0.4	12
2009	Flood	Karnataka, Andhra Pradesh, Maharashtra	2.2	0.1	2
2013	Flood	Multiple States	1.1	0.5	45
2014	Flood	J&K	16	0.2	1
2014	Storm	Andhra Pradesh, Orissa	7	0.5	8
2015	Storm	Multiple States	0.9	0.1	12
2015	Drought	Multiple States	3	0.4	13
2015	Flood	Andhra Pradesh, Tamil Nadu	2.2	0.8	34
2016	Storm	Tamil Nadu, Andhra Pradesh	1	0.2	20
2016	Flood	Andhra Pradesh, Telangana	0.6	0	7
2017	Flood	Mumbai, Thane	0.3	0.1	26
2019	Flood	Multiple States	10	0.2	2
2020	Flood	Multiple States	7.5	0.8	11
Total			67.6	5.7	8

Source EM-DAT; SBI research

of 78.523 lakh hectares. It alone represents 9.40% of the entire flood-prone territory in the nation[8]. The recurring disasters in these two states are classical cases of how risk insurance operates and shares the risks. Crop insurance is a strategy to reduce the risk of farming under natural disasters (Keskar, 2012). Cariappa et al. (2017) argue that insurance offers farmers a safety net in the event of crop loss with operational efficacy. Ifft et al. (2024) argue that when revenue declines, crop insurance increases the possibility that loans will be repaid, protecting lenders. Crop insurance is an economic support scheme for farmers. Ifft et al. (2015) argue that farmers who employ crop insurance borrow more money, especially for short-term operating loans in the United States, to compensate for some risk reduction.

Droughts, which have a 35% likelihood of occurring nationwide and vary from 20% in dry-humid regions to 40% or higher in desert parts, pose a threat to more than two-thirds of India's land area (Government of India, 2009)[2]. Birthal et al. (2015) observed that droughts are prone to occurring across over two-thirds of India's geographical area; they have a 35% chance of happening nationwide and can occur in 20% of dry-humid regions and 40% or more of arid areas (Kumar et al., 2014). Climate risk will likely push the value of uninsurable losses high in India (Costa et al., 2023). Indian Council of Agricultural Research's study shows that 19% of Indian districts fall under very high-risk, while 201 are risk districts. Mohanty et al. (2021) assessed that 17 out of 20 people in India are vulnerable to extreme hydrometeorological disasters. A study on an Indian district's level of vulnerability to undue weather risk shows the severity of flood and drought risks in India. See Tables 2.3 and 2.4.

Insurance is an inevitable source of sustainment in farming, and it ensures the farming of marginal farmers. Raju and Chand (2008)

Table 2.3 Vulnerability of districts in India

Indicator	*Frequency*
High	72
Low	95
Moderate	113
Very high	60
Very low	123
Total	463

Source Mohanty et al. (2021)

Table 2.4 Disaster events in districts

Disaster	*Frequency*
Cyclone	3
Drought	185
Drought and cyclone	12
Flood	93
Flood and cyclone	18
Flood and drought	110
Flood, drought and cyclone	42
Total	463

Source Mohanty et al. (2021)

observed that crop insurance protects farmers against financial loss incurred by crop failure caused by uncontrollable natural calamities, such as fires, pests, illnesses, weather, floods. Since agriculture in India is regarded as a high-risk sector of the economy, farmers are shielded against unforeseen and uncontrollable natural disasters that may have an impact on crop output by crop insurance. It is a financial tool that shares the loss load by combining several uncertainties that impact crop yields, hence lowering the probability of crop yield loss (Rao, 2002). Initiatives for agricultural adaptation are also implemented in the villages most vulnerable to climate change (Panda, 2016). Institutional support, such as credit and risk-coping finance, limits the farmers' fight for adaptation. This may be the cause of the growing acclaim among farmers for crop insurance programs like PM Fasal Bima Yojana. However, the study carried out as part of a research project in one area devastated by flooding in Assam and two districts afflicted by drought in Maharashtra provides insight into the fact that impoverished marginal farmers are looking for insurance because they are vulnerable to debt. See Fig. 2.10, to get an idea of the indebtedness of farmers, who have opted for this particular insurance scheme. So for them, crop insurance is an institution that keeps them in farming while the state and the insurance company share the risks.

The marginal and small farmers have to opt for this scheme for two reasons: the lack of macro-level government support and insurance subsidies. Under PM Fasal Bima Yojana, farmers do not need to pay any premium as they have to pay only one Indian rupee, and the rest of the amount would flow from the government to the insurance company as a subsidy. It is like a humanitarian assistant, as Ahmed (2021) assesses the efficacy of novel sovereign disaster insurance systems for humanitarian

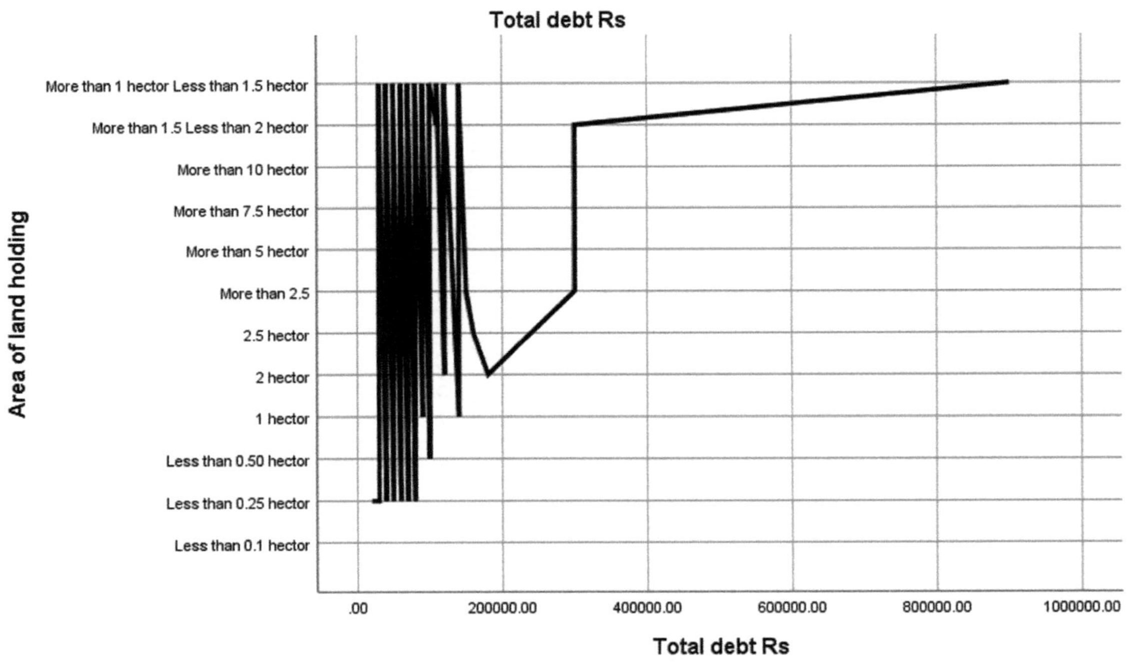

Fig. 2.10 Debt of farmers and land ownership in Jalna

assistance. The farmer has to choose this insurance to survive as they are affected by drought.

Figures 2.11 and 2.12 show that small and marginal farmers are subject to the risk of drought and experience lower income. For them, the government is the only agency to share the risk of drought risks. The farmers need to share the economic risk and protect their livelihood. In crop insurance, the government prefers public–private partnership initiatives, which have been done through a network of private-sector insurance firms. Public–private partnerships ensure efficient risk management in insurance (Jametti & Ungern-Sternberg, 2010). Privatization of the insurance sector was the biggest opportunity for the new actors to invest in insurance-based risk sharing. There is a clear distinction between public- and private-sector insurance concerning risk sharing. The insurance trust evolved with public sector insurance companies as part of the larger welfare state initiatives. Insurance is also a game, so, every firm involved in insurance is expected to maximize its profits. The simple logic of insurance is the ability to gain and reduce losses.

$$\text{Expected Loss} = P \times L \left(P \text{ probability of loss, } L \text{ amount of loss}\right)$$

$$\text{Expected Gain} = Pm - EL \left(\text{premium charged, expected loss}\right)$$

Every insurance firm is prepared to increase its losses, and these two options determine the institutional structure of insurance in disaster contexts. The expectation of loss over gain is why insurance for disaster

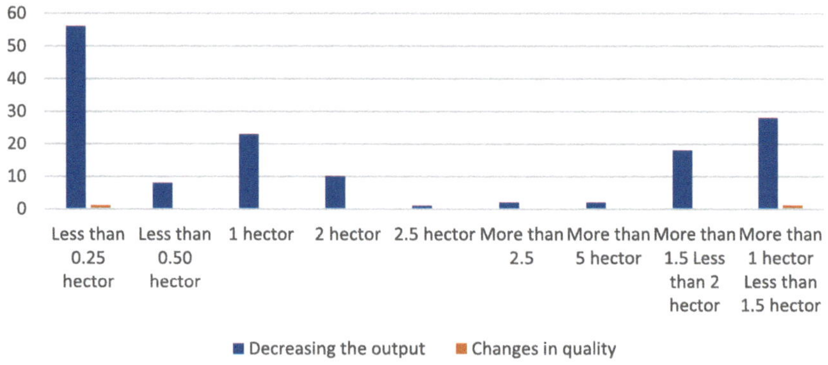

Fig. 2.11 Drought affect the farming in Jalna District

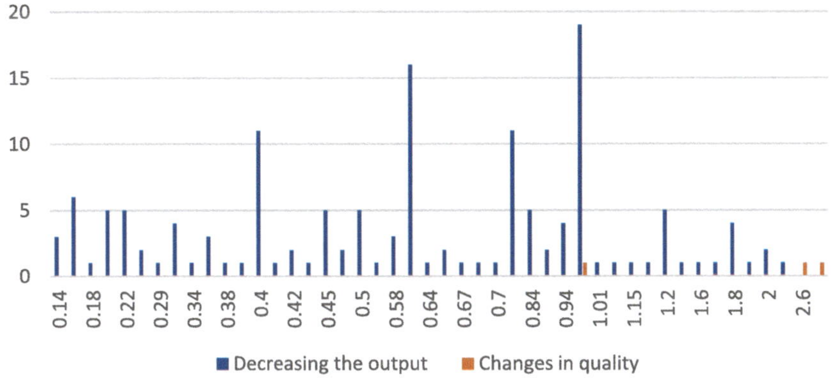

Fig. 2.12 Drought affect the farming in Aurangabad District

risk management is not very popular in India. In a country like India, where poverty and disaster risk are interrelated, insurance is a financial instrument that takes care of the economic implications of the risks. This is evident in the case of PM Fasal Bima Yojana, in which the poor farmers have a significant dependency on insurance. For small and marginal farmers, the insurance kept them in farming and continued their livelihood. The deprivation of the farmers has been the source of income for the insures. See Table 2.5.

Insurance firms profit from the business. However, the farmers also make gains since the government bears the premium. Risk tolerance rather than risk sharing is happening here; the government tolerates the risks. However, the exciting aspect of this process is that insurance replaced other farming sector subsidies. So, this example also shows that equilibrium can be possible in vulnerable situations. The economic condition of the vulnerable farmers remains the same; however, the risk of exposure remains with the sharing of financial risks. No insurance company in India is willing to offer disaster insurance precisely due to the lack of methods to make a proper economic loss of risks. The Fifteenth Finance Commission of India tried to establish a new method to share the economic risk between India's union government and state governments. The commission has prepared a disaster risk index for state governments to distribute the union government financial support. It proposed a scoring method that combined the number of below-poverty line populations in the state and geographical areas exposed to natural calamities.

Table 2.5 Date collected through Right to Information Act 2005 from Pradhan Mantri Fasal Bima Yojna office

Insurance company	*Year*	*Premium (in Cr)*	*Claim (in Cr)*	*Government subsidy (in Cr)*
AICIL	2020	253.84	157.72	126.31
	2021	93.45	252.01	43.8
	2022	61.68	11.77	34.83
Total		155.13	421.5	204.94
SBI GICL	2021	10.55	4.1	4.67
	2022	17.55	0.73	9.65
Total		28.1	4.83	14.32
HDFC ERGO	2020	52.28	34.51	40.13
	2021	25.65	14.46	12.48
	2022	51.42	4.86	23.27
Total		77.07	53.83	75.88
Future General	2021	9.33	10	5.74
	2022	11.3	1.44	7.83
Total		20.63	11.44	13.57
Reliance General	2021	7.09	4.1	3.34
	2022	8.19	0.73	4.56
Total		15.28	4.83	7.9

Source

For instance, in terms of flood risks, if more than 20% of the geographical location is exposed to flood, that region would get a score of 15. If the area vulnerable to flood is between 10 and 20, it will assign a value of 10, and less than 10% of the geographical area susceptible to flood would get a score of 5. Combined with poverty, this score enables the government to share the public funds. It is a fund for response, and only 20% of the funding is allocated to mitigate expenditures.

Still, it is the source of response funding, including temporary support, emergency response, and administrative costs. However, recovery costs should be at the expense of large-scale development expenditures. So, the vulnerable disasters and climate change victims have no resources to share the risks rather than depend on the state in a country like India. This heavy dependency on the state for risk sharing is the biggest constraint on India's economy of risk sharing.

One needs to do a simple analysis of the combined ratio analysis here,

$$\text{Combined Ratio} = \frac{\text{IL} + E + D}{\text{EP}}$$

IL = incurred losses, E = expenses, D = dividends, EP = earned premiums (EP).

A combined ratio below 100% indicates underwriting profitability. In comparison, a ratio above 100% indicates underwriting losses for a country like India where the incurred losses are high; however, with less asset value and high dependency, poor expenses from the affected and poor dividends push the combined ratio above 100%. In a developing country like India, only state/public finance can ensure a combined ratio below 100%; however, advanced market economies often adopt market-based risk sharing. Catastrophic bonds are one among them, and it is a reliable method for directly transferring the financial effects of catastrophic events (hazards) into the financial market through the use of catastrophe (CAT) risk bonds (Shao et al., 2015). CAT bonds are usually parametric (e.g., wind speed during a hurricane or ground movement during an earthquake) or non-indemnity (e.g., indemnity-based) bonds that specify industry loss estimates or events that trigger the bond's terms (Lee and Yu, 2007). CAT bonds, as they are now called, are among the most significant financial instruments associated with insurance. The issuer offers CAT bonds to investors, special-purpose vehicles that concurrently engage in a reinsurance agreement with a reinsurance provider (Egami & Young, 2008). Even while catastrophe bonds are unlikely to replace reinsurance, they have a place in the larger market for risk transfer (Lakdawalla & Zanjani, 2011). Insurance securitization instruments, known as catastrophe (Cat) bonds, are designed to shift underwriting risk associated with catastrophes from issuers to capital markets (Hagendorff et al., 2014). Cat bonds are financial claims that, in the event of a specific catastrophe loss occurrence, allow the issuing company to forfeit principal or coupon payments, thus shielding it from catastrophic losses (Cummins et al., 2002; Froot, 2001; Froot & O'Connell, 2008). It organizes financial instruments well and is linked to lower insurance risk, so regulators ought to support their use. This is especially crucial because several prominent insurance companies are becoming more and more relevant to the system (Billio et al., 2012). A catastrophe-link (CAT) bond is a type of debt commitment where the repayment of principal and interest is contingent upon an insurance company's payout conditions (Kish, 2016). Some assessments show that the global catastrophic bond market increased by 4% per annum, see Table 2.6.

World Bank is one of the significant issuers of catastrophe bonds, and it has initiated innovative methods to promote catastrophe bonds in low-income countries. Unlike developed economies with established financial markets, promoting catastrophe bonds in low-income countries is challenging. See Table 2.7.

The OECD report (2024) added that catastrophic bonds are financial instruments that utilize securitization to put natural disaster risk into a tradable format. Only a few economies in which the financial market is vulnerable to disasters and private funding for risk mitigation. So, risk reduction and response influence the interest rate. The calamities also

Table 2.6 Alternative capital deployment, 2002–2023E, USD billions

Year	*Total*	*Cat bonds*	*Other insurance-linked securities*
2002	5.4	2.9	2.5
2003	7.4	4.4	3
2004	8.4	4.4	4
2005	10.5	5.5	5
2006	17.1	9.6	7.5
2007	21.8	16	16
2008	18.9	14.4	4.5
2009	22.2	14.6	7.7
2010	23.5	13.7	9.8
2011	27.5	13.9	13.6
2012	44	27.5	16.5
2013	49.7	29.4	20.3
2014	63.8	39.5	24.3
2015	68.3	44.9	23.4
2016	79.5	57	22.5
2017	97.3	71.6	25.7
2018	97.6	67.9	29.7
2019	94.8	64.8	30
2020	93.6	61.6	32
2021	96.3	62.3	34
2022	92.7	56.7	36
2023	100	59	41

Source https://www.swissre.com/institute/research/sigma-research/Economic-Insights/catastrophe-bond-issuance.html

Table 2.7 Enabling factors for and challenges to the widespread issuance of sovereign CAT bonds in the Philippines

Enabling factors	*Challenges*
Presence on the CAT bond market through the World Bank issuance	High transaction costs Narrow investor base
Strong legal and institutional frameworks for disaster risk management, including provisions on risk transfer mechanisms	Short-term coverage Need to recalibrate existing models to reflect local practices
Availability of models for several types of catastrophe events	Lack of data and statistics on the probability and severity of a catastrophe event

Source OECD., 2024. Fostering catastrophe bond markets in Asia and the Pacific, the development dimension, OECD Publishing, Paris, https://doi.org/10.1787/ab1e49ef-en

influence the adaptive capacity of the firms (Seetharam, 2017), and such ability is connected with market risks. So, to save the market from further risk, market economies prefer catastrophic bonds as a source of secured capital. See Fig. 2.13.

Catastrophe bonds enable risk trading as risk sharing; however, in a country like India, disaster risk cannot be tradable, as the calamities are

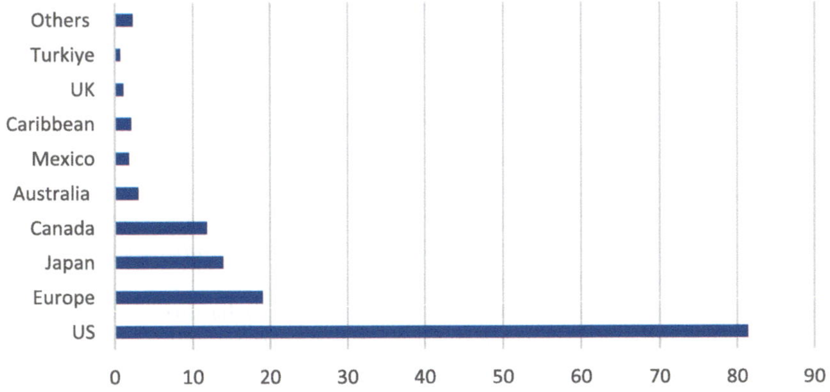

Fig. 2.13 Geographical coverage of CAT bonds issued from 1996 to 2022 in % of total issuance (*Source* OECD., 2024. Fostering catastrophe bond markets in Asia and the Pacific, the development dimension, OECD Publishing, Paris, https://doi.org/10.1787/ab1e49ef-en)

connected with structural vulnerabilities. Also, risk sharing through financial instruments necessitates the identification of risks that are susceptible to natural disasters. It could include credit, liquidity, market, and systemic risks. In a risk trading system, risks often get priority in risk sharing. Systemic risks refer to the risk or probability of a financial system as a whole or market being affected by risks (Acharya et al., 2017a, 2017b). Those types of risk classification enable better risk sharing through financial instruments. Risk exposure triggered by structural causes cannot be classified and traded with insurance in a society where calamities displace a large population. So, risk sharing becomes an economic process in those countries wherein the risk disrupts the everyday financial process; however, for larger vulnerable populations, risk sharing is government ownership of the economic impact of risks.

The number of disaster events is increasing; hence, all risk sharing apprehensions become agents of change in disaster risk reduction. In developing economies like India, state ownership of risk sharing, i.e., state investment in risk reduction, is inevitable for a country like India. So, any debate on risk sharing is closely associated with the differential impact of economic risks due to calamities. It is not simply the financial risks alone; instead, it is a complex system in which life, livelihood, asset price, the value of resources, and social mobility are the matters for debate. Risk sharing could also be an institutional process. Hence, institutions, including financial institutions, should follow adaptive governance to engage with the economy of risk sharing in disaster contexts.

References

Aase, K. K. (2021). Optimal risk sharing in society. *Mathematics, 10*(1), 161. https://doi.org/10.3390/math10010161

Acharya, V. V., Pedersen, L. H., Philippon, T., & Richardson, M. (2017a). Measuring systemic risk. *The Review of Financial Studies, 30*(1), 2–47. https://doi.org/10.1093/rfs/hhw088

Acharya, V. V., Pedersen, L. H., Philippon, T., & Richardson, M. (2017b). Measuring systemic risk. *The Review of Financial Studies, 30*(1), 2–47.

Achtnicht, M., & Osberghaus, D. (2017). The demand for index-based flood insurance in a high-income country. *German Economic Review*. https://doi.org/10.1111/geer.12142

Ahmed, M. (2021). Humanitarian funding in crisis and the rise of innovative humanitarian finance. In *Innovative humanitarian financing. Palgrave studies in impact Finance*. Palgrave Macmillan. https://doi.org/10.1007/978-3-030-83209-4_2

Al-Harran, S. (1999). Introduction: Cases in Islamic Finance. *Arab Law Quarterly, 14*(3), 193–202.

Aoki, M. (1984). *The cooperative game theory of the firm*. Oxford University Press.

Apergis, N., & Poufinas, T. (2020). The role of insurance growth in economic growth: Fresh evidence from a panel of OECD countries. *The North American Journal of Economics and Finance, 53*, 101217. https://doi.org/10.1016/j.najef.2020.101217

Aradau, C., & Van Munster, R. (2007). Governing terrorism through risk: Taking precautions, (un)knowing the future. *European Journal of International Relations, 13*(1), 89–115.

Arrow, K. J. (1971). The theory of risk aversion. In Y. J. S. Helsinki (Ed.), *Aspects of the theory of risk bearing, reprinted in essays in the theory of risk bearing* (pp. 90–109). Markham Publ Co.

Arrow, K. J., & Debreu, G. (1954). Existence of an equilibrium for a competitive economy. *Econometrica, 22*(3), 265–290.

Askari, H., Iqbal, Z., & Mirakhor, A. (2015). *Introduction to Islamic economics theory and application*. Wiley.

Averchenkova, A., Crick, F., Kocornik-Mina, A., Leck, H., & Surminski, S. (2016). Multinational and large national corporations and climate adaptation: Are we asking the right questions? A review of current knowledge and a new research perspective. *Wiley Interdisciplinary Reviews: Climate Change, 7*(4), 517–536.

Balli, F., Kalemli-Ozcan, S., & Sørensen, B. E. (2012). Risk sharing through capital gains. *The Canadian Journal of Economics/revue Canadienne D'economique, 45*(2), 472–492.

Baran, P. A., & Sweezy, P. M. (1966). *Monopoly capital: An essay on the American economic and social order*. Monthly Review Press.

Baumol, W. J. (1959). *Business behavior, value and growth*. Macmillan.

Baye, M. R., & Prince, J. T. (2017). *Managerial economics & business strategy*. London: McGraw-Hill Education.

Beard, R. E., Pentikainen, T., & Pesonen, E. (1969). *Risk theory: The stochastic basis of insurance*. Chapman And Hall.

Beckert, S. (2015). *Empire of cotton: A global history*. Vintage Books Trade.

Belhaj, M., Bourlès, R., & Deroïan, F. (2014). Risk-taking and risk-sharing incentives under moral hazard. *American Economic Journal: Microeconomics, 6*(1), 58–90.

Bernard, C. (2013). Risk sharing and pricing in the reinsurance market. *Handbook of Insurance*. https://doi.org/10.1007/978-1-4614-0155-1_21

Biais, B., Heider, F., & Hoerova, M. (2016). Risk-sharing or risk-taking? Counterparty risk, incentives, and margins. *The Journal of Finance, 71*(4), 1669–1698.
Billio, M., Getmansky, M., Lo, W. A., & Pelizzon, L. (2012). Econometric measures of connectedness and systemic risk in the finance and insurance sectors. *Journal of Financial Economics, 104*(3), 535–559.
Birthal, P. S., Negi, D. S., Khan, M. T., & Agarwal, S. (2015). Is Indian agriculture becoming resilient to droughts? Evidence from rice production systems. *Food Policy, 56*, 1–12. https://doi.org/10.1016/j.foodpol.2015.07.005
Borch, K. (1974). *The mathematical theory of insurance*. Lexington Books.
Botzen, W. W., & Van Den Bergh, J. C. (2008). Insurance against climate change and flooding in the Netherlands: Present, future, and comparison with other countries. *Risk Analysis: An International Journal, 28*(2), 413–426.
Boulatov, A., & Dieckmann, S. (2013). The risk-sharing implications of disaster insurance funds. *The Journal of Risk and Insurance, 80*(1), 37–64.
Bourdeau-Brien, M., & Kryzanowski, L. (2017). The impact of natural disasters on the stock returns and volatilities of local firms. *The Quarterly Review of Economics and Finance, 63*, 259–270. https://doi.org/10.1016/j.qref.2016.05.003
Bower, J. L., Leonard, H. B., & Paine, L. S. (2011). *Capitalism at risk: Rethinking the role of business*. Harvard Business Review Press.
Boyes, W. J. (2003). *The new managerial economics*. London: Houghton Mifflin.
Broner, F., & Ventura, J. (2011). Globalization and risk sharing. *The Review of Economic Studies, 78*(1), 49–82. https://doi.org/10.1093/restud/rdq015
Brousseau, E., & Glachant, J.-M. (2004). The economics of contracts and the renewal of economics. In E. Brousseau & J.-M. Glachant (Eds.), *The economics of contracts-theories and applications*. Cambridge University Press.
Buckham, D., Wahl, J., & Rose, S. (2010). *Executive's guide to solvency II*. London: Wiley.
Cao, G., Xu, W., & Guo, Y. (2015). Effects of climatic events on the Chinese stock market: Applying event analysis. *Natural Hazards, 77*(3), 1979–1992. https://doi.org/10.1007/s11069-015-1687-9
Cariappa, A. G. A., Lokesh, G. B., & Ramesh, G. B. (2017). Progress of crop insurance and Pradhan Mantri Fasal Bima Yojana in India. *Agricultural Economics Research Review, 30*, 1.
Carmichael, D., & Gartell, S. (1994). Insurance and disaster planning. *Facilities, 12*(1), 9–11. https://doi.org/10.1108/02632779410004997
Cettolin, E., & Tausch, F. (2015). Risk taking and risk sharing: Does responsibility matter? *Journal of Risk and Uncertainty, 50*(3), 229–248.
Chen, H., Joslin, S., & Tran, N. K. (2012). Rare disasters and risk sharing with heterogeneous beliefs. *The Review of Financial Studies, 25*(7), 2189–2224.

Chen, Y., & Hamwi, I. S. (2012). Why some disaster insurance does not exist. *Asia-Pacific Journal of Risk and Insurance*. https://doi.org/10.1515/2153-3792.1111

Chen, Z., & Xie, W. (2020). Sharing the value-at-risk under distributional ambiguity. *Mathematical Finance, 31*(1), 531–559. https://doi.org/10.1111/mafi.12296

Cherry, T. L., Howe, E. L., & Murphy, J. J. (2015). Sharing as risk pooling in a social dilemma experiment. *Ecology and Society, 20*(1), 1.

Chiles, T. H., & McMackin, J. F. (1996a). Integrating variable risk preferences, trust, and transaction cost economics. *The Academy of Management Review, 21*(1), 73–99.

Chiles, T. H., & McMackin, J. F. (1996b). Integrating variable risk preferences, trust, and transaction cost economics. *The Academy of Management Review, 21*(1), 73–99. https://doi.org/10.2307/258630

Clarke, S. (1990). The Marxist theory of over accumulation and crisis. *Science and Society, 54*(4), 442–467.

Coase, R. H. (1937). The nature of the firm. *Economica, 4*, 386–405. https://doi.org/10.1111/j.1468-0335.1937.tb00002.x

Coate, S. (1995). Altruism, the Samaritan's dilemma, and government transfer policy. *American Economic Review, 85*(1), 46–57.

Costa, F., Forge, F., Garred, J. and Pessoa, J.P. (2023). The impact of climate change on risk and return in Indian agriculture. *Environmental and Resource Economics, 85*(1), 1–27.

Cristea, M., Marcu, N., & Carstina, S. (2014). The relationship between insurance and economic growth in Romania compared to the main results in Europe—A theoretical and empirical analysis. *Procedia Economics and Finance, 8*, 226–235.

Cummins, J. D., Doherty, N., & Lo, A. (2002). Can insurers pay for the "big one"? Measuring the capacity of the insurance market to respond to catastrophic losses. *Journal of Banking and Finance, 26*, 557–583.

Dao, H., & Delacroix, A. (2018). Diminishing returns and labor market adjustments. *Macroeconomic Dynamics, 22*(8), 2088–2106. https://doi.org/10.1017/S1365100516001012

Devereux, M. B., & Smith, G. W. (1994). International risk sharing and economic growth. *International Economic Review, 1994*, 535–550.

Dierker, E., & Grodal, B. (1996). Profit maximization mitigates competition. *Economic Theory, 7*, 139–160. https://doi.org/10.1007/BF01212187

Durand-Lasserve, A., Selod, H., & Durand-Lasserve, M. (2013). *A systemic analysis of land markets and land institutions in west African cities: rules and practices—The case of Bamako, Mali Policy research working paper 6687*. World Bank, Washington, DC.

Egami, M., & Young, V. R. (2008). Indifference prices of structured catastrophe (CAT) bonds. *Insurance: Mathematics and Economics, 42*(2), 771–778. https://doi.org/10.1016/j.insmatheco.2007.08

Fatmawatie, N., Natalina, S. A., & Fauza, H. (2021). Effect of net profit margin and company size on risk disclosure. *Management and Economic Journal., 5*(2), 2021.

Faure, M.G., & Heldt, T. (2016). Resilient compensation mechanisms: The role of government intervention in the insurance of catastrophic risks. In *Law and the management of disasters* (pp. 224–244). Routledge.

Foss, N. J. (1996). Knowledge-based approaches to the theory of the firm: Some critical comments. *Organization Science, 7*(5), 470–476.

Foster, J. B., & McChesney, R. W. (2012). *The endless crisis: How monopoly-finance capital produces stagnation and upheaval from USA to China*. Monthly Review Press.

Franco, G. (2021). Earthquake mitigation strategies through insurance. In M. Beer, I. Kougioumtzoglou, E. Patelli, & I. K. Au (Eds.), *Encyclopedia of earthquake engineering*. Berlin: Springer. https://doi.org/10.1007/978-3-642-36197-5_401-1

Franklin, J. (2001). *The science of conjecture: evidence and probability before pascal*. Johns Hopkins University Press.

Froot, K. (2001). The market for catastrophe risk: A clinical examination. *Journal of Financial Economics, 60*, 529–571.

Froot, K. A., & O'Connell, P. G. J. (2008). On the pricing of intermediated risks: Theory and application to catastrophe reinsurance. *Journal of Banking and Finance, 32*, 69–85.

Ganderton, P. T., Brookshire, D. S., McKee, M., Stewart, S., & Thurston, H. (2000). Buying insurance for disaster-type risks: Experimental evidence. *Journal of Risk and Uncertainty, 20*(3), 271–289. https://doi.org/10.1023/a:1007871514658

GDV. (2016). *Naturgefahrenreport 2016*. Gesamtverband der Deutschen Versicherungswirtschaft e. V.

Gollier, C., Koehl, P., & Rochet, J. C. (1997). Risk-taking behavior with limited liability and risk aversion. *The Journal of Risk and Insurance, 64*, 347–370.

Grislain-Letrémy, C. (2018). Natural disasters: Exposure and underinsurance. *The National Institute of Statistics and Economic Studies*. https://doi.org/10.15609/annaeconstat2009.129.0053

Grove, K. (2012). Preempting the next disaster: Catastrophe insurance and the financialization of disaster management. *Security Dialogue, 43*(2), 139–155. https://doi.org/10.1177/0967010612438434

Hagendorff, B., Hagendorff, J., Keasey, K., & Gonzalez, A. (2014). The risk implications of insurance securitization: The case of catastrophe bonds.

Journal of Corporate Finance, 25, 387–402. https://doi.org/10.1016/j.jcorpfin.2014.01.00

Hague, D. C. (1958). Alfred Marshall and the competitive firm. *The Economic Journal, 68*(272), 673–690. https://doi.org/10.2307/2227279

Hansen, A. H. (1939). Economic progress and declining population growth. *The American Economic Review, 29*(1), 1–15.

Harrington, S. E., & Niehaus, G. (2016). *Risk management and insurance*. London: McGraw-Hill Education.

Hassan, A., & Saleem, S. (2017). An Islamic microfinance business model in Bangladesh: Its role in alleviation of poverty and socio-economic well-being of women. *Humanomics, 33*(1), 15–37.

Hawley, F. B. (1907). *Enterprise and the productive process*. https://www.survivorlibrary.com/library/enterprise_and_the_productive_process_1907.pdf

Hawley, F. (1893). The risk theory of profit. *Quarterly Journal of Economics, 7*(4), 459–479.

He, Q., & Faure, M. G. (2023). Mitigation of long-term risks and the role of insurance: A behavioural law and economics perspective. *European Journal of Risk Regulation, 14*(4), 779–792. https://doi.org/10.1017/err.2023.13

Hirsch, R. (2020). Risk and trouble: Adam Smith on profit and the protagonists of capitalism. *American Journal of Political Science, 65*(1), 166–179. https://doi.org/10.1111/ajps.12556

Holzmann, R., Packard, T., & Cuesta, J. (2000). *Extending coverage in multi-pillar pension systems: Constraints and hypotheses, preliminary evidence and future research agenda*. Social protection discussion paper series, pp. no. SP 0002. Washington, DC: The World Bank.

Hunter, J. R. (1994). Insuring against natural disaster. *NAIC Journal of Insurance, 12*, 467.

Hwang, J.-T., Ping, C., & Wang, C.-H. (2010). Debt overhang, financial sector development and economic growth. *Hitotsubashi Journal of Economics, 51*, 13–30.

Ifft, J., Kuethe, T. H., Lyons, G., Schultz, A., & Zhu, J. Y. (2024). Crop insurance's impact on commercial bank loan volumes: Theory and evidence. *Applied Economic Perspectives and Policy, 46*(1), 318–337. https://doi.org/10.1002/aepp.13388

Ifft, J. E., Kuethe, T., & Morehart, M. (2015). Does federal crop insurance lead to higher farm debt use? Evidence from the agricultural resource management survey (arms). *Agricultural Finance Review, 75*(3), 349–367.

Iqbal, Z., & Mirakhor, A. (2011). *An introduction to Islamic finance: Theory and practice*. London: Wiley.

Irac, D. M., & Minoiu, C. (2006). Risk insurance in a transition economy. *Economics of Transition, 15*(1), 153–173. https://doi.org/10.1111/j.1468-0351.2007.00275.x

Islam, A., Matthew Leister, C., Mahmud, M., & Raschky, P. A. (2020). Natural disaster and risk-sharing behavior: Evidence from rural Bangladesh. *Journal of Risk and Uncertainty, 2020*(61), 67–99.

Islam, R., & Ahmad, R. (2019). Applicability of Mudarabah and Musharakah as Islamic micro-equity finance to underprivileged women in Malaysia. *The European Journal of Development Research*. https://doi.org/10.1057/s41287-019-00225-3

Islam, R., & Ahmad, R. (2020). Applicability of Mudarabah and Musharakah as Islamic micro-equity finance to underprivileged women in Malaysia. *European Journal of Development Research, 32*, 176–197. https://doi.org/10.1057/s41287-019-00225-3

Jaffee, D. M., & Russell, T. (1997). Catastrophe insurance, capital markets, and uninsurable risks. *Journal of Risk and Insurance., 64*(2), 205.

Jametti, M., & von Ungern-Sternberg, T. (2010). Risk selection in natural-disaster insurance. *Journal of Institutional and Theoretical Economics JITE, 166*(2), 344–364. https://doi.org/10.1628/093245610791343021

Kahneman, D., & Tversky, A. (1979). Prospect theory: An analysis of decision under risk. *Econometrica, 47*(2), 263–292.

Kalemli-Ozcan, S., Luttini, E., & Sørensen, B. (2013). Debt crises and risk-sharing: The role of markets versus sovereigns. *The Scandinavian Journal of Economics, 116*(1), 253–276.

Kalemli-Ozcan, S., Sørensen, B. E., & Yosha, O. (2003). Risk sharing and industrial specialization: Regional and international evidence. *American Economic Review, 93*(3), 903–918.

Kaushalya, H., Karunasena, G., & Amarathunga, D. (2014). Role of insurance in post disaster recovery planning in business community. *Procedia Economics and Finance, 18*, 626–634. https://doi.org/10.1016/s2212-5671(14)00984-8

Kelly, M., & Kleffner, A. E. (2003). Optimal loss mitigation and contract design. *Journal of Risk and Insurance, 70*(1), 53–72.

Keskar, S. A . (2012). *Study of the problems and prospects in the implementation of crop insurance schemes in the state of Maharashtra*. Ph.D. thesis. SNDT Womens University.

Keynes, J. M. (1937). Some economic consequences of a declining population. *Eugenics Review, 29*, 13–17.

Kilström, M., & Roth, P. (2024). Risk-sharing and entrepreneurship. *Journal of Comparative Economics, 52*(1), 341–360. https://doi.org/10.1016/j.jce.2023.12.002

Kindleberger, C. P., & Aliber, R. Z. (2011). *Manias, panics, and crashes: A history of financial crises*. Palgrave Macmillan.

Kish, R. J. (2016). Catastrophe (CAT) bonds: Risk offsets with diversification and high returns. *Financial Services Review, 25*(2016), 303–329.

Kleindorfer, P. R., & Kunreuther, H. (1999). The complementary roles of mitigation and insurance in managing catastrophic risks. *Risk Analysis, 19*(4), 727–738. https://doi.org/10.1111/j.1539-6924.1999.tb00442.x

Klugman, S. A., Panjer, H. H., & Willmot, G. E. (2012). *Loss models: From data to decisions*. Wiley.

Knight, F. H. (1921). *Risk uncertainty and profit*. https://oll-resources.s3.us-east-2.amazonaws.com/oll3/store/titles/306/Knight_0192.html

Kononovych, T., & Myasoid, P. (2020). Prospects theory and individual style of economic decision making. *Problems of Psychology in the 21st Century, 14*(1), 54. https://doi.org/10.33225/ppc/20.14.54

Krueger, D., & Perri, F. (2011). Public versus private risk sharing. *Journal of Economic Theory, 146*(3), 920–956.

Kull, A. (2009). Sharing risk—An economic perspective. *ASTIN Bulletin: THe Journal of the IAA, 39*(2), 591–613.

Kumar, P., Joshi, P. K., & Aggarwal, P. K. (2014). Projected effect of droughts on supply, demand, and prices of crops in India. *Economic and Political Weekly, 49*(52), 54–63.

Kunreuther, H. (2006). Disaster mitigation and insurance: Learning from Katrina. *The ANNALS of the American Academy of Political and Social Science, 604*(1), 208–227. https://doi.org/10.1177/0002716205285685

Lakdawalla, D., & Zanjani, G. (2011). Catastrophe bonds, reinsurance, and the optimal collateralization of risk transfer. *Journal of Risk and Insurance, 79*(2), 449–476. https://doi.org/10.1111/j.1539-6975.2011.01425.x

Lamond, J., & Penning-Rowsell, E. (2014). The robustness of flood insurance regimes given changing risk resulting from climate change. *Climate Risk Management, 2*, 1–10.

Lee, J.-P., & Yu, M.-T. (2007). Valuation of catastrophe reinsurance with catastrophe bonds. *Insurance: Mathematics and Economics, 41*(2), 264–278. https://doi.org/10.1016/j.insmatheco.2006.11

Leibenstein, H. (1969). Organizational or frictional equilibria, X-efficiency, and the rate of innovation. *The Quarterly Journal of Economics, 83*(4), 600–623.

Levy, J. S. (1992). An introduction to prospect theory. *Political Psychology, 13*(2), 171–186.

Linnerooth-Bayer, J., Mechler, R., & Hochrainer-Stigler, S. (2011). Insurance against losses from natural disasters in developing countries, evidence, gaps and the way forward. *Journal of Integrated Disaster Risk Management IDRiM, 1*(1), 1.

Lobo-Guerrero, L. (2010). *Insuring security: Biopolitics, security, and risk*. Routledge.

Lowe, R., & Teece, D. (2000). Diversification and economies of scope. *International Encyclopedia of the Social & Behavioral Sciences*. https://doi.org/10.1016/B0-08-043076-7/04263-7

Lowry, J., Rawlings, P. J., Merkin, Q. C. R., & Merkin, R. (2011). *Insurance law: Doctrines and principles*. London: Bloomsbury Publishing.

Madan, D. B. (2009). Capital requirements, acceptable risks and profits. *Quantitative Finance, 9*(7), 767–773. https://doi.org/10.1080/14697680903314456

Maghrebi, N. E., Mirakhor, A., Akın, T., & Iqbal, Z. (2023). The risk-sharing organizing principle of Iqtiṣād. Palgrave Studies in Islamic Banking, Finance and Economics Palgrave Macmillan.

Magni, D. (2019). *New perspectives of profit smoothing empirical evidence from China*. London: This Palgrave Macmillan.

Mankiw, N. G. (2014). *Principles of microeconomics*. Cengage Learning.

Markowitz, H. (1952). Portfolio selection. *The Journal of Finance, 7*(1), 77–91.

Martynov, A., & Schepker, D. J. (2017). Risk preferences and asset ownership: Integrating prospect theory and transaction cost economics. *Managerial and Decision Economics, 38*(2), 125–143. https://doi.org/10.1002/mde.2746

Marx, K. (1887). *Capital a critique of political economy volume I*. https://www.marxists.org/archive/marx/works/1867-c1/

Masci, P. (2011). The history of insurance: Risk, uncertainty and entrepreneurship. *Journal of the Washington Institute of China Studies, 5*(3), 25–68.

Mayers, D., & Smith, C. (1982). On the corporate demand for insurance. *The Journal of Business, 55*(2), 281–296.

McGuire, T. G., & Van Kleef, R. C. (2017). Risk sharing. *Risk Adjustment, Risk Sharing and Premium Regulation in Health Insurance Markets*. https://doi.org/10.1016/B978-0-12-811325-7.00004-X

Michel-Kerjan, E. O. (2010). Catastrophe economics: The national flood insurance program. *Journal of Economic Perspectives, 24*(4), 165–186.

Miller, K. D. (1998). Economic exposure and integrated risk management. *Strategic Management Journal, 19*(5), 497–514.

Mirakhor, A., & Hamid, I. S. (2011). Risk sharing and public policy. In *5th international Islamic capital market forum, securities commission of Malaysia*, November (Vol. 10).

Mishra, S., Vyas, V., & Meena, V. K. (2021). Abnormal returns and impact of information of natural disaster on the Indian stock market. *Journal of Commerce and Accounting Research, 10*(3), 1.

Mohanty, A., & Wadhawan, S. (2021). Mapping India's climate vulnerability: A district-level assessment. New Delhi: Council on Energy, Environment and Water.

Nacol, E. C. (2016). *Age of risk: Politics and economy in early modern Britain*. Princeton University Press.

Nguyen, T., & Chaiechi, T. (2021). The effects of natural disasters on stock market return and volatility in Hong Kong. *Economic Effects of Natural Disasters, 2021*, 11–20.

Obrinsky, M. (1983). *Theory and capitalism*. University of Pennsylvania Press.
Outreville, J. F. (1998). *Theory and practice of insurance*. New York: Springer.
Pagnottoni, P., Spelta, A., Flori, A., & Pammolli, F. (2022). Climate change and financial stability: Natural disaster impacts on global stock markets. *Physica a: Statistical Mechanics and Its Applications, 599*, 127514. https://doi.org/10.1016/j.physa.2022.127514
Panda, A. (2016). Vulnerability to climate variability and drought among small and marginal farmers: A case study in Odisha. *India. Climate and Development, 9*(7), 605–617.
Paradine, T. J. (1995). Business interruption insurance: A vital ingredient in your disaster recovery plan. *Information Management and Computer Security, 3*(1), 9–17.
Pauly, M. (1968). The economics of moral hazard: Comment. *American Economic Review, 58*, 531–536.
Peleckienė, V., Peleckis, K., Dudzevičiūtė, G., & Peleckis, K. K. (2019). The relationship between insurance and economic growth: Evidence from the European Union countries. *Economic Research-Ekonomska Istraživanja, 32*(1), 1138–1151. https://doi.org/10.1080/1331677X.2019.1588765
Petak, W. (1998). Mitigation and insurance. In H. Kunreuther & R. J. Roth (Eds.), *Paying the price: The status and role of insurance against Natural disaster in United States*. London: Joseph Henry Press.
Picard, P. (2008). Natural disaster insurance and the equity-efficiency trade-off. *The Journal of Risk and Insurance, 75*(1), 17–38.
Purcell, J. R., & Edward, A. (2016). *Capitalism and risk: Concepts, consequences, and ideologies*. https://digitalcommons.nyls.edu/cgi/viewcontent.cgi?article=1432&context=fac_articles_chapters
Raju, S. S., & Chand, R. (2008). *Agricultural insurance in India problems and prospects*. NCAP working, paper no. 8.
Rao, K. N. (2002). Crop insurance in India: Past, present, and future. *Vision the Journal of Business Perspective., 6*(2), 29–39.
Raschky, P., & Weckhannemann, H. (2007). Charity hazard—A real hazard to natural disaster insurance? *Environmental Hazards, 7*(4), 321–329. https://doi.org/10.1016/j.envhaz.2007.09.002
Raviv, A. (1979). The design of an optimal insurance policy. *The American Economic Review, 69*(1), 84–96.
Reinhart, C. M., & Rogoff, K. S. (2009). *This time is different: Eight centuries of financial folly*. Princeton University Press.
Ren, K., Qin, T., & Yuandong, M. (2023). The role of aggregate risk aversion in the pricing of economic uncertainty. *Applied Economics Letters, 30*(14), 1896–1903. https://doi.org/10.1080/13504851.2022.2083561
Reuten, G. (1991). Accumulation of capital and the foundation of the tendency of the rate of profit to fall. *Cambridge Journal of Economics, 15*(1), 79–93.

Ricardo, D. (1817). *Principles of political economy and taxation*. https://www.marxists.org/reference/subject/economics/ricardo/tax/index.htm
Rothschild, M., & Stiglitz, J. (1976). Equilibrium in competitive insurance markets: An essay on the economics of imperfect information. *The Quarterly Journal of Economics, 90*(4), 629–649.
Sakshi, V. (2009). Catastrophic risk and insurance. *Revue Management and Avenir, 27*, 225–240.
Sawa, R. (2021). A prospect theory Nash bargaining solution and its stochastic stability. *Journal of Economic Behavior and Organization, 184*, 692–711.
Sawyer, M. (2023). Secular stagnation and monopoly capitalism. *Journal of Post Keynesian Economics, 46*(4), 545–565. https://doi.org/10.1080/01603477.2023.2270949
Scott, S. (2011). Risk and insurance in early modern England: People, politics, and culture, 1500–1800. *Journal of Interdisciplinary History, 42*(3), 471–473.
Seetharam, I. (2017). *Environmental disasters and stock market performance*. https://web.stanford.edu/~ishuwar/Disasters_Stocks_Current.pdf
Shao, J., Pantelous, A., & Papaioannou, A. D. (2015). Catastrophe risk bonds with applications to earthquakes. *European Actuarial Journal, 5*(1), 113–138. https://doi.org/10.1007/s13385-015-0104-9
Shavell, S. (1979). On moral hazard and insurance. *The Quarterly Journal of Economics, 93*(4), 541–562.
Shiller, R. J. (2005). *Irrational exuberance*. Princeton University Press.
Siddiqi, M. N. (2006). Islamic banking and finance in theory and practice: A survey of state of the art. Islamic economic studies. *The Islamic Research and Training Institute (IRTI), 13*, 2–48.
Simon, H. A. (1955). A behavioral model of rational choice. *The Quarterly Journal of Economics, 69*(1), 99–118.
Smith, A. (1776). *The wealth of the nation*. https://www.rrojasdatabank.info/Wealth-Nations.pdf
Sopha, B. M., Arvianto, A., & Tjahjono, B. (2022). Survival strategies of traditional retailers during the COVID-19 pandemic: Some insights from a developing country. *Journal of Industrial Engineering and Management, 15*(2), 185–201. https://doi.org/10.3926/jiem.3698
Stiglitz, J. E. (1974). Incentives and risk sharing in sharecropping. *Review of Economic Studies, 41*, 219–255.
Stiglitz, J. E. (1983). Risk, incentives and insurance: The pure theory of moral hazard. *The Geneva Papers on Risk and Insurance, 8*(26), 4–33.
Swastika, P., & Mirakhor, A. (2021). Risk sharing economy: A framework. In Applying risk-sharing finance for economic development. Political Economy of Islam. Palgrave Macmillan. https://doi.org/10.1007/978-3-030-82642-0_3

Tate, W. L., & Ellram, L. M. (2022). Transaction cost economics. In W. Tate, L. Ellram, & L. Bals (Eds.), *Handbook of theories for purchasing, supply chain and management research*. London: Edward Elgar.

Temin, P. (1976). *Id monetary forces cause the great depression?* Norton.

Thomas, C. R., & Maurice, S. C. (2019). *Managerial economics* (13th ed.). London: McGraw-Hill Education.

Townsend, R. M. (1994). Risk and insurance in village India. *Econometrica, 62*, 539–591.

Usmani. (1999). The concept of Musharakah and its application as an Islamic method of financing. *Arab Law Quarterly, 14*(3), 203–220.

Vaughan, E. J. (1997). *Risk management*. Wiley.

Willett, A. H. (1901). *The economic theory of risk and Insurance*. London: Columbia Univxhsity.

Williams, E. (1943). *Capitalism and slavery*. The University of North Carolina Press.

Williamson, O. E. (1962). Managerial discretion and business behavior. *American Economic Review, 52*(2), 103–112.

Williamson, O. E. (1981). The economics of organization: The transaction cost approach. *American Journal of Sociology, 87*(3), 548–577.

Williamson, O. E. (1985a). *The economic institutions of capitalism firms, markets, Relational Contracting*. China Social Sciences Publishing House Chengcheng Books Limited.

Williamson, O. E. (1985b). *The economic institutions of capitalism*. Free Press.

Williamson, O. E. (1998). *The economic institutions of capitalism*. London: The Free Press.

Zajac, E. J., & Olsen, C. P. (1992). From transaction cost to transactional value analysis: Implications for the study of interorganizational strategies. *Journal of Management Studies, 30*(1), 131–145. https://doi.org/10.1111/j.1467-6486.1993.tb00298.x

Zhang, C., Yang, C., & Liu, C. (2021). Economic policy uncertainty and corporate risk-taking: Loss aversion or opportunity expectations. *Pacific-Basin Finance Journal, 69*, 101640. https://doi.org/10.1016/j.pacfin.2021.101640

CHAPTER 3

Risk and Economic Governance

Risk governance has emerged as a discipline and an institution in itself. It evolved out of environmental crises, nuclear risks, and political conflicts. It is still growing due to macro- and micro-level development and economic changes. Governing 'risk' is defined as controlling the agent of uncertainty and exposures. Risk governance is about applying the core idea of governance in making decisions related to risk and uncertainties. Marchi (2003) argues that risk governance is a popular expression associated with the precautionary principle, which can be interpreted as a bridge, combining the idea of 'sound' science with democratic participation. So, risk governance is a combination of science and social rights in the specific context of democracy. The political system in which the risk manifests and governs matters since the use of scientific rationality in dictating human and social behaviour is a question of power and power relations. So, democratic governance is widely recognized as the best institutional environment to govern the risks, including political crises. Risk governance is a multi-actor process encompassing risk assessment, management, and communication. It also involves information gathering, analysis, communication, and decision-making through rules, procedures, and mechanisms (Figueroa, 2016). Mitchell (2006) argues that risk governance is a project of public arrangement for preventing, avoiding, and mitigating technology and natural risks, which is referred

S. M. Irshad, *Economics of Disasters and Climate Change*, Sustainable Development Goals Series,
https://doi.org/10.1007/978-981-97-9415-7_3

to as risk governance. It typically refers to an all-encompassing, methodical strategy that makes use of scientific instruments and is integrated with other public policies that are economically and environmentally sustainable. By making risk analysis a fundamental component of governance and by taking into account the likelihood and consequences of potential negative outcomes, risk-based approaches to governance aim to enhance the logic, efficacy, and calibre of governance regimes (Rothstein et al., 2013). Vermeulen (2005) put another argument that risk governance is neither a risk method of governance nor an addition to the efficiency of risk management. Risk governance needs an independent perspective to ensure that relevant and efficient risk modelling and institutions exist to manage it. Risk governance is also a polycentric process; hence, each institution must adapt to the situation and the emerging perception of risks.

Risk governance is also subject to political criticism and scientific rationality. Objectivity and empirical facts determine the rationality of science; however, such rational objectivity does not endorse the social perception of risks and risk governance. Governing risk is possible through adopting empiricism in decision-making, and the accuracy of decisions depends on social and political consensus. Scientific information provides access to various actor groups as it permeates several societal domains (Lange & Garrelts, 2013). Furthermore, methodically producing information results in both increased knowledge and increased ignorance. Other catchphrases that target various forms of ignorance are positioned next to the term "knowledge society", such "risk" and "uncertainty", the latter of which refers to the absence of predictive power in open systems (Schiller, 2005: 46). Politics and related issues are typically the backdrop for contemporary calls on research to produce knowledge that is actively beneficial in various spheres of society (Hirsch-Hadorn et al., 2002: 285). In forming risk assessments, public views, attitudes, and concerns regarding dangers are vital. Risk perceptions and attitudes in society can diverge significantly from scientific evaluations (Slovic, 1987). So, the empiricism of science often intercepts social choices and interpretations of risk and uncertainty. It is a critical part of communicating risk perception and arriving at well-informed decision-making; scientists, legislators, and the general public must communicate openly and clearly about risks and uncertainties (Fischhoff & Kadvany, 2011). Incorporating diverse knowledge is essential for resolving the shortcomings of conventional risk assessments that rely only on computer models and expert calculations (De Marchi, 2014). Risk governance is indeed an interface of a diverse set of knowledge and even epistemologies. Risk governance brings a diverse group of actors together, particularly integrated risk governance. Globally and nationally, each box is complex in structure and at the basic structural level. Local and regional actors are crucial in many situations regarding risk-related activities (Assmuth et al., 2010). One set of rationalities often interfaces with other sets of rationalities and choices, so a single-prong approach to risk governance does not ensure effective control and regulation of risk. Notwithstanding the different viewpoints, it is evident that risk management entails more than merely technical evaluation and risk optimization as quantifiable entities. Risks are influenced by political systems, cultural elements, political ideologies, and other social and psychological aspects (Felt et al., 2007; Kasperson et al., 1988). The effectiveness of risk governance is closely associated with the critical location and application of discursive knowledge and epistemologies. Risk governance is a project governing the interface between society and risks, including environmental risks. Environmental risks are often local-specific and do not necessarily adhere to the global discourse of risk and uncertainties. It is as Habermas (1987: 131) articulated the governing the life world of individuals and society. The life world is intuitively present, in this sense, familiar and transparent. At the same time, a vast and incalculable web of presuppositions must be satisfied if an actual utterance is to be at all meaningful, that is, valid or invalid. Risk governance follows a discursive practice as its method is subject to the socio-political context of the regions and economy. Here, we use a discursive approach of risk governance, subject to the social process of locating risks in the given socio-political system. Discursive also means engaging with the different power dynamics of the system, which generate risks and its willingness to own it up.

So, the idea of governance in diverse contexts, as Rose and Miller (1992) argue, political power exercised through a profusion of shifting alliances between diverse authorities in projects to govern a multitude of facets of economic activity, social life, and individual conditions determine the risk governance. Scholars define risk governance as the 'translation' of governance's fundamental ideas and content to the context of risk and risk-related decision-making, known as 'risk governance' (Renn, 2008). Renn's theory has deeply influenced the risk governance in the Global South. The Global South often perceives risk as a result of uneven and irrational development and sciences. The diversity and differences further influence the perception of risk in the Global South.

Governing risk and uncertainty are meant to reduce their effect on risk on utility and value of assets and prevent negative externalities. Risk governance is about monitoring, disciplining, and removing ineffective management teams to ensure stakeholders' interests (Ben Naceur & Kandil, 2009). The management team could use human resources to engage in risk-induced decision-making. The critical focus of risk governance is the demonstrated impact or effect of risk and uncertainty on expected utilities. So, governance is possible in the context of information symmetry and transparency in decision-making. Risk governance is defined as a firm's capability to initiate a collaborative process of interaction and decision-making among different actors to control the risk-related complexity in its internal and external environment (Stein et al., 2019). There are critical observations on the risk governance of capitalist organizations. Stein et al. (2019) observed that organizations will be able to manage the risk-related complexity of open organizations thanks to risk governance, which will also serve as a conceptual framework to improve the rigour of research on corporate loss minimization and value creation in the modern, multi-political dynamic environments. A firm's capability is an integral part of risk sharing and risk governance, as it represents the ability of the firm to understand and assess the impact of uncertainty on an everyday basis. Scholars argue that risk governance 'combines two separate concepts, but belong to spheres of investigation and practical interest that are strictly intertwined and partially overlapping' (Marchi, 2003). Risk governance implies an institutional capability to push for a risk mitigation process and transform the institutions. As Rosa () defined risk, 'risk is a situation or event where something of human value (including humans themselves) is at stake and where the outcome is uncertain'. Rosa's definition of risk gives a broader understanding of risks, so risk governance depends on how society and the economy perceive the risks regarding the expected outcome. Economists consider risks as a source that intercepts the market and pushes the value and utilities down, so risk governance from an economic perspective is to control the economic transaction and decision on values. Economists' risk perception and assessment are much more specific than any other risk assessment regarding outcome. It could be production loss and output loss in terms of economic cost. So, economic risk often dominates the perception of risk and decision-making in emerging market economies, including the perception of disaster and climate risks. Risk governance in the financial sector is the procedure to identify the risks and initiate measures to correct them accordingly. So, one could argue that risk governance is beyond the traditional risk analysis as it comprises legal, political, social, and economic factors that influence risk generation and creation (Nahar et al., 2016). The political economy of risk governance is located in the process between risk generation and risk governance. Risks are an inevitable outcome of the development process, and contemporary capitalist development has proved its inability to balance risk and profits. Risks are associated with profitability; hence, risk governance should consider the profitability of the economic value addition. This is evident in the case of urbanization and solid waste management in countries like India. According to government sources, about 4400 towns and cities exist in India. India's urban population will reach 600 million by 2030 (National Institute of Urban Affairs, https://nudm.mohua.gov.in/about/).

The Central Pollution Control Board of India (2016) states that Mumbai alone generates more than 11,000 tonnes per day of solid waste, and the dumping yards in Mumbai have crossed their capacities. Mumbai is the financial capital of India and one of the expanding cities. There is a positive correlation between city expansion and solid waste generation. However, this huge risk of waste management falls on the informal solid waste management workers in the city. Informal labour drives this livelihood process. Studies proved the involvement of informal sector labour in waste management worldwide. Afon's (2007) study observes that informal initiatives play an important role in solid waste management in Cities of African nations. Macro-level studies also prove informal sector labours' critical role in solid waste segregation and management. Solid waste collection and disposal is an essential source of income diversification for the poor in cities (Dan Tong et al., 2021). A sophisticated and modern method of solid waste management is not affordable to developing countries, and informal sector involvement is the primary instrument for waste management (Wilson et al., 2012). These academic studies establish the linkages between urban risk management and informal labour. They collect, segregate, and dump the waste in the dumping grounds, which are close to the informal labour settlements in Mumbai. These informal labourers are managing waste management risk at the cost of low wage rates and occupational hazards. City municipal corporations and urbanization do not stop or control waste generation; however, they effectively employ informal labour to manage the waste and govern the risk. This complexity in risk governance is seen in almost all economic decision-making.

Risk governance as a concept and theory evolved out of European discourse on risk, and it's rooted in transdisciplinary work in the interface between risk assessment, risk management, regulatory sciences, and policy analysis, focusing on European situations (van Asselt and Renn, 2011). European idea of risk governance has influenced the global discourse on risk governance. Different jurisdictions differ in their perceptions of and sensitivity to risk when risk and regulation are considered part of political discourse (Haines, 2017). Developed economies have risk governance perspectives and institutions suited to their jurisdiction and local political and economic systems. Market economies prefer risk governance close to protecting the market interest, whereas developing and underdeveloped economies prefer risk reduction and environmental security as part of public interests. This does not mean that developing countries do not consider the market while governing risks; risk governance as a public choice is primarily associated with vulnerability and deprivation. Where the vulnerability is concentrated, the risk governance gets the nature of public choice. Society and economies with vulnerable populations prefer inclusive risk governance based on a normative assumption that integrating knowledge and value could lead to the involvement of all stakeholders in decision-making on risk (Renn & Schweizer, 2009). It is challenging to practice risk governance as a single-prong strategy as it requires multiple approaches and needs to consider the heterodox experience of risk and risk impacts.

Governing risk is otherwise engaging with the complexities of experiences and the people's lived experiences. Risk governance refers to identifying, controlling, moderating, and communicating risks, particularly complex and ambiguous ones (Jacobson et al., 2013). Each aspect of risk governance has a differential impact when engaging with risks in different contexts. Decisions on risk governance are often taken at the micro-level and connected with the adaptive capacity (Elrick-Barr et al., 2014). Smit and Wandel (2006) defined adaptive capacity as a system's capacity to anticipate shocks and changes or to adapt and react to their consequences. The ability of a system to alter or adjust its traits or behaviour to better withstand current or predicted external shocks is known as adaptive capacity (Adger et al., 2004: 28). One facet of resilience is adaptive capacity, which represents the ability of a system to learn in the face of disruption (Carpenter et al., 2001: 766). The ability of a system to reconfigure and regenerate itself in the face of change is also known as the system's adaptive capacity in place (Fazey et al., 2007: 375). The prerequisites for adaptation, such as the ability to mobilize social and physical components, are known as adaptive capacity. It is exemplified by the array of resources, the system's resilience to disruptions, and the ability to plan and carry out efficient adaptation techniques to deal with upcoming or present occurrences (Nelson et al., 2007: 397, 400). Adger and Vincent (2005) defined 'adaptive capacity as a vector of resources and assets that represent the asset base from which adaptation actions and investments can be made'.

Governing risk is a project closely associated with the adaptive capacity of the institutions to engage with the expected impact of risk and uncertainty. Risk governance for the vulnerable community is the human system's ability to improve (or at least preserve) each member's quality of life in a particular environment or range of environments, which is synonymous with adaptive capacity (Gallopin, 2006: 300). A society and economy expose to sever risk would imagine risk governance as an institutional intervention to reduce their exposure to risks. A system's capacity to adapt so that it is better able to control how exposed to and sensitive it is to climatic effects (Preston & Stafford-Smith, 2009: 12). Risk governance is possible through building institutions. Also, it makes institutions accessible to the vulnerable community and even to the market. This observation reflects the larger socio-political importance of risk governance; however, every risk governance tool is not accessible to society at risk. An 'at risk' society evolved out of vulnerability and hazardous development preferred to inclusive risk governance, which, as said before, is risk reduction as a public good. Everybody is not in favour of the market, and some are questioning market-driven risk governance, which emphasizes value protection and business continuity as risk governance.

The market is the most adaptive institution since it exists through adapting to the risks. Market control is one of the adaptation strategies, and it includes monopoly and competitive pricing systems. Market logic may not be appropriate for understanding the impact of governing environmental risks and uncertainties. So, the complexities of risk governance allow us to see the interface of risk governance with the political economy of governance.

3.1 Risk Governance and Governing Adaptations

Risk governance does not fully operate under the idea of instrumental rationality. Rather, it is evolved through the specific context of the economy. Risk governance could be read as solutions and responses, so a rigid approach is never possible in practising risk governance. Risk governance is the collaborative accomplishment of actors with different roles, goals, and levels of awareness of their respective duties (Boholm et al., 2012). It is a framework and an approach rather than an institution-driven method. Frameworks for risk governance can occasionally be inconsistent, path-dependent, and fragmented (Hood et al., 2001). The idea of looking at risk governance as a fragmented project necessitates integrating multiple stakeholders and approaches in risk governance.

The networks in question involve many stakeholders, and any governance approach to risk policy formulation ought to explore "channels and systems by which important and capable actors synchronize their actions and assets to achieve mutually specified goals" (Pierre, 2005, 452). The theoretical foundation for modern risk governance comes from neoclassical approaches to resource management. Some historians argue that the idea of risk governance originated with the ancient Greeks, who made efforts to suppress and regulate hazards. The general perception that hazards could be measured and controlled followed this (Bernstein, 1996). Recognizing uncertainty as a scientific notion is the first step towards risk governance. Other components of risk governance include improving resilience and lowering risk (Collingridge, 1996). Marijke et al. (2012) argue that the term "risk governance" describes the various approaches taken by many people, organizations, and public and private entities to manage risks surrounded by complexity, ambiguity, or uncertainty.

Building institutions for risk governance is a path-dependent phenomenon and is close to how people understand risk as a determinant of everyday life. The foundation of people's understanding of risk is their ability to construct contingent linkages between an object at risk and a risk object (Boholm & Corvellec, 2011). Public perception of risk is essential in deciding the risk governance policy (Thompson & Rayner, 1998). Paradoxically, the neoliberal period is also the age of the regulatory state as states allocate more resources to regulation. We have more regulation than deregulation, most often for capitalism and markets (Levi-Faur, 2005). Policy for governing risk depends on the policy of governance. Specifically, the academic discourse on governance has become popular along with neoliberal policies. The countries that are moved into neoliberal policies prefer a political consensus to operate the state during the neoliberal period. Rhodes (1996, p. 652) argues that "governance signifies a change in the meaning of government, referring to a new process of governing; or a changed condition of ordered rule; or the new method by which society is governed". It was in the 1980s that the phrase "governance" first appeared. The phrase essentially refers to "the action of governing" on one level (Oxford Shorter). It is also crucial to recognize that the phrase has been seized by neoliberals, who have succeeded in imposing their definition. Because of this, the term "governance" refers to a particular type of management that was first employed in the private sector but is being increasingly adopted by the government. This type of management replicates the mechanics of a free market to make decisions (Ives, 2015). Governance became a popular terminology during the neoliberal regime, and the government adopted the language of neoliberalism. Neoliberalism requires multilevel governance to fully realize its objectives (Harmes, 2006). The neoliberal state has become a normal entity now, and every government is forced to follow the rules and regulations of neoliberal governance. Governance is a process of enabling stakeholder coordination in decision-making to facilitate the development of shared values (Stewart & Jones, 2003). The challenge of governance in a neoliberal context is the integration of shared values of multiple agents. Community, individuals, and civil society influence risk governance; hence, governance requires strong institutional realizations.

As said before, governing demonstrated uncertainties does mean controlling and regulating the agents of risk, so the public perception of the effectiveness of governance matters. On a national scale, governance describes structures and processes for collective decision-making involving governmental and non-governmental actors (Neye & Donahue, 2000). Nonstate actors' involvement in risk governance is an established debate. However, it is as complex as the risks. Governing choices in modern societies are seen as an interplay between governmental institutions, economic forces, and civil society actors (such as NGOs). At the global level, governance embodies a horizontally organized structure of functional self-regulation encompassing state and non-state actors, bringing about collectively binding decisions without superior authority

(Rosenau, 1992; Wolf, 2002). Some scholars argue that civil society organizations should be part of risk governance (Halachmi, 2005). Hegelian interpretation of civil society gives more clarity on the role of civil society. For Hegel (1896, 1952), the creation of civil Society is the achievement of the modern world, *which has, for the first time, given all determinations of the Idea their due. If the State is represented as a unity of different persons, as a unity that is only a partnership, then what is meant is only civil society.* Hegel interprets civil Society as a space between the State and the family, emphasizing the importance of civic articulation of rights between the State and the private space (family). Hegel's interpretation of civil society articulates the right to develop a political space between the state and family to engage in the decision-making process. It could also be a decision on development, and hence, its civil society can articulate risk in accordance with the context and the perception of the society. Theoretically, civil society involvement in risk governance makes risk regulation or control a public choice.

Alexander (2006) explained that civil society is an aggregate of multiple institutions engaged in non-state activities, which could be read as private, friendly, and part of the public sphere. It could create a risk-informed public sphere that looks for better and more effective governance for making security a collective right. Baker (2002) also referred to civil society as pluralists' demand for an active role of a democratic state to meet the needs of the citizens. The liberal thinkers, however, argue that it is civil society's responsibility to prevent the over-concentration of power in society. So, risk reduction projects could result in the integration of multiple choices in defining social responsibilities. Robinson (1995) observed civil society as a political discourse that emerged during the middle of the 1980s. Robinson emphasized both the neoliberal and neo-populist paradigms of civil society to promote democratic values and challenge the State's domination. The core argument is that civil society could be an effective counterbalance to state power, and in risk governance, it challenges the state's narrative of risks. States in the market and developing economies like India often see states ignoring risks in economic decision-making, so civil society movements could play an essential role in determining the implementation of risk governance. This is evident in the case of poor pollution control measures. Though civil society has the potential even to challenge the state and its narration of

Box 3.1 Kathikudam Struggle and Risk Governance

The local community of the Chalakudy area of Ernakulam-Thrissur area of Kerala state found dead fish on the Chalakuddy River in the month of May and June in the year 2013. It was found in the area where the Nitta Gelatin India Limited operates and releases the wastewater into the river. The local community suspects the factory. This factory, which produces Ossine from animal bonds, started in 1979 in Kathikudam village in the Chalakudy area. The water consumption is high, and wastewater, along with chemical particles, is released to the Chalakudy River, affecting the local groundwater conditions. The local community started a protest movement, and the local Panchayat did not favour the company. However, the company got approval from the Kerala State Pollution Control Board, and later on, the National Green Tribunal, a unique system for hearing environment-related legal disputes, also issued a judgement in favour of the company. The company got scientific support from the state pollution control board, which said that the pollutants found in Chalakudy River were not as harmful as Binoy (2021) in the study argues that the expert knowledge produced by state pollution control boards of Kerala, influenced by the ideology of power and hegemony and which is in favour of the state and ignore the local lived experiences. It is primarily against the principles of deliberative democracy in risk governance

Source Binoy, P. (2021). Pollution Governance in the time of disasters: Testimonials of Caste/d Women and the Politics of Knowledge in Kathikudam, Kerala. *Geoforum*, *124*, 175–184. https://doi.org/10.1016/j.geoforum.2021.06.008. Keeralyeem Mazika, April May 2018

risk and uncertainties, it still operates in a society that accepts democracy as the fundamental method of governance and also recognizes deliberative democratic principles. See Box 3.1

3.2 Risk Governance as Deliberative Democratic Practice

Risk governance encompasses more than just the three commonly acknowledged components of risk analysis: risk assessment, risk management, and risk communication. It also involves issues related to institutional design and function, organizational capability, stakeholder engagement, cooperative decision-making, political accountability on the part of public entities, and corporate responsibility on the part of private businesses (Renn, 2008). So, such a complex project needs to be located within the context of the democratic process. The deliberative model of democracy holds that a polity's institutions must be set up in such a way that processes of collective deliberation conducted fairly and rationally among free and equal individuals produce what is deemed to be in the best interests of all (Benhabib, 1996: 69) for such processes to achieve legitimacy and rationality. Deliberative democratic principles operate in governing the impact of environmental risks as well.

Conditions for the expression and consideration of the diversity of environmental (and other) values are provided by deliberative democracy (Smith, 2003). For more respectable and reliable forms of political power to arise, two essential requirements must be met: inclusivity and unrestricted discourse (Smith, 2003). Governing risks often need contestations of existing discourse on development, disaster, and risks, as well as new discourses on governing uncertainties. The ability of the political representative to think and make decisions on behalf of others is the foundation of the principal-agent form of representation, which is so common in liberal democracies (Pitkin, 1967: 42–3). A system follows or accepts the principles of deliberative democracy. The idea of inclusivity in risk governance could be possible through a deliberative democratic practice. The importance of connecting risk governance with deliberative democracy is that the economic cost of risk governance at the expense of capitalist development has the potential to be selective in risk reductions. Risk governance for large sections of vulnerable populations is nothing but establishing institutions for risk reduction and having access to it.

The differential impact of risk is quite common in developing and backward economies, so a multiple-knowledge system needs to be imparted to build resilience and adaptation. A vulnerability paradigm has driven approaches to disaster for a long time, and it perceives disaster impact as being driven by social and economic vulnerability. The vulnerability paradigm emerged in the 1970s in response to the hazard paradigm. The hazard paradigm describes disaster as the consequence of extraordinary hazards (Gaillard, 2019; Hewitt, 1983). The vulnerability paradigm influences the institutional structure that largely focuses on community and social vulnerabilities. Discourse on the vulnerability paradigm has influenced the academic and policy-making of risk governance. It is quite evident in the case of natural calamities; the vulnerability paradigm undermines the local political economy of disasters and follows the Western understanding of disaster as an individual crisis. Some studies argue that the Global South's local narratives of disasters counter-hegemony against the capitalist narratives of disaster risks (Gaillard, 2019). The theory of risk evolved from industrialized capitalist economies based on the science of risks, which is increasingly becoming popular in developing and underdeveloped countries.

Beck (1992) introduced risk as a reflection or an after-effect of capitalist developments in Western economies. The theories of risk are subject to multiple inquiries and debates; for instance, some studies connect risk to the expected loss (Willis, 2007), so this is very much connected with risk governance in the Global North, where the value of the loss is high. So, their risk perception is primarily associated with capital loss. Governing risk as capital saving is indeed a complex task, however, this is an integral part of risk governance in emerging market economies. Risk is considered equal to the expected disutility (Campbell, 2005), i.e., loss of utility on resource and asset base of the community and economy. So, risk governance under this perception is about building institutions to reduce economic losses, which could be insurance and market resilience. Other scholars argue that risk is an adverse outcome's probability (Graham & Weiner, 1995; Lowrance, 1976). Scholars also observe that risk is equal to the two-dimensional combination of events/consequences and associated uncertainties (Aven, 2007); risk is also considered as the uncertainty of the outcome of actions and events (Cabinet Office, 2002). Expected outcome influences risk governance to a great extent and results in institutional challenges as well. In the technical literature, the risk is frequently described in terms of expected values, but it is also frequently characterized in terms of the whole probability distribution of the outcomes or the combination of probabilities and consequences (outcomes) (Ale, 2002; Aven, 2003). According to constructivism and cultural theory, danger is the same as risk perception (Jasanoff, 1999). Risk perception also changes with the impacts and implications on the community and economy, so governing that uncertainty again moves along with the macro and micro effects of risks.

The macro- and micro-economic variables and economic structures matter in deciding the institution of risk governance. Excessive risk exposure frequently creates a financial crisis, leading to the collapse of banks and currencies. So, the financial market perceives risk accordingly and governs risk as preventing market imperfections. Due to a change in the production function, these hazards have spread throughout society and impact the environment and human health (Alexander et al., 2004). Risk governance is a project of building an institutional consciousness so that institution building could be either structural or non-structural. It has to deal with the public's perception of risk and uncertainty that evolved out of environmental risks. People's perceptions of risk and trust are affected by how the information on uncertainty is presented

(Johnson & Slovic, 1995). It could have an economic impact in terms of slowing down GDP and decreasing the capital assets of natural capital and economic processes. Uncertainties could be manifest in the public and private spheres of society. One of the challenges of risk governance is society's unequal socio-economic character, which often disowns the idea of risk governance that does not resolve the inequality issue. In addition, it is a project to regulate the relationship between risks and society, including environmental risks. It's close to Habermas's (1987: 131) theory of engaging and controlling the life world. In this sense, the world is naturally present, recognizable, and straightforward. Still, it is also a vast and endless snare of presuppositions that must be satisfied for a genuine expression to be meaningful or at least valid or invalid. Gregory et al. (1993) observed that people have well-defined values only for familiar goods; they proposed a constructivist procedure to support respondents when valuing environmental goods. The social context in which risk perceptions of environmental and technological dangers are embedded cannot be reified or evaluated independently. The negative impact of risk perception may be mitigated by perceptions of benefit, particularly to oneself or the environment (Frewer, 1999).

There is a strong correlation between belief and risk perception (Sjöberg, 2007), and it is very important in societies that follow traditional value systems. The organization and norms play an important role in creating the impression of risk and utilities (Siegrist et al., 2000). Institutions could govern and influence the perception of risks. Institutions must engage with the epistemic uncertainties, i.e., diversity of knowledge practices and perceptions. Scholars observe that it is difficult to identify, evaluate, and manage outcome risks, i.e., the various adverse outcomes that might or might not occur as a result of decisions due to the epistemic uncertainty that causes epistemic risks (Sahlin, 2012). Epistemic risk assessment values scientific facts, and it follows a rigorous process (Wandall, 2004). However, the people of the Global South experience risk as the socio-economic crisis deeply impacts their very existence. The Global South state plays a critical role in governing risks; hence, the nature of state intervention determines the effectiveness of deliberative democracy. Bohman and Rehg (1997) argue that deliberative democracy is based on Rawls' theory of justice and is about securing the best use of resources for the citizens. Deliberative democracy follows multiple methods; it could be in the form of a constitutional state with institutions or a participatory approach, which leads the people directly to influence the decision-making (Bohman, 2004). The members of deliberative democracy are conditioned to share a joint resolution for collective issues and choice options. It pushes for public reasoning as the basis for institutions to establish deliberative democracy (Cohen, 1989).

Deliberative democratic politics is indeed an inclusive model for countries operating under democracy, and for the Global South, it is essentially a project of practising welfare state policies. Deliberative democracy acknowledges that people's preferences and value orientations might change during the process of interaction; nevertheless, it shares with liberal theories the goal of establishing political structures that will settle disagreement (Miller, 1992; Phillips, 1995). The risk governance in developing countries with vulnerable populations often perceives risk reduction as democratic justice delivery. Risk-induced exclusion from the institutions of risk reduction is an everyday reality in countries like India. See Box 3.2.

Smith (2003) argues that the institutions that engage in deliberation must be aware of and vigilant against manipulative and strategic tactics in engaging with society. The high degrees of complexity, uncertainty, and collective action issues are associated with many modern environmental problems, are likely to be more "ecologically rational" than other social choice mechanisms (Dryzek, 1987). Dryzek (1987) argues that ecological rationality requires a political system to incorporate negative feedback and coordination in environmental decision-making. Fearon (1998: 49) and Torgerson (1999) discuss Dryzek's ideas and highlight how democratic

Box 3.2 Caste and exclusion from disaster relief

There are various studies show that depressed caste Indians (Dalits) are discriminated against in disaster relief in India. One of the victims of Cyclone Gaja affected Nagapattinam district in Tamil Nadu, shared his experience of not getting relief materials as their villages are located away from the main road and relief vehicles have to cross the upper caste villages. National Dalit Watch and NGO working on the issue of disaster and exclusion in their periodic report explains caste discrimination in disaster situations, particularly in the light of the experiences during the 2004 tsunami and the 2007 Kosi floods in Bihar. These communities are most vulnerable and have no land asses to loss, so their loss in terms of person days and income never account in the damage and loss assessment report and hence not eligible for any compensation rather than access to temporary shelters

Source Jain, Mahima A. 2019. Despite being hit hardest by natural disasters, landless Dalits are the last to get relief. IndiaSpend.com. National Dalit Watch. 2012. Caste discrimination in disaster situations in India—Reports by National Dalit Watch. https://www.indiawaterportal.org/

deliberation might mitigate the issue of bounded rationality by acknowledging '*the fact that our imaginations and calculating abilities are limited and fallible*'. Through applying each other's skills, knowledge, and experience, deliberation provides the framework for actors to expand their own constrained and prone-to-error viewpoints. The interface of deliberative democracy and risk governance is possible only when government institutions have the ability to adapt to the perception of risk reduction as vulnerability reduction and regulating hazards. It needs broader institutional interventions by the state and other actors.

3.3 Governmentality of Risk Governance

As mentioned above, risk governance is possible through the interface of vulnerability and hazard paradigm of risk analysis. It requires multiple institutionalism and the involvement of various actors and agents other than the state. Discursive use of knowledge and power in decision-making necessitates a Fouaultain discourse analysis. Governmentality was first used by Foucault (1991) to describe governance as occurring not only through actions of the state but also across society. His emphasis was on the technologies of power that formed, directed, and regulated people's ideas, desires, lives, and behaviours rather than the official laws and institutions of the contemporary state. Governmentality is the intersection between governance (government) and the mentalities (frameworks) that guide governance. It encompasses a vast range of organizations, practices, and knowledge systems that go beyond the state machinery with the intention of influencing public behaviour (Bevir, 2011). The effectiveness of risk governance is a reduction in hazards and also control of the secondary impact of any risk-induced disasters or calamities. Governmentality refers to the art of governing beyond just the political and administrative, encompassing the management of individuals and populations through a combination of institutions, procedures, analyses, reflections, calculations, and tactics. It's not limited to the state but includes a variety of actors such as institutions, NGOs, and private entities. Governance is about practices and making decisions to involve the concerned stakeholders in dealing with risks (Benn et al., 2009). Risk governance is a project of governmentality in practice as it does not follow any linear process in governing risks. Rather, it is a project of making every agent own up to the cause and effects of risk reduction. It is not about making stakeholders cooperate. As Heriard-Dubreuil

(2001) argues, cooperation among the stakeholders makes traditional risk governance a complex process. Coordination issues are more likely to be resolved by thoughtful institutional arrangements. It is better to think of deliberative democracy as a "desirable ingredient" of democracy rather than as a stand-alone "model of democracy" (Saward, 2000: 68). Rather than being harmful to political freedom as some detractors fear, the epistemic dimension of deliberative democracy serves to uphold it. The idea that everyone should have the chance to participate and the freedom to reject information they are not persuaded is accurate or correct is fundamental to individual learning, internal and public autonomy, and both (Rostbøll, 2008). Proper communication of risks to the larger community is the core of risk governance, and risk communication is driven by a systemic knowledge of environmental risks. Language and epistemology matter in risk communication; it is the transformation of knowledge from the scientific community to the masses, and it has to enable the masses to connect risk with their capability to respond and act. Institutions like the Indian Meteorological Department (IMD) are essential in this regard. Everybody recognizes and accepts IMD's data as authentic since they use the language of science and communicate the risk to different categories of the population. Earlier, IMD used to communicate the risk through formal communication methods, and it was mainly on general climate conditions. Later on, the advent of technology and the inclusion of people facing differential risk impact makes risk communication an everyday institutional norm. For instance, the special warning to fishermen in India is a sign of deliberative democracy. This community section needs proper communication or early warning on weather changes, including cyclones. Risk communication is essential for fishers as their life and livelihood in the sea are subject to risks. There are incidences in which risk communication disrupts risk governance. See Box 3.3.

3.4 Institutions, a Coproduction of Knowledge and Risk

Institutions make disaster mitigation decisions effective (Kenny, 2012), and it depends on the context and political situations of the region where risk is manifest. Institutions can also mandate specific conduct in repeating situations, which can be enforced by self-regulatory organizations or by outside authorities (Allegret & Dulbecco, 2002). Institutions can make rules as knowledge for practices. Here, risk has to be viewed as part of the

Box 3.3 Ockhi cyclone: conflicts over articulation

Ockhi cyclone hit the Kerala coast on 27 November 2017. The local fishermen in the Vizhinjam area of Thiruvananthapuram district noticed some unusual weather changes in the sea. They informed the local church leaders, who tried to contact the administration. There were no signs of a major disaster up to this point. Meanwhile, the Kerala State Disaster Management Authority (KSDMA) sent the fishermen constant warnings of turbulent weather and advised them to avoid fishing. There was total negligence and a lack of proper assessment of a potential threat in the first three days. Indian Meteorological Department's (IMD) weather alerts did not mention the cyclone in its weather report from 27th November to 29th November; however, on 30th November, the IMD declared it a cyclone by the time the 102 local fishers lost their life. The local anglers were turned against the Kerala State Disaster Management Authority (KSDMA) for not acting on time and delivering warning messages. However, KSDMA defended its position by stating that IMD did not release any proper cyclone warning. Rather, it mentioned deep depressions, which KSDMA declined to interpret at cyclone. IMD released information, but KSDMA did not apply its knowledge and logic to analyse the cyclone. It was an improper risk communication between authority and society. This improper communication results in human and economic loss to the local fishermen

Source Irshad, S. Mohammed. 2020. 'Early Warning and Risk Management: A Case Study of the Ockhi Cyclone in Kerala.' The Indian Journal of Social Work. Volume 81, Issue 3 July 2020

systemic understanding. For example, the recurring flood risk in Assam, India, forces communities and local institutions to perceive it as an integral part of the local system and learn to live with it. About 40% of the entire land area in Assam, i.e., 3.1 million hectares—is in flood-prone zones (Coelho, 2013). Flash floods and recurring floods cause displacement and homelessness of a large number of vulnerable populations in Assam (Das et al., 2009). One major cause of recurring floods in Assam is the Brahmaputra and Barak rivers and their tributaries overflowing into the sea, affecting Assam's economy (Phukan, 2016: Mohapatra & Singh, 2003). The Brahmaputra River experienced geological disruptions due to the 1950s earthquake (EPW, 1968). When discussing the causes of Assamese floods, Borah and Borthakur (2003) noted that a significant amount of the water was released into the rivers due to the melting of the Himalayan snow and the monsoon season's rainfall in the upper hills catchment areas. The Brahmaputra River's silt load rose, raising the riverbed's level. The river is silting up because of the numerous landslips and fractures caused by the earthquake (Guha, 1981). Increased flooding and deforestation have resulted from the growing population along the Brahmaputra River (Guha, 1981). While floods cannot be averted entirely, their damaging effects can be lessened with advance notice (Sinclair & Pegram, 2003). The number of people living in flood-prone areas is rising despite significant investments in flood defence, which is increasing the amount of money lost to flood damage in many countries (Smith & Ward, 1998). The flood created differential impacts on the community and local economy of Assam. Studies have observed that the urban centres of Assam benefit more from flood management measures than rural areas (Das, 2014). Among them, many studies prove that the semi-nomadic Mishing community has received little attention in flood risk governance, whereas the revenue-generating lands were protected by embankments (Das, 2014). Sand casting, waterlogging, soil erosion caused by floods, and damage to standing crops impact Assams' endogenous resources (Goyari, 2005). Such exceptional support evolves out of the political economy of risk governance and reflects the Assam government's narrative of risks that do not match with the multiple realities of flood risk in the area. Each institution applies its own logic in governing the risks, which could also be instrumental. The disaster management authority of Assam and the Water Resource Ministry of the Government of India planned various programs. However, the number of people affected has increased over some time (ASDMA Flood report multiple years). It is evident that the Farmer in the flood-affected areas of Assam adopt a risk-averse technique to prevent crop losses, and as a result, rabi foodgrains and vegetables have increased in acreage share, whereas kharif foodgrains have decreased (Mandal, 2010). A study conducted among the marginal and small farmers farming in the recurring flood-affected district of Assam, known as Dhemaji, by these authors, shows that there has been a continued decline in farm income in the last 10 years. See Figs. 3.1 and 3.2.

Figures 3.1 and 3.2 explain that the community experiences risks in their everyday life as permanent risks, and governing the risks is a private choice as defined by neoliberal philosophy. The community perceived this recurring flood risk as an institution of uncertainty, and it reflects the system theory of risks, which holds that human societies are structured as a variety of self-referential or autopoietic (self-organizing) systems that form both their reality and an image of the outside world (Luhmann, 1984). It is evident in the Assam flood, in which the Government of India, the Government of Assam, Non-Governmental Organisations, and the community have shared scientific, and socially constructed risk perception. However, the government of India's and Assam government's

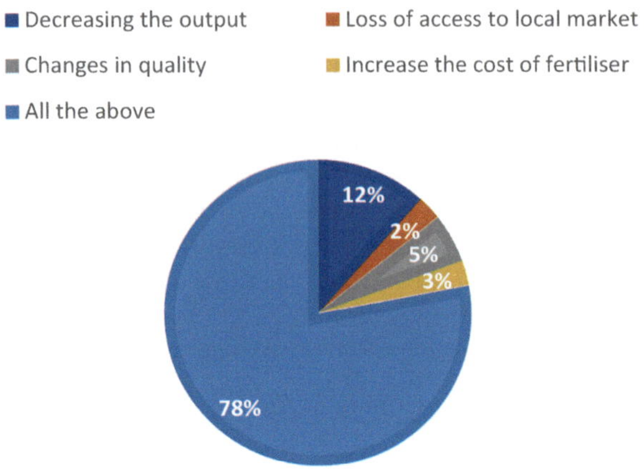

Fig. 3.1 Flood affect the farming (*Source* Fieldwork from 2023-November to 2024 January)

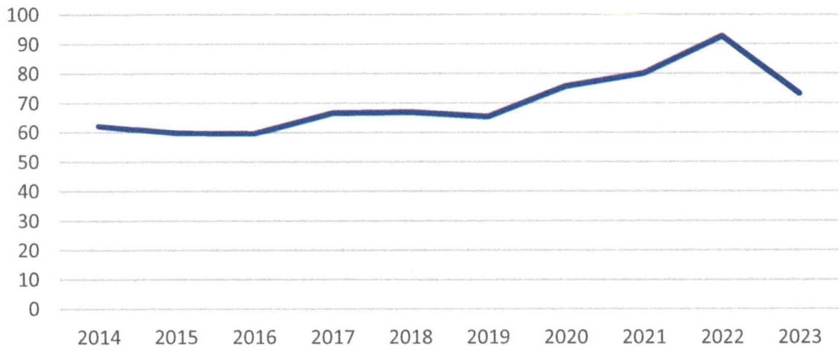

Fig. 3.2 Percentage loss of crops from 2014 to 2023 among marginal and small farmers in Flood Prone areas of Dhemaji District, Assam (*Source* Fieldwork from 2023-November to 2024 January)

perception of flood risk governance is close to the ability of the government institutions to reduce the impact of floods in the short run. It could be read as the organized form of risk governance, which is close to the ability of the institutions to engage with the structural and non-structural causes of risks.

The theories of institutions talk about an organized form of thinking to have a defined outcome. In the case of the Assam flood, the government wanted the specific outcome of reducing the human causalities and also local communities' ownership of flood risk governance. The government prefers an evolution of a system to govern as system theory defines institutions as rule-based spheres, which means that formal organizations embed norms, routines, or systems (Morgan & Yeung, 2007: 53). Institutions for risk management reflect how society perceives risks and the expected outcome of uncertainty and there is no standard or general agreement on the anticipated outcome of a disaster. As said before, risk governance is possible through institutions; hence, it has to follow an evolutionary approach of institutions in risk governance. As explained in Chapter 1, sustainable development is an institutional evolution to tackle environmental risks and uncertainties. Uncertainty on expected utility is instrumental in evolving institutions, and those institutions do not necessarily follow a share value; it could also be individual perception. Individual behaviour matters, and in the context of disaster and climate change, it becomes a rational choice as response and resilience are connected with such complex decisions. Institutions evolved to encourage users to invest in information to lessen ambiguity about ecological functions by reducing tenure uncertainty (Hanna, 1996). Institutions often proliferate on mutually beneficial terms to all stakeholders (Bowles et al., 2003). People do approach institutions to seek rent, and rent-seeking could be a reason for the evolution of institutions (Gifford, 1999). In climate discourse, adaptation and resilience manifest the institutional consciousness of the society and economy. Scholars argue that individuals within particular communities draw upon a shared basis of knowledge and moral standards in making decisions (Douglas, 1986). Increasing disaster events and the unprecedented impact of climate risk demands outcome-oriented institutions. Instrumental logic alone does not meet the institutional requirements of societies affected by disaster events and climate risks. Institutions for disaster risk reduction and climate action should create stakeholders and produce insight for furthering the risk mitigation by itself. Instrumental approaches to co-production risk overlooking the political, cultural, and historical determinants as well as the underlying science–society relations that were at the heart of the original co-production framework (Goldman et al., 2018). The co-protectionist approach is indeed a complex one in governing risk, yet it is an essential component in risk governance. It has to be looked at from an environmental risk perspective and be specific to disaster and climate risk contexts. Since these risks can affect the social and economic structure of the society, governing it requires knowledge and often contestations of expertise as well. Contestations could be rejecting the global macro-narrative of risks and its theorization and accepting the discursive knowledge practices. Governing risk is possible through producing and coproducing knowledge to control and reduce risks. It is essentially disaster and climate risk reduction.

Disaster and climate risk challenges the economic, social, and political structure of society. Hence, institutions should co-produce knowledge to reduce the risk and build adaptations. Who can make such institutions? This is the fundamental question. The discursive practices of community and state policies often restrict the evolution of co-protectionist approaches to institutions. The core concept here is value articulating institutions (Jacobs, 1997). The type of institutions invoked in the process of expressing values influences both the values that come forward and the conclusions that can be drawn based on them. Disaster governance creates institutions for relief and recovery. However, those institutions follow the rationality of an agency. In a country like India, the state is the rational agent that meets the requirements of institutions. Rationality is perceived as an individual experience, and it demands that preferences are complete, transitive, and continuous (Hausman, 1998). The victims of disaster or climate risk have to think along with those institutions to rationalize the institutional requirements. Communication of risk with probable outcomes only makes these institutions possible. It is otherwise called risk communication. The institution itself should be an agency that communicates risk to stakeholders. Risk communication is asymmetric, and there are epistemic blocks in perceiving risks. The work of Berger and Luckman (1967) is essential to the cognitive position. In their understanding, the fundamental problem is how people can communicate and cooperate in a complex world that cannot explain itself to us. So, governing a complex set of relationships and approaches requires institutions to regulate and govern the risks. It could also be in the form of a legitimizing regulatory state since state regulation on development, environment, and politics of decision-making are critical for practising risk governance. The need for regulatory state and management should be discussed in the larger context of neoliberal regimes, which denounce the state ownership and responsibility of risk creation.

3.5 Institutions as Risk Regulation

The idea of a regulatory state is one of the most important contributions of liberal economic regimes. Scholars who study the idea of a regulatory state observed that Americans have invented this idea of a regulatory state in which businesses are controlled by legislative methods rather than through government ownership (Moran, 2002: 392). The World Bank, in its 1997 reports, suggests the idea of the state in the changing world, in which the state has to be a facilitator rather than own the business; it was a game change in development discourse and governance. The regulatory state has become popular, along with economic reforms in countries like India. Regulation becomes a necessary policy instrument to ensure the very political existence of the state in democratic countries wherein the public imagines development as deliberative justices. Regulation refers to a mechanism in which any intervention is capable of producing behavioural change (Baldwin et al., 1998: 4). It is an essential polity tool for a country like India, wherein the huge, vulnerable population does not endorse market-driven economic policies that push a large section of the population into risks. So, regulatory institutions otherwise act as agents of change in governance and also build consensus for economic reforms. Regulation theories focus on public and private interest, and such interest-based theories often contrast with institution-based theories (Baldwin et al., 2012). Regulation as a governance system is subject to the interest of multiple agencies other than the public.

State-promulgated laws and rules have traditionally been associated with regulation. Scott defined regulation as "*any process or set of processes by which norms are established, the behavior of those subjected to norms monitored or fed back into the regime, and for which there are mechanisms for holding the behavior of regulated actors within the acceptable limits of the regime*" (Scott, 2001: 330–331). Regulation is larger project of putting instrumental logic over authority society interface. Selznick defines regulation as "*sustained and focused control exercised by a public agency over activities that are valued by the community*" (Selznick, 1985: 363). The public agency, otherwise called the state, defines the method of regulation and defines the structure of regulation. The idea of regulation became popular after 1990, especially in the era of economic reforms in India.

The institutions of regulation are outcomes of regulatory capitalism, and it undermine the institutional rationale of the welfare state. Regulatory capitalism encapsulates the spread of regulation across all spheres as an institutional design, a practice, and a discourse (Braithwaite, 2008; Levi-Faur, 2005). Majone asserts that a change in the mode of governance has occurred with the rise of the regulatory state (Majone, 1997). This transition takes place from the welfare or redistribution model of governance to the regulatory model. A shift from "direct state intervention, supported by the power to tax and spend" to "rule-making and extensive delegation of powers to institutions operating at arm's length from government" (Majone, 1997). The regulatory state is a political shift in developing countries like India wherein the public largely imagines the state as an agent of welfare rather than dictating rules for capitalist governance. The idea of risk regulation evolves out of regulatory capitalism. Regulatory capitalism attempts to strike a balance between the market and economic welfare, so it introduces legislative interventions to ensure that capitalism survives even with public support. Regulatory capitalism is an outcome of economic reforms in the Global South. Unlike the Western system, capitalism is still not able to displace state-driven welfare in a country like India. This dilemma is still quite visible in disaster and climate risk mitigation interventions in countries like India. State funding for disaster relief and rehabilitation in India displaces all the market-driven risk governance frameworks. Though the government of India and state governments are increasingly pushing for privatization and state withdrawals from public utilities, institutional logic still fails in risk governance. Risk governance in India is a welfare state activity that promotes risk-induced development policies. It is indeed a political task.

The concept of 'risk regulation' is the most recent addition to our knowledge of the regulatory state (Hood et al., 2001; Moran, 2002). Ensuring that organizations and societies can foresee, plan for, and respond to potential dangers entails the formation of rules, policies, and procedures to identify, assess, monitor, and control risks (Hopkin, 2018; Kaplan & Garrick, 1981). The rapidly expanding industrial society creates several risks. Teamwork will be needed to create new frameworks and regulatory mechanisms to address these hazards. Regulations are being demanded as a result of these risks. This strengthens the state's regulatory role in controlling and determining the risks in the context of disaster and climate risks.

Disaster response and interventions are treated as a merit good in economically weaker sessions, so as a parliamentary democracy, a country like India still follows a welfare approach to disaster risk mitigation. The rationale of government spending in India is that disasters affect poor and marginal communities, and no private sector, insurance, or capital base of the community is available for disaster responses. Still, India is an emerging world market economy. This is a critical challenge ahead of climate and disaster risk management in emerging market economies. As discussed in Chapter 1, disaster and climate risks displace the growth path of an economy, and hence, it needs enormous replacement capital to overcome the economic consequences. The replacement capital volume depends on the countries' Gross Domestic Product (GDP). It is pretty evident in the capital market fluctuations in developed market economies like the United States and India during disasters. High-income countries have to spend capital for replacement at the cost of market expansion; however, for a country like India, replacement capital should come from public sources or government budgets. The value of replacement capital makes disaster risks an economic crisis and influences the approaches to risks. Disaster and climate risks create more economic risks in developed market economies, and hence, regulating risk becomes a survival method in such economies.

In its broadest sense, the idea of the regulatory state (Yeung, 2010) suggests a greater dependence on organizations that function independently of the government, free from the constant constraints of politics, and that base their judgements on technical knowledge. Phillips (2006: 24) argues that "the emergence of the regulatory state… is characterized *by an increasingly rule-based, technocratic, and juridical approach to economic governance, in which there is a greater emphasis on institutional self-regulation*". We must place the regulatory state in its historical perspective to comprehend it better. Additionally, it has to be better understood in the context of the theory of the capitalist state and the "South" specifically (Levi-Faur, 2013). The idea that purpose-governed states are incapable of using rules to further their goals is implied by the comparison between rule-governed and purpose-governed states. It makes no sense to utilize it because of this. The states of development and regulation are, or at least have the potential to be intertwined government systems. This broader concept of regulatory state needs studies with reference to governing risk and uncertainties. Risk is a probability, so its impacts and outcomes are not predictable.

Probability is a measure in statistical terms and is determined by multiple variables, including socio-economic situations. The impact of risk could be discursive. However, risk governance and management are often treated as an organized intervention aiming at a common goal. Risk management is an essential component of governmentality because it incorporates ways of thinking through which the state asserts that it is attempting to safeguard the populace from danger (Crawford et al., 2002). The need for a globally and even locally acceptable risk regulation has become a common agenda in the last three decades. Neoliberal policies and market-driven policies force the countries to frame risk regulation instruments at the national level and agree to be part of international treaties as well. For instance, the Montreal Protocol 1987, the Kyoto Protocol 1997, the Sendai Framework for Disaster Risk Reduction, the 2030 Agenda for Sustainable Development, and the Paris Agreement are examples of global disaster governance initiatives. These treaties are indeed legitimate institutional forms, and concerned governments should promote them as part of their national priorities. These treaties are non-binding and do not make any institution liable to implement them. It often enables the countries to plan for local institutional interventions; however, the global treaties want to make countries accountable for risk governance. There is a clear distinction between the Global South and the North when implementing these treaties. For instance, the Montreal Protocol of 1987 proposes to protect against the depletion of the Ozone Layer. The biggest concern of the agreement was the reduction of the use of hydrochlorofluorocarbons (HCFCs) in refrigerators and air conditions. Still, no country that signed the agreement is able to explain its HCFC reduction plan or strategy as it is connected with the market economy. The Kyoto Protocol wants to reduce carbon emissions. Like the Montreal Protocol, the Kyoto Protocol is also subject to market and economic interests. Studies revealed that the 38 industrialized countries are unable to reach their Kyoto Protocol commitments within the time frame specified (Huang et al., 2008). See Fig. 3.3.

Similarly, the Sendai Framework, Agenda of Sustainable Development, and Paris Agreements remain as global risk reduction advocacy rules, and national neoliberal development often overlooks these treaties. The extensive deforestation and destructive industrial policies, etc., prove that risk governance without institutional forms is never implemented. Governments across the world agree to the idea of risk regulation and

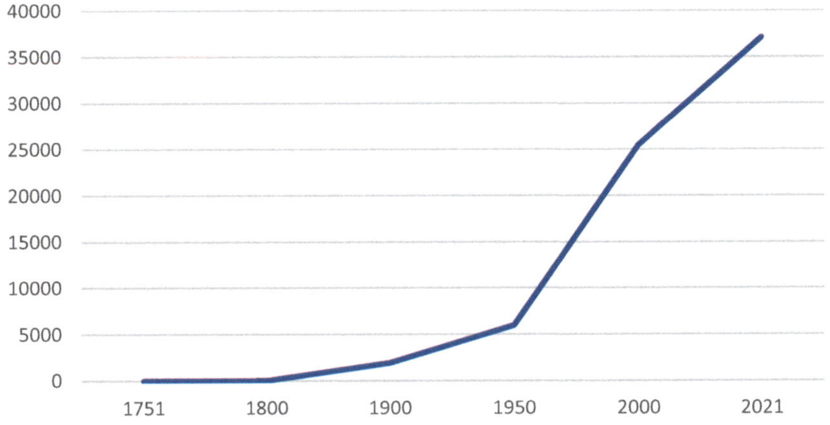

Fig. 3.3 Global CO_2 Emission (*Source* https://ourworldindata.org/co2-emissions)

demonstrate their willingness to be signatories to risk regulation policies. Risk regulation is inherently multidisciplinary, so it is difficult to devise a universally applicable framework (Fisher, 2013). As said before, the public good nature of safety, as well as disparities in risk levels and risk perception among community members, investments in catastrophe mitigation, and preparedness in particular, are challenges in disk governance (Charveriat, 2000). Both developed and developing countries equally agree with the idea of safety as a public good, and hence, it itself is a challenge to build the institutions. Natural disasters are intricate, diverse phenomena brought on by poorly and improperly managed risks that take into account both current circumstances and historical variables (Alexander, 2006).

The vulnerable population and the need to ensure risk reduction as a collective right make risk regulation a complex institutional process in developing countries. Institutional geography, rules, practice, and animating ideas complicate the regulation of a specific risk or hazard (Hood et al., 2001: 9). Collective rights and action dictate the risk regulation approaches in developing countries. The major concern of regulations is to put people and the collective rights of the community ahead of other factors. It is also about governing the conflict arising out of rights over resources, such as collectivization and capitalist use. Olson

(1965: 6) has defined the theoretical foundation of collective action. Olson explains that *labour unions are expected to strive for higher wages and better working conditions for their members; farm organizations are expected to strive for favourable legislation for their members; cartels are expected to strive for higher prices for participating firms; the corporation is expected to increase the interests of its stockholders, and the State is expected to increase the common interests of its citizens (though in this nationalistic age, the State often has interests and ambitions apart from those of its citizens)*. Every institution and approach wants to have maximum utility for its members. Hence, there is a chance that collectivization will lead to maximization of utility in the context of natural resource use. Collective action for risk reduction is a popular idea in developing countries like India; primarily, it promotes community participation in risk reduction. Community-based disaster risk reduction practices in countries like India depend on this collective action concept. Community-based risk governance is popular among vulnerable communities. It aims to ensure the inclusion of community members in the risk response and recovery. Community-based risk reduction is indeed a challenge as it reflects the institutional failure to ensure social and environmental security for vulnerable populations. Theoretically, it follows the concepts of social capital and citizen participation in decision-making and the implementation of governance principles. Arnstein (1969) argues about citizen participation as '*it is the redistribution of power that enables the have-not citizens, presently excluded from the political and economic processes, to be deliberately included in the future*'. Citizens' participation in governing risks is possible only when the citizens have the information on the risk and its consequences on their lives, livelihoods, and political existence. It is otherwise called a project to prevent exclusion from risk reduction programmes. It is to ensure the proper utilization of community resources and prevent the exclusion of community actors in mainstreaming disaster risk reduction. Bonner (2007: 4) defined social exclusion as "*social inclusion occurs when those in need engage with and begin to benefit from statutory and no statutory support structures and services. However, inclusion involves more than 'support'; participation in the community is a key aspect of meaning and belonging*". The community-based method is being promoted by international agencies like UNISDR, and they suggest that this method could enable the community to use all the available resources and capacities of the community. It does not have a universal model.

Box 3.4 Disaster risk reduction in dryland area of Niger

Niger, one of the most backward economies, is a landlocked dryland country located in the Sahel region. The country is poor partly because of the geophysical/climatological specificities and partly because of poor development prospects. Drought is the biggest challenge for Niger, accompanied by civil war and terrorism. International NGOs began work in the area with food security and nutrition as their primary target. It was later associated with the DRR, which focuses on food security. DRR was integrated with the emergency response and mitigation program. The lack of government intervention led to the flow of NGO funds into the area, which gained importance for the local community. Though NGOs undertake work for a short period, the community has to find its own institutional support to enhance and sustain the benefits. Therefore, the success of the project depends on community involvement, including financial contribution. This proves that CBDRR can be limited by resources. CBDRR is often projected as a success story, but putting the entire responsibility on the community does not always yield positive outcomes

Source Concern disaster risk reduction—coastal areas. USC Dublin. Centre for Humanitarian Action

Rather, it is closely connected with the local risk demonstration and development dynamics. See Box 3.4.

The success of community and collective action-based risk governance is entirely local-specific and limited to the local conditions and articulation of risks. Also, the institutional form of collective action for risk governance has to follow the rules and regulations imposed by state agencies. State interventions could be read as institutional collective actions to protect the environment by regulating individual use. Citizens' choices often interface with the government's narrative of risk within its institutional capabilities to deal with it. Within this perspective, political culture—governmental or regulatory frameworks—represents a significant component of risk governance. Every nation pursues a different approach to risk management, as do, frequently, several risk domains within a nation (Renn, 2008).

Studies also argue that politically marginalized groups' interests and viewpoints are often ignored, or at the very least, inadequately addressed, due to the impact of party interests and the absence of their presence or "voice" in political decision-making processes. Policies "are unlikely to engage all relevant concerns when they are worked out for rather than with a politically excluded constituency" (Phillips, 1995: 13). State and its institutions are powerful enough to regulate the environmental risk through legislative interventions. Such legislative interventions are critical in the present context as every agency of capitalism claims ownership of resources. As explained in the tragedy of the common's thesis and capitalization of resources, modern capitalism necessitates an institutional structure to save the interests of its members. This critical position of resource endorsement changes the narratives of disaster and climate risks. The neoliberal economic order has its interests in protecting and governing the risk accordingly.

3.6 Risk Regulation and Its Neoliberal Contestations

Disaster risk reduction (DRR) is an economic process; it is about capital investment to maintain the economy's growth path. In principle, DRR refers to the investment to prevent deviation from the growth path of the concerned economy. Deviating growth path: a grand theoretical framework. In their studies, kuznets (1955) and Lewis (1954) argue that an economy's growth path is determined by the relationship between economic investment and income distribution and by shifting people from unproductive to more productive economic activities. Risk governance in the context of disaster risk reduction could be defined as a policy framework to prevent risk from deviating from the existing growth path of the economy and reduce vulnerability to prevent risk manifestations. So, disaster risk reduction is, in principle, a method to govern the risk with reference to anticipated economic losses. The anticipation of economic losses further depends on the production and production relations of the economy. Not every economy is concerned about economic risks; market economies, emerging economies, economies expecting higher capital investments, and backward economies are anxious about risks. Disaster and climate risk make some countries more vulnerable to capital losses and plan for disaster risk reduction measures. Disaster risk reduction is again a complex institutional process with responsibilities. It is otherwise called an outcome-based investment; risk reduction and growth are the outcomes. In countries like India, government institutions and agencies prefer the term mitigation rather than DRR. The term mitigation has larger public acceptance in terms of demonstrated impacts. Sustainable development goals (SDGs) are another demonstration of the mitigation. The public perception of SDGs is a policy of conservation and non-exploitative use of natural resources. In the form of a pre-disaster response from the government and community, mitigation and preparations get a consensus; for instance, the drought and flood mitigation plans of the state government in India before monsoon season. However, risk reduction is a complicated term for the government and international lending agencies. Risk reduction is an empirical program of risk regulation. Regulation is possible through state-driven programs in developing economies suspectable to climate risks. However, the same state has to promote neoliberal policies. This institutional dilemma is quite visible in a country like India. The emerging market economies of the Global South have adopted neoliberal policies as state policies and have to introduce risk regulation measures. Neoliberal economic policies are risk-generating in terms of extensive exploitation of resources, so states that promote neoliberalism find it difficult to fully endorse risk reduction principles and prefer a risk-regulating regime. Risk reduction is more complex than risk regulation as the former is subject to public auditing, and vulnerable populations can themselves make initiatives or institutions for risk reduction. Common and permanent structures or institutions are quite impossible, so they need multiple or polycentric approaches. One does not prefer risk nor avoid it, so risk regulation does not necessarily follow a linear approach. Rather, it looks for a polycentric approach.

Polycentric systems, which she characterized as *multiple governing authorities at different scales rather than a mono-centric unit. Each unit within a polycentric system exercises considerable independence to make norms and rules within a specific domain (such as a family, a firm, a local government, a network of local governments, a state or province, a region, a national government, or an international regime*) (Ostrom, 2010: 552). Risk and uncertainty make every institution an autonomous agent in determining the actions and responses. For instance, in a country like India, flood risk management and control are restricted to the water resource ministry, and the irrigation department within the water resource ministry is assigned to look into the drought risks. The Ministry of Agriculture has to look into the overall impact of flood and drought in rural areas with reference to agricultural production. Institutions often dictate policies and norms to regulate risk and engage with risk-creating environments. So, developing countries like India, which adopts neoliberal economic policies, often find it difficult to practice the same instrumental logic in risk governance.

The most critical concern is that the neoliberal system never offers a free environment. However, it needs institutions to operate. Unlike the supply-driven model or centralized economic policy, neoliberalism requires institutions to run the policies. Neoliberal policies primarily engage with the perception of society, and they propose a method to liberate people from state regulation. Neoliberal policies undermine the welfare state and also the old capitalist institutional structures and constitute a new institutional structure to govern the policies. Neoliberalism becomes an ideology of the state, and those states develop or define the institutions of development. It is otherwise called a neoliberal state. Many scholars attempt to interpret the nature and ideology of the neoliberal state. Plant (2010) argues that there is, in fact, no clear distinction between social democracy and neoliberalism, particularly not in terms of the rule of law. Social democracy never denies liberalism and private capital interests. It also agrees with Marxian political theory and liberalism, so defining social democracy is a complex process as every democratic government endorsing capitalist ideologies categorizes itself as social democracy. There is a wider social acceptance of social democracy, and it has been largely perceived as a movement against inequality in the context of capitalism. Kołakowski (1982: 11) defined social democracy as merely '*an obstinate will to erode by inches the conditions which produce avoidable suffering, oppression, hunger, wars, racial and national hatred, insatiable greed and vindictive envy*'. Kołakowski's definition of social democracy has indeed become the popular explanation, and even the capitalist economies identified themselves with it. Oakeshott (2006) drew a distinction between a nomocracy (a rule-governed order that was not devoted to the attainment of particular ends) and a democratic order of society, also known as a democracy (an order devoted to the pursuit of some overall end, goal, or purpose). Oakeshott (2006) gives a theoretical justification for social democracy and the form of governance. Social democracy often operates as democracy and evolves institutions to engage with the developmental process; hence, neoliberalism fully endorses social democratic policies as it permits object-oriented institutions to evolve. Neoliberalism itself is a diverse collection of institutions with distinct ideas, social and economic policies, and organizational strategies for political and economic activity. It ought to include formal institutions like programs for taxation, business regulation, and a minimal welfare state; decentralized capital-labor relations and flexible labour markets, free of strong unions and collective bargaining; and the absence of obstacles to the movement of international capital (Campbell & Pedersen, 2001).

Striking a balance between neoliberalism and risk governance needs institutional transformation and changes.

The neoliberal state is, in fact, more powerful than even the socialist and monopoly capitalist state. Capitalism prefers a neoliberal state to operate rather than a command or centralized government. The neoliberal state is a challenge to society because the state makes laws to regulate the lives and perceptions of the people. The ideological success of the neoliberal state is that it never lets the public question the minimum welfare state. The state is established as an overarching entity and starts communicating with people on governance, commitment, and promoting markets. Neoliberal state equally influences risk governance, and state-driven risk reduction becomes an economic good. Welfare as an economic good is a capitalist concept, and institutions like the World Bank encourage it. Reducing public expenditure is the guiding principle of economic good; however, in an environmental context, public investments reduce the exposure of risk to vulnerable communities. Willingness to pay and cost recovery are the method of implementing economic good concepts. Neoliberal states develop institutions to govern disaster risk reduction as an economic good. Public–Private Partnership is an example of this. A neoliberal state creates institutions and transforms risk-regulating policies. The emphasis shifts from risk reduction to regulation. Risk regulation substitutes acceptable risk for unacceptable risk, not risk elimination (Heyvaert, 2011). The neoliberal state and its institutions look at risk within the private sphere and put economic values on externalities of risks. Risk regulation uses the 'regime' to link risk with the regulatory systems that are meant to show how risk is controlled in a particular risk domain (Denney, 2005: 37). Neoliberalism influences risk governance and also changes the perception of risks and prefers to legitimize the vulnerability paradigm in risk governance. It proposes to focus on the non-structural and individual conditions as the driving forces of risks. It adopts the following methods.

3.6.1 Utilitarian Risk Perspective

The major institutional contribution of neoliberal policies on risk governance is that they look at risk from a utilitarian perspective. As Mill (2001: 15) argued, "*Utility includes not solely the pursuit of happiness, but the prevention or mitigation of unhappiness; and if the former aim is chimerical, there will be all the greater scope and more imperative need for the latter, so long at least as mankind think fit to live"*. Mill's idea of utilitarianism is derived from man's pursuit of happiness, and the pursuit of happiness is often attached to choices. It is not a single entity; it is connected with the larger social process. It is also associated with how different social actors determine human interactions. Mill (*ibid: 41–42*) further elaborated, "*In all ages of speculation, one of the strongest obstacles to the reception of the doctrine that Utility or Happiness is the criterion of right and wrong has been drawn from the idea of justice"*. It explains that utility or happiness is a relative concept, i.e., dependent on the practice of justice. Hence, risk reduction is also a relative phenomenon. It is important to contextualize Mill's theory of utilitarianism with disaster risk. There are both subjective and objective experiences of disaster risk. Therefore, the risk depends on how the society experiences it. The liberal choices extended by neoliberal policies offer multiple avenues to view disaster risk as a personal experience and give a sense of permanence. Mill's view is about the relationship between justice and utilitarianism. The failure to deliver justice affects the level of human satisfaction; thus, justice does mean a collective consciousness in which the State ensures the maximum possible level of satisfaction to people. However, justice and the level of satisfaction do not correlate with hazard and risk management. The disaster and climate risks result in unprecedented impacts on society and the economy, and hence, justice does mean maximum possible institutional support to prevent the risk from devastating the lifeworld and economic system. The neoliberal system creates a socio-political situation in which the society realizes its risk tolerance level and finds a better tradeoff between risks and benefits. Geiger (2005) analysed the Royal Society approach to risk and argued that a community's risk tolerance expresses individuals and groups' willingness to accept and live with the risk to obtain certain benefits. Risk tolerance rather than acceptance is the most critical aspect of disaster risk management in the contemporary neoliberal policy.

Excessive utilization of environmental resources and its consequences prove this relationship in detail. Risk tolerance and justice are inversely correlated. Risk tolerance is a utility since the level of tolerance is equal to the level of material satisfaction, for instance, the Kerala Conservation of Paddy Land and Wetland Bill, 2008, Kerala, India. This act was enacted in Kerala in the context of the extensive diversion of paddy fields and its implications on the local ecology in terms of groundwater depletions in the state. There were massive local movements for paddy field conservation, and this act was the result of such massive local protests. As per the Act, "*the owner, occupier or the person in custody of any paddy land shall not undertake any activity for the conversion or reclamation of such paddy land except in accordance with the provisions of this Act*". However, the Act also recommended for a committee to look into the implementation of the Act. It further stated, "*provided that the Committee shall not recommend for filling of paddy land of more than ten cents in a Panchayat or five cents in a Municipality/Corporation, as the case may be, for the construction of a residential building for the owner of the paddy land*". This loophole of the Act has been heavily misused in Kerala and resulted in the reclamation of the wetland ecosystem, severely affecting the water bodies. Acres of paddy land have been reclaimed for construction purposes, badly hitting the drinking water sources of Kerala. The farmers are selling their land in pieces to escape the rule of the Act. The risk tolerance level of the individual is, in fact, a threat to collective justice, yet the Kerala government does not intervene to correct the system in favour of larger goals. It is extremely difficult to measure the risk tolerance level of the individual in such critical scenarios. The willingness to engage with risk in the neoliberal context invalidates all the regulatory mechanisms for risk. In this peculiar case, people's willingness to tolerate environmental risk influences the utility of resources in the area. The tolerance level determines the level of engagement with risks and uncertainties. Neoliberal policies are opening up various avenues to engage with risks. The most important among them is the liberal market value system. The rent-seeking behaviour of capitalism offers better monetary value for resources, so risk tolerance will be high. Lyng et al., (2005: 22) observed that risk-taking is an ascendant theme in consumer culture. It could reflect the special function of consumption practices within late capitalism. Risk-taking or risk tolerance has become a practice in itself and has been integrated as part of development. The origin of risk tolerance lies within the engagement of the State and the individual.

3.6.2 Risk Blaming and Risk Trade-Off

Another major effect of neoliberal policy on risk reduction is risk blaming and trade-offs. As mentioned before, it is the society that determines the nature of disaster risk, and it is also the society that makes technology and intervention possible. As Douglas (2003: 9–10) observed, "*Science has not produced a run of people who do not wish to dominate one another. Industrialization has not produced a race of human beings disinclined to use danger in the rhetoric that protects the public good. The difference is not in the quality of knowledge but in the kind of community that we want to make, or rather, the community we are able to make, or I should say, the community that technology makes possible for us"*. Although Douglas focuses on society's evolution and existence, the argument is about how a community evolves and perceives risk. The crux of the argument is that it is not the technology or science that creates risk; society determines the nature of risk. It is the project of putting the onus on society for the risk and the perception of it. Such responsibility shifting is similar to individualization of risk in that it helps set aside the reasons for risks. For instance, if a community is affected by environmental degradation, the risk-bearing responsibility would shift to the community and individuals. Douglas (2003: 16) further explained that risk reduction has become another form of blaming system, which has replaced the moralist condemning of victims with the condemnation of their incompetence as responsible for risk exposure. It obviously redefines the public responsibility in risk reduction interventions. Neoliberal policies are actually the most important beneficiaries of this sort of knowledge on risk. The incompetence of the community effectively justifies the risk and, naturally, also affects risk reduction. It is true that the level of competence of the communities is relative. It is directly associated with the knowledge of risk and support systems provided by the State. Douglas's analysis of risk blaming is a reflection of the impact of neoliberal policies on risk reduction. The idea of risk trade-off is an important contribution to neoliberal development policies. It is generally considered in the framework of impact assessments. However, it is not limited to that and should be viewed in the larger context of risk acceptance vis-à-vis benefits.

Risk trade-off is generally associated with compromising the process of risk reduction. The expansion of choices and the pressure of competition in the era of neoliberalism led to individual rationality in determining decisions. Limited opportunities for development and resource competition force the community to trade-off development with risks. Development needs to be read as benefits as well as risk tolerance. The World Bank report on water security (2014) observed that "currently, 1.6 billion people live in countries and regions with absolute water scarcity, *and the number is expected to rise to 2.8 billion people by 2025"*. This report warns of a future disaster and is critically important for disaster risk management programs. However, it remains silent on the overexploitation and privatization of water resources, which are indeed causes of crises. The report's content gives a detailed account of the patterns of water resource use and water-related risks. It predicts a severe water scarcity shortly but does not suggest any sustainable solutions. Drinking water is not substitutable, meaning that this crisis is severe. However, the report does not get much media attention except for a few regional language dailies. This indicates the nature of disaster risk perception in the present-day system. Neither the Government of India nor the Ministry of Water Resources have paid any attention to these findings, even though they are expected to come up with a solution. The ability to neglect such a critical warning is not simply an administrative reason; it is the result of a changing state policy towards such risks. The solution to the problems is to strictly control water use and stop the exploitation of ground and surface water sources. Market-driven choices lead the State to negotiate with risk, which leads to risk trade-offs for the community.

Neoliberal policies on risk governance put the onus on the individual, and the State becomes a silent partner in risk creation. It is not a simple transfer of power to the community; it entails a larger change in the perspective towards risk governance. It includes the widening of the life world of the individual in accordance with the market. Such change in the life world forces them to accept the risk as an individual experience. It also transforms the state policy towards risk acceptance and tolerance. This complex linkage could be analysed with reference to the contemporary financial capitalist's method of expansion of prospects. This theorization does not reject the fact that climate and disaster risks push the utility down; hence, economic decisions are largely influenced by the risks.

Still, the neoliberal economic policies drive economic decision-making; hence, state institutions are adapting to the institutional requirement for neoliberal capitalism. Risk-induced or informed decision-making is context-specific and depends on how the authority is capable of engaging with liberal capitalism. Specifically, state institutions in market economies like India find it difficult to challenge neoliberal economic policies, often taken without democratic debate and discussion in the legislative bodies. In developed capitalist economies, the state market decides on investment and risks. As discussed in the second chapter, developed market economies like the US market are highly volatile to climate and disaster risks, and in developing countries, public finance becomes volatile to climate and disaster risks. In developing countries like India, there is an institutional dilemma in governing risks; i.e., the institutions that facilitate financial capitalism have to make decisions to govern the risks.

In addition to increasing profit potential, the evolving global financial markets have also raised transaction risk, which could affect systemic stability (Crockett, 2000). According to Axelrod (1984), institutions are commonly understood to be social norms that all members of a society agree upon. It could be otherwise defined as institutional adaptation. A system's ability to adapt is a collection of traits that enable it to recognize change or potentially dangerous situations, assess them, choose a course of action, and create and implement procedures and instruments to control the risk, so remaining intact throughout (Wall & Marzall, 2006: 378). Risk governance is about governing the sustainable use of resources, and hence, the essential component of resource management is the adaptive capacity of the agencies, which is defined as the ability to experiment and foster innovative solutions in complex social and ecological circumstances while reflecting learning (Armitage, 2005: 703–704). Theories of adaptation defined adaptability, i.e., the collective ability of a group to adapt to and cope with climate change over time in a way that maximizes well-being, the definition of adaptive capacity in the context of environmental risk (Mendis et al., 2003: 29; 62).

3.7 Risk Governance as Adaptive Governance

The established idea of risk governance is that it comprises assessment, management, and communication of risks as Jasanoff (1999: 150) suggested that '*the social sciences have deeply altered our understanding of what "risk" means—from something real and physical, if hard to measure, and accessible only to experts, to something constructed out of history and experience by experts and laypeople alike. Risk, in this sense, is culturally embedded in texture and meaning that vary from one social grouping to another. Trying to assess risk is, therefore, necessarily a social and political exercise, even when the methods employed are the seemingly technical routines of quantitative risk assessments… Environmental regulation calls for a more open-ended process, with multiple access points for dissenting views and unorthodox perspectives*'. Risk perception is autonomous and often subject to individual capabilities. However, risk governance is not an independent activity. Rather, it is subjected to the society and economy, which value risks and their externalities. As mentioned above, it could be part of the system itself. Systemic risk is another force that creates a negative externality on society in terms of the financial behaviour of firms (Eatwell & Taylor, 2000). Aven and Renn (2010) defined systemic risk as the embeddedness of environmental and public health hazards within a broader framework of social, financial, and economic risks and possibilities.

When something humans value is involved, the risk is the degree of uncertainty about the events and outcomes (or consequences) of a certain activity (Aven & Renn, 2009). Emerging systemic risks are a new concept of risk due to recent trends and the effects of hazards on society. "The systems on which the society depends—health, transport, environment, telecommunications, etc." are at risk from these threats (OECD, 2024). When the negative impacts of a causative factor cannot be immediately recognized, risk assessment becomes more complex (Kolluru, 1995; Bedford & Cooke, 2001). The economic notion also considers risk attitudes like risk aversion and risk proneness. According to Luce and Weber (1986), economic rationality suggests that varying risk attitudes are acceptable components of risk management.

In economics and many other social sciences, the idea that rational choice serves as the conceptual foundation for understanding risk has grown to be the most widely accepted and significant theory of risk (Jaeger et al., 2001: 20). The reflexive modernization approach dates back to the foundational writings of Giddens (1990) and Beck (1992) and combines the macro and micro levels. The foundation of reflexive modernization theory is the idea that modernity's meta-rationality—that is, its instrumental rationality, efficiency, and justice through economic growth, as well as its steady advancement of science and technology and consequent improvement of individual living conditions—has lost its ability to justify modernity. The complex nature of risk manifestations in the era of extreme disaster and climate risk necessitates looking at risk governance from adaptive governance. Conflict over rationality, science, and social constructions equally influence risk governance. So, adaptive governance offers a wider theoretical and conceptual framework to risk governance in the neoliberal governance contexts.

A notion from institutional theory called 'adaptive governance' addresses how institutions have changed over time to manage shared resources, especially common pool resources and other types of natural capital. For this reason, it talks about how institutions have changed over time (Hatfield-Dodds et al., 2007). Luhmann (1980) observed that governance systems are made up of "organizations" that share "decisions" that are essential to directing governance. Thus, conceptions of adaptation must be examined in theories of adaptive governance, and the study of organizations has much to contribute in this area. Capitalizing on current adaption processes and forms is crucial for adaptive governance (Van Assche et al., 2022). Scholz and Stiftel (2005) describe adaptive governance as *'the evolution of new governance institutions capable of generating long-term, sustainable policy solutions to wicked problems through coordinated efforts involving previously independent systems of users, knowledge, authorities, and organized interests'*. Djalante et al. (2011) found four adaptive governance traits that are very crucial for constructing disaster resilience: institutions that are polycentric and multilayered; (ii) participation and teamwork; (iii) networks and self-organization; and (iv) learning and creativity. The conceptual framework of adaptive governance refers to the theory of adaptation. Adaptive governance is about making institutions adapt to the need for risk governance.

The design recommendations outlined in prior research on adaptive governance are similar to what adaptive governance does in practice. These recommendations include building social capital, empowering and engaging communities, connecting knowledge and decision-making through data collection and monitoring, fostering leadership capacity, and taking advantage of or creating governance opportunities (Sharma-Wallace et al., 2018). Aadaptive governance has become a fascinating field of study and application for comprehensively handling challenging environmental issues (Dietz et al., 2003; Folke et al., 2005; Walker et al., 2004). The increasing number of disaster and climate risk necessitates adaptive governance a framework and method to interface with environmental risk and community vulnerability.

Adaptive governance explicitly rejects a narrow focus on linear management for ecosystem outcomes in response to the failure of previous management regimes to implement governance structures strong enough to achieve ecological sustainability and develop community capacity in uncertain times (Brunner et al., 2005; Pahl-Wostl, 2009). Adaptive governance is also important in dealing with social vulnerability in country like India. A country which adopt the three-tier governance system is institutionally capable to have an adaptive risk governance. Scholz and Stiftel (2005) discuss adaptive governance from a planning perspective, and recognize the need for constitutional level institutional reforms to improve the practice of adaptive management on the ground. Risk governance needed to be integrated with risk reduction planning which include livelihood support and ecosystem restorations. So, adaptive governance offers a broader institutional structure to govern the agencies of risks and uncertainty. From an institutional perspective, adaptive management and adaptive governance can be thought of as nested rule structures, Also had an explicit normative focus on the goal of serving the common interest (Steelman, 2022).

Scholars engaging with adaptive governance discus the idea of 'co-productive governance', it is essentially a project to response to the social, ecological and institutional changes to connect knowledge and power. It offers a critical ways to interface with science, power and governance (Wyborn, 2015). This perspective of adaptive governance very much close to disaster and climate risk governance. Climate and disaster often expose the limitations of institutional knowledge and its applications. The risk of climate and disaster manifest on the given social, economic and political system, and hence it subject to the interpretations of diverse epistemologies as well. As Mehta et al. (2001) observed that one need to look for more situated and critical understanding of adaptive governance which take into the consider the dynamic interplay of governance with history, context, process, practice, and agency. It enables greater emphasis on negotiation, power, and contestations of knowledge and practices.

Adaptation is popular in disaster and climate risk governance; however, adaptive governance is possible through stakeholder participation. Participation from several stakeholders can enable adaptive governance (Djalante, 2012). "Less rigid, less uniform, less prescriptive and hierarchical, and promising a more innovative but effective way of dealing with complex environmental problems" is how adaptive governance describes the new governance structures being called for (Holley, 2010). Various philosophical traditions impact the evolution of theories related to adaptive governance. Holling (1978) also observes that adaptive management and social-ecological systems shaped the concepts of collaborative governance and cooperative management. Stakeholders' involvement in risk governance is theoretically possible. However, there are many assumptions that guide the stakeholder's involvement. It could be the conflict of the expected outcome. However, adaptive governance is possible if the stakeholders agree on risk impacts. It is otherwise called governance through a polycentric system, McGinnis (1999); polycentric government systems essentially involve multiple governing authorities at different levels. As a result, many of the functions that a central government once performed are now performed by non-state actors, including management, administration, regulation, and mediation.

Adaptive governance in risk governance ensures an integrated governance system in which each actor agrees to demonstrate the risk of their choice and to the extent to which they can tolerate the risks. It is normatively desirable for adaptive governance to have polycentric institutional arrangements (Wyborn et al., 2023). Adaptive governance is a co-management system that includes the integrative role of social capital, trust, and leadership. It is quite possible to practice adaptive governance in a society where the risks result in differential impacts; however, adaptive risk governance is critical if the risks are being approached on its differential economic interests. Folke et al. (2005) addressed the larger social circumstances that support ecosystem-based management by focusing on adaptive governance instead of just ecosystem management. A hybrid construction of risk based on perception and reality is made possible by adaptive governance (a weak constructionist approach) (Gupta et al., 2003). Adaptive and democratic governance must encompass a variety of democratic associations, groups, or communities rather than relying just on official organizations (Assche et al., 2022). The need for adaptive risk governance is that it risk governance is it adopts the rationality of hazards and politics of vulnerability approaches. A broad range of stakeholders working at various social and ecological scales in multilevel institutions and organizations must collaborate to implement an adaptive governance framework (Olsson, Folke, & Berkes, 2004). To put it succinctly, adaptive governance is a tool, not an aim in and of itself, in the policy sciences (Brunner, 2010).

Risk governance is not a tool alone. Rather, it is a practice that needs to be adopted in the environmental, economic, and political governance of a country. Risk is an everyday reality; hence, all institutions engaging with the socio-political of the time need an institutional framework to engage with risks. It is evolving and needs timely adaptions to the risks. Risk governance is not an independent method, viz., general political governance; rather, risk governance needs an integrationist approach. One needs to see risk governance in the context of disaster and climate change. The following chapters discuss it in detail.

References

Adger, N., Brooks, N., Bentham, G., Agnew, M., & Eriksen, S. (2004). *New indicators of vulnerability and adaptive capacity*. Technical Report 7, Tyndall Centre for Climate Change Research.

Adger, N., & Vincent, K. (2005). Uncertainty in adaptive capacity. *Comptes Rendus Geoscience, 337*, 399–410.

Alexander, J. C. (2006). *The civil sphere*. Oxford University Press.

Allegret, J. P., & Dulbecco, P. (2002). Global governance versus domestic governance: What role for international institutions? *European Journal of Development Research, 14*(2), 173–192.

Arnstein, S. R. (1969). A ladder of citizen participation. *Journal of the American Institute of Planners, 35*(4), 216–224. https://doi.org/10.1080/01944366908977225

Armitage, D. (2005). Adaptive capacity and community-based natural resource management. *Environmental Management, 35*(6), 703–715.

Assche, K. V., Beunen, R., Verweij, S., Evans, J., & Gruezmacher, M. (2022). "No time for nonsense!": The organization of learning and its limits in evolving governance. *Administration & Society, 54*(7), 1211–1225.

Assmuth, T., Hildén, M., & Benighaus, C. (2010). Integrated risk assessment and risk governance as socio-political phenomena: A synthetic view of the challenges. *Science of the Total Environment, 408*(2010), 3943–3953.

Alexander, K., Dhumale, R., & Eatwell, J. (2004). *Global governance of financial systems: The international regulation of systemic risk*. OUP.

Ale, B. J. M. (2002). Risk assessment practices in The Netherlands. *Safety Science, 40*, 105–126.

Aven, T., & Renn, O. (2010). *Risk management and governance concepts*. Springer.

Aven, T. (2007). A unified framework for risk and vulnerability analysis and management covering both safety and security. *Reliability Engineering and System Safety, 92*, 745–754.

Aven, T. (2003). *Foundations of risk analysis: A knowledge and decision-oriented perspective*. Wiley.

Aven, T., & Renn, O. (2009). On risk defined as an event where the outcome is uncertain. *Journal of Risk Research, 12*, 1–11.

Axelrod, R. (1984). *The evolution of cooperation*. Basic Books.

Barro, R. J. (2006). Rare disasters and asset markets in the twentieth century. *The Quarter Journal of Economics, 121*(3), 823–866.

Baker, G. (2002). *Civil society and democratic theory: Alternative voices*. London: Routledge.

Baldwin, R., Martin, C., & Martin, L. (2012). *Understanding regulation: Theory, strategy, and practice*. Oxford University Press.

Baldwin, R., Colin, S., & Christopher, H. (1998). Introduction. In S. Baldwin & F. Hood (Eds.), *A reader on regulation*. Oxford: Oxford University Press.

Bedford, T., & Cooke, R. (2001). *Probabilistic risk analysis: Foundations and methods*. Cambridge: Cambridge University Publishing.

Benhabib, S. (1996). Toward a deliberative model of democratic legitimacy'. In S. Benhabib (Ed.), *Democracy and difference*. Princeton University Press.

Bevir, M. (2011). Governance and governmentality after neoliberalism. *Policy & Politics, 39*(4), 457–471. Retrieved May 19, 2024, from https://doi.org/10.1332/030557310X550141

Benn, S., Dunphy, D., & Martin, A. (2009). Governance of environmental risk: New approaches to managing stakeholder involvement. *Journal of Environmental Management, 90*(2009), 1567–1575.

Ben Naceur, S., & Kandil, M. (2009). The impact of capital requirements on banks cost of intermediation and performance: The case of Egypt. *Journal of Economics and Business., 61*(1), 70–89.

Beck, U. (1992b). *Risk society towards a new modernity*. Sage publications.

Berger, P., & Luckman, T. (1967 [1991]). *The social construction of reality. A treatise in the sociology of knowledge*. Penguin Books

Boholm, Å., Corvellec, H., & Karlsson, M. (2012). The practice of risk governance: Lessons from the field. *Journal of Risk Research, 15*(1), 1–20. https://doi.org/10.1080/13669877.2011.587886

Bohman, J., & Rehg, W. (1997). *Deliberative democracy: Essays on reason and politics*. MIT Press.

Bohman, J. (2004). Realizing deliberative democracy as a mode of inquiry: Pragmatism, social facts, and normative theory. *The Journal of Speculative Philosophy, 18*(1), 23–43.

Boholm, Å., & Corvellec, H. (2011). A relational theory of risk. *Journal of Risk Research, 14*(2), 175–190.

Bonner, A. (2007). *Social exclusion and the Way out: An individual and community response to human social dysfunction*. Wiley.

Borah, R. C., & Borthakur, A. J. (2003). Floods in Assam: Causes and remedies. In P. C. Sabhapadit (Ed.), *Flood problem of Assam: Causes and remedies.*. Omsons Publication.

Brunner, R. D. (2010). Adaptive governance as a reform strategy. *Policy Sciences 43*, 301–341. https://doi.org/10.1007/s11077-010-9117-z

Brunner, R. D., Steelman, T. A., Coe-Juell, L., Cromley, C. M., Edwards, C. M., & Tucker, D. W. (2005). *Adaptive governance: Integrating science, policy, and decision making*. Columbia University Press.

Braithwaite, J. (2008). *Regulatory capitalism: How it works, ideas for making it work*. Cheltenham: Edward Elgar. https://doi.org/10.4337/9781848441262

Bowles, S., Choi, J.-K., & Hopfensitz, A. (2003). The co-evolution of individual behaviors and social institutions. *Journal of Theoretical Biology, 223*(2), 135–147. https://doi.org/10.1016/s0022-5193(03)00060-2

Carpenter, S., Walker, B., Anderies, J., & Abel, N. (2001). From metaphor to measurement: Resilience of what to what? *Ecosystems, 4*, 765–781.

Charveriat, C. (2000). *Natural disasters in Latin America and the Caribbean: An overview of risk.* Working paper no. 434. Washington, DC: Research Department, Inter-American Development Bank.

Collingridge, D. (1996). Resilience, flexibility, and diversity in managing the risks of technologies. In C. Hood & D. K. C. Jones (Eds.), *Accident and design: Contemporary debates in risk management* (pp. 40–45). UCL Press.

Cohen, J. (1989). The economic basis of deliberative democracy. *Social Philosophy and Policy, 6*(2), 25–50.

Crawford, A. (2002). *Crime and insecurity*. Routledge.

Coelho, S. (2013). *Assam and the Brahmaputra: Recurrent flooding and internal displacement*. The-State-of-Environmental-Migration, 63–73. http://labos.ulg.ac.be/hugo/wp-content/uploads/sites/38/2017/11/The-State-of-Environmental-Migration-2013-63-73.pdf. Accessed on 19/2/2024.

Campbell, S. (2005). Determining overall risk. *Journal of Risk Research, 8*, 569–581.

Campbell, J. L., & Pedersen, O. K. (2001). The rise of neoliberalism and institutional analysis. In J. L. Campbell & O. K. Pedersen (Eds.), *The rise of neoliberalism and institutional analysis.* Princeton: Princeton University Press.

Office, C. (2002). *Risk: Improving government's capability to handle risk and uncertainty (strategy unit report).* Cabinet Office.

Crockett, A. (2000). *Why is financial stability a goal of public policy?* Working paper. Basel: Bank for International Settlements.

Das, P. J., Chutiya, D., & Hazarika, N. (2009). *Adjusting to floods on the Brahmaputra plains, Assam, India.* ICIMOD and Aaranyak.

Tong, D., Yen, T. D. X., & Dungkhong, T. (2021). Understanding the role of informal sector for sustainable development of municipal solid waste management system: A case study in Vietnam. *Waste Management, 124*(1), 118–127.

Das, D. (2014). Majuli in Peril: Challenging the received wisdom on flood control in Brahmaputra River Basin, Assam (1940–2000). *Journal of International Water History Association, 6*(2), 15–58.

Dryzek, J. S. (1987). *Rational ecology: Environment and political economy.* Blackwell.

Denney, D. (2005). *Risk and society*. Sage Publications.

Dietz, T., Ostrom, E., & Stern, P. C. (2003). The struggle to govern the commons. *Science, 302*(5652), 1907–1912. https://doi.org/10.1126/science.1091015

Djalante, R. (2012). Adaptive governance and resilience: the role of multi-stakeholder platforms in disaster risk reduction. *Natural Hazards and Earth System Sciences, 12*(9), 2923–2942

Djalante, R., Holley, C., & Thomalla, F. (2011). Adaptive governance and managing resilience to natural hazards. *International Journal of Disaster Risk Science, 2*, 1–14.

Douglas, M. (1986). *How institutions think*. Syracuse University Press.

Douglas, M. (2003). *Risk and blame: Essays in cultural theory*. London: Routledge.

De Marchi, B. (2014). Risk governance and the integration of different types of knowledge. In *Risk governance: The articulation of hazard, politics and ecology* (pp. 149–165). Springer.

Eatwell, J., & Taylor, L. (2000). *Global finance at risk*. Free Press.

Elrick-Barr, C. E., Preston, B. L., Thomsen, D. C., & Smith, T. F. (2014). Toward a new conceptualization of household adaptive capacity to climate change: Applying a risk governance lens. *Ecology and Society, 19*(4), 12. https://doi.org/10.5751/ES-06745-190412

Economic and Political Weekly. (1968). *Taming the Brahmaputra*. July 27, 1968.

Felt, U., Wynne, B., Callon, M., Gonçalves, M. E., Jasanoff, S., Jepsen, M., Joly, P. B., Konopasek, Z., May, S., Rip, A., & Neubauer, C. (2007). *Taking European knowledge society seriously*. Report of the expert group on science and governance to the Science, Economy and Society Directorate, Directorate-General for Research, European Commission.

Figueroa, R. (2016). Risk governance: Concepts, frameworks, and applications. In *Handbook of risk theory* (pp. 123–145). Springer

Giddens, A. (1990). *The consequences of modernity*. Stanford University Press.

Graham, J. D., & Weiner, J. B. (Eds.). (1995). *Risk versus risk: Tradeoffs in protecting health and the environment*. Harvard University Press.

Gifford, A., Jr. (1999). Being and time: On the nature and the evolution of institutions. *Journal of Bioeconomics, 1*(2), 127–149. https://doi.org/10.1023/a:1010026613577

Goldman, M. J., Turner, M. D., & Daly, M. A. (2018). Critical political ecology of human dimensions of climate change: Epistemology, ontology, and ethics. *Wires Climate Change, 2018*(9), e526. https://doi.org/10.1002/wcc.526

Fazey, I., Fazey, J., Fischer, J., Sherren, K., Warren, J., Noss, R., & Dovers, S. (2007). Adaptive capacity and learning to learn as leverage for social-ecological resilience. *Frontiers in Ecology and the Environment, 5*(7), 375–380.

Fisher, E. (2013). Framing risk regulation: A critical reflection. *European Journal of Risk Regulation, 4*(2), 125–132.

Fearon, J. D. (1998). Deliberation as discussion. In J. Elster (Ed.), *Deliberative democracy*. Cambridge: Cambridge University Press.
Fischhoff, B., & Kadvany, J. (2011). *Risk: A very short introduction*. Oxford: Oxford University Press.
Foucault, M. (1991). Governmentality. In G. Burchell, C. Gordon, & P. Miller (Eds.), *The foucault effect: Studies in governmentality* (pp. 87–104). London: Harvester Wheatsheaf.
Folke, C., Hahn, T., Olsson, P., & Norberg, J. (2005). Adaptive governance of social-ecological systems. *Annual Review of Environment and Resources, 30*(1), 441–473. https://doi.org/10.1146/annurev.energy.30.050504.144511
Frewer, L. (1999). Risk perception, social trust, and public participation in strategic decision making: Implications for emerging technologies. *Ambio, 28*(6), 569–574.
Gallopin, G. (2006). Linkages between vulnerability, resilience, and adaptive capacity. *Global Environmental Change, 16*, 293–303.
Geiger, G. (2005). Risk acceptance from non-linear utility theory. *Journal of Risk Research, 8*(3), 225–252.
Gaillard, J. C. (2019). Disaster studies inside out. *Disasters, 43*(S1), S7–S17.
Goyari, P. (2005). Flood damages and sustainability of agriculture in Assam. *Economic and Political Weekly, 40*(26), 2723–2729.
Gregory, R., Lichtenstein, S., & Slovic, P. (1993). Valuing environmental resources: A constructive approach. *Journal of Risk and Uncertainty, 7*, 177–197.
Guha, S. (1981). Once more unto the breach. *Economic and Political Weekly, 16*(34), 1.
Gupta, J., Olsthoorn, X., & Rotenberg, E. (2003). The role of scientific uncertainty in compliance with the Kyoto Protocol to the Climate Change Convention. *Environmental Science and Policy, 6*(6), 475–486. https://doi.org/10.1016/j.envsci.2003.09.001
Huang, W. M., Lee, G. W., & Wu, C. C. (2008). GHG emissions, GDP growth and the Kyoto Protocol: A revisit of Environmental Kuznets Curve hypothesis. *Energy Policy, 36*(1), 239–247. https://doi.org/10.1016/j.enpol.2007.08.035
Hewitt, K. (1983). *Interpretations of calamity from the viewpoint of human ecology*. Allen and Unwin.
Heyvaert, V. (2011). Governing climate change: Towards a new paradigm for risk regulation. *The Modern Law Review, 74*(6), 817–844.
Hatfield-Dodds, S., Nelson, R., & Cook, D. C. (2007). Adaptive governance: An introduction and implications for public policy. In 2007 conference (51st), February 13–16, 2007, Queenstown, New Zealand 10440, Australian Agricultural and Resource Economics Society.

Harmes, A. (2006). Neoliberalism and multilevel governance. *Review of International Political Economy, 13*(5), 725–7491.
Hegel, G. W. F. (1896/1952). *Philosophy of right*. https://www.marxists.org/reference/archive/hegel/works/pr/philosophy-of-right.pdf
Hirsch-Hadorn, G., Kissling-Naf, I., & Pohl, C. (2004). How to design Interfaces between Science and society: Lessons from platforms for knowledge communication in Switzerland. In F. Biermann, S. Campe & K. Jacob (Eds.), *Proceedings of the 2002 conference on the human dimensions of global environmental change "knowledge for the sustainability transition. The challenge for social sciences"* (pp. 285–291). Global Governance Project.
Hood, C., Rothstein, H., & Baldwin, R. (2001). *The government of risk: Understanding risk regulation regimes*. Oxford University Press.
Halachmi, A. (2005). Governance and risk management: Challenges and public productivity. *International Journal of Public Sector Management, 18*(4), 2005.
Hanna, S. (1996). Designing institutions for the environment. *Environment and Development Economics*. https://doi.org/10.1017/s1355770x00000462
Habermas, J. (1987). *The theory of communicative action: Lifeworld and system: A critique of functionalist Reason*. Beacon Press.
Heriard-Dubreuil, G. F. (2001). Present challenges to risk governance. *Journal of Hazardous Materials, 86*(2001), 245–248.
Hausman, D. M. (1998). Rationality and knavery. In W. Leinfellner, E. Köhler (Eds.), *Game theory, experience, rationality. Vienna Circle Institute Yearbook [1997]* (Vol. 5). Springer. https://doi.org/10.1007/978-94-017-1654-3_6
Haines, F. (2017). Regulation and risk. In P. Drahos (Ed.), *Regulatory theory: Foundations and applications* (pp. 181–196). ANU Press. http://www.jstor.org/stable/j.ctt1q1crtm.19
Holling, C. S. (1978). *Adaptive environmental assessment and management*. https://pure.iiasa.ac.at/id/eprint/823/1/XB-78-103.pdf. Accessed on 12th January 2024.
Hopkin, P. (2018). *Fundamentals of risk management: Understanding*. Kogan Page Publishers.
Ives, A. (2015). Neoliberalism and the concept of governance: Renewing with an older liberal tradition to legitimize capital's power. *Open Edition Journal*. https://doi.org/10.4000/mimmoc.2263
Jaeger, C. C., Renn, O., Rosa, E. A., & Webler, T. (2001). *Risk uncertainty and rational action*. Earthscan.
Jacobs, M. (1997). Environmental valuation, deliberative democracy and public decision-making institutions. In J. Foster (Ed.), *Valuing nature? Economics, ethics and environment* (pp. 211–231). Routledge.
Jasanoff, S. (1999). The songlines of risk. *Environmental Values: Special Issue on Risk, 8*(2), 135–152.

Jacobson, P. D., McHugh, S. J., & Tran, V. K. (2013). Risk governance and population health. *Jurimetrics, 53*(3), 279–292.

Johnson, B. B., & Slovic, P. (1995). Presenting uncertainty in health risk assessment: Initial studies of its effects on risk perception and trust. *Risk Analysis, 15*(4), 485–494.

Kaplan, S., & Garrick, B. J. (1981). On the quantitative definition of risk. *Risk Analysis, 1*(1), 11–27.

Kenny, C. (2012). Disaster risk reduction in developing countries: costs, benefits and institutions. *Disasters, 36*(4), 559–588.

Kolluru, R. V. (1995). Risk assessment and management: A unified approach. In R. V. Kolluru, S. Bartell, R. Pitblado, & S. Stricoff (Eds.), *Risk assessment and management handbook for environmental, health, and safety professionals* (p. 1.3-1.41). New York: McGraw-Hill.

Kasperson, R. E., Renn, O., Slovic, P., Brown, H. S., Emel, J., Goble, R., Kasperson, J. X., & Ratick, S. (1988). The social amplification of risk: A conceptual framework. *Risk Analysis, 8*(2), 177–187.

Kołakowski, L. (1982). What is living (and what is dead) in the social-democratic idea? *Encounter, 58*, 11–17.

Lange, H., & Garrelts, H. (2013). Risk management at the science-policy interface: Two contrasting cases in the field of flood protection in Germany. In *Governance for sustainable development* (pp. 71–87). Routledge.

Kuznets, S. (1955). Economic growth and income inequality. *The American Economic Review, 15*, 1.

Levi-Faur, D. (2013). The regulatory state and the developmental state: Towards polymorphic comparative capitalism. In N. K. Dubash & B. Morgan (Eds.), *The rise of the regulatory state of the south: Infrastructure and development in emerging economies*. London: OUP.

Levi-Faur, D. (2005). The global diffusion of regulatory capitalism. *The Annals of the American Academy of Political and Social Sciences, 598*(1), 12–32.

Lowrance, W. W. (1976). *Of acceptable risk: Science and the determination of safety*. Los Altos: William Kaufman.

Luce, R. D., & Weber, E. U. (1986). An axiomatic theory of conjoint expected risk. *Journal of Mathematical Psychology, 30*, 188–205.

Luhmann, N. (1980). *Trust and power*. Wiley.

Luhmann, N. (1984). Soziale Systeme. Frankfurt/Main: Suhrkamp.

Lewis, W. A. (1954). Economic development with unlimited supplies of labour. *The Manchester School, 22*(2), 139–191.

Lyng, S., et al. (2005). *Edgework: The sociology of risk taking*. Routledge.

Miller, D. (1992). Deliberative democracy and social choice. *Political Studies Special Issue: Prospects for Democracy, 40*, 54–67.

Majone, G. (1997). From the positive to the regulatory state. *Journal of Public Policy, 17*(2), 139–167.

Mandal, R. (2010). Cropping patterns and risk management in the flood plains of Assam. *Economic and Political Weekly, 45*(33), 78–81.
Marchi, B. D. (2003). Risk governance: Public participation and risk governance. *Science and Public Policy, 30*(3), 171–176.
Marijke, A. H., Fox, T., & van Asselt, M. B. A. (2012). Risk governance. In S. Roeser, R. Hillerbrand, P. Sandin, & M. Petersen (Eds.), *Handbook of risk theory, epistemology, decision theory, ethics and social implications of risk*. Heidelberg: Springer.
McGinnis, M. D. (Ed.) (1999). *Polycentricity and local public economies: Readings from the workshop in political theory and policy analysis*. University of Michigan Press.
Mendis, S., Mills, S., & Yantz, J. (2003). *Building community capacity to adapt to climate change in resource-based communities*. Report from the University of Saskatchewan and University of Manitoba, prepared for the Prince Albert Model Forest, Prince Albert, Canada.
Mehta, L., Leach, M., & Scoones, I. (2001). Editorial: Environmental governance in an uncertain world editorial: Environmental governance in an uncertain world. *IDS Bulletin, 32*(4), 1–14.
Mill, J. S. (2001). *Utilitarianism Batoche books*. Canada.
Mitchell, J. K. (2006). Risk governance: Public arrangements for technological and environmental risks. *Environment: Science and Policy for Sustainable Development, 48*(10), 30–43.
Morgan, B., & Yeung, K. (2007). *An introduction to law and regulation: Text and materials*. Cambridge University Press.
Moran, M. (2002). Review article: Understanding the regulatory state. *British Journal of Political Science, 32*, 391–413.
Mohapatra, P. K., & Singh, R. D. (2003). *Flood management in India*. London: Kluwer Academic Publishers.
Nahar, S., Jubb, C., & Azim, M. I. (2016). Risk governance and performance: A developing country perspective. *Managerial Auditing Journal, 31*(3), 250–268.
Nelson, D., Adger, W., & Brown, K. (2007). Adaptation to environmental change: Contributions of a resilience framework. *Annual Review of Environment and Resources, 32*, 395–419.
Neye, J. S., & Donahue, J. (Eds.). (2000). *Governance in a globalizing world*. Washington: Brookings Institution.
OECD. (2024). *Fostering catastrophe bond markets in Asia and the Pacific, the development dimension*. OECD Publishing.
Oakeshott, M. (2006). *Lectures in the history of political thought*. T. Nardin & L. O'Sullivan (Eds.). Imprint Academic.
Olson, M., Jr. (1965). *The logic of collective action: Public goods and the theory of groups*. London: Harvard University Press.

Olsson, P, Folke, C., & Berkes, F. (2004). Adaptive co-management for building resilience in social-ecological systems. *Environmental Management, 34*, 75–90. https://doi.org/10.1007/s00267-003-0101-7

Ostrom, E. (2010). Polycentric systems for coping with collective action and global environmental change. *Global Environmental Change, 20*(4), 550–557. https://doi.org/10.1016/j.gloenvcha.2010.07.004

Phillips, N. (2006). States and modes of regulation in the global political economy. In M. Minogue & L. Carino (Eds.), *Regulatory governance in developing countries*. Cheltenham: Edward Elgar Publishing Ltd.

Phillips, A. (1995). *The politics of presence*. Oxford University Press.

Pitkin, H. (1967). *The concept of representation*. University of California Press.

Phukan, K. (2016). Impacts of flood in economy of Assam, India and the changing cropping practices. *South Asian Journal of Multidisciplinary Studies, 3*(5), 64–75.

Pierre, J. (2005). Comparative urban governance: Uncovering complex causalities. *Urban Affairs Review, 40*(4), 446–462.

Plant, R. (2010). *The neo-liberal state*. Oxford: Oxford University Press.

Preston, B., & Stafford-Smith, M. (2009). *Framing vulnerability and adaptive capacity assessment: Discussion paper*. CSIRO climate adaptation flagship working paper no. 2.

Pahl-Wostl, C. (2009). A conceptual framework for analysing adaptive capacity and multilevel learning processes in resource governance regimes. *Global Environmental Change, 19*(3), 354–365.

Rhodes, R. A. W. (1996). The new governance: Governing without government. *Political Studies, 44*(3), 652–667.

Renn, O. (2008). White paper on risk governance: Toward an integrative framework. In O. Renn & K. Walker (Eds.), *Global risk governance: Concept and practice using the IRGC framework*. London: Springer.

Renn, O., & Schweizer, P.-J. (2009). Inclusive risk governance: Concepts and application to environmental policy making. *Environmental Policy and Governance, 19*(3), 174–185. https://doi.org/10.1002/eet.507

Robinson, M. (1995). Strengthening civil society in Africa: The role of foreign political aid. *IDS Bulletin, 26*(2), 1–8.

Rosenau, J. N. (1992). Governance, order, and change in world politics. In J. N. Rosenau & E. O. Czempiel (Eds.), *Governance without government: Order and change in world politics* (pp. 1–29). Cambridge: Cambridge University Press.

Rostbøll, C. F. (2008). *Deliberative freedom: Deliberative democracy as critical theory*. State University Press.

Rothstein, H., Borraz, O., & Huber, M. (2013). Risk and the limits of governance: Exploring varied patterns of risk-based governance across Europe. *Regulations Gov, 7*, 215–235.

Sahlin, N. E. (2012). 18 Unreliable probabilities, paradoxes, and epistemic risks. In S. Roeser, R. Hillerbrand, P. Sandin, & M.Peterson (Eds.), *Handbook of risk theory*. Springer.

Saward, M. (2000). Less than meets the eye: Democratic legitimacy and deliberative theory. In M. Saward (Ed.), *Democratic innovation: Deliberation, representation and association*. London: Routledge.

Schiller, F. (2005). *Diskurs uber Nachhaltigkeit–Zur Dematerialisierung in den industrialisierten Demokratien*. München: Okom-Verlag.

Scholz, J. T., & Stiftel, B. (2005). The challenges of adaptive governance. In J. T. Scholz & B. Stiftel (Eds.), *Adaptive governance and water conflict: New institutions for collaborative planning*. Washington, DC: Resources for the Future.

Scott, C. (2001). Analysing regulatory space: Fragmented resources and institutional design. *Public Law, Summer, 2001*, 329–352.

Selznick, P. (1985). 1985, Focusing organisational research on regulation. In R. Noll (Ed.), *Regulatory policy and the social sciences* (pp. 363–368). University of California Press.

Sharma-Wallace, L., Velarde, S. J., & Wreford, A. (2018). Adaptive governance good practice: Show me the evidence! *Journal of Environmental Management, 222*, 174–184. https://doi.org/10.1016/j.jenvman.2018.05.067

Siegrist, M., Cvetkovich, G., & Roth, C. (2000). Salient value similarity, social trust, and risk/benefit perception. *Risk Analysis, 20*(3), 353–362.

Sinclair, S., & Pegram, G. (2003). A flood nowcasting system for the e-Thekwini Metro, vol. 1: Urgent now casting using radar—An integrated pilot study. Water Research Commission (WCR), South Africa: Silowa Printers.

Sjöberg, L. (2007). Emotions and risk perception. *Risk Management, 9*(4), 223–237.

Slovic, P. (1987). Perception of risk. *Science, 236*(4799), 280–285.

Smit, B., & Wandel, J. (2006). Adaptation, adaptive capacity and vulnerability. *Global Environmental Change, 16*(3), 282–292. https://doi.org/10.1016/j.gloenvcha.2006.03.008

Smith, G. (2003). *Deliberative democracy and the environment*. Routledge.

Smith, K., & Ward, R. (1998). *Floods: Physical processes and human impacts*. Wiley.

Steelman, T. (2022). Adaptive governance. In C. Ansell & J. Torfing (Eds.), *Handbook on theories of governance*. London: Edward Elgar Publishing Limited.

Stein, V., Wiedemann, A., & Bouten, C. (2019). Framing risk governance. *Management Research Review, 42*(11), 1224–1242.

Stewart, J., & Jones, G. (2003). *Renegotiating the environment* (1st ed.). The Federation Press.

Thompson, M., & Rayner, S. (1998). Risk and governance part I: The discourses of climate change. *Government and Opposition, 33*(2), 139–166.

Torgerson, D. (1999). *The promise of green politics*. Dukes University Press.

Van Assche, K., Valentinov, V., & Verschraegen, G. (2022). Adaptive governance: learning from what organizations do and managing the role they play. *Kybernetes, 51*(5), 1738–1758.

van Asselt, M. B. A., & Renn, O. (2011). Risk governance. *Journal of Risk Research, 14*(4), 431–449. https://doi.org/10.1080/13669877.2011.553730

Vermeulen, F. (2005). On rigor and relevance: Fostering dialectic progress in management research. *Academy of Management Journal, 48*, 978–982.

Wall, E., & Marzall, K. (2006). Adaptive capacity for climate change in Canadian rural communities. *Local Environment, 11*(4), 373–397.

Walker, B., Holling, C. S., Carpenter, S. R., & Kinzig, A. (2004). Resilience, adaptability and transformability in social–ecological systems. *Ecology and Society, 9*(2), 1.

Wandall, B. (2004). Values in science and risk assessment. *Toxicology Letters, 152*(3), 265–272. https://doi.org/10.1016/j.toxlet.2004.05.010

Willis, H. H. (2007). Guiding resource allocations based on terrorism risk. *Risk Analysis, 27*(3), 597–606.

Wolf, K. D. (2002). Contextualizing normative standards for legitimate governance beyond the state. In J. R. Grote & B. Gbikpi (Eds.), *Participatory governance: Political and societal implications* (pp. 35–50). Opladen: Leske Und Budrich.

Wilson, D. C., Rodic, L., Scheinberg, A., Velis, C. A., & Alabaster, G. (2012). Comparative analysis of solid waste management in 20 cities. *Waste Management and Research, 30*(3), 237–254.

Wyborn, C. (2015). Co-productive governance: A relational framework for adaptive governance. *Global Environmental Change, 30*, 56–67. https://doi.org/10.1016/j.gloenvcha.2014.10.0

Wyborn, C. A., van Kerkhoff, L. E., Colloff, M. J., Alexandra, J., & Olsson, R. (2023). The politics of adaptive governance: water reform, climate change, and First Nations' justice in Australia's Murray-Darling Basin. *Ecology and Society, 28*(1).

Yeung, K. (2010). The regulatory state. In R. Baldwin, M. Cave, & M. Lodge (Eds.), *The Oxford handbook of regulation*. Oxford: Oxford University Press.

CHAPTER 4

Disaster Economics

A disaster is an event that disrupts the normative aspects of the economic system, and every event has a history of making. An event is the result of cumulative risks and losses over a while; for instance, the Joshimad landslide in Uttarakhand, India, in the year 2023, made massive discussions on the impact of landslides. Another critical discussion around the Joshimad incident was the National Geological Survey of India's report on probable risk in Joshimand in 1976. It took 46 years for the event to happen. So, disaster economics should be looked at from an evolutionary perspective. An economist perceives a natural disaster as an event that causes perturbation to the operations of the economic system and includes negative impacts on assets, production process, output and consumption employment, or consumption (Hallegatte, 2014, p. 9). Disaster should not be treated as an event alone; instead, it is a project leading to a transition in economic decision-making. Every financial decision is made on the assumptions of a stable economic process that follows a linearity. The fundamental economic principle is demand and supply, and these two concepts determine the existence of economics as an academic discipline. It is the theory of wealth creation and surplus generation. No economic activity is possible without a surplus, and wealth depends on the surplus. Economic theories evolve from the process of wealth creation and the method of it. Alfred Marshall (1890: 1920) defined wealth as 'all wealth

S. M. Irshad, *Economics of Disasters and Climate Change*, Sustainable Development Goals Series,
https://doi.org/10.1007/978-981-97-9415-7_4

consists of desirable things; that is, things which satisfy human wants directly or indirectly: but not all desirable things are reckoned as wealth'. Marshall further adds that wealth could be transferable or nontransferable goods. Wealth is something measurable and attached to values and utilities.

Classical growth models aim to avoid a stagnant state in which wealth creation or capital expansion gets affected. They exist on the idea of profit, which needed to be protected, and any challenge to profit expansion was treated as a threat to the State and its power. Adam Smith's (1776) 'The Wealth of the Nation' explains the classical economist view on development. The classical economy was primarily built on multiplying and concentrating wealth, which was inevitable for the survival of classical economic thought. Today, it is still so relevant that no economy would survive with capital loss. Classical economy preferred to position labour and capital in a specific order to generate wealth. It was about controlling and regulating labour for potential use or exploitation. Contemporary economic policies and government initiatives favour putting labour and resources under a single command that ensures maximum use.

Smith further elaborated the concept of limit to the division of labour. According to him, '*as it is the power of exchanging that gives occasion to the division of labour, so the extent of this division must always be limited by the extent of that power, or, in other words, by the extent of the market. When the market is tiny, no person can have any encouragement to dedicate himself entirely to one employment for want of the power to exchange all that surplus part of the produce of his labor, which is over and above his consumption, for such parts of the produce of other men's labour as he has occasion for* (Smith, 1776, p. 21)'. Smith's perception was based on the view of the classical economists on market and labour. It also focuses on the process of making wealth and profit.

Smith's perception of wealth creation largely depends on the idea of the effective utilization of resources. According to him, '*though the whole annual produce of the land and labour of every country is no doubt ultimately destined for supplying the consumption of its inhabitants, and for procuring a revenue to them; yet when it first comes either from the ground or from the hands of the productive labourers, it naturally divides itself into two parts. One of them, and frequently the largest, is, in the first place, destined for replacing a capital or for renewing the provisions, materials, and finished work which had been withdrawn from a capital; the other for constituting a revenue either to the owner of this capital, as the profit of his stock, or to some other person, as the rent of his land* (Smith, 1776: p. 212)'. Adam Smith pioneered classical economic thinking on wealth and wealth creation. It was a period in which capitalist production did not evolve much to consider multiple factors in production. So, land and labour were the means of production; hence, rent and wages were the critical focus of the classical theory of wealth creation.

Classical economists followed a rigid method to maintain the wealth creation process, so the issue of population and land became a matter of concern. Wages and rent were the core factors that made wealth creation possible in classical methods. Adam Smith's thinking on rent, Ricardian theory of rent, and Malthusian theory of populations were the core theoretical contributions to rent theory and the idea of rent-seeking behaviour. Smith's idea of rent is closely connected with prices of commodities; for him, '*when the price of any commodity is neither more nor less than what is sufficient to pay the rent of the land, the wages of the labour, and the profits of the stock employed in raising, preparing, and bringing it to market, according to their natural rates, the commodity is then sold for what may be called its natural price*' (Smith, 1776, p. 51). Adam Smith's proposition of rent is above the price, i.e., surplus. Rent is neither price determining nor price determining because neither rent nor price is a system basic determinant (Wessel, 1967). In his work, Theories of Surplus Value (1861), Marx critiques Smith's theory of rent and puts forward a different method to define and theorize the rent. Marx defined rent as a surplus over the natural price, and Marxian theory did not distinguish between the surplus value and rent. Marx claims that less-productive land will be cultivated as the population grows and the need for agricultural products grows. Rent emerges as a result of the differential in productivity between more fertile (higher quality) and less fertile (lower quality) lands (Marx, 1894). He also attempted to examine the concept of absolute rent, which derives from owning land with a monopoly position due to specific factors such as location or access to natural resources. The landowner is entitled to more rent than differential productivity warrants (Marx, 1894). So, rent and prices determine the wealth and its accumulation. In the early days of modern capitalism, the risk of high rent and wealth was the low supply and restricted demands.

This chapter's critical question is the linkages of rent, wealth, and disaster risks. Smith's perception of wealth creation largely depends on the idea of the effective utilization of resources. According to him, '*though the whole annual produce of the land and labour of every country is no doubt ultimately destined for supplying the consumption of its inhabitants, and for procuring a revenue to them; yet when it first comes either from the ground or from the hands of the productive labourers, it naturally divides itself into two parts. One of them, and frequently the largest, is, in the first place, destined for replacing a capital or for renewing the provisions, materials, and finished work which had been withdrawn from a capital; the other for constituting a revenue either to the owner of this capital, as the profit of his stock, or to some other person, as the rent of his land* (Smith, 1776: Chap. 3: 212)'. A capitalist economy should keep reserve resources to maintain future production. Putting this concept into an abnormal context, such as a disaster, gives a different contextual meaning to the entire theoretical proposition. Disaster displaces the value of physical capital, and emerging climate risks push the value of natural resources down. Value is related to its existence. Simmel (1978: 62) explains that '*value is in a sense the counterpart to being, and is comparable to being as a comprehensive form and category of the world view*'. Simmel's theorization of value is indeed a philosophical approach to determining value. Simmel (Simmel, 1978: 65) further added that 'in whatever empirical or transcendental sense the difference between objects and subjects is *conceived, value is never a 'quality' of objects, but a judgment upon them which remain inherent in the subject'*. The beingness of value could be called price; it could be market and non-market prices. This could be why first-world developed economies are deeply concerned about disaster and climate risks, as they affect the value of resources and wealth. Wealth protection was one of the major concerns of the classical and neoclassical economists. Classical economics theories originated in a specific historical period in which natural resources and labour were the source of capital; hence, any challenges on profits or surplus accumulation were perceived as a challenge. Malthusian theory of population is, in fact, more popular even now in terms of its theorisation of population and wealth.

4.1 Malthusian Theory of Population—A Disaster Approach

Malthusian theory of population begins with an argument that the rate of population, if not checked, increases geometrically, and the subsistence for man grows arithmetically. Malthusian growth model was strictly limited to the iron law of wages and the slavery theory of population. It is based on a demographically-driven labour market theory, which effectively supports accumulating capitalist wealth. The model is primarily meant to ensure long-term subsistence wages to increase profits and capital accumulation. Malthus defines that (1798), *yet in all societies, even those that are most vicious, the tendency to a virtuous attachment is so strong that there is a constant effort towards an increase in population. This constant effort tends to subject the lower classes of the society to distress and prevent any permanent amelioration of their condition*. Malthus attempted to justify the iron law of wages and believed that the agents of destruction of capitalist wealth accumulation were the lower-class population, i.e., workers. Malthusian model anticipates that better wage leads to pleasure among the worker population, which increases underemployment. The primary focus of the model is the subsistence of food production and the contribution of unskilled labour in the capitalist production function.

Though it is a dated capitalist labour exploitation model, it has some critical relevance to disaster- and climate-risk-affected economies and communities. The affected community, indeed, has to accept the iron law of wages for subsistence survival. The number of people affected by disasters is significantly high in third-world countries. Hence, the population growth rate is often called the primary cause of vulnerability. Vulnerability is a core aspect that disaster research has been dealing with. Vulnerability refers to the proclivity to be damaged, in this case by a hazard, and to be unable to deal with that injury in tandem with the social processes that create and perpetuate that proclivity. Vulnerability includes human decisions, values, governance, attitudes, and behaviours that create settings in which risks may cause harm (Kelman et al., 2016). Vulnerability can be seen as a probability of falling into poverty soon (Chaudhuri, 2003). Scholars attempt to explain the correlation between population and disaster exposure.

For instance, Asia occupies 60% of the world's population and accounts for 85% of people killed and affected by disasters as of 2011 (Islam & Lim, 2015). Scholars use the popular pressure and release (PAR Model) model developed by Wisner et al. (1994); the Pressure and Release Model (PAR model) emphasizes various root causes of vulnerability, and the population is one among them. Wisner et al. (1994) developed the argument based on other scholarly studies and explained that the exercise and distribution of power in a society are reflected in root causes. People who are economically marginal (such as urban squatters) or who live in environmentally 'marginal' environments (isolated, arid or semi-arid, flood-prone coastal or forest ecosystems; steep, flood-prone urban areas) are also of marginal importance to those in positions of economic and political power. Studies prove that population growth, composition, and distribution are the most critical factors that increase the vulnerability to disaster (Donner & Rodríguez, 2008). Population pressure and climate risk become an everyday debate now than ever before.

Intergovernmental Panel on Climate Change (2018) report explains that population expansion has been identified as a 'key impediment' to the critical aim of reducing global warming to 1.5 degrees Celsius over pre-industrial levels. Also the Intergovernmental Panel on Climate Change, Sixth Assessment Report, Climate Change 2022: Mitigation of Climate Change, argues that globally, GDP per capita and population increase have been the most potent drivers of CO2 emissions from fossil fuel use in the recent decade (high confidence). Trends from 1990 to 2019 were maintained, with GDP per capita and population growth increasing emissions by 2.3% yr − 1 and 1.2% yr − 1, respectively. This expansion surpassed global reductions in energy consumption per unit of GDP (− 2% year − 1) and improvements in energy carbon intensity (− 0.3% yr − 1). Lamb et al. (2023) study proved the linkages between carbon emissions and population growth. It is common and general that population increases demand, leading to carbon emissions. Also, the diversion of forests and vegetation results in high emissions. Chancel (2022) argues that a one-percent population growth leads to a 23% increase in emissions.

There is a clear distinction between income and carbon emissions. Assessments are showing the inequality in emissions. Unequal emissions rate is a challenge in practising development. Bruckner et al. (2022), the study assessed that the average carbon emissions of low-income sub-Saharan countries are less than 0.2 tCO_2, while for the United States, it is 14.5 tCO_2. Low-income people are not responsible for emissions, although their number is high. Oxfam's (2020) report revealed that the wealthiest 10% of the population is responsible for 52% of carbon emissions and used 31% of the carbon budget in the last 25 years. On the contrary, 50% of the poor population is responsible for only 7% of carbon emissions and uses only 4% of the carbon budget. This stark inequality in carbon emissions is a reality of the time. However, the impact is still on the people only. For instance, climate change-induced displacement is an example to prove the unequal impact of carbon emissions. See Box 4.1

The related impact of climate change on land degradation also pushes many into extreme poverty, so all these impacts are on the poor rather than the rich. The countries in the Global South and people with low

Box 4.1 Climate-induced displacement

Countries in the Global South are seeing increased displacement, with estimates putting the figure at 250 million by 2050. They are also losing a large number of people owing to natural calamities rather than fighting and violence. Weather-related disasters will account for over 97% of disaster-induced relocations in 2022. In 2022, the Intergovernmental Panel on Climate Change (IPCC) warned that a minimum of 3.3 billion people worldwide are severely susceptible to climate change. Sea-level rise alone might displace millions by 2100. Estimates of displacement caused by sea-level rise differ significantly due to differing definitions of who is 'at risk.'

Source Sarkar, Sampurna and Anamitra Anurag Danda. 2023. Climate-Induced displacement and Migration: A proposed framework for G20 Collaboration. T20 Policy Brief. Observer Research Foundation

incomes are indeed blamed for the negative impact of climate risks as public funds are spent on mitigation. So, the number of populations often restricts even the mitigation policy. Governments in the Global South seem 'people are the threat' as mitigation expenditure is from public sources and economic decisions are taken in favour of the private sector. So, there is an inclination towards endorsing Malthusian theory in defining risk, vulnerability, and population—higher rate of fatality due to the geographical and economic vulnerability of the community. Hence, the demand for resources is often higher than the supply. Such lack of supply persuades the community to live with risk and exposure to disaster. Malthus's analysis is perfectly proper to this community and situations where the real challenge is the population. However, 'the population problem' in these areas should be discussed in the context of structural exclusion of the community and other socio-economic backwardness. The poor quality of life and lack of institutional support push people into a vulnerable situation. Hence, Malthus's theory of population explosions becomes a reality and a burden on society. Malthus's perception of the supply-side model works in disaster-prone and affected areas, where no production is possible in the short run. Hence, all resources must be supplied and reach out to everyone, and the number matters for the distribution of resources. Minimum support and services extend to disaster-affected, and climate is an example of Malthusian influence in decision-making. The rationale of such bare minimum support to the vulnerable population matches poor institution-driven supply and high-risk induced demands. Here, the supply of resources does not mean a real crisis, but the lack of economic incentives to supply resources as private goods is the concern. The state or any agency wanting to invest in disaster-affected areas has to follow it up as public goods supply with minimum quality. The biggest challenges are the population and low-priced labour. Sometimes, this low-priced labour helps to make investments in disaster-affected areas.

Person-days loss due to disaster is a neglected activity in the Global South. It is a severe issue that impedes disaster recovery in India. The International Labour Organization (ILO) 2019 report explains that heat waves as extreme weather risk events push informal labour in developing and backward countries into poverty and risks. The ILO report argues that exposure to excess heat affects workers' natural defensive mechanisms, such as slowing down, taking more frequent and prolonged breaks, and limiting their work hours. It specifies that labour has no control or authority over their body and labour. As a result, productivity, economic production, and family income are all reduced. ILO's narrative of heat waves reflects the reality of risks and distributional inequality. ILO's articulation reflects the scenarios of the Global South where the labour force with low productivity and low wages is increasingly exposed to disaster and climate risks. What is needed is a different perspective to look at the impact of disaster and climate risk. See Box 4.2

This loss of income and losses are increasingly becoming an everyday reality in countries like India. This massive labour force has to live with this risk as the governments in developing and backward economies do not have any specific income support projects for this labour force as their number is directly proportional to the population. Also, the fact that iron law of wages does not work in terms of classical theory, because these labours are getting minimum wages only. The classical development and

Box 4.2 Climate risk and employment

In 1995, high heat levels cost the world 1.4% of total hours worked, which equates to around 35 million full-time jobs. Assuming a 1.5 °C rise in global temperature by the end of the century (the best-case scenario), estimates based on labour force trends suggest that by 2030, the percentage of total hours of work lost due to heat stress may rise to 2.0%, a labour productivity loss equivalent to 72 million full-time jobs. This is an underestimate because it is based on a worldwide mean temperature increase of no more than 1.5 °C and assumes that agricultural activity is done in the shade

Source International Labour Organisation. 2018. The employment impact of climate change adaptation Input Document for the G20 Climate Sustainability Working Group. Geneva, ILO

growth models are primarily aimed at ensuring and legitimizing the profitability of the capitalist class, and labour is the only means of production. The classical models have attempted to explain the importance of cheap labour and maintaining subsistence wages to ensure better surplus capital. There are some critical correlations between the subsistence wage and disaster impacts. Most disaster-affected communities earn low wages, and disaster often forces them to live on a subsistence wage. Such minimum wage does not ensure any new employment to the community, and the survivors are forced to live with the crisis. Low wages due to risk limit the capital replacements and delay recovery. Still, some scholars critique the Malthusian theory of population. Malthusian approach ignores regional diversity; instead, it is a theory of Western society (Ford & Adamson, 1995). David Ricardo also emphasized the importance of wages and labour.

Like other classical growth models, the Ricardian model also emphasizes that labour is a commodity like any other transferable commodity. Hence, labour can be purchased and sold, and its quantity can be diminished or increased. The model envisaged a free-floating labour force with less control over movements and rights. Like other classical economists, his model focuses on labour and wage. Ricardo's argument focuses on the limited survival of the workers. The Ricardian model also demands a natural salary (price), which depends on the food price, necessaries, and other conveniences required to support the labourers and their families. Hence, any rise in the price of these can increase the wage and vice versa. The classical perception of development was primarily on surplus value. Accordingly, Ricardo also argued for subsistence wages for the workers. He argued that high wages increase the population and lead to colossal labour availability; hence, wages can fall to their natural price level (natural wage). Malthus and Ricardo were equally concerned about population and its proportional increase on labour. Classical economic thinking and theories reflected the capitalist process of wealth accumulation. They had a very selective approach to the population and labour. The classical economists' understanding of labour is deeply associated with the slavery of the century. Smith (1776) was not very specific about the abolition of slavery; for him, '*slavery continued to take place almost universally for several centuries afterward, till it was gradually abolished by the joint operation of the two interests above mentioned; that of the proprietor on the one hand, and that of the sovereign on the other*'. Smith did not see any law to abolish but rather believed that it was an economic system in which labour productivity is less than free labour. Enslaved people were perceived as a valuable capital asset who could be forced to work for less than market wages. Enslavers could successfully tax enslaved people's leisure since they were the remaining claims to the fruits of their labour (Magness et al., 2023). The debates around slavery in classical economists were mainly focused on the 'productivity and profitability of slave labour'. The work of Tullock (1967) argues that to make slave enterprises function, the enslaved people should be prevented by fleeing and killing their masters. He adds that the cost of running slave enterprises should be shifted from enterprises to the general community. Classical economists believed in the iron law of wages and were otherwise proposed to have slave labour as the source of capitalist development.

Classical economists' iron law of wage theory was otherwise called slave labour theory. European interest in slave labour started with the plantation sector. The plantation sector never gives up the slave labour system and always used specific methods of slavery to keep the labour with them (Mandle, 1973). European labour was unwilling to work in tropical countries, which led to the slave trade (Chew & Mohayidin, 1995). British Parliament's decision to abolish slavery led to a massive economic crisis for plantation owners, and it was not acceptable to the planters in countries like India (Reno, 1964). It was like near slavery, and labourers had to accept the low wages to live and exist. It was the period when the slave trade was legal, and classical economists did not question its rationale. Enslaved people labour on cotton, sugar, tobacco, and other plantations under harsh conditions and intense exploitation (Eltis & Richardson, 2017). Slave labour and the Iron law of wage otherwise ensured the value of capital and wealth.

4.2 Rent-Seeking and Capital Assets

Economic rent was the primary concern of classical economists, and it is base of capitalist expansion. Adam Smith (1776) defines that '*rent, it is to be observed, therefore, enters into the composition of the price of commodities in a different way from wages and profit. High or low wages and profit are the causes of high or low prices; high or low rent is the effect of it. It is because high or low wages and profit must be paid to bring a particular commodity to market that its price is high or low.* Smith's idea of rent is closely related to wealth creation and protection. Smith's view of rent and profit has a different meaning regarding a disaster—an affected area where the rent value keeps changing by the impact of disasters. Classical economics established an objective theory of value based on a normative examination of what types of work should be deemed productive and what should be considered rent-seeking. Activities might be defined as falling within or outside of a 'production boundary', with those falling outside not being included in assessments of a country's growth and prosperity (Christophers, 2013; Mazzucato et al., 2023). Rents, according to Mill (1848: 429), are earnings from ownership earned 'without working, risking, or economizing', illustrating how the rentier elite 'grows richer, as if in their sleep.' Classical economics argued for the majority of state revenue to be levied on landowners who reaped unearned income from ground rent rises caused by economic development that had nothing to do with their labour (Ryan-Collins et al., 2017). The classical considered income from land ownership and much banking sector activity as rent since it included a transfer of capital from one activity to another rather than contributing to total wealth (Mazzucato et al., 2023). Higher economic rent was considered to mean less profit and further investments. So, the classical economists believed the low rent was a source of further investments. Classical economists were not bothered about calamities while engaging with concepts, and it was the period of mercantile and feudal capitalism. The economic rent plays a critical role in determining disaster loss in the Global South and north. Information asymmetry and local specific use value of resources in the Global South play an important role in fixing economic rents. However, the nature of capitalistic exploitation there and the resulting social relations depend on the untapped resource value and the community's poverty. The case of land acquisition in disaster-prone areas mentioned below proves this (See Box 4.3).

The higher use value of assets in developed economies is more concerned about environmental risk since it pushes the economic rent down. In the Global South market, states are equally worried about climate risk and disaster owing to their impact on pushing economic rent down. It is quite known that environmental risk can extend human suffering, especially to those who have less command over the resources. In countries in the Global South, such as India, disaster and climate risks affect the consumption pattern of a large population, and hence, the economic rent would fall. Disasters can negatively influence consumer behaviour, which can be severe enough to damage social integrity (Kar et al., 2022). The classical economist suggests that individuals should distribute their income between consumption and savings based on their

Box 4.3 Land acquisition in disaster-prone areas

Acquiring land for major development projects in disaster-prone areas is comparatively hassle-free. The Jayakwadi Project stage—I, in 1965, envisaged the construction of Paithan dam across the river Godavari in Paithan Tehsil of Aurangabad district, Maharashtra. The dam was 9997 metres long (excluding the spillway) with 37.73 metres of maximum height. About 35,000 hectares of land was submerged for the project including agricultural land. Irrigation department undertook initiatives in rehabilitation and relocation of people from 96 affected villages. The drought and sugar cultivation in the State has been used to justify land acquisition for dams, resulting in Maharashtra having the largest number of dams in the country i.e. 1845. And yet, drought management is a pertinent issue. Dams have the potential to store water but no policy is effectively implemented there. This increases drought risks and pushes people into uncertainties

Source http://www.india-wris.nrsc.gov.in. http://shodhganga.inflibnet.ac.in/bitstream/10603/149447/14/13_chapter%204.pdf

long-term preferences and predicted future income (Marshal, 1980; Mill, 1848). Friedman (1957) created the Permanent Income Hypothesis, which proposes that people's consumption decisions are driven by their long-term average income rather than short-term volatility. Based on their perceived constant income, people are considered to smooth out their spending across their lifespan. Disasters and any environmental risk will have negative impacts on consumption. In a country like India, disaster-induced consumption has a different effect. It is ranching from consumer to capital goods consumption—also, the state consumption of materials for relief and responses. Environmental risk changes the consumption pattern and may negatively impact the capital goods sector.

The interface of disaster and consumption is global discourses, and every region often identifies a correlation between disaster and resource consumption. Consumption in a disaster context could be otherwise called overconsumption or over-exploitation. The interface of consumption and disaster do a mutual correlation. Concerns about food insecurity, population growth, and shifting consumption habits could make environmental sustainability difficult. When consumer habits alter, they typically gravitate towards goods that are either uncommon or not produced locally in sufficient quantities (Sharma et al., 2018). Consumption can then be viewed as either material provisioning, where risks rise with increasing distance from the resource; background, mis-consumption, or overconsumption; or as a series of decisions that force "producers" to

Box 4.4 Mulgao mining disaster

The Mulgao Mining Disaster happened in the Indian state of Goa, near the village of Mulgao, in the Bicholim taluka. This catastrophe illustrates the adverse effects of widespread, unrestricted mining activity in the area on 16th July, 2011. Terrible mining pit collapse accidents have destroyed large swathes of the village's productive fields and water bodies. A huge amount of dirt dropped into a water-filled pit. The displaced water destroyed a retaining wall, which also pushed stones and boulders into the horticultural fields below. Many trees were uprooted and the farms of Gaonkarwada-Mulgao were inundated as the water fell with tremendous velocity. The surrounding homes, farms, and infrastructure were destroyed due to landslides caused by the collapse of mining pits. The disaster resulted in significant flooding in the hamlet and surrounding regions because of the accumulation of water in the mining pits and the blocking of natural water flow. Residents had health difficulties due to the tragedy and its aftermath, such as respiratory disorders from dust and debris and waterborne infections from contaminated water

Source http://www.minesandcommunities.org/

exhibit behaviours of restraint and resistance (Princen, 1999). See the Box 4.4.

Overconsumption of the capital goods sector, including natural resources, results in declining marginal utility and negative returns. Another critical fact is that consumption habits, in general, can be severely and immediately disrupted by disasters. For instance, the 2011 earthquake and tsunami in Japan resulted in extensive devastation, sharply reducing household consumption because of the destroyed homes, infrastructure, and economic uncertainty (Noy & Vu, 2010). Such poor consumption results from the declining capital value and poor capitalization of resources. It also influences public spending priorities, such as food, water, and medical supplies, which are examples of necessities that households may value more highly than non-essential products and services (Sawada & Shimizutani, 2008). These changes in public consumption result in income and wealth losses, further reducing one's ability to consume. Consumption shocks are more likely to affect households with lower incomes and savings (Skidmore & Toya, 2002). Consumption shock reflects the wealth effects of disaster, since the massive destruction of physical assets, such as houses, infrastructure, and productive assets like cattle and machinery, are frequently destroyed in disasters. Also, disasters reduce household wealth and the ability to consume. The wealth effect of disasters severely impacts the poor and marginal section of the disaster victims more than the wealthy class. In order to deal with the immediate aftermath of a disaster, communities and households could spend all of their savings or sell off investments. Long-term effects on wealth accumulation and economic stability may result from this. According to a research on Hurricane Katrina's effects, households that were impacted, especially those without insurance, saw considerable declines in wealth (Gallagher & Hartley, 2017). Insurance often acts as an economic agent to prevent the wealth and income effects of disaster in developed market economies; however, this option is hardly available for the people of developing and underdeveloped countries. Disaster insurance has yet to be developed in underdeveloped economies. Chapter two of this book explains it in detail. Loss of asset value could affect the wealth of households and may be further depleted by this decline in property values (Bin & Landry, 2013). Agarwal et al. (2024) study on the Chennai flood of 2015 found that the consumption decreased by 11%; 65% of that amount was regained afterwards. The annual decline in consumption per person was $312 on average or almost 5% of GDP. Furthermore, we demonstrate that rather than causing price shocks, natural disasters reduced consumption through income shocks. Cantelmo et al. (2019) study proved that for over 30 years, private consumption and private investment in disaster-prone areas were 40% lower than in non-disaster-prone countries. Mainstream economic analysis often ignores the micro and macro level implication of disaster and consumptions. It is not restricted to consumption goods alone, one needs to locate this capital logic with reference to capital good sector as well.

The negative impact of capital goods consumption pushes the economic rent down. Public consumption of society would not be normal in a risky situation. Disaster-affected or disaster-prone areas seldom offer any substantial rent to the land and better labour productivity. Disaster-prone areas are otherwise known as areas with poor carrying capacity. Using carrying capacity as the baseline, the ecological limitations evaluated enabled quantifying human effect and the amount the ecosystem could withstand (Świąder et al., 2020). The most significant population, density, or biomass that a given area can sustainably support is known as carrying capacity. This probably changes over time and is influenced by habitat, available resources, and the presence of predators, disease agents, and rivals (Hartvigsen, 2016). Hence, the resource inequality would remain. If land and labour offer higher rent and productivity, it results in faster economic recovery. Smith (1776) also emphasized the issue of changing rent and productivity. Smith's theory evolved out of the classical period theory; however, it could apply to modern-day environmental contexts. Smith argued that there are some sections of land output for which demand must always be such that it can afford a higher price than what is required to bring them to market and others for which demand may or may not be such that it can afford this higher price. The former must always pay the landlord's rent. Depending on the circumstances, the latter may or may not occur at all. Smith's argument was based on the nineteenth-century mercantilist economic perspective. Applying this value system to disaster-prone areas in developing countries will explain the rationale of Smith's perception. Disaster-prone regions of India justify this argument. Economic recovery from disaster loss depends on land value and labour productivity. The economic impact of a disaster varies according to the economic relations within the land/geographical area where it strikes. It is evident from the various global disaster loss assessment reports. The huge differences in economic loss are primarily due to the high use and material value of resources. The value of final output is comparatively high in developed countries, while the poor economic conditions in backward economies never offer such a high output value. The output value is closely related to economic rent, so any risk that changes the output also impacts the economic rent.

Smith's concept of rent is significant for analyzing the economic impact of natural disasters. It is about the values that offer better income and returns from using resources. Smith defined rent as a *'composition of the price of commodities in a different way from wages and profits. High or low wages and profit or low wages and profit must be paid in order to bring a particular commodity to be the cause of high or low prices; high or low rent is the effect of it. It is because high market, that is price is high or low. However, it is because its price is high or low, a great deal more, or very little more, or no more, than what is sufficient to pay those wages and profit, that it affords a high rent, a low rent, or no rent.* Smith's theoretical position on rent and profit is derived from production relations. Thus, an effective and highly capitalized production process creates high rent value, whereas backward economies create comparatively less rent. According to Schumpeter (1942), Rents are a natural and vital characteristic of a dynamic capitalist economy. This is why economic loss due to disaster is high in developed economies, and the recovery cost also changes according to these economic relations. Smith's theory of rent is most visible in case of recurring disasters in developing countries[1], and hence, the rent and profit determine the long-term impact of the disasters. Smith had no reason to anticipate a critical reflection of his theory in the twenty-first century based on the impact of natural disasters. As said before, the attempt to engage with Adam Smith's theory in the context of a natural disaster gives a different perception of classical economic thinking. It revisits Smith's classical perception of wealth creation as a linear process, which would ensure better and effective utilization of labour and land. Natural disaster never offers such a linear project of engaging with wealth creation. The wealth creation in pre and post-disaster situations proves Smith's theory of rent-seeking; however, it puts the production process of backward economies into crisis. The structural weakness of these economies pushes them to focus on rebuilding a high-value production process, including livelihood practices.[2]

The economic perspective of disaster is primarily related with wealth, so economic rent is an important area of disaster economics. Like Smith, David Ricardo explained about the differential rent, i.e., the productivity gap between the most fertile land (the 'best' land) and marginal land (the least fertile land), as agriculture grew and less-productive land was used, gave rise to economic rent (Ricardo, 1817). Ricardian theory of differential rent is associated with the capitalist use of land; for Ricardo (1817), '*rent is that portion of the earth's produce, which is paid to the landlord for the use of the original and indestructible powers of the soil. It is often, however, confounded with the interest and profit of capital, and, in popular language, the term is applied to whatever is annually paid by a farmer to his landlord*'. Ricardian theory of rent was also associated with iron law of wages. Ricardian model also emphasizes that labour is a commodity like any other transferable commodity. Hence, labour can be purchased and

[1] The declining value of land in drought prone areas in India proves this. The declining value is also attributed to low wage rate and income from farming. Government support to the farmers depends on the economic value attached with the land, and hence, it is minimum.

[2] Getting media attention on urban flooding in India is an example wherein the rural backward regions keep on neglecting.

sold, and its quantity can be diminished or increased. The model envisaged a free-floating labour force with less control over movements and rights. Like other classical economists, his model focuses on labour and wage. Ricardo's argument focuses on the limited survival of the workers. The Ricardian model also demands a natural wage (price), which depends on the food price, necessaries, and other conveniences required to support the labourers and their families. Hence, any rise in the price of these can increase the wage and vice versa. The classical perception of development was primarily on surplus value. Therefore, Ricardo also argued for subsistence wages to the workers. He argued that high wages increase the population and lead to huge labour availability; hence, wages can fall to their natural price level (natural wage).

The secondary impact of environmental risk manifests mainly as the loss of value of natural resources. Which land is more vulnerable to disaster risks? One factor contributing to declining land value is an area's greater susceptibility to disaster and environmental harm. For instance, places with a history of earthquakes, those near nuclear power plants, and those at risk of flooding and inundation typically have poor land values (Nakagawa et al., 2009). There are multiple economic reasons for declining land prices, which is a theoretical challenge. The productivity of land is affected due to environmental risks. Disasters like earthquakes make land uneconomic for further investments. Conditions connected to climate change are responsible for geographical differences in land prices of more than an order of magnitude (Bandyopadhyay et al., 2022). A study on flood risk and land value proves that the increase in flood risk pushes land prices down in China (Wei & Zhao, 2022). Another study based on Malayais proves that a metre increase in flood depth decreases 44.6% of the property value (Ismail et al., 2019)—the price of natural resources like land, where the supply is fixed. Figure 2.1 explains the demand–supply debates around land.

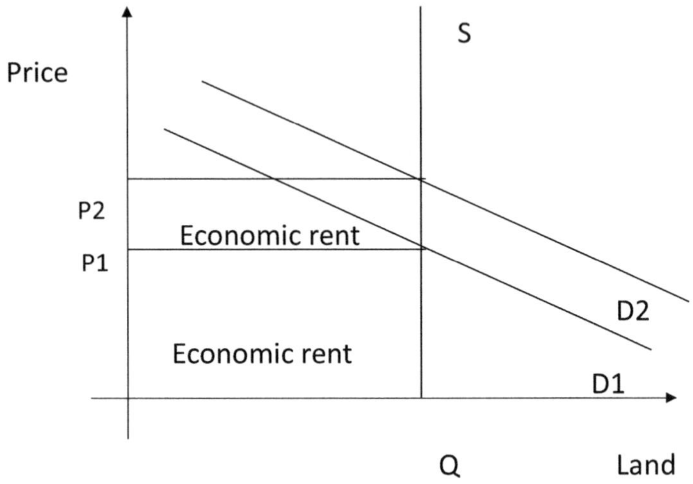

Natural disasters and climate changes are the factors that change the demand for land; it could also be up and down. Increasing demand pushes the rent up, and vice versa, and this is why resource-dependent communities get affected by disasters in different ways. Disaster never affects land supply in absolute terms; however, land fertility would be a significant concern. Risks that devalue the rent are an economic crisis, too. Classical economic theories are more concerned about the value of resources and wealth protection, so they cannot engage with risk and uncertainties in resource management. Also, it was a period of colonial power, and the Industrial Revolution started, and the significant risk factors were war and natural calamities. There were natural calamities in those periods; the economic interest of the time was feudal and colonial wealth. The mercantilist idea of wealth creation was an idea of colonialism; hence, economic theories of the time wanted to protect the wealth and wealth creation process. Any discussion on classical economics also necessitates a detailed discussion of post-classical or neoclassical economics.

Engaging with neoclassical theorisation concerning environmental risk offers multiple kinds of institutional perspectives to study disaster and climate risks. Wolff and Resnick (2012) argued that neoclassical thinking is based on two guiding principles: one is to endow and protect each individual with the complete freedom to act according to her self-interest, and the second is to establish the institutional framework and structure, which ensures that freedom (competitive markets and private property).

The modern theorisation of risk economics traces back to this neoclassical approach to economics. Wolff and Resnick (2012: 52) observed that neoclassical theory primarily centres on the belief that innate human nature determines economic outcomes. This notion further assumes that humans naturally possess particular rational and productive abilities to create wealth. Neoclassical economics defines individuals as making rational judgements based on their desires and available choices (Becker, 1965). In the context of a crisis, this means that people will choose actions that maximize their utility, considering the costs and advantages of various options.

The neoclassical economic theory focuses on the individual consumption of goods and services at the maximum level. Risk disrupts the linearity of decision-making, and consumers found it difficult to practise rational choice in economic decision-making. Recovering from risk directly correlates to the utility maximization behaviour of individual consumers. Neoclassical economics views the human actor as rational in economic terms (homo economics), primarily in the market arena, frequently only in producer behaviour and entrepreneurial behaviour, and not in all social domains (Zafirovski, 2000). Market and even state institutions expect the rational market behaviour of individuals and production systems when confronting disasters. Recovery from losses depends on the rational behaviour of individuals. The neoclassical definition of the innate ability that human beings possess is indeed the core aspect of disaster recovery. However, unlike under normal conditions, it is rather challenging to put in practice the innate coping ability in a crisis. Directly engaging with the state is necessary for the affected communities' bare minimum survival. Neoclassical models, especially their institutional applications, come quite close to the conditions of disaster-affected communities. This does not mean that a neoclassical framework can help analyze the crisis. Still, the model helps one locate institutions' absence in the larger economic recovery framework. The institutional importance of neoclassical economics is essential in risk economics as it refers to external capital and resource interventions.

For the first time, the new Keynesian macroeconomics rationalized the importance of fiscalism via government deficit spending; this was implemented at first in the United States, then in Europe and finally introduced to third-world countries. The new Keynesian macroeconomic model revisits the 'opulence' philosophy of national wealth. Neo Keynesian macroeconomic governance favours active State intervention through deficit financing and depends on the magic of the multiplier to cure the deficiency of aggregate demand. Neoclassical thinking had brought a hitherto unknown analysis of the modern capitalist economy. It put forth the following assumptions: (i) the people had rational choices and preferences; (ii) individuals wanted to maximize utility, and firms wanted to maximize profits; and finally, (iii) people act based on full and given information.

The three major postulates of neoclassical approaches evolved as the theoretical foundations of risk economics. Risk results in asymmetric information, so rational choice of commodities becomes challenging. Some studies prove that individuals and groups weigh evacuation risks and advantages. Also, people at risk and the targets of emergency warnings prefer information from multiple sources rather than a single spokesman (Mileti & Peek, 2000; Turner et al., 1986). State, public, and individuals become more rational while confronting disasters. Individuals, communities, and states will likely prefer a risk-weighted expected utility in every economic decision-making. Public and private choices are evolved under certainties, so shifting the decision-making from certainty to uncertainties is not unform. The neoclassical theory discusses rational decision-making under uncertainties. Buchak (2013) argues that consistency or instrumental rationality, as well as reasonableness, governs decisions. The former imposes structural constraints on preferences, whereas the latter imposes content constraints on desires.

Individuals fail to be rational and become more independent during a natural disaster. Everybody acts according to will, and such freedom is critical for the operations of disaster rehabilitation. Though freedom promotes rational choices, it is a fact that the choices are framed and controlled by external agencies and actors. There exists a conflict of engagement with the rational choices of survivors and agencies. For instance, the sphere standard is a guiding principle for ensuring the fulfilment of bare minimum needs for disaster-affected communities. The choices are very rational and not driven by individual decisions. An external agency makes decisions based on minimum consumption, and they are accepted across communities and countries to a great extent. The human nature of survival conditions such interventions. The idea of utilitarian behaviour of individuals connects with the severity of disasters. The community with less access to institutional support would burden the agencies responding to disasters. Hence, choices driven by the capacity of agencies decide the nature of support, and the marginal utility of support would be high. This is the significance of Malthus's theory in the context of disasters. All living species must be able to detect and escape dangerous environmental situations to survive. The ability to codify and learn from prior experience also helps with survival. Humans have an additional skill that permits them to change and respond to their surroundings (Slovic, 2000). Neoclassical economics expressed trust in individual ability and decision-making to overcome the crisis. It was a big contribution to the field of economic analysis of crisis and later post-war neoclassical economics introduced further concepts to deal with the crisis. Still, the crisis according to classical and even neoclassical approaches was the crisis of capitalism and wealth accumulation.

4.3 Post-war Neoclassical Models

The post-war neoclassical models put forward different explanations for the operations of capitalist economic models. As Cornwall and Cornwall (2001: 39) observed, the neoclassical paradigm evolved from an assumption that the private sector of a capitalist economy is self-regulating in the undefined long run. Neoclassical economists argue that capitalism is subject to economic and political conflict and the structural change that leads to periodic episodes of poor performance. The post-war neoclassical primarily traces capitalism's undefined and unstructured engagement with the politics of State rule and puts faith in capitalism's capacity to engage with such crises. Ferguson (2008: 3) explained that neoclassical theory is based on the assumption that there are no fixed and no augmentable factors of production. This assumption contradicts with the classical assumption of a fixed supply of land and it also assumes that population growth is an exogenous factor. The neoclassical production function is smooth and continuous based on changes in production factors. The normal production function model of $\Upsilon = (K, L)$ represents only the general production idea. The neoclassical model assumes multiple points where input factors create efficient production. It uses an aggregate production method, which explains that Υ depends on capital K, labour L, and technology A. Therefore, the production function will be:

$$Y = F(K, AL)$$

Neoclassical production function proposes that factors of production can be substituted for one another. Hence, combining different factors for K and AL can produce a given output. Neoclassical production function is based on the project of the diminishing return of capital. It has both positive and diminishing marginal productivity of the factors of production. It further assumes that the marginal product of capital leads to infinity as capital and labour move to zero and vice versa. It defined that the marginal product of capital and labour declines since the labour and capital increase towards infinity. The neoclassical model redefines the concepts of population and capital. It explained that the declining marginal utility of labour and capital results from the continuous engagement of labour with the same amount of capital goods without any new uses, which leads to additional capital becoming redundant. One of the essential contributions of neoclassical production function is the law of diminishing marginal utility. This is a simple assumption. It explains that every additional input of factors of production increases the production, yet the output per factor input becomes lesser as the factor input goes up. This process is defined as the marginal productivity of the factor input. It is an essential aspect of risk-based investments in developing countries, wherein the marginal productivity of factor inputs fluctuates with the extent of disasters. Investments in factor inputs in disaster-affected or disaster-prone areas seldom ensure higher initial factor output. It requires a higher rate of factor inputs to maintain a high output rate and recover the economy. Such protections for capital have different manifestations in disaster contexts, and they never agree with the core concept of investments in a capitalist framework. The poor and slow economic recovery after disasters is often attributed to less factor outputs. The neoclassical production function has further expanded the law of variable proportion. The law of variable proportion is an expanded version of the law of diminishing returns. The law of variable proportion is primarily meant to assess the extent of marginal productivity of each factor input by keeping other inputs constant. It depends on multiple assumptions. It assumes that the production technique remains constant and that the variable factor inputs are homogeneous. It also depends on the assumption that labour is a single variable factor input. The law of variable proportion is a short-term model since all factors of production keep changing in the long run, and the factor inputs will change due to changes in production and production function. The basic assumptions of the law of variable proportion have multiple reflections when applied in a natural disaster context. Every factor input varies in a disaster context, and nothing remains constant. It isn't easy to maintain homogeneous factors of production and keep the technology intact to produce the factor inputs. It is true that labour is a single variable input, even in disaster recovery projects. It is often the only input available in disaster contexts in developing countries, wherein recovery and rehabilitation depend on the availability of labour. Any change in factor output depends on the use of labour force. Thus, the required increase in factor output for disaster recovery is only attained in the long run, and it further depends on higher factor inputs. The production function must be changed to attain economic recovery after a disaster and reduce future disaster risk.

Another critical dimension of the neoclassical model is the importance of the idea of return to scale. It assumes that a change in the factor inputs leads to a change in output. There are three categories of return to scale: (i) constant return to scale, which explains that every additional factor input leads to double the output; (ii) increasing return to scale, which means double the factor inputs and gain, double is the output; and (iii) decreasing return to scale, which is about every additional factor input leading to less output. These three can be applied to disaster situations. The rate of economic recovery after a disaster depends on these three returns to scale. A slow recovery rate in developing countries such as India is attributed to decreasing return to scale. The cost of factor inputs plays an important role. A higher rate of factor inputs due to poor supply and access reduces the outputs. A production function with an increasing rate of return is required for disaster recovery in developing countries. It is a challenge since the poor incentive prevents investments in such areas. State incentives for investments could be an option; however, there are challenges in ensuring such incentives. There should be extra tax or borrowings for that, and the local economy of disaster-affected areas seldom ensures any such tax income for the state. Therefore, the burden shifts to the government to invest or provide extra incentives to private investments, which is still challenging.

The Neo-Classical Revolution did not just change the perception of classical doctrines but led to a larger change in the development approaches. The Great Depression of the 1930s questioned the classical notion that supply creates demand. For the first time, the neoclassical perception of economic growth recognized the importance of marginal utility of factor input along with return to scale and the role of technology in the production function. The classical understanding of economic growth challenges the concept of elasticity. It talked about elasticity of supply, price elasticity of demand, and the elasticity of factor input substitution. It implied that price changes would impact the demand and supply of goods, considerably changing production. The universal application of the model could not capture the regional specificities and disparities while explaining the growth models. The theory of marginal utility, elasticity, and return of the scale play a critical role in disaster recovery investments. Unlike general investments, disaster-induced investments require specific targets to be achieved. They must be a time-bound investment, and their marginal utility is comparatively high. The absence of other support systems and poor financial conditions force the survivors to utilise the given support system quickly. The use values of investments are comparatively high for the community, which pushes the marginal utility up. It also connects with the marginal productivity of land and labour.

The marginal productivity of land and labour are the biggest challenges of disaster recovery. The huge supply of unemployed workers after the disaster due to the loss of livelihoods reduces the marginal productivity of the workers. This large number of less-productive workers needs to be employed. The marginal utility of lands affected by natural calamities must also be considered in post-disaster rehabilitation programmes. The low productivity of land due to natural calamities often pushes the general economic development down and affects the elasticity of demand. The low price of factor inputs and the low wage rate must be accepted in post-disaster recovery investments. Variable proportions of factor inputs must be followed due to low availability and price elasticity. Higher labour participation is often necessary for the survival of the affected community. The neoclassical model's basic assumptions often apply to post-disaster recovery investments. Yet, its application depends on how agencies define and place post-disaster investments. Like classical notions, the neoclassical model also puts a thrust on a capitalist mode of production. Hence, State or public investment has zero references in the model.

State or public institutions have an essential role in post-disaster recovery investments in developing countries. Such investments seldom take into consideration the marginal productivity of the factor inputs. The investment aims to create marginal productivity in the short run, irrespective of its long-term impacts. In the short run, no other agency except the State can be engaged with the production process in the disaster area. State investments often lead to loss-making as per the conventional capitalist method of assessments, but the State still has to make those investments. The final output of a production process after a disaster in a short period never creates much economic value. Hence, private-sector investments have a limit on releasing capital to these areas. Imbalances in the short run can hamper the long-run equilibrium of the affected regions and communities. Disasters generally dismantle the equilibrium of production functions of the region in the short run, and the community and the region are pushed into zero marginal productivity. The long-run equilibrium of such regions and communities depends on the projects that are meant to maintain short-run equilibrium. Such investments seldom come from the private sector, except for capitalizing on disasters through huge supplies of reconstruction materials and land grabbing. It has been proved that only state funding can maintain the short-run equilibrium. However, the neoclassical model does not give much thought to it. The survivors' purchasing power is also less compared to normal economic conditions. The lack of collective purchasing power is the biggest threat to the economic recovery of disaster-affected communities. Post-disaster recovery investments' success depends on the higher purchasing power of affected communities.

4.4 Risk, Wealth, and Surplus

The classical and neoclassical economics standpoint on risk is particular and about saving the value of wealth. Post-Keynesian economics offers a diverse set of economic theories to approach wealth creation. Post-Keynesian economics is very much concerned with the idea of effective demand proposed by Keynesian economics. One of the prominent post-Keynesian economics theories was the debate on the importance of monetary policy and the market in determining the money supply. It was assessed that the financial system appears to be essentially endogenous to the money supply (Niggle, 1991). Neo Keynesian scholars argue that the Keynes model failed to understand that in a real-world market economy with decentralized decision-makers, it is in principle impossible to supply economic agents with the information they need to engage in a set of individual commitments and acts that would ensure continual full employment. Money holders must make vital decisions regarding the financial forms to store their money over time, and organizations must make critical decisions about real capital investment and finance (Crotty, 1980). The post-Keynesian economy is the economy of growth of wealth. See Fig. 4.1. Figure 4.1 also refers to why the post-Keynesian economists are increasingly concentrating on effective demand. The increasing concentration of wealth makes the theory of effective demands more critical for capitalism. Wealth has grown exponentially over these periods, and so has income inequality.

Many national and international sources are available to assess income inequality worldwide. Global wealth growth needs to be assessed for global inequality. In 2013, the cut-off for the richest 10% of the globe was 14,500 int-$, while the cut-off for the lowest 10% was 480 int-$. The proportion is 30.2. While global inequality remains high, we are living in a time of declining inequality. This ratio was 37.6 in 2003. In addition, the Gini coefficient has decreased from 68.7 to 64.9 (Roser, 2017). Inequality and wealth growth move together, so the modern capitalist economy always expects a recession. The risk according to modern capitalism is recession due to consumption reduction. Some studies prove that global income inequality has always been extremely high, suggesting the longevity of a highly hierarchical global economic structure (Chancel & Piketty, 2021). Post-Keynesians also overestimate the impact of deep or extended recessions on inflation. Rising unemployment jeopardizes job security and affects working circumstances for millions of employed people (Crotty, 1980). See Fig. 4.2.

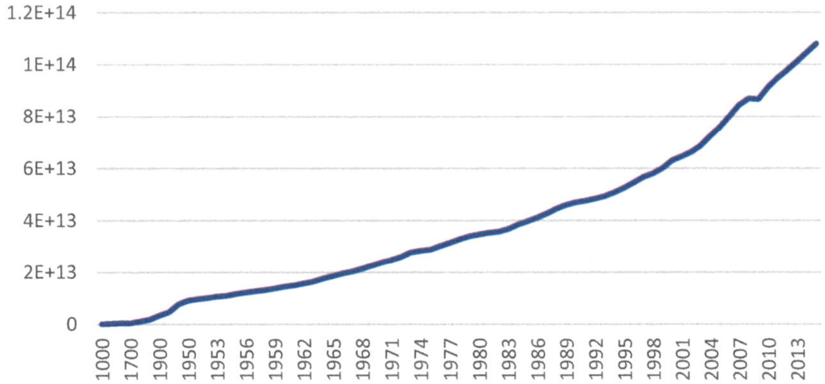

Fig. 4.1 World GDP in 2011 Int.$ [OWID based on World Bank & Maddison (2017)] (*Source* https://ourworldindata.org/grapher/world-gdp-over-the-last-two-millennia)

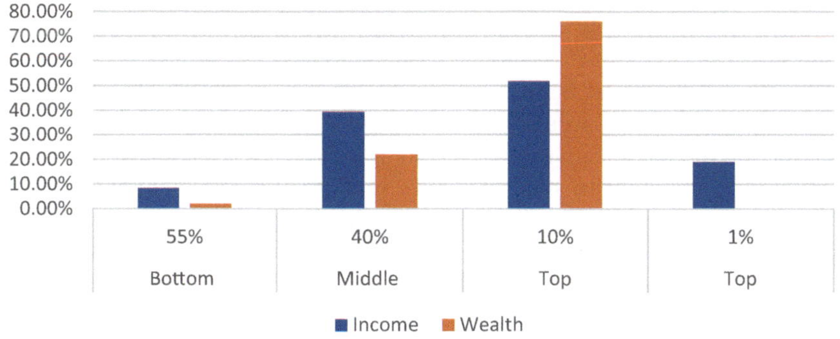

Fig. 4.2 Global income and wealth inequality, 2021 (*Source* World inequality report 2022)

Figure 2.2 shows that over time, the wealth of the rich has increased, and it is true that the wealth of people at the bottom has never grown to a larger extent. It takes generations to grow. Economic institutions indeed follow the capitalist growth path and models. Williamson (1985), who studied the institutions of capitalism, explains that economic institutions, particularly huge conglomerate firms, allude to transaction cost economization. Williamson was referring to the new institutional economics that engages with capitalism. New institutional economics carry forward the neoclassical concept and build law and institutions (Swedberg, 1992). Here, one needs to refer to Schumpeter (1943), who introduced the term 'creative destruction', which Schumpeter used to describe the process through which new inventions, technologies, and business practices overthrow and replace pre-existing economic structures and systems, was first used by him. He believed that capitalism is characterized by this ongoing process of creative destruction, in which innovators and businesspeople challenge the current system for economic advancement. Creative destruction applies in a disaster context; however, a few economies have overcome the crisis. Schumpeter (1943: 82) argues that, '*Capitalism, then, is by nature a form or method of economic change and not only never is but never can be stationary. And this evolutionary character of the capitalist process is not merely because economic life goes on in a social and natural environment which changes and, by its change, alters the data of economic action; this fact is important, and these changes (wars, revolutions, and so on) often condition industrial change, but they are not its prime movers. Nor is this evolutionary character due to a quasi automatic increase in population and capital or to the vagaries of monetary systems of which exactly the same thing holds true'*. Schumpeter's theory talks about the fundamental philosophy of wealth accumulation in capitalism.

The theory of creative destruction is otherwise a capitalist method; however, it is proper to state that not every wealth is resilient to destruction. Wealth creation associated with institutions, policies, and adequate surplus would survive the devastation. Wealth inequality plays an essential role in evolving a resilient capital. Some capitals do not create a surplus, only a bare minimum surplus to existing capital. We need to consider two types of capital in this context: the capital, which creates surplus and grows, and the capital, which results in scarcity and devaluation. So, environmental risk and uncertainty would affect wealth and capital based on its surplus-generating capability.

4.5 Risk, Uncertainty, and Wealth

Evolving capital, as Schumpeter states, considers risk and uncertainty as critical factors since they may disrupt the evolutionary process. The practical difference between risk and uncertainty is that in the former, the distribution of the outcome in a group of instances is known (either through a priori calculation or from statistics of experience), whereas, in the case of uncertainty, this is not true, because it is impossible to form a group of instances. After all, the situation dealt with is essentially unique (Knight, 1921). Modern economic processes consider risk a destruction of growth path and risk of surplus accumulation. In the Marxian perspective, surplus value is '*the product value is exactly equal to the value of the capital advanced. The value so advanced has not expanded, no surplus value has been created, and consequently, money has not been converted into capital* (Marx, 1887)'. It explains that if the value of the capital is increased and distributed, it is called surplus value. It exists in most of the advanced capitalist economies. Without it, capital expansion is not possible. The capital accumulation of every capitalist economy depends on these huge profits. It is quite interesting to apply the Marxian framework to post-disaster capital investments, where only labour resources are surplus. Human resources are available in developed and developing countries to start the recovery. The pre-disaster economic vulnerability still influences the disaster recovery process. The low capital base of society and huge labour resources should be put into creating assets for survival. Both Schumpeter and Marx discussed the potential crisis of capitalism, which may lead to a lower surplus. The risk, according to them, is the risk of falling into a stationary state of economy. The ability of capitalism to overcome the stationary state is associated with multiple processes, including the market, institutions, consumption, and profits. The capital or economic resources, which the society's vulnerable sections never hold, can overcome the risks. Marx had discussed environmental risk in a larger context. Marx (1887) explains that '*capitalist production collects the population together in great centres, and causes the urban population to achieve an ever-growing preponderance … it disturbs the metabolic interaction between man and the earth, i.e., it prevents the return to the soil of its constituent elements consumed by man in the form of food and clothing; hence it hinders the operation of the eternal natural condition for the lasting fertility of the soil*'. Marx was trying to explain how capitalism undermines the metabolic relationship between humans and nature, resulting in environmental degradation; however, Marx did not elaborate on this concept in detail. Later on, Marxian scholars engaged with these concepts in detail. Also, Marx (1844) argued that '*man lives from nature, i.e., nature is his body, and he must maintain a continuing dialogue with it if he is not to die. To say that man's physical and mental life is linked to nature simply means that nature is linked to itself, for man is a part of nature*'. The marxian approach was to establish the relationship between nature and labour. Human beings are part of nature, and there is no other existence of human beings.

Every economy, irrespective of its developmental status, is now identifying the vulnerable geographic areas within the country and preparing action plans to reduce the risks. The method to assess this area is essentially a manifestation of environmental risks and not of poverty and vulnerabilities alone. For instance, in India, the website of the National Disaster Management Authority of India (NDMA) gives a detailed account of the hazard and vulnerability profile of India. It explains the region's vulnerability to disasters and identifies the areas prone to natural disasters. According to NDMA, more than 58.6% of India's land mass is prone to earthquakes having moderate to high intensity, meaning that a majority of the people live with risks. However, the economic and social impact and risk perception may differ. The NDMA classifications are generally based on physical assessment and not related to the vulnerabilities of the communities and poverty prevailing in the area. As per the NDMA classification, about 12% of India's land area is prone to floods and river erosion. Floods and droughts are recurring phenomena in India that cause severe economic loss. The economic cost is one of the consequences of the recurring flood; the significant impact is on livelihood security of the community living in flood-prone areas. Studies prove that, in the Indian states of Bihar, Uttar Pradesh, and West Bengal, all of which are located along the Ganges River, a total of 196 million people live in high-risk flood zones, accounting for 33–53% of the population of the respective states.

Foster (2000) later elaborates on the concept of metabolic rift; according to Foster, the large-scale capitalism civilization caused a metabolic rift between humans and the land, suggesting that nature-imposed sustainability conditions had been broken. The Marxian and Foster's elaboration is again based on the late industrial revolution period's conflict over agricultural land and the expansion of towns. Kautsky (1899), a Marxian theorist, engages with the idea of metabolic rift and argues that '*the growth of towns and the expansion of industry, which increasingly exhausts the soil and imposes new burdens on agriculture in the form of the fertilisers needed to combat this exhaustion, does not rest content with this achievement. It also robs agriculture of its labour-power*'. Kautsky was deeply concerned about the loss of agriculture labour and it not about the declining soil fertility alone. Later, scholars will discuss pesticide risk as a continuation of this critical concern. Bosso argues (1987: 28) that pesticides were primarily associated with agricultural advancement in the 1940s. Environmental or safety concerns did not impact the economy of pesticides. The classical work of Carison has changed the perception of pesticide use in the world. Carison (1962) asserted that the Second World War created the pesticide industry. It is a byproduct of creating chemical warfare agents since it was discovered that some of the developed compounds could also be used to kill pests. The negative impact of pesticides on soil fertility and livelihood has influenced the academic and policy discourses on risk. It reflected the period and had no critical engagement with the growing capitalist development worldwide.

There were natural calamities and environmental risk reporting; however, those were treated as independent events and had no linkages effects. Over time, increasing disaster events and fatalities necessitate an inquiry into the risk and impact. The classical work of Beck (1992) brought a new approach to the risks and risk paradigm. The risk paradigm has redefined the concept of wealth creation and challenges the modern capitalist wealth creation method. Beck (1992: 19) has argued that *'in advanced modernity the social production of wealth is systematically accompanied by the social production of risks'*. Beck's theory offered a new perspective on modern economic production. Beck's core argument is that economic inequalities in risk and class often overlap and can produce the former later. Beck argued that wealth accumulates at the top and risks at the bottom, and they also said that wealth can purchase safety. Beck's risk theory encompasses modern capitalism as the root cause of risks. Beck's theory also reflects the metabolic rift concept and develops a discourse on social groups' wealth and capital. As Beck (1992: 41) narrates, *'the proletariat of the global risk society settles beneath the smokestacks, next to the refineries and chemical factories in the industrial centres of the third world'*. So, the risk and value of wealth are correlated in the modern-day economy. Beck was referring to pollution; however, the environmental risk is reaching out to every aspect of the production process. Capitalism, which creates risks, also assesses the risks. As Covello and Merkhofer (1993: 3) argue, risk assessment generates a probability distribution of uncertainties about the timing and magnitudes of possible environmental impacts associated with specific events or actions. Uncertainty disrupts the economic growth path of the capitalist system since it has a specific method to explore the market, commodity, and resource access. So, the modern capitalist economic system wants to build resilience against risk. Chapter one of this book discusses economic resilience; however, for capitalism, resilience is possible through institutional interventions. As discussed before, capitalism builds institutions to create resilience. Also, as Piketty (2020) explains, an ownership society has evolved with wealth over time. Piketty attempts to explain the historical evolution of ownership societies in European societies, but it still has continuity in the non-western developing economies. Beck's theory of class society deals with an impacted society having poor access to and ownership of resources. Ownership society is more capable of building resilience to overcome the crisis; however, on the contrary, non-ownership risk society falls into the crisis. Disaster and climate risk hardly affect ownership of society; hence, the risk is being articulated from their perspective. Naomi Klein (2007) gives us the details of this practice without any theoretical and ideological underpinnings; she wrote, *'I traveled to Sri Lanka, several months after the devastating 2004 tsunami, and witnessed another version of the same maneuvre: foreign investors and international lenders had teamed up to use the atmosphere of panic to hand the entire beautiful coastline over to entrepreneurs who quickly built large*

resorts, blocking hundreds of thousands of fishing people from rebuilding their villages near the water'. Klein's narrative has to be studied in the context that the Tsunmi killed about 7500 fishermen in Sri Lanka, and over 5600 are still missing. Over 5000 Sri Lankan fishing families have been relocated, and 80% of coastal fishing vessels, including around 19,000 boats, have been destroyed or severely damaged. Seventy-five percent of the fishing fleet was lost, and salinity harmed about 25,000 acres of arable land. In total, 150,000 people lost their primary source of income (Relief Web, 2005; World-Habitat, 2008). Srilanka got bilateral and multilateral aid for rehabilitation; however, these investments created or expanded the wealth of ownership society. There is no institution-driven cooperation to ensure economic resilience. Cooperation breaks down when there is resource inequality and a higher relative risk for the poorer individuals. This is because when they are less in danger, the wealthy invest proportionately less in halting environmental risks (Burton-Chellew et al., 2013).

Literature proves the correlation between income inequality and flood disasters in 67 middle- and high-income countries between 1990 and 2018, and the study found that unequal countries tend to suffer more flood fatalities (Lamb et al., 2023). Interestingly, resource-owned society seldom faces long-term economic impacts; somewhat, their wealth increase or is never affected by disaster. The critical question is why the risk and uncertainty do not restrict the growth of the wealth of ownership society and increase income inequalities (Bista, 2020; Pleninger, 2022). Also, some studies show that economic growth declines in the short run due to climatic and geological disasters (Botzen et al., 2019). The wealth that cannot connect with institutions of modern capitalism and has the internal ability to maintain resilience is immense and more vulnerable to natural risks and uncertainties. See Box 4.5.

The case study presented in the box is about the United States, one of the richest industrial economies in the world, and it shows that they do have the problem of 'vulnerable wealth'. Being in a powerful market economy does not convert the capital into multiple values. Marxian analysis of the circulation of capital explains this context in detail. The Marxian theory of the circulation of commodities C–M–C explains the transformation of commodities into money and converting money into commodities. It also elaborates on the process that it entails. Marx explained that M–C is a purchase, i.e., money is changed into a commodity, and later, the commodity is sold for money (C–M). Hence, it

Box 4.5 Insult to injury: natural disasters and residents' financial health

The study discovered that residing in a natural disaster-affected area results in significant and permanent declines in credit scores, on average, when compared to living in an unaffected area with otherwise similar individuals. These impacts are visible in the first year after a tragedy strikes, last for 4 years, and tend to expand with time. Credit score drops following Hurricane Sandy and other large and medium-sized calamities. It is also possible to uncover more significant credit-score losses among residents affected by medium-sized catastrophes (up to 22 points by the fourth year after the disaster) than among residents affected by massive disasters such as Hurricane Sandy (10 points in year four). Drops of 22 points for people in this range could make them substantially poor credit risks, limiting their access to traditional credit, limiting their capacity to recover from natural disasters, and resulting in more extraordinary expenses if they seek loans from other sources

Source Ratcliffe, Caroline; William J. Congdon; Alexandra Stanczyk; Daniel Teles; Carlos Martín and Bapuchandra Kotapati. 2019. Insult to Injury: Natural Disasters and Residents' Financial Health. Urban Institute. https://www.urban.org/research/publication/insult-injury-natural-disasters-and-residents-financial-health

again comes back as money. This is a circulation of capital, and it is a part of a capitalist economy. It establishes that the circuit C–M–C begins with one commodity and finishes with another. Consumption is the end. M–C–M begins with money and ends with money. Marxian analysis explains the logic of capitalist production, which is essentially the core of both socialist economies; however, the ownership of the mode of production and distribution matters. Marx further divided the net profit of the capitalist into variable capital (V) and constant capital (C). Capital C depends on (a) the sum of money spent on means of production and (b) the money spent on labour power. Surplus value from assets interfaced with risk and uncertainty is primarily possible only with non-capitalist investments, which is never possible in a capitalist economic system. In Marxian analysis, the production that does not create a surplus is useless, so in a disaster context, not all variables, including labour do not make a surplus, hence in the Marxian perspective, they remain idle. Economic surplus or additional value makes capital assets; however, some assets remain idle and hardly make any surplus in the capitalist sense. The fact is that capitalism survives with the existence of such non-surplus-generating assets. It is true that apart from inevitable temporary crises, modern capitalism explored various ways and means to survive and continue capital accumulation at a higher rate. The declining rate of profit is a reality unless the cost of investment becomes less and effective demand becomes high; as discussed above, the reproductive value of such capital is comparatively low, and a considerable labour force with a low wage rate has all the possibilities to lead to a situation of a declining rate of return. See Box 4.6.

The case in Box 2.2 explains that the economic theory of surplus never applies to all sectors and there are assets including labour which survive without generating any surplus. These assets are not resilient as well, economic resilience is not common across all categories of wealth rather it is an internal method of capitalism to save capital. These poor and vulnerable assets do not generate a surplus to grow, however, they continue to serve the capital to generate a surplus. Mounting environmental risks devalue the assets base and eliminate economies' Gross Domestic Product (GDP). See Box 4.7.

The case explained in Box 2.3 discusses the interface of climate risk and asset base, and the reality is that massive environmental risk displaces the GDP of vulnerable economies. In countries like this, it applies to regions in which the asset base of local communities is affected by climate risks. Climate-related risk pricing must account for this heterogeneity by assessing asset exposure to climate-related risks as well as the firm's sensitivity, or ability to respond and adapt to the exposure (Campiglio et al., 2023). Being vulnerable to natural and technology disasters is primarily a public health issue because these events usually affect communities rather

Box 4.6 Asset of landslide affected labour in a private plantation land

On 6 August 2020, there was a landslide in Pettimudi, Idukki in the South Indian state of Kerala which took 70 lives. It happened in a tea plantation estate owned by Kanan Devan Hills Plantations (KDHP) Company. Its origins can be found in the colonial history of Indian plantations. Therefore, the landslip occurred in a densely populated area where the landowners, including workers, had control over the resources. The workers were live in layam (one-bedroom houses given by the planation company). Layams where the land-slide victims lived were built during the British period (pre-independence). It was in poor condition, and it is one of the major tea plantations in South India. The economic loss due to this landside was minimal compared to the company's asset base. The total loss in partially destroyed layam was ₹139,400. The total economic loss was Rs 7,663,000, of which the community owned Rs 5,301,000 vehicles. The total assets of the labour who were serving the tea plantation were Rs 2,362,000 only. It is a known fact that the plantation sector survives because of labour and it is a kind of bonded labour. This landslide did not affect the tea plantation, and the company continued its operation without any impact

Source Irshad, S. M and Christin Solaman, S. S. 2022. Identity, Space and Disaster: A Case Study of Pettimudi Landslide in Kerala. *Sociological Bulletin*. https://doi.org/10.1177/00380229221094785

Box 4.7 Climate change and GDP loss

An assessment of the climate-vulnerable countries (V20 Group of Finance Ministers representing 55 of the world's most climate-vulnerable economies) groups experiences shows that in the last two decades, these countries lost half of their economic growth due to human-induced climate change; in another world, if there is no climate change, these economies would be 20% wealthier today. For instance, without climate change, Ghana's actual average growth rate of 4% for the period would have been 4.5%. Climate change-attributable losses average 0.92% of a given level of yearly economic growth and a total 20% of GDP during the last two decades (2000–2019) for all V20 economies

Source Vulnerable 20. 2019. Climate Vulnerable Economies Loss Report. Economic losses attributable to climate change in V20 economies over the last two decades (2000–2019). www.v-20.org/wp-content/uploads/2022/06/Climate-Vulnerable-Economies-Loss-Report_June-14_compressed-1.pdf

than lone people. Likewise, actions taken to lessen vulnerability are largely considered public goods (Boyce, 2000).

It could be otherwise defined as the challenges of capital asset pricing in economics. The Capital Asset Pricing Model (CAPM) is a popular financial theory that proposes a linear link between an investment's expected return and its systematic risk.

$$\text{Capital Asset Pricing Model (CAPM)} = \text{ER} = \text{Rf} + (\beta \times (\text{Rm} - \text{Rf}))$$

ER is the expected return on the asset. Rf is the risk-free rate. β (beta) is the asset's sensitivity to market movements. Rm is the expected return of the overall market.

It is an economic model that intent to see risk-free investment and high net present value. It does not necessarily engage with the context of disaster or climate risk. Bai et al. (2019) looked at the CAPM in a disaster context, and it shows that when disasters occur, the predicted market beta better accounts for the substantial covariation between the value-minus-growth return and the pricing kernel. Some scholars elaborate on the CAPM and argue that aside from the physical risk that impacts the entire market, we also consider the transition risk of climate change, which is the danger of being exposed to stringent environmental rules that reduce the returns on carbon-intensive assets (Karydas & Xepapadeas, 2019). Β (beta) is sensitive to risk in some economic systems and non-sensitive in certain contexts. Rm is quite sensitive to natural calamities. Disasters and climate risk create stranded assets and vulnerable capital assets, so the investment to generate surplus to push the growth up is determined by multiple economic factors. Some studies based on the Western industrial economies argue that both aggregate consumption and investment are reduced by calamity. Wealth-poor households raise their precautionary savings in response to an increase in overall risk, which significantly explains the consumption response. Wealthy households that initially hold more wealth in high-yielding, illiquid assets are the primary drivers of response investment (Kim, 2022). Natural calamities create a scarcity of resources and capital assets, so the economic risk otherwise has to interface with scarcity.

4.6 Scarcity and Vulnerable Assets

The Box 2.3 explains the very specific case of disaster to certain economies, primarily it results scarcity due to devaluation of resources. Capitalisation of those resources becomes a critical challenges in developing economies. For instance, the Report Of The Survey On Climate Risk And Sustainable Finance by Reserve bank of India (2022) observed that climate risk or green financing required a drastic change in the banking system. The poor creditworthiness due to climate change weakens the banking institutions in drought-affected areas, increasing the dependency on direct financial support from the government. The Reserve Bank of India's assessment explains that banks are reluctant to lend to the farmers affected by or from drought-prone areas of Western Mahrarahstra State, India. Western Maharashtra is known for severe drought for generations. The commercial banks of India follow the economic logic of rent and marginal productivity in determining the credit policy. The rent from natural resources is linked with marginal productivity (Devarajan & Fisher, 1982). The Physiocrats regarded rent as the only true net product, and they considered rent as surplus over any necessary to landowners (Lackman, 1976).

However, the core concern of this concept is highly significant for the economic recovery of a climate change and disaster-affected economy i.e. replacing capital resources. Chapter I gives a detailed account of replacement capital to recover the economic impact of disasters or climate risks. It is otherwise called wealth and economy and is concerned about disasters and climate risk precisely because of the negative impact on rent and surplus value of resources. Poor surplus value and poor rent result in scarcity in the economies and areas prone to disasters. Scarcity is otherwise a property that emerges from human interventions or social factors.

Also, scarcity can be absolute or relative scarcity (Barbier, 1989). Daly (1977: 39) defines absolute scarcity as, *'refers to the scarcity of resources in general, the scarcity of ultimate means. Absolute scarcity increases as population growth and per-capital consumption push us ever closer to the biosphere's carrying capacity. The concept presupposes that all economical substitutions among resources will be made [this is relative scarcity]. While such substitutions will certainly mitigate the burden of absolute scarcity, they will not eliminate it nor prevent is eventual increase'*. Marshall (1890: 1920) emphasized that scarcity requires individuals and societies to decide how to use limited resources to satisfy their infinite demands. It also leads to other kinds of deprivations. Natural disasters increase people's susceptibility to poverty, making poverty a measurable and significant problem (Hallegatte et al., 2020). So scarcity is not only a modern creation, it is a modern dilemma too (Xenos, 1987). When resources are low relative to needs, the sense of scarcity emerges and influences the decision-making changes in how they make decisions (Mullainathan & Shafir, 2013). Scarcity influences the capitalization of resources and economic decision-making. See Box 4.8.

Classical economist have discussed the issue of scarcity in detail and attempted to explain it with reference to surplus generation and resource mobilization. There are limitations in measuring resource scarcity based on shadow prices (Halvorsen and Smith, 1984). Scarcity is the core debate in economic theory, however, it definitions are complex when it confront natural resource availability (Smith, 1978). Scarcity has an impact on the basic economic forces of supply and demand. When a resource is rare, its price rises due to high demand and restricted supply (Marshall, 1890: 1920). Simon (1955) argues that, individuals and businesses' rational decision-making is influenced by scarcity. He emphasized that individuals make rational decisions within the restrictions of limited knowledge,

Box 4.8 Drought and poverty

A study on drought in Rajasthan proves that during a drought, the number of poor climbs significantly in areas where poverty is normally low. In a drought year, the share of individuals who are infrequently poor and prone to poverty rises from 19 to 27%, with the number of those suffering from chronic poverty doubling. This is seen in agricultural and non-agricultural households alike

Source Dasgupta, Purnamita and Smita Sirohi. 2019. Drought but why: How poverty is aggravated. Down to Earth. 15 March 2019

cognitive limits, and time. These theories articulate that scarcity influences the economic decision-making and in natural calamity context, scarcity influences the rational economic decision-making of all economic agents. For instance, the studies prove that disaster often changes the consumer behaviour of individuals (Kunreuther, 1967). Other effects of the scarcity are as mentioned above inequalities. Direct impact of disasters results indirect economic losses and well-being of the people (Edmonds & Noy, 2018). Environmental risk-induced resource scarcity increasingly affects a large section of the population. For instance, with reference to climate risk, it is estimated that approximately 90% of the heat emitted into the atmosphere as a result of global warming is deposited in the seas, and this heat storage contributes significantly to mean sea-level rise. Based on the earth system model output, recent research on primary production in the Indian Ocean predicts a 20% reduction in marine phytoplankton over the previous six decades (Roxy et al., 2016). Scientific and scholarly research is being conducted to determine the impact of climate change on beaches and coastal communities. According to Cheung et al. (2016), ocean warming caused by climate change affects the distribution and behaviour of marine species. Fish stocks and availability for fishing communities suffer as a result. There is a direct linkage between disasters and resource scarcity or devaluation of resources. See Box 4.9.

Disaster-induced scarcity also pushes the marginal productivity down and hence economic growth and progress will be at stake. So, the developed market economies depend on market sources, however, in countries

Box 4.9 Drought and resource scarcity

Droughts affect an estimated 55 million people worldwide each year, constituting the most serious threat to animals and crops in practically every corner of the world. Drought endangers people's livelihoods, raises the risk of sickness and death, and drives mass migration. Water scarcity affects 40% of the world's population, and up to 700 million people may be displaced due to drought by 2030. In Somalia, the worst drought in 40 years. There were 42,000 extra deaths in 2022 alone, while at least 3.5 million animals have been destroyed, and an estimated 1.4 million people have been displaced since 2021. It is estimated that 1.54 billion population is affected by drought and desertification. A terrible drought is producing Ethiopia's worst food crisis in 30 years, placing millions at danger of famine and disease

Source www.who.int/health-topics/drought?; www.reliefweb.int; Bai ZG, Dent DL, Olsson L, Schaepman ME. 2008.Proxy global assessment of land degradation. Soil Use Manag 24:223–234; ww.oxfam.org

like India public prevent the resource scarcities. In developing economies, the government follows a public finance approach in which tax money spend for disaster risk mitigation. In India the national disaster response fund and national disaster mitigation fund are the major source of capital support. The government also borrows from international lending agencies for disaster relief. It has been followed the method of capital replacement. Let us revisit the CAPM model for country where public finding will support Rf. Then, the model would be

$$\text{Capital Asset Pricing Model}\,(CAPM) = E(\text{Ri}) = \text{Rf} + \beta i \cdot (E(\text{Rm}) - \text{Rf})$$

$E(\text{Ri})$ is the expected return on asset. Rf is the risk-free rate now, it is public funding with zero expectations on returns. βi is the beta coefficient of asset and i is the measurement of its systematic risk (volatility relative to the market). $E(\text{Rm})$ is the expected return on the overall market.

$\text{Rf} + \beta i$ is a determining factor of developing economies. The Capital Asset Pricing Model is subject to various scholarly inquiries; for instance, Bai et al. (2019) argue that value stocks are more vulnerable to a disaster than growth stocks in a general equilibrium production economy with heterogeneous companies and disasters. The pricing kernel experiences severe nonlinearity due to the disaster risk. Research indicates that riskier investments may require higher necessary returns due to possible catastrophic losses (Barro, 2006). Acharya et al. (2017) also observed that an increased correlation between asset returns following a disaster is a common indicator of systemic risk. Elevated systemic risk can potentially affect the total market return and risk premium, influencing the estimated return on all assets. The changing value of assets and risk influence the β i and hence the asset value. This correlation is more complex in backward economies having vulnerable assets with poor asset value with higher use value. In a country like India, disaster and climate risk as public finance crises as the source of mitigation and responses are from budgetary sources. Fresh investment is required to endure the economic impact of natural disasters (Marto et al., 2018). Disasters deplete capital, but new investment boosts marginal production (Hallegatte et al., 2022). India's state investment is to increase the marginal productivity of assets affected by disaster and climate risks. No private sector is interested in disaster mitigation, responses, and rehabilitation in a country like India. The private sector contributes under corporate social responsibility (CSR) and charity-based livelihood support, not for any significant investment for capital replacement. The major impediment of poor private-sector investment is the assets' vulnerability and poor marginal efficiency of vulnerable assets.

Keynes' marginal efficiency theory of capital (1936) defined the marginal efficiency of capital as the discount rate at which the present value of the series of annuities resulting from the returns anticipated from the capital asset during its lifetime is precisely equal to its supply price. We can now calculate the marginal efficiencies of specific categories of capital assets. Consequently, the highest of these marginal efficiencies is the marginal efficiency of capital. In disaster-affected areas, the marginal efficiency of capital will be extremely low, making private-sector investment impossible. The Keynesian hypothesis of potential returns from capital investments in disaster-prone or impacted areas is misguided. A low capital's marginal efficiency is crucial when investing in fragile regions. The Keynesian model is an essential framework for analyzing how disaster-affected populations and even socially and economically weak areas of the third world are faring economically. Affected communities frequently depend on Keynes' contribution to the short-run model to survive. Vulnerable assets are primarily exposed to disasters and extreme weather risks in developing and backward economies; hence, only capital not expecting surplus would ensure marginal efficiencies.

Damage and loss assessment reports and post-disaster need assessments are expressly framed to locate vulnerable assets in backward economies. In India, the revenue department evaluates each sector's loss after a natural disaster and assesses the loss in economic terms on a temporal basis. The Economic Commission for Latin America and the Caribbean (ECLAC) has pioneered catastrophe assessment, developing and disseminating a disaster assessment methodology. It is one of the popular assessment frameworks since it assesses the real-time economic impact of a natural calamity. The ECLAC method is used to assess the cost involved in recovery and reconstruction cost. Another popular framework is The Post-Disaster Needs Assessment (PDNA), an internationally recognized approach for calculating the physical damages, economic losses, and expenses of satisfying recovery needs following a natural disaster using a government-led procedure. Since the European Union (EU), the United Nations Development Programme (UNDP), and the World Bank (WB). ECLAC and PDNA are used to assess the economic implications of calamities and the cost of reconstruction. It is active and popular in developing and backward economies rather than developed industrialized economies. See Fig. 4.3, which explains the relationship between income and disaster loss in different income categories of the global economy. Low-income countries have less income to lose but face more disaster events, see Table 4.1.

As said, the number of disaster events is increasing; however, it creates a differential impact based on the macroeconomic structures. Figure 2.4 details one case of absolute numbers and percentage of people affected by disasters. The higher implication of disaster risk, except in high-income countries, indicates poor economic resilience and vulnerable assets.

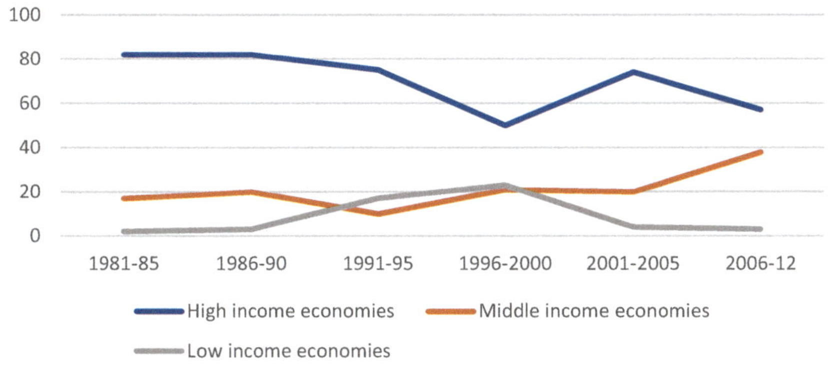

Fig. 4.3 Relative distributions of direct loss between high-, middle-, and low-income countries across time (as percent of total annual direct loss) (*Source* World Bank. 2014. Financial protection against natural disasters: from products to comprehensive strategies. An operational framework for disaster risk financing and insurance)

Table 4.1 Percentage of disaster reports by national income groups at GAUL 1st and 2nd unit levels 2000–2017

	1st admin unit/low precision	*2nd admin unit/low precision*	
High income	60%	40%	100%
Upper-middle income	56%	44%	100%
Lower-middle income	38%	62%	100%
Lowe-income	36%	64%	100%

Source Economic Losses, Poverty, and Disasters 1998–2017. UNISDR

Figure 4.5 is associated with Figs. 4.4 and 4.5 represents the world's present and emerging risk scenario. Lower-middle-income and lower-income countries are experiencing colossal GDP loss, eventually pushing these economies into the poverty trap. Making an economic production with vulnerable assets with poor economic resilience is impossible. Some vulnerable assets within middle-income countries are equally susceptible to risks and create inequality. Economic theory considers lower GDP as an indication of the macroeconomic health of the economy since it consists of Consumption (C), Investment (I), Government spending (G), and Net Exports (Exports–Imports) (NX). Economic growth is determined by GDP. So, changes in GDP indicate the growth prospects of the economy, and risk could influence each of these variables; hence, eventually, investment will reach negative. Also, government spending to increase the marginal efficiency of capital would be low due to disaster risks in lower-income countries. Marginal efficiency of capital remains low; hence, growth would stagnate due to disaster risks. The impact of the disaster on food production is a classic example that proves the interface of disaster and the declining marginal efficiency of capital assets. The FAO (2023) report explains that the frequency and intensity of disasters es have increased over the past 20 years, from 100 annually in the 1970s to over 400 events annually. This harms agrifood systems in many ways, jeopardizing food security and eroding the agriculture sector's sustainability. It is otherwise called the declining marginal efficiency of natural capital, leading to low food production and price inflation. Wright (2011) also observed that the volatility of the world's food markets is exacerbated by catastrophic weather occurrences, which drive up the cost of staple foods like rice, wheat, and maize. Ultimately, these risks push a vulnerable population into further risk and uncertainty and are also excluded from property ownership later. So, this critical interface of disaster and productivity loss of capital is an emerging risk in the Global South and regions prone to disaster risks.

This chapter intends to see the theoretical base of disaster economics in the context of emerging disasters and climate risks. No single theoretical framework can engage with disaster economics, so the chapter discusses the evolution of approaches from classical to neoclassical approaches to wealth concerning disasters and climate risks. The critical focus is on wealth and risk in wealth creation prospects. Developed and developing economies are exposed to disasters and climate risk; however, the data proves that the impacts differ. Also, the chapter discussed the vulnerable

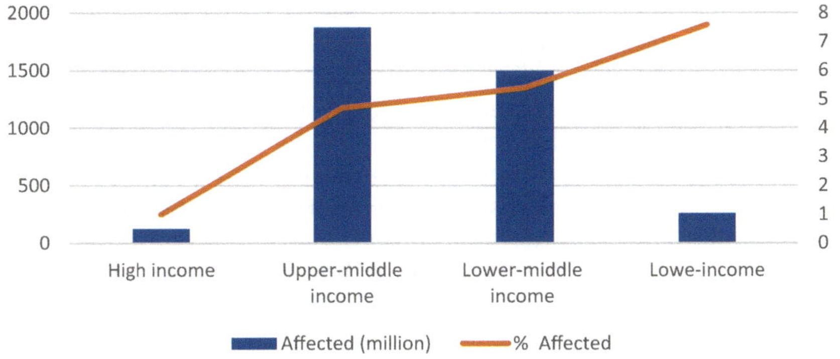

Fig. 4.4 Climate-related disaster affected totals in absolute numbers and percentage of population potentially exposed (PPE) 2000–2017 (*Source* Economic Losses, Poverty, and Disasters 1998–2017. UNISDR)

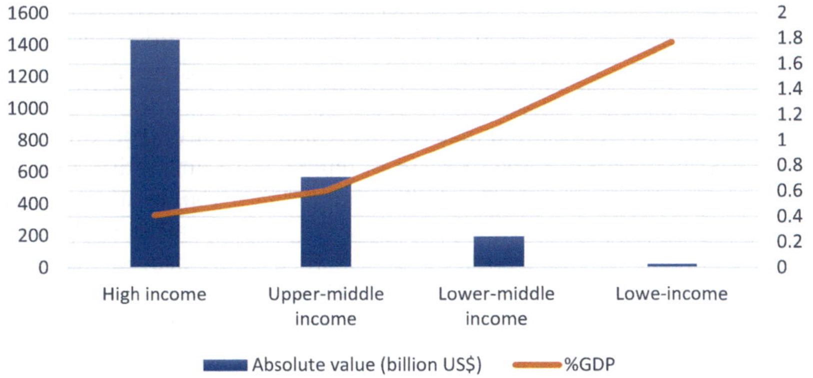

Fig. 4.5 Recorded climate-related disaster losses per income group compared to GDP losses 1998–2017 (*Source* Economic Losses, Poverty, and Disasters 1998–2017. UNISDR)

assets and how risk has resulted in the loss of GDP and eventually widened the inequality between the countries and within communities. The experiences of countries like India proved the importance of the Keynesian approach of marginal efficiency of capital to prevent the accumulation of vulnerable assets. Public investment plays a vital role in increasing the marginal efficiency of vulnerable assets; however, it is pretty tricky except in countries like India. Disaster and climate risk should be examined from a broader economic perspective, and market-driven models help locate the crisis within the linkages effects of capitalist assets. Capitalism has market-driven responses to risk; however, those approaches are ineffective for backward economies. This is an economic crisis for low-income economies adopting market economic policies. Hence, a new economic epistemology of risk must be arrived at, focusing on vulnerable non-capitalist assets.

References

Acharya, V. V., Pedersen, L. H., Philippon, T., & Richardson, M. (2017). Measuring systemic risk. *The Review of Financial Studies, 30*(1), 2–47. https://doi.org/10.1093/rfs/hhw088

Agarwal, S., Ghosh, P., & Zheng, H. (2024). Consumption response to a natural disaster: Evidence of price and income shocks from Chennai flood. *Energy Economics, 131*, 107323. https://doi.org/10.1016/j.eneco.2024.107323

Bai, H., Hou, K., Kung, H., Li, E. X., & Zhang, L. (2019). The CAPM strikes back? An equilibrium model with disasters. *Journal of Financial Economics, 131*(2), 269–298. https://doi.org/10.1016/j.jfineco.2018.08.009

Bandyopadhyay, S., Bandyopadhyay, S., Dasgupta, S., Mallik, C., & Wheeler, D. (2022). Discounting disaster: Land markets and climate change in the Indian sundarbans. *Ecology, Economy and Society—the INSEE Journal, 5*(2), 43–66.

Barbier, E. B. (1989). *Economics, natural-resource scarcity and development: Conventional and alternative views*. Earthscan.

Barro, R. J. (2006). Rare disasters and asset markets in the twentieth century. *The Quarter Journal of Economics, 121*(3), 823–866.

Beck, U. (1992). *Risk society: Toward a new modernity*. London: Sage. Translated by Mark A. Ritter (originally published 1986).

Becker, G. S. (1965). A theory of the allocation of time. *The Economic Journal, 75*(299), 493. https://doi.org/10.2307/2228949

Bin, O., & Landry, C. E. (2013). Changes in implicit flood risk premiums: Empirical evidence from the housing market. *Journal of Environmental Economics and Management, 65*(3), 361–376.

Bista, R. B. (2020). Does disaster change income and wealth distribution towards extremity of inequality and poverty? Analysis of flood and landslides in the vulnerable locations of Nepal. *ForumforSocialEconomics, 2020*, 1–18.

Bosso, C. J. (1987). *Pesticides and politics: The life cycle of a public issue*. University of Pittsburgh Press.

Botzen, W., Wouter, J., Olivier Deschenes and Mark Sanders. (2019). The economic impacts of natural disasters: A review of models and empirical studies. *Review of Environmental Economics and Policy, 13*(2), 167–188. https://doi.org/10.1093/reep/rez004

Boyce, J. K. (2000). Let them eat risk? Wealth, rights and disaster vulnerability. *Disasters, 24*(3), 254–261. https://doi.org/10.1111/1467-7717.00146

Bruckner, B., Hubacek, K., Shan, Y., Zhong, H., & Feng, K. (2022). Impacts of poverty alleviation on national and global carbon emissions. *Nature Sustainability, 5*, 311–320. https://doi.org/10.1038/s41893-021-00842-z

Buchak, L. (2013). *Risk and rationality*. OUP.

Burton-Chellew, M. N., May, R. M., & West, S. A. (2013). Combined inequality in wealth and risk leads to disaster in the climate change game. *Climatic Change, 120*(4), 815–830. https://doi.org/10.1007/s10584-013-0856-7

Campiglio, E., Daumas, L., & Monnin, P. (2023). Climate-related risks in financial assets. *Journal of Economic Surveys, 37*(3), 950–992. https://doi.org/10.1111/joes.12525

Cantelmo, A., Melina, G., & Papageorgiou, C. (2019). *Macroeconomic outcomes in disaster-prone countries*. IMF working paper WP/19/217.

Chancel, L. (2022). *Global carbon inequality over 1990–2019*. Nature Sustainability | Vol. 5 | November 2022, 931–938.

Chancel, L., & Piketty, T. (2021). Global income inequality, 1820–2020: The persistence and mutation of extreme inequality. *Journal of the European Economic Association, 19*(6), 3025–3062. https://doi.org/10.1093/jeea/jvab047

Chaudhuri, S. (2003). *Assessing vulnerability to poverty: Concepts*. Columbia University.

Cheung, W. W., Jones, M. C., Reygondeau, G., Stock, C. A., Lam, V. W., & Frölicher, T. L. (2016). Large benefits to marine fisheries of meeting the 1.5 °C global warming target. *Science, 354*(6319), 1591–1594.

Chew, T.-A., & Ghazali Mohayidin, M. (1995). Plantation agriculture: Its genesis, management, and role in the Malaysian Economy. *Agribusiness, 11*(2), 139–145.

Christophers, B. (2013). *Banking across Boundaries: Placing finance in capitalism*. John Wiley & Sons.

Cornwall, J., & Cornwall, W. (2001). *Capitalist development in the twentieth century an evolutionary-Keynesian analysis*. Cambridge University Press.

Covello, V. T., & Merkhofer, M. W. (1993). *Risk assessment methods: Approaches for assessing health and environmental risks*. Springer.

Crotty, J. R. (1980). Post-Keynesian economic theory: An overview and evaluation. *The American Economic Review, 70*(2), 20–25. Papers and proceedings of the ninety-second annual meeting of the American economic association.

Daly, H. E. (1977). *Steady state economics: The economics of biophysical equilibnum and moral growth*. Freeman.
Devarajan, S., & Fisher, A. C. (1982). Exploration and scarcity. *Journal of Political Economy, 90*(6), 1279–1290.
Donner, W., & Rodríguez, H. (2008). Population composition, migration and inequality: The influence of demographic changes on disaster risk and vulnerability. *Social Forces, 87*(2), 1089–1114.
Edmonds, C., & Noy, I. (2018). The economics of disaster risks and impacts in the Pacific. *Disaster Prevention and Management: an International Journal*. https://doi.org/10.1108/DPM-02-2018-0057
Eltis, D., & Richardson, D. (2017). *Atlas of the transatlantic slave trade*. Yale University Press.
Ferguson, C. E. (2008). *The neoclassical theory of production and distribution*. Cambridge University Press.
Food and Agriculture Organization (FAO). (2023). *The impact of disasters on agriculture and food security 2023—Avoiding and reducing losses through investment in resilience*. FAO website (accessed on 28th July, 2024).
Ford, R. E., & Adamson, K. T. (1995). The population-environment nexus and vulnerability assessment in Africa. *GeoJournal, 35*(2), 207–216. https://doi.org/10.1007/bf00814067
Foster, J. B. (2000). *Marx's ecology materialism and nature*. Monthly Review Press.
Friedman, M. (1957). *Theory of the consumption function*. Princeton University Press.
Gallagher, J., & Hartley, D. (2017). Household finance after a natural disaster: The case of Hurricane Katrina. *American Economic Journal: Economic Policy, 9*(3), 199–228.
Hallegatte, S., Charl, J., & McIsaac, F. (2022). *Macroeconomic consequences of natural disasters: A modelling proposal and application to floods and earthquakes in Turkey*. Policy research working paper 9943. World Bank.
Hallegatte, S. (2014). *Natural disasters and climate change: An economic perspective*. Springer.
Hallegatte, S., Vogt-Schilb, A., Rozenberg, J., Bangalore, M., & Beaudet, C. (2020). From poverty to disaster and back: A review of the literature. *EconDisCliCha, 4*, 223–247.
Halvorsen, R., & Smith, T. R. (1984). On measuring natural resource scarcity. *Journal of Political Economy, 92*(5), 954–964.
Hartvigsen, G. (2016). Carrying capacity, concept of. *Reference Module in Life Sciences*. https://doi.org/10.1016/B978-0-12-809633-8.02393-1
Islam, M. S., & Lim, S. H. (2015). When "nature" strikes: A sociology of climate change and disaster vulnerabilities in Asia. *Nature and Culture, 10*(1), 57–80.

Ismail, N. H., Abd. Karim, M. Z., & Hasan Basri, B. (2019). A hedonic modelling of land property value based on the effect of flooding: A case for peninsular Malaysia. In *Proceedings of the second international conference on the future of ASEAN (ICoFA) 2017* (Vol. 1, pp. 167–179). https://doi.org/10.1007/978-981-10-8730-1_17

Karydas, C., & Xepapadeas, A. (2019). *Pricing climate change risks: CAPM with rare disasters and stochastic probabilities*. Economics working paper series, no. 19/311, ETH Zurich, CER-ETH—Center of Economic Research, Zurich. https://doi.org/10.3929/ethz-b-000320545

Kautsky, K. (1899). *The agrarian question*. Zwan Publications.

Kelman, I., Gaillard, J. C., Lewis, J., & Mercer, J. (2016). Learning from the history of disaster vulnerability and resilience research and practice for climate change. *Natural Hazards, 82*(S1), 129–143. https://doi.org/10.1007/s11069-016-2294-0

Keynes, J. (1936). *The general theory of employment, interest and money*. Macmillan.

Kim, H. (2022). Inequality, disaster risk, and the great recession. *Review of Economic Dynamics, 45*, 187–216. https://doi.org/10.1016/j.red.2021.06.006

Klein, N. (2007). *The shock doctrine: The rise of disaster capitalism*. London: Metropolitan Books.

Knight, F. H. (1921). *Risk uncertainty and profit*. https://oll-resources.s3.us-east-2.amazonaws.com/oll3/store/titles/306/Knight_0192.html

Kumar, K., Sujita, A. A., & Singh, N. (2022). Disaster and consumption behavior. In S. M. Yasir-Arafat, S. K. Kar, & R. Kabir (Eds.), *Panic buying and environmental disasters: Management and mitigation approaches*. London: Springer.

Kunreuther, H. (1967). The peculiar economics of disaster. *Papers on Non-Market Decision Making, 3*(1), 67–83.

Lackman, C. L. (1976). The classical base of modern rent theory. *The American Journal of Economics and Sociology, 35*(3), 287–300.

Lamb, F. W., Wiedmann, T., Pongratz, J., Andrew, R., Crippa, M., Livier, J. G. J. O., Wiedenhofer, D., Mattioli, G., AlKhourdajie, A., House, J., Pachauri, S., Figueroa, M., Saheb, Y., Slade, R., Hubacek, K., Sun, L., Ribeiro, S. K., Khennas, S., Can, S. R., … Di Baldassarre, G. (2023). The wider the gap between rich and poor the higher the flood mortality. *Nature Sustainability, 6*(8), 995–1005. https://doi.org/10.1038/s41893-023-01107-7

Magness, P. W., Carden, A., & Murtazashvili, I. (2023). Gordon Tullock and the economics of slavery. *Public Choice*. https://doi.org/10.1007/s11127-023-01100-w

Malthus, T. R. (1798). *Principle of population*. https://www.bertie.ccsu.edu/naturesci/Evolution/Unit12OriginSpecies/Malthus.html

Mandle, R. (1973). The re-establishment of the plantation economy in the south 1865–1910. *The Review of Black Political Economy, 3*(2), 68–88. https://doi.org/10.1007/bf03040532

Marshall, A. (1890:1920). *Principles of economics*. https://www.econlib.org/library/Marshall/marP.html

Marto, R., Papageorgiou, C., & Klyuev, V. (2018). Building resilience to natural disasters: An application to small developing states. *Journal of Development Economics, 135*, 574586.

Marx, K. (1844). *Economic and philosophical manuscripts*. https://www.marxists.org/archive/marx/works/1844/manuscripts/preface.htm

Marx, K. (1887). *Capital a critique of political economy volume I*. https://www.marxists.org/archive/marx/works/1867-c1/

Marx, K. (1894). *Capital, volume III*. https://www.marxists.org/archive/marx/works/download/pdf/Capital-Volume-III.pdf

Mazzucato, M., Ryan-Collins, J., & Gouzoulis, G. (2023). Mapping modern economic rents: The good, the bad, and the grey areas. *Cambridge Journal of Economics, 47*(3), 507–534. https://doi.org/10.1093/cje/bead013

Mileti, D. S., & Peek, L. (2000). The social psychology of public response to warnings of a nuclear power plant accident. *Journal of Hazardous Materials, 75*(2–3), 181–194. https://doi.org/10.1016/s0304-3894(00)00179-5

Mill, J. S. (1848). *The principles of political economy*. https://www.cooperative-individualism.org/mill-john-stuart_on-rent-1848.htm

Mullainathan, S., & Shafir, E. (2013). *Scarcity: Why having too little means so much*. Henry Holt and Company.

Nakagawa, M., Saito, M., & Yamaga, H. (2009). Earthquake risks and land prices: Evidence from the Tokyo metropolitan area. *The Japanese Economic Review, 60*, 208–222.

Niggle, C. J. (1991). The endogenous money supply theory: An institutionalist appraisal. *Journal of Economic Issues, 25*(1), 137–151.

Noy, I., & Vu, T. B. (2010). The economics of natural disasters in a developing country: The case of Vietnam. *Journal of Asian Economics, 21*(4), 345–354.

Oxfam. (2020). *Confronting carbon inequality: Putting climate justice at the heart of the COVID-19 recovery*. 21 September 2020.

Piketty, T. (2020). *Capital and ideology*. London: The Belknap Press of Harvard University Press.

Pleninger, R. (2022). Impact of natural disasters on the income distribution. *World Development, 157*, 105936.

Princen, T. (1999). Consumption and environment: Some conceptual issues. *Ecological Economics, 31*(3), 347–363. https://doi.org/10.1016/S0921-8009(99)00039-7

Rachel, C. (1962). *Silent spring*. Penguin Books.

Relief Web. (2005). *Tsunamis destroyed tens of thousands of fishing boats: Marine fisheries and aquaculture infrastructure in many coastal areas destroyed or damaged*. https://www.reliefweb.int/report/malaysia/tsunamis-destroyed-tens-thousands-fishing-boats-marine-fisheries-and-aquaculture. Accessed on 15th September, 2023.

Reno, P. (1964). The ordeal of British 'Guiana.' *Monthly Review, 16*, 5.

Reserve Bank of India. (2022). *Discussion paper on climate risk and sustainable finance*. RBI

Ricardo, D. (1817). *Principles of political economy and taxation*. https://www.marxists.org/reference/subject/economics/ricardo/tax/index.htm

Roser, M. (2017). *The history of global economic inequality*. Published online at OurWorldInData.org. Retrieved from: 'https://ourworldindata.org/the-history-of-global-economic-inequality' [Online Resource].

Roxy, M. K., Modi, A., Murtugudde, R., Valsala, V., Panickal, S., Prasanna Kumar, S., Ravichandran, M., Vichi, M., & Lévy, M. (2016). A reduction in marine primary productivity driven by rapid warming over the tropical Indian Ocean. *Geophysical Research Letters, 43*(2), 826–833.

Ryan-Collins, J., Lloyd, T., & Macfarlane, L. (2017). *Rethinking the economics of land and housing*. Zed Books.

Sawada, Y., & Shimizutani, S. (2008). How do people cope with natural disasters? Evidence from the great Hanshin-Awaji (Kobe) Earthquake in 1995. *Journal of Money, Credit and Banking, 40*(2–3), 463–488.

Schumpeter, J. A. (1943 (2010)). *Capitalism, socialism and democracy*. Routledge.

Schumpeter, J. A. (1942). *Capitalism, socialism and democracy*. Harper & Row.

Sharma-Wallace, L., Velarde, S. J., & Wreford, A. (2018). Adaptive governance good practice: Show me the evidence! *Journal of Environmental Management, 222*, 174–184. https://doi.org/10.1016/j.jenvman.2018.05.067

Simmel, G. (1978). *The philosophy of money*. Routledge.

Simon, H. A. (1955). A behavioral model of rational choice. *The Quarterly Journal of Economics, 69*(1), 99–118.

Skidmore, M., & Toya, H. (2002). Do natural disasters promote long-term growth? *Economic Inquiry, 40*(4), 664–687.

Slovic, P. (2000). The perception of risk. In P. Slovic (Ed.), *The perception of Riskp*. London: Earthscan.

Smith, A. (1776). *The wealth of the nation*. https://www.rrojasdatabank.info/Wealth-Nations.pdf

Swedberg, R. (1992). Can capitalism survive? Schumpeter's answer and its relevance for new institutional economics. *European Journal of Sociology, 33*(02), 350. https://doi.org/10.1017/s0003975600006500

Świąder, M., Szewrański, S., & Kazak, J. K. (2020). Environmental carrying capacity assessment—The policy instrument and tool for sustainable spatial

management. *Frontiers in Environmental Science, 8*, 579838. https://doi.org/10.3389/fenvs.2020.579838
Tullock, G. (1967). The economics of slavery. *Left and Right, 3*(2), 5–16.
Turner, R. H., Nigg, J. M., & Paz, D. H. (1986). *Waiting for disaster: Earthquake watch in California*. University of California Press.
Wei, F., & Zhao, L. (2022). The effect of flood risk on residential land prices. *Land, 2022*(11), 1612. https://doi.org/10.3390/land11101612
Wessel, R. H. (1967). A note on economic rent. *The American Economic Review, 57*(5), 12211226.
Williamson, O. E. (1985). *The economic institutions of capitalism firms, markets, Relational Contracting*. China Social Sciences Publishing House Chengcheng Books Limited.
Wisner, B., Blaikie, P., Cannon, T., & Davis, I. (1994). *AT RISK natural hazards, people's vulnerability and disasters*. Routledge.
Wolff, R. D., & Resnick, S. A. (2012). *Contending economic theories: Neoclassical, Keynesian, and Marxian*. MIT Press.
World-Habitat. (2008). *Post-tsunami Reconstruction and Rehabilitation in Sri Lanka*. world-habitat.org. Accessed on 15th September, 2023.
Wright, B. D. (2011). The economics of grain price volatility. *Applied Economic Perspectives and Policy, 33*(1), 32–58. https://doi.org/10.1093/aepp/ppq033
Xenos, N. (1987). Liberalism and the postulate of scarcity. *Political Theory, 15*(2), 225–243.
Zafirovski, M. (2000). The rational choice generalization of neoclassical economics reconsidered: Any theoretical legitimation for economic imperialism? *Sociological Theory, 18*(3), 448–471.

CHAPTER 5

Climate Risk Economics

Climate Change is an everyday reality and not just a slow-onset environmental risk. United Nation's definition of climate change has gotten wider recognition. UN climate action defined climate change as long-term changes in temperature and weather patterns, referred to as climate change. These fluctuations may be caused by significant volcanic eruptions or variations in the sun's activity. However, human activity has been the primary cause of climate change since the 1800s, primarily due to fossil fuels like coal, oil, and gas combustion. Climate change became a state concern in 1988 when the General Assembly resolution declared climate change a common concern of human beings. The Hague Summit 1989 called for new institutions to preserve the environment and global warming. Until 1990, the states intrigued by environmental change were fundamentally Western industrialized nations, and these nations had the most active ecological constituencies and ministries, as well as the majority of the scientific research on climate change (Bodansky, 2001). The Global South countries often follow developed economies' approaches to environmental conservation. Global agreements and treaties dictate the worldwide risk and climate action. United Nations Framework Convention on Climate Change in 1992 proposed a broader definition of climate change. It is defined as, 'adverse effects of climate change", which means changes in the physical environment or biota resulting

S. M. Irshad, *Economics of Disasters and Climate Change*, Sustainable Development Goals Series,
https://doi.org/10.1007/978-981-97-9415-7_5

from climate change that have significant harmful effects on the composition, resilience, *or productivity of natural and managed ecosystems or the operation of socio-economic systems or on human health and welfare. "Climate change" means a change of climate that is attributed directly or indirectly to human activity that alters the composition of the global atmosphere and is in addition to natural climate variability observed over comparable periods.* Climate change does create severe implications for ecology, public health, and the socio-economic system (Zhuang & Zhang, 2020; Li et al., 2019; Hosseinzadehtalaei et al., 2020; Yang et al., 2020). Climate change will impact numerous climatic characteristics and varying effects on numerous sectors (both market and nonmarket). Therefore, the breadth or completeness of the estimates of climate change impacts is a crucial concern (Watkiss, 2011). Despite the widespread belief that climate change results from natural processes, economics is the cause and solution for climate change (Nordhaus, 2013). Finding "the optimal path of carbon pollution" requires balancing the environmental and economic goals (Jaccard, 2014). The financial incentive may facilitate and encourage low-carbon behaviour (Whiteman, 2013).

Climate economics as a concept is colossally related with environmental economics, yet one of the differences in terms of validating the manifestation of risks. Climate economic is another theoretical debate to engage with the impact of climate risk and its economic impacts. Climate economics is an evolutionary-inspired way of thinking combined with a systemic and historical perspective of technology change is necessary to analyze the economics of climate change. It offers a very informative alternative to orthodox economics (Maréchal, 2007). The combination of ideas like "bounded rationality" with an emphasis on economic dynamics brought about by innovation, selection, and accumulation is made possible by evolutionary economics, which results in fresh perspectives on how environmental policy should be framed (van den Bergh et al., 2006). There are studies further assessing that technological advancements are needed to combat climate change, especially in the areas of sustainable practices, energy efficiency, and renewable energy. According to evolutionary economics, policy frameworks should encourage innovation dispersion, technical diversity, and experimentation (Foxon, 2011). Also many economies are "locked-in" to infrastructures and technology that are high in carbon. It will take significant adjustments to cultural norms, investments, and regulations to break out of this lock-in (Unruh, 2000). Societies and economies must become more resilient to the effects of climate change. A framework for comprehending how systems might acquire adaptive capacity through diversification and innovation is provided by evolutionary economics (Folke et al., 2010).

Chapter one of the book explains the need for looking at disaster from an evolutionary perspective. It enables to an integrationist approach to economic impact of climate change. Climate economics links science and politics, converting scientific forecasts about physical systems into easily understood projections about human welfare and economic growth. (Ackerman & Stanton, 2013). It is also assessed that climate economics is also a project integrating various risk assessment model to assess the impacts (Heal, 2017). Scholas examines the financial and job prospects offered by a green economy, emphasizing the room for expansion and innovation in sustainability-related fields (Saha, 2024). Studies also emphasize how crucial mitigation efforts are for lowering greenhouse gas emissions and containing global warming. These tactics include switching to renewable energy sources, enhancing energy efficiency, putting in place carbon pricing mechanisms, and investing in low-carbon technologies (Singla, 2024). A major concern of climate economic is to link the economic decision-making with sustainable development. It highlights the necessity of making demand-side mitigation alternatives more widely available, appealing, and visible rather than depending exclusively on laws or economic policies (Silvi, 2024). The application of sustainability, environmental justice, and precautionary principles to the economic analysis of climate change policies; according to Nordhaus, this suggests a swift and drastic reduction in emissions rather than the idea of "economic optimality", which suggests a sustained increase in emissions over several decades (Roca & Padilla, 2023). Studies also explain how the effects of climate change are linked to human progress, highlighting the reciprocal relationship between environmental issues and financial security (Pan, 2022). Joseph et al. (2020) explains that connection between economics and climate change, emphasizing the direct and indirect financial impacts of climate change. It highlights the importance of these expenses, which are affected by things like the selection of the discount rate. By examining many economic viewpoints on climate change, studies challenge the prevailing narratives in mainstream economics and provide a platform for more in-depth comprehension and sophisticated policy conversations (Roos & Hoffart, 2021).

UN involvement in climate change discourse has influenced global action and made climate change a threat to the 'public good'. It is also an environmental risk, and climate change has influenced the global discourse on the environment, society, and economy. Climate can be defined as a statistical construct derived from the average meteorological phenomena (such as temperature, atmospheric pressure, precipitation, and solar radiation) over 35 years. Without the natural phenomena known as the greenhouse effect, which has existed for millions of years, the Earth would be too cold to support life as we know it (Moffatt, 2004). The greenhouse gas idea has a pretty lengthy history of being a cause of climate change (Plass, 1956; Ramanathan et al., 1985). For instance, Fourier (1827) proposed in 1827 that the atmosphere might be able to hold onto the heat and compared the result to that of a hothouse (greenhouse). Tyndall (1861) investigated the ability of carbon dioxide, water vapour, and other gases to absorb heat in the 1860s. Climate science has extensively researched the natural and human causes of climate risks. Climate change discourse is a relatively recent debate via pollution and other critical environmental risks. The idea and implications of climate change risk move evolutionarily, specifically along with modern developmental discourses. The theory of global warming in the late 1950s began popularizing climate change discourse in industrial capitalist countries and developing economies, which had to wait a few decades to interface with climate risk debates. There are a couple of approaches to climate change, such as the Greenhouse Effect, Anthropogenic Global Warming, Clouds, Albedo and Cosmic Rays, Human Forcings Besides Greenhouse Gases, Ocean outgassing of CO_2, Solar Variability, Ocean Currents, Planetary Motion, Volcanic Activity, and Biological and Chemical Processes. The emissions and warming considerably dictate the climate change discourse, and climate risk economics revolves around these two fundamental indicators. Economic decision-making on emissions also moves around the rate of growth of emissions. It is evident in the mean temperature assessment and is widely accepted as the agent of climate change discourse. There has been an increasing trend of these emissions and global warming over an extended period. The IPCC report (2018) explains that human activities are the primary causes that push 1.0°C of global warming above pre-industrial levels, and global warming is likely to reach 1.5 °C between 2030 and 2052 if it continues to increase at the current rate (IPCC 2018). See Fig. 5.1, which shows the increasing ocean temperature. Figure 5.2 explains the global sea level anomalies, one of the signs of climate change risk.

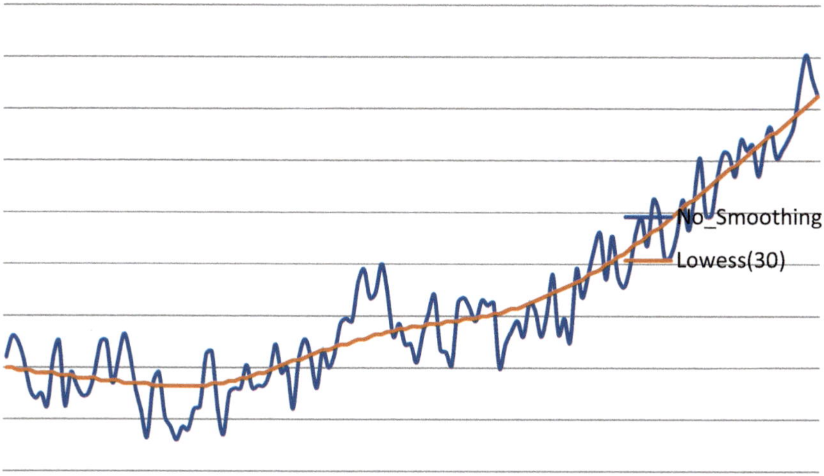

Fig. 5.1 Land–ocean global means temperature (*Source* https://ourworldindata.org/)

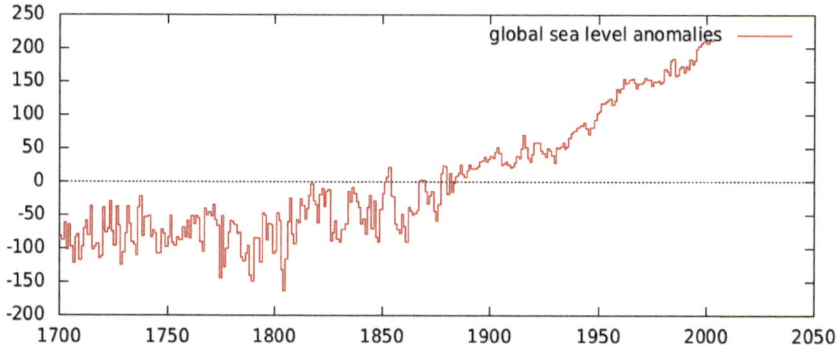

Fig. 5.2 Global sea level rise anomalies (*Source* World Meteorological Organization)

Figures 5.3 and 5.4 refer to the changing nature of climate risk and its relative impact on natural capital regarding risk and depreciation costs. So, its effects are associated with the economic policies and approaches of the area and the country. Therefore, its governance, finance, and actors are highly diverse, complex, and operating at different scales (Rabe, 2007).

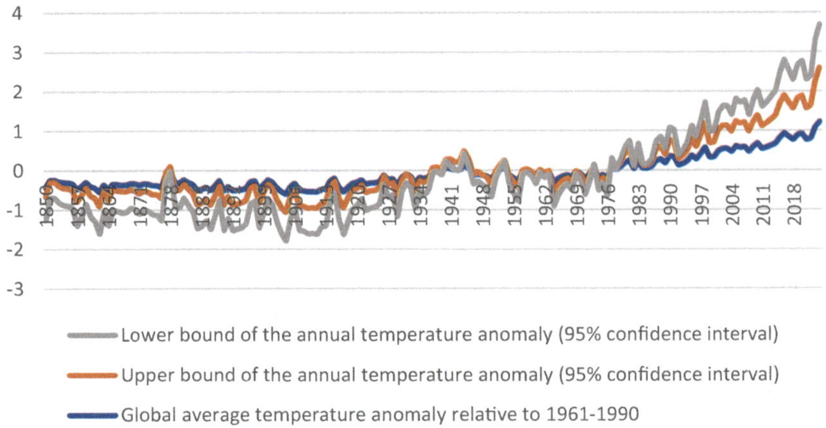

Fig. 5.3 Average temperature anomaly, global (*Source* https://ourworldindata.org/)

Issues related to climate change don't simply fit into one industry. Because climate change affects all aspects of development policy and practice, there are constant requests to mainstream or integrate the issue (Reid et al., 2003). Greenhouse gas emissions from human activity represent a real and immediate threat to the stability of our climate system. We must quickly and strictly shift our consumption patterns to stay below the 2-degree Celsius warming threshold and prevent the worst effects of climate change (Park, 2015). At the global level, CO_2 emission has increased over decades, indicating a growth path and economical use of natural resources.

The gradual increase in emissions could be attributed to industrial and capital-intensive development. Studies argue that, after the industrial revolution, human activities, including combustion, urbanization, automobiles, land-use changes, and the mining of fossil carbon, have significantly increased CO_2 accumulation, which has resulted in climate change (Falkowski et al., 2000; Riahi et al., 2017). Apart from industrial development, urbanization and consumption further added emissions. Parikh and Shukla (1995) study the effect of urbanization and increased resource consumption on greenhouse gas emissions after empirical analysis of the link (Parikh & Shukla, 1995). Since the 1990s, the energy-related CO_2 emissions of newly industrialized economies have

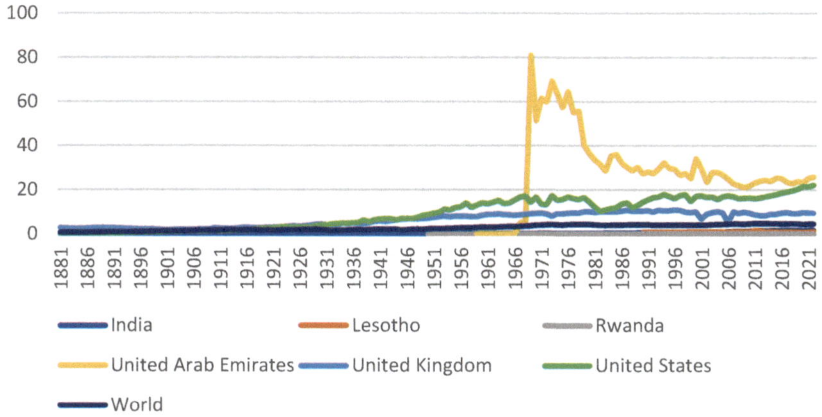

Fig. 5.4 Annual CO_2 emissions (per capita) (*Source* https://ourworldindata.org/)

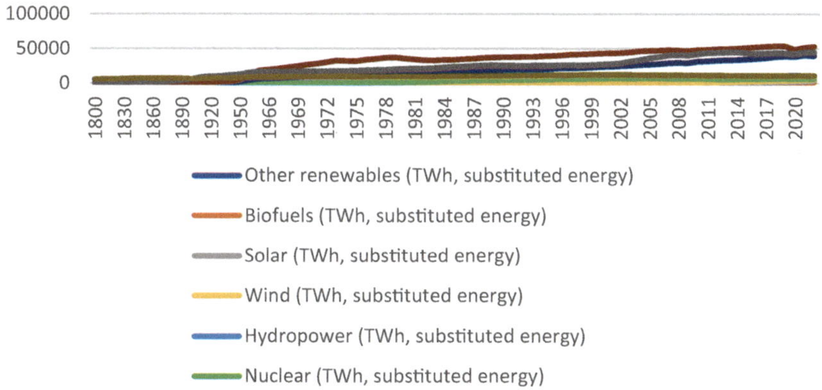

Fig. 5.5 Global electricity production by source

increased significantly compared to those in industrialized nations (Mitić et al., 2023)—energy consumption as part of capital and consumer goods consumption. High carbon-intensive electricity production still dominates global energy production. See Fig. 5.5; these figures indicate the nature of emission, climate, and development risk.

The economy of climate change is located in this critical relationship between emissions, warming, and output of development. Studies also observe that Energy consumption is responsible for extensive carbon emissions (Farhani & Tiwari, 2019). This rising emission needs to be considered as an outcome of an economic process (Yang et al., 2023), which argues that urbanization results in higher concentrations of CO_2. Because of energy-related human activities that are impacted by economic development, CO_2 emissions have been rising (Sadorsky, 2010). A simple correlation between GDP and Carbon emission gives a higher correlation. Nothing is new in that emissions are the outcome of unsustainable economic development.

A central theme in economic and environmental research has been the relationship between GDP and carbon dioxide (CO_2) emissions. The two generally have a positive link, especially in the early phases of economic development. However, as economies develop and move towards more sustainable practices, this relationship may alter. This higher correlation between GDP and CO_2 emission brought sustainable development back to developmental discourses. The idea of sustainable development is, in fact, one of the most popular concepts that has influenced academia, civil society, and the government. No other development programme has such a broad mass appeal and academic imagination in the present-day global economy. However, much more considerable academic appeal and deliberations have not translated into an action mode. No consensus has been reached on putting sustainable development into practice. Popular imagination and pragmatic action are not moving together. One could ascribe this to an institutional failure or inefficiency of the policy. Sustainable development is critically associated with the practice of conserving natural resources. The National Environmental Policy Act of 1969 by the United States of America was considered the first state-level initiative to put administrative instruments on conservation. An attempt by the US government could be read as the first attempt to institutionalize the prevention of environmental damage. The root of sustainable development is traced to the capitalist economic crisis of the early 1960s and the massive public outrage against governments in developing countries. In 1983, the United Nations (UN) came forward. They constituted an expert commission led by Gro Harlem Brundtland to create a framework to persuade the member countries to revisit their approaches to development. It led to the compilation of world-recognized, however, the commission report 'Brundtland Commission Report of 1987' has yet to be implemented. The academia still refers to this report to teach the fundamental ethos of sustainable development, and perhaps this is one of the most celebrated UN reports worldwide. Since the UN assigned it, the commission was not bound by any national interest, and hence, it proposes a globally recognized approach to environmental and development. Though it was not bound by national interest, the report still hardly held capitalism responsible for the ecological crisis. The commission believed that the consumption poor were accountable for the environmental destruction. Though this report by the commission inspired academia and civil societies to a great extent in promoting a concept of responsive capitalism, there are still many critical perspective crises in it. For the first time, the commission recognized the overutilization of resources and accepted that there exists an inequality in accessing resources. Studies validate the environmental Kuznets curve in terms of energy consumption and economic growth (Acaravci & Ozturk, 2010). The EKC hypothesis was found to be valid for China and while FDI inflows had a beneficial influence on China's carbon emissions, the exchange rate and services trade had a negative impact (Zhang & Zhang, 2018). Another study investigates the connection between Vietnam's GDP and CO_2 emissions and finds evidence in favour of the Environmental Kuznets Curve theory (Al-Mulali et al., 2015). Ang (2007) suggests a bidirectional causal relationship between CO_2 emissions and output by examining the long-term relationship between CO_2 emissions, energy consumption, and output. Zhang et al. (2009), in a similar study, observed the connection between China's energy use, carbon emissions, and economic expansion, revealing signs of long-term equilibrium. It is found that global emissions generally tend to slow down as per capita incomes rise. It's possible that affluence drives up demand for environmental conservation. Proposals for reducing emissions that guarantee earnings won't be negatively impacted, especially for less developed nations (LDCs), will have the best chance of being implemented (Tucker, 1995). This study examines the relationship between energy consumption, financial development, economic growth, and CO_2 emissions in Malaysia, emphasizing the contribution of financial development to emissions reduction (Shahbaz et al., 2013). The correlation between consumption and GDP creates long-term economic implications in terms of widening income gap. This income gap determines the long-term impact of climate change.

The period in which the Brundtland Commission came up was critical, and it was the period in which the global economies were subjected to a significant shift. The fall of the Berlin Wall in 1989 and the disintegration of the Soviet Union in 1991 significantly influenced the international political economy. The fall of the socialist block in the worldwide economy ended the state-controlled economy and let the market take over the economy. The institutional form of command economy took centralized decisions, and in a socialist economy, it constituted a system to distribute the resources. The fall of the Berlin Wall and the disintegration of the Soviet Union forced many countries to follow state control and have a mixed economy. The countries that the USSR supported in terms of technology and socialist development patterns influenced the public imagination of development in the third world as well. The welfare state was the most important among them.

Interestingly, the approach of the socialist countries to production was not critically different from other capitalist countries. Mass production and consumption were the strategies of development even in socialist economies. Socialist economies were primarily concentrated in capital goods exports. India was one of the beneficiaries of the USSR's external affairs policy. USSR had extended the technology and capital goods sector in India to a great extent. The socialist and capitalist methods have not made any substantial differences in emission control and sustainable use of resources. However, it is also a fact that modern capitalist development has engaged with climate risk and evolved institutions to deal with risk and develop tools to ensure that climate risk does not stop capital investment. The costs of nonreplaceable and reproducible environmental assets, such as biodiversity and, most likely, species and ecosystems, account for most long-term costs with the extensive capital investment process (Philibert, 1999). The inequality of global economic production has influenced the outcome of the development, including carbon emissions. Capitalism wants to balance emissions and project economic return as the final necessity. Emission is a risk out of development, so governing this risk determines the growth path of an economy. Governing climate risk is first advised at a macro-level as a global advocacy framework, and later on, local strategies are added to the climate risk governance. The following part discusses some treaties concerning emission governance and economic growth.

5.1 The Montreal Protocol 1987

As discussed in chapter three, the Montreal Protocol proposes to protect against the depletion of the Ozone Layer as a regulatory strategy; the protocol states that it '*determined to protect the ozone layer by taking precautionary measures to control equitably total global emissions of substances that deplete it, with the ultimate objective of their elimination based on developments in scientific knowledge, taking into account technical and economic considerations*'. The agreement listed the number of substances that cause the depletion of the ozone layer. The agreement aimed to reduce and finally eliminate the use of ozone-depleting substances. Some scholars observe that bilateral trade agreements can support international environmental governance rather than undermine it (Morin & Bialais, 2018). Montreal protocol is an extended strategy of the standard pool resource theory (Epstein et al., 2014). It emphasizes that common pool resource conservation is necessary for people to survive. It is one of the most flexible treaties and has been amended multiple times. The agreement's biggest concern was the reduction of hydrochlorofluorocarbons (HCFCs) in refrigerators and air conditions. Still, no country that signed the deal can explain its HCFC reduction plan or strategy as it is connected with the market economy. There is a phase-out strategy or HCFC. Studies show that by 2050, the global HCFC emissions will be 9–19% of CO_2 emissions, which is one of the core components of greenhouse gas emissions (Velders et al., 2009; Xiang et al. The government of India has claimed that it could reduce the HCFC considerably. The Government of India report claims that the government would plan to reduce HFCS in four steps from 2032 onwards, and it would reduce to 10% in 2032, 20% in 2037, 30% in 2042, and 85% in 2047 (Press Information Bureau, 18 Aug. 2021). See Fig. 5.6.

Figure 5.6 indicates the emerging trend in global responses towards ozone-depleting emissions. The Montreal Protocol is indeed one of the most successful international environmental treaties. However, scholars have identified various reasons for the success of HCFC reduction. Hydrofluorocarbons (HFCs) have been introduced as replacement substances for both chlorofluorocarbons (CFCs) and hydrochlorofluorocarbons (HCFCs) as a result of the Montreal Protocol and its revisions since they do not destroy stratospheric ozone. (Fortems-Cheiney et al., 2015). Their study shows a seasonal cycle in the HFC-134a emissions 2002, which becomes enhanced over time. The ozone reduction project

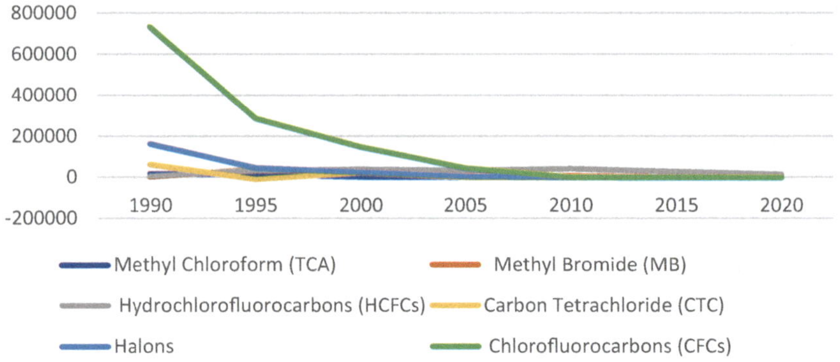

Fig. 5.6 Emissions of substances that deplete the ozone layer (*Source* https://ourworldindata.org/ozone-layer)

got more comprehensive policy and technical support and has been considered a shared pool of resources. Atmospheric air is treated as a common good, and countries plan their policies and projects accordingly. Still, there were apprehensions about the approaches to the Montreal Protocol. Bach and Jain (1990) assess that the current initiatives to reduce chlorofluorocarbons (CFCs) are insufficient. As a result, the Protocol's provisions will be strengthened in 1990. The urgency of revising the Protocol is heightened because ozone-depleting CFCs also have a high greenhouse potential, contributing significantly to climate change. There are multiple perspectives on the zone protection approaches. However, as DuPuis and Gareau (2008) argue, the capitalist knowledge regime influences decision-making. State and capitalists influence policy-making to ensure environmental regulations do not interfere with the market economy. It is a complex governance system, and developing and backward economies are transforming their institutions to move along with market reforms. Market-driven economic policies are increasingly redefining climate action policies, so institutions for implementing climate action programmes, like the Montreal Protocol, are becoming ineffective or weak. Global discussions on climate action include the Kyoto Protocol of 1997 and The Montreal Protocol of 1987.

5.2 Kyoto Protocol and Climate Politics 1997

The Kyoto Protocol was another global commitment to agree with environmental sustainability. It was expected that 192 signatories, in addition to the European Union, would come together to ensure energy efficiency and maintain equity in national economies. The protocol forces industrialized countries to limit greenhouse gas emissions to mitigate global warming. Through the equalization of marginal abatement costs across regions, international trading in emissions dramatically reduces the total costs of Kyoto compliance (Böhringer & Löschel, 2002).

This provision signifies the commitments of relevant international environmental agreements and the promotion of sustainable forest resource management, including afforestation and reforestation. Another feature of the protocol is the promotion of sustainable agriculture with reference to climate change. This is an essential aspect of the climate change debate in India since sustainable agriculture is perhaps the most neglected area in emerging agricultural practices. India's farming community depends on monsoon rains, especially the most vulnerable farmers. Inequality in land ownership and lack of proper irrigation force small and marginal farmers to leave farming to become agricultural workers who continue with subsistence farming or join other informal sectors as workers. Sustainable agriculture is also about the sustainable use of groundwater based on the fact that it is a common property and about suitable coping patterns that can adapt to the changing environment. However, this is the least prioritized in the contemporary Indian farming system. The marginal farmers or workers have adapted to the crisis faster than big farmers. Their adaptation is generally at the cost of the production quantity and not by any displacement from farming alone. Climate change risks in terms of economic and social existence are more visible in the case of marginal farmers. Hence, the need for sustainable farming cannot be denied. It is an inevitable requirement. The protocol reiterates the rationale for having sustainable agriculture more than ever before; however, the responsibility is with the State to implement it.

Kyoto Protocol recommends a policy–level intervention to phase out market imperfections and offers tax benefits and fiscal support to reduce emissions of greenhouse gases in various sectors. The protocol aims to regulate the emissions and transfer technology and money from countries emitting more greenhouse gas to developing countries to set up industries with less emission. The United Nations Environment Programme

(UNEP) (2013) has defined this treaty as '*the goal to lower overall emissions from six greenhouse gases—carbon dioxide, methane, nitrous oxide, sulfur hexafluoride, HFCs, and PFCs—calculated as an average over the 5 years of 2008–2012. National targets range from 8% reductions for the European Union and some others to 7% for the US, 6% for Japan, 0% for Russia, and permitted increases of 8% for Australia and 10% for Iceland*'. This treaty aims to have a global agreement on governing the environment and sharing responsibilities. Hence, any decision by a particular country will have a global impact.

Like the Montreal Protocol, the Kyoto Protocol is also subject to market and economic interests. Studies revealed that the 38 industrialized countries cannot reach their Kyoto Protocol commitments within the specified time frame (Huang et al., 2008). The international community has the challenge of ensuring the implementation of genuine GHG reductions—achieving the Protocol's technical standards without honouring the spirit of the Convention or its long-term goals is feasible. Studies suggest that we require manageable and effective enforcement for the climate change regime to be implemented successfully (Gupta et al., 2003). Like other international commitments, national environmental policies must adapt institutionally to global needs. Emission trading, suggested in Article 17 of the Kyoto Protocol, is subject to multiple interpretations. Under the protocol, countries have to initiate domestic policies to implement the protocol. It is a voluntary, non-enforceable agreement, so the countries decide their priorities. Many countries' Emissions continue to rise despite emission caps under the Kyoto Protocol (Aichele & Felbermayr, 2013). One of the core institutional interventions of the Kyoto Protocol is that it introduced market-based solutions to ensure environmental security. Emission trading opened up another method of 'commodity trade' on behalf of risk reductions. Kyoto Protocol constitutes the concept of cap and trade in which blanket permission to pollute and trade or buy risk is the most significant contribution of the neoliberal system. The World Bank (2023) report explains that the revenue from carbon taxes and emission trade grow over 10% in 2022, reaching almost USD95 billion globally. A carbon tax has been promoted as a practical economic tool for reducing CO_2 emissions by a number of nations, notably China, the nation with the highest carbon emissions worldwide. But reducing carbon emissions cannot be achieved at the expense of economic expansion. To determine the best course for sustainable growth, a careful balance between the two must be found.

It's possible that Northern Europe was the first area to impose a carbon price in order to lower CO_2 emissions. Other nations or areas have also imposed carbon taxes and attained some degree of reduction in carbon emissions, including France, Italy, the Colorado Board in the United States, Quebec, and British Columbia in Canada (Liu et al., 2017). Researchers also show that (Jeff & Owen 2009; Wang et al., 2016), applying a carbon tax has a greater effect on reducing emissions than carbon trading, but it also comes with a lower implementation cost (Cao & Wang 2015). Pereira et al. (2016) demonstrate the necessity of a carbon price in order to cut Portugal's CO_2 emissions by 40% by 2030 compared to 1990 levels using a dynamic general equilibrium model. Evidence from empirical studies indicates a positive and significant long- and short-term relationship between GDP and energy consumption and CO_2 emissions. Lastly, it is advised that governments concentrate on lowering pollution, particularly in nations with high carbon emissions. In addition, nations that require a reduction in the use of coal and oil as a source of energy could contribute to lowering CO_2 emissions in order to save the environment (Choudhury et al., 2023). The success of a market-driven emission reduction depends on multiple factors, and trading alone hardly makes emission reduction possible. Studies demonstrate that the carbon market efficiently reduces carbon emissions. However, the market mechanism does not achieve this policy outcome (Lin & Huang, 2022). Also, it is argued that emission trading results in the world's greatest-ever privatization of natural assets (Hepburn, 2007). Carbon trading promotes emissions and prevents the development of policy alternatives such as carbon taxes and control (Meckling, 2011). Emission trading has become another commodity, a legitimate tool for pollution. The effectiveness of carbon trading in reducing environmental risk has not yet been demonstrated.

The Kyoto Protocol made government and economic agencies accountable for risk reduction. However, the method adopted by the protocol is market-driven, entirely in tandem with the neoliberal idea of the market. The significant contribution of this protocol is that it brought an international market-based consensus on environmental regulation, especially demonstrating the roles and responsibilities of governments, cutting across geopolitical and economic differences. The carbon market and the financial benefits put undue responsibility and restrictions on developing countries. Some examples prove that carbon trading benefits sustainable development. See Box 5.1

Box 5.1 Carbon trade and local conservation in backward economies

A carbon financing program in Kenya, which protects over 500,000 acres of vulnerable forest and helps animal conservation by securing a migration corridor, benefits thousands of people. Between Kenya's two most significant protected areas, Tsavo East and Tsavo West National Parks, which comprise 4% of the nation's total land area, is where Wildlife Works' Kasigau Corridor REDD + Project is located. Throughout the project's 30-year lifespan, 30 million tonnes of CO_2 emissions are anticipated to be saved

The Kenyan government is also working to reduce charcoal production and illegal logging. According to Rose Akombo, Assistant Director of the Kenya Forest Service, "the Kenyan government has considered charcoal production as a serious issue, which led to the enactment of 2009 rules to regulate the production of charcoal." The Kenya Forest Service can now encourage sustainable charcoal production in the dryland areas, which comprise more than 80% of Kenya's land mass. Tim Christophersen, the UN-REDD coordinator at UNEP, said, "The governments in Eastern Africa have recognized the importance of the charcoal trade and the illegal timber trade and have asked the United Nations for support

The project produces over 1 million Voluntary Emission Reductions, a carbon offset that may be purchased or sold. Nearly 150,000 rural residents receive water and educational benefits from the offset sales revenue. It has also led to 300 locals receiving direct work; some are former poachers and illegal loggers

Source Communities and Forests Reaping Benefits of Carbon Trading. 2015. https://www.unep.org/news-and-stories/press-release/communities-and-forests-reaping-benefits-carbon-trading

It also recognizes the importance of the conservation of resources as part of carbon crediting. This protocol would help reduce the risk of hazards and vulnerability related to climate change. It is still ironic that the Kyoto Protocol has been unable to regulate carbon emissions in developed industrial countries or persuade them to reduce them at the cost of business interests. Third-world economies have become responsible for implementing the protocol and imposing regulations. The risk is not equally shared among the countries; the burden is more on low-income people. Kyoto Protocol is increasingly losing its significance concerning persistent risk to low-income people. For people with low incomes in third-world countries, the state policy is closer to them rather than this protocol. Over time, the Kyoto Protocol has offered economic incentives to poor countries to participate in the carbon market. The neoliberal approach to carbon trading does not give any substantial option for carbon justice, and the market idea of carbon trading impacts the negotiations at the cost of environmental risk and disaster. Montreal Protocol and Kyoto Protocol have colossal potential to regulate environmental risks; however, implementing these tools is neoliberal. Every climate treaty since the Kyoto Protocol discusses various options to reach a consensus on emission reduction; however, the consensus is determined by the economic interests of the countries and the sectors leading global capitalist production. The Paris Agreement in 2015 again discusses the possibilities of reducing global greenhouse gas emissions to keep the rise in global temperature to well below two °C above pre-industrial levels and pursuing efforts to limit it to 1.5 °C above pre-industrial levels. Also, suggest financial support to build resilience and capacity to reduce the emission target. Paris Agreement connects climate change, sustainable development, and poverty. The implementation of the agreement is dependent on the political will and economic efficiency of the countries. Developed industrial countries prefer not to take responsibility for the emission risks, and risk is unequally spread, and financial benefits are concentrated in high-income countries. The Paris Agreement encouraged the countries to share a long-term vision about the significance of fully implementing technology development and transfer under Article 10 of the Paris Agreement. Another agreement is defined in Article 11 of the Paris Agreement, which provides a significant and sustainable capacity-building framework to enable developing nations to mitigate and adapt to climate change effectively. There is enough data available to prove that the parties, i.e., countries, are not able to make policies and programmes at the national level to reduce the temperature and emissions. The climate agreement, including the Paris Agreement, is a non-binding political commitment (Durney, 2017). It is voluntary, so as said, it needs political obligations; however, the political economy does matter in determining climate action.

5.3 Climate Change and Asset Risks

Unlike disasters, climate risks such as emissions result in a gradual decline in economic output. Hence, the financial risk of climate change is a decisive factor in countries experiencing higher factor output. These climate impacts exacerbate weather and land conditions for agriculture, resulting in production losses due to natural disasters (Deryugina & Hsiang, 2014). The global discourse on climate economics concerns fluctuating GDP and emissions. By 2050, rising temperatures and altered monsoon rainfall patterns brought about by climate change in India might cost the country 2.8% of its GDP and lower living standards for almost half of its people (Mani et al., 2018). Climate change could cause India to lose between 3 and 10% of its GDP yearly by 2100 (Kompas et al., 2018). Taking into account direct spillover and capital losses, climate change has resulted in a population-weighted GDP loss of 6.3% worldwide in 2022. It is estimated that the unweighted percentage of lost global GDP is 1.8%, or roughly $1.5 trillion. The disparity between those two figures indicates the unequal distribution of impacts (Rising, 2023). A study based on a panel data set of 174 countries from 1960 to 2014 found that per capita actual output is adversely affected by changes in temperature (Kahn et al., 2019). Economic losses due to weather-induced disasters are a reality, and they impact economic decision-making as well. See Fig. 5.7, which demonstrates the impact of climate change on GDP, a critical aspect of climate change at the time.

One could prove the linkages of climate change and development to see the implications of emissions on everyday aspects of the economy. Chapter four gives a detailed account of the relationship between disaster and vulnerable assets. Climate risk is another factor that pushes the marginal productivity of the output down.

$$GDP(t) = (GDP)\_(0.e) \int\_o^\wedge t(g - d(\Delta T(t)))\mathrm{d}\tau$$

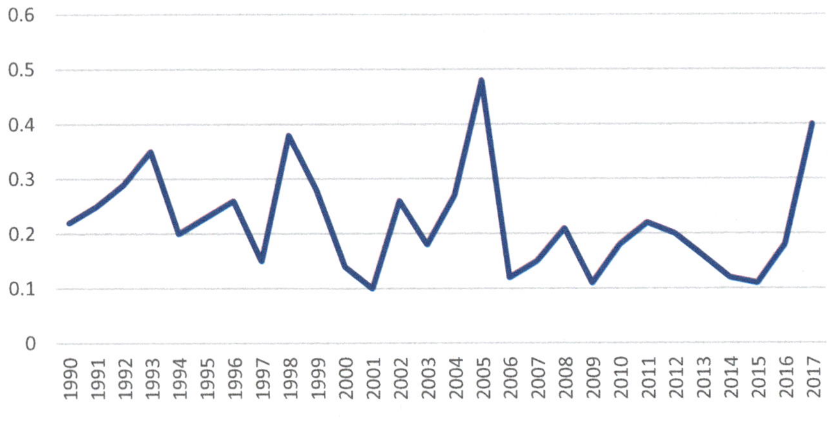

Fig. 5.7 Weather disaster losses as % of global GDP (Munich Re) [*Source*: https://ourworldindata.org/grapher/weather-losses-share-gdp (accessed on 06/13/2024)]

$GDP\_(t)$ is the initial GDP, g is the natural growth rate of the economy without climate impact, and $d(\Delta T)$ represents the negative impact of temperature change on economic growth. $d(\Delta T)$ could be sectoral losses Economies prefer a sustained GDP to indicate progress; hence, higher marginal efficiency of capital and Keynesian theory of practical demands are logically correlated. Still, the trade-off between emissions and capital assets determines the economic impact of climate risk. Higher capital growth leads to emissions; emission reduction is otherwise called controlling supernormal profits. The excess returns a company generates above and above the typical profit threshold are called supernormal, economic, or abnormal profits. Average profit, often known as the opportunity cost of capital, is the minimal profit required for a business to stay competitive. When total revenue (explicit and implicit expenses combined) exceeds total costs, supernormal profits result. Since there are no entry barriers and all items are similar, businesses in entirely competitive marketplaces usually make average profits over the long term. Any transient supernormal gains draw in new competitors, which raises supply and drives down prices until only average profits remain (Mankiw, 2020). On the other hand, because of entry hurdles, product differentiation, and market dominance, businesses can maintain supernormal profits in imperfectly competitive markets, including oligopolies, monopolies, and monopolistic competition (Pindyck & Rubinfeld, 2018; Varian, 2014). The correlation also proved the higher significance of GDP and emissions, and one could argue that the extent of risk the global economy is facing now is, indeed, the negative externalities of supernormal profit-making. This logical connection between profits and emissions poses multiple challenges to economic policy-making, and various climate summits show unequal negotiations on emission reduction. This could be why climate change discourse dictates and overrules environmental discourses. The economist has done various assessments and developed a framework to engage with the climate risks. Nordhaus (1992) developed a Dynamic Integrated Model of Climate and the Economy (DICE) to see how climate change influences economic decision-making. The DICE model offers a comprehensive framework to connect economic output and climate change. The DICE model starts with assessing the economic outcome

$$Y_t = A_t K_t^{\alpha} L_t^{1-\alpha}$$

Y_t = Economic output, A_t is the total factor productivity at time t, k_t is the capital stock at time t, L_t is the labour (or population) at time t, α the capital share in income.

The combination of production factors determines the economic output of an economy. However, this model is standard across all financial systems, and the capitalist production process controls the production process. Expanding the economy's capital base does not mean total public capital only, and in the current global economy, it is also largely private capital.

$$K_{t+1} = (1 - \delta)K_t + I_t$$

K_t is the cpaital stock evoble over a period of time,
δ the depreciation value of capital assets, I_t investment at time t.

The economy constantly assesses the depreciation value, an integral part of production. Depreciation is a deduction; the economy keeps capital to replace the depreciation cost. The depreciation value is deducted from the profit. In the context of climate risks, depreciation happens as a reduction in the marginal efficiency of capital assets and is not always reflected in the immediate economic return. Also, the fact that, like disasters, climate-induced marginal utility loss is critical for those assets (including natural capital) that are vulnerable to environmental risks. The DICE model needs to be discussed in this very crucial context, which added emission into this linear production function. As said before, emission is an inevitable outcome of capital accumulation, so reducing or mitigating it is another economic activity. Emission reduction is possible either by cutting short the capitalist output or by a new source of capital to invest in mitigation. Conventional disaster management discourses consider mitigation as a broader perspective that starts with risk identification. Mitigation recognizes possible risks and evaluates their impact and likelihood. This stage is essential for prioritizing mitigation activities and determining what needs to be mitigated (Smith, 2013). Risk mitigation plans are indeed structural and local or regionally specific. However, climate change discourses outsource mitigation methods, and they become transferable commodities. Disaster management focuses on the area-specific items of 'disaster-prone' areas. A geographical area prone to disaster is otherwise defined as an area wherein the natural resource values are less and marginal productivity is low. Risk-prone areas are where hazards are demonstrated, and risk is manifested in different forms. A disaster-prone area could be defined as a geographical region prone to multiple hazards. In such areas, hazard risks are considered inevitable, meaning that hazards occur at a particular frequency and can potentially harm human life. This is not just about people who are vulnerable due to socio-economic reasons; vulnerability is beyond the conventional understanding of poverty and inequality. Disaster-prone areas are where most people with low incomes live and make a living. However, climate-induced risk and uncertainty create other disaster-prone areas that differ from the conventional method of classifying disaster-prone areas. Changes in weather due to climate variability spread the risk and uncertainty across the community, and it often moves beyond administrative boundaries. The administrative and physical areas focus on disaster risk assessment and will not survive for long. Climate risk widened the boundary of disaster beyond geographical and administrative intervention, and hence, the classification of 'disaster-prone area' needs to be reclassified. In climate change discourses, mitigation is not restricted to the physical boundary of the disaster-prone area or place of origin of the hazards. The shifting of the mitigation process from a specific area or a physical boundary to larger areas beyond a given territory. This shifting of mitigation space resulting a situation in which the agent or cause of risk becomes a neutral agent. It could not make a system to identify a particular agent or cause that results in climate risk. It is a huge business success and enables the capitalist industrial economies to transfer risk. Transfer of risk is otherwise called emission trade. Emission is an economic output, i.e., depreciation costs. So, the replacement cost, otherwise called mitigation costs and economic production, should include the mitigation costs. So, if we use Nordhaus's (1992) model, the Emission E_t would be,

$$E_t = \sigma_t(1 - \mu_t)\,Y_t \text{ Sigma } \sigma_t \text{ is the emissions intensity of output.}$$

$$\mu_t \text{ is the emissions reduction rate } \left(\text{mitigation effort}\right) \text{ at time } t.$$

Emission reduction rates determine the supranormal profit of industrial capitalism. The DICE model gives a normative structure. However, it is not as simple and regular as the model envisages; the cost of mitigation or profit from the carbon trade governs the mitigation risk. It isn't easy to make a statistical correlation between profit and emissions. Emission reduction itself is a capital investment in developed industrial capitalist countries, and for developing and underdeveloped countries, mitigation is cost means regulation of industries and conservation of natural capital.

The carbon cycle formation, as explained by Nordhaus (1992), is defined as,

The atmospheric concentration of CO_2 creation

$M_{t+1} = M_t + E_t - \beta(M_t - M_{\text{Pre}})$, M_t is the atmospheric CO_2 Concentration at the time t, β is the rate at which CO_2 is removed from the atmosphere, M_{Pre} is the pre-industrial CO_2 concentration.

M_t is the profit of capitalism and β is the cost of risk mitigation. The critical question is the cost of risk sharing and compromised profits. Capitalism seldom surrenders profits; however, it is institutionally capable of finding tools for economic risk governance.

Carbon removal is a globally accepted and celebrated process, and there are many techniques for removing carbon dioxide from the atmosphere directly, including extracting the gas straight from the atmosphere. In addition to more technological and engineered methods like direct air capture and carbon mineralization, biomass with carbon removal and sequestration, and ocean-based carbon removal, these include natural methods like tree restoration and agricultural soil management. The degree to which emissions are decreased, how quickly they do so, and the degree to which the temperature "overshoots" the 1.5-degree objective will determine how much CO_2 removal (CDR) or harmful emissions are needed (Naimoli, 2021). The IPCC report explains the scenarios that keeping global warming to less than two °C is possible through carbon dioxide removal techniques in addition to decreases in greenhouse gas emissions from human activities like burning fossil fuels and changing land use (Smith et al., 2016). β i.e., could also be the rate at which carbon removal needs economic planning and investments. β is otherwise defined as mitigation. This chaperone discusses this in detail.

Figure 5.1 gives a detailed account of rising global mean temperatures and carbon emissions. Song et al. (2023) use statistical tools to see the correlation between temperature and GDP, and their study agrees with the fact that rising temperature affects the economy. Bansal and Ochoa (2011), in their research, argue that temperature is a source of aggregate financial risk. Some studies demonstrate that increased temperature lowers GDP per capita growth, but only for poor countries' total factor productivity (Dell et al., 2012; Henseler & Schumacher, 2019). Some studies demonstrated that increased temperature hurts GDP growth but do not find differential impacts between rich and poor countries (Burke et al.,

2015). Like emissions, global mean temperature influences the GDP, and one needs to see the economic differences in the sources of increasing temperature. See Fig. 5.8.

Figure 5.8 explains that high-income countries are responsible for more than 50% of global warming, which causes increases in global mean temperature. Though the high-income countries are responsible for global warming, it does not mean that these economies are exposed to economic risks. Economists and international and economic forums have expressed concern about this complex issue. Bilal and Känzig (2024) study observed that a one °C increase in global temperature leads to a 12% decline in world GDP. Hallegatte et al. (2016) observed that just 0.8% of the world's CO_2 emissions were produced in 2011 by the 900 million people (or 13% of the total population) who resided in the 50 poorest nations. It is also estimated that 10% of the wealthiest population in the world is responsible for 49% of carbon emissions (Kartha et al., 2020). These data sources demonstrate that climate risks such as carbon emission and global warming create an unequal society and economy.

Figure 5.9 demonstrates the critical aspect of climate risk discourse about its unequal impacts, and the percentage-wise calculation cannot capture the low-income countries' consumption base emissions. It's pretty low compared to the high-income countries. The international negotiations on climate change often set aside this crucial fact about climate

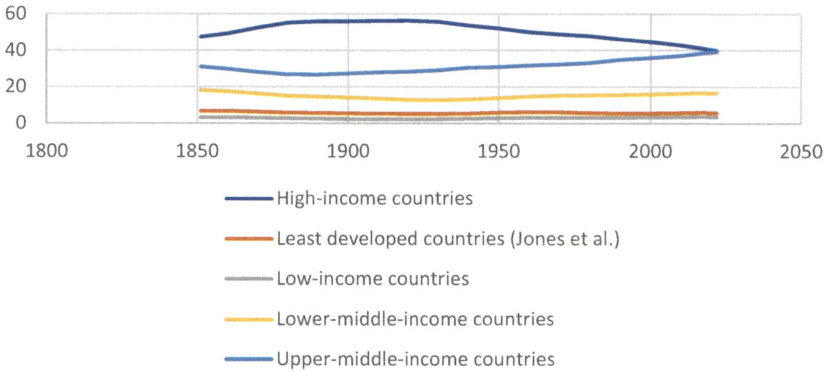

Fig. 5.8 Global warming: contributions to the change in global mean surface temperature, 1851–2022 in % terms (*Source* https://OurWorldInData.org/co2-and-greenhouse-gas-emissions)

risks. The DICE model offers a broader perspective on understanding the increasing temperature dynamics. The DICE model discusses the need to optimize the temperature. It demonstrates the changes in global mean temperature.

Temperature Dynamics

$$T_{t+1} = T_t + k(F_t - \lambda(T_t - T_{Pre}))$$

where T_t is the global mean temperatuer at the time of t, k is the climate sensitivity parameter, F_t is the radiative force at the time of t, λ is the feedback parameter, T_{Pre} is the pre-industrial temperatuer.

This model is generally used to predict the temperature provided if the system assesses or gives a specific value for k, λ and T_{Pre}. Vale of these three parameters depends on the history of events and data. The values indeed represent economic interests and local dynamics in governing the environment. It explains that temperature is a decisive factor in determining the value, and again, these values are influenced by economic decisions.

The economics of climate change is about the economic damage due to climate change and its externalities. Nordhaus (1992), in the DICE

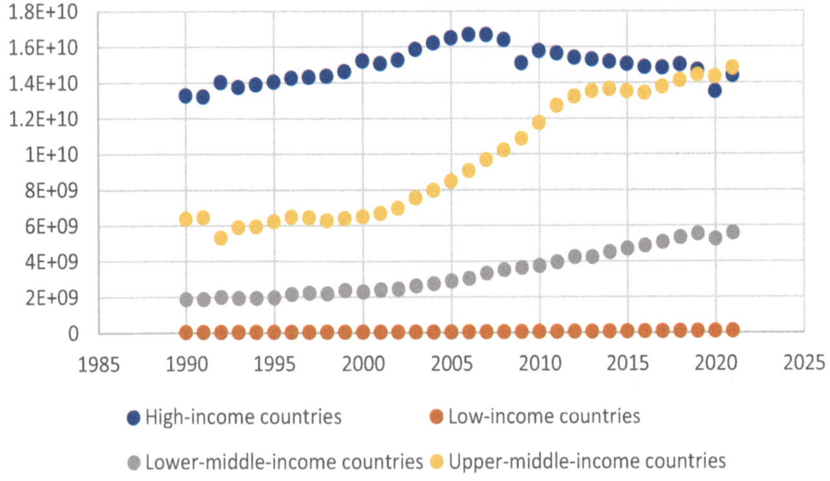

Fig. 5.9 Consumption-based CO_2 emissions, 2021 [*Source* https://ourworldindata.org/grapher/consumption-co2-emissions (accessed on 19-06-2024)]

model, defines economic damage due to climate risk. D_t as

$$D_t = \Omega(T_t)Y_t$$

where $\Omega(T_t)$ is the relationship between temperature at time t (T_t) and economic damage.

$$\Omega(T_t) = \frac{1}{1 + \theta_1 T_t + \theta_2 T_t^2}$$

θ_1 and θ_2 are parameters, Y_t the economic output at the time of t.

It demonstrates that economic damage is a function of temperature and a product of economic output. The function $\Omega(T_t)$ modifies the economic damage caused by temperature fluctuations. This model can calculate the potential economic effects of temperature variations brought on by climate change. This model is a brilliant articulation of financial damage due to climate risks. However, the economic damage depends on the asset value and dependencies. A developed capitalist economy perceives the function $\Omega(T_t)$. In the given capitalist framework in which it wants to protect the asset value and global share of economic production. For developing and underdeveloped economies, the function $\Omega(T_t)$ represent both negative and positive externalities in terms of emission, temperature, and carbon trade so that it could be

$$\Omega(T_t) - R$$

R could be the economic return from carbon trade and the cost of mitigation, if any; the cost of mitigation depends on the size and nature of the economy in terms of investment and governing the risks. Nordhaus (1992) emphasizes social welfare in the DICE model. However, its application needs to be examined in light of the changing nature of climate change. Social welfare has a different meaning in developed and developing market economies and in poor and underdeveloped economies. The society in these economies connects social welfare to climate justice. The informed and economically capable society of developed capitalist economies prefers effective risk governance to price the risk and wants to focus on risk trading as the social impact of climate risks. According to Nordhaus, maximize the social welfare in which the present value of utility over time.

$$w = \Sigma_{t=0}^{T} \frac{U(C_t, L_t)}{(1 + p)^t}$$

W is the social welfare. Whereas

$$U(C_t, L_t) \text{ is the utility function in the form of} U(C_t, L_t) = L_t \frac{c^{1-\eta} - 1}{1^{-\eta}}$$

C_t is the consumption at the time of t, p is the pure rate of social time preference, η is the elasticity of marginal utiiyt of consumption.

The DICE model uses these equations to solve for the optimal path of variables such as consumption, C_t, investment I_t, and mitigation efforts η_t. At maximizing social welfare while considering the economic and climate dynamics. Social welfare is a broader concept associated with the welfare state approach. It is still in the imagination of people in developing countries like India, which has implemented privatization and marketization; however, it still needs to ensure the public good.

Climate justice represents the political economy of climate damage management. Climate justice represents global inequality in emissions. The bulk of past carbon emissions have come from the developed nations of the Global North, so it is their responsibility to frame climate justice from this historical perspective (Gignac & Matthews, 2015). Some scholars support both attempts to increase economic fairness and a climate change accord. However, they present a compelling argument that leaving out provisions intended to correct past wrongs against developing nations or transfer wealth is the best—and maybe the only—way to achieve an effective climate deal (Posner & Weisbach, 2010). Climate justice is a project to correct historical injustices against poor countries and marginal communities. Low-income groups are more likely to reside in locations susceptible to catastrophic weather occurrences and frequently lack the means necessary to adapt to climate change (Bullard, 2007). Given the enormous harm caused by climate change, it emphasizes how urgent it is to resolve climate change mitigation as a question of justice. It involves splitting the cost of adaptation and mitigation (Moellendorf, 2015).

Climate justice could be conceived as

$$J = k(Q, S, D)$$

J is the climate justice index, Q is the quality of life, S is the social welfare, and D is the damage.

$$J = \alpha\left(\frac{Q}{D}\right) + \beta S - \gamma C$$

α, β, and γ are value and C mitigagtion costs.

It suggests that climate justice is related to good quality of life and social welfare and negatively correlates with damage. So, the economic process pushes the emission and damage, which does not ensure climate justice, though it is a requirement. Climate justice is not about an organized reduction plan; rather, it could be regulated by current consumption.

5.4 Climate Risk and Economics of Mitigation

Climate change triggers natural calamities and economic losses. Extreme occurrences are known to be triggered by rapidly changing climatic circumstances and are predicted to increase in frequency shortly. There is a chance that frequent climate-related calamities could make it more difficult for a nation to recover and get ready for future occurrences, which would eventually make vulnerable populations even more vulnerable (Cappelli et al., 2021). The Intergovernmental Panel on Climate Change (IPCC) predicts that as greenhouse gas concentrations in the atmosphere rise, these occurrences will become even more frequent and powerful (IPCC, 2018). IPCC (2012) report explains that the frequency, severity, length, timing, and spatial extent of weather and climatic extremes are all affected by climate change, which can produce previously unheard-of extremes. The effects of climate change will balance out and become more negative as time goes on, with an increasing number of irreversible effects like ecosystem loss (Van Aalst, 2006). There is a rising number of disaster events in general, along with extreme temperatures and weather events. See Fig. 5.10.

Figure 5.9 explains disaster events, including extreme weather and temperature events. Figure 5.11 tells another case in which climatological disasters impact the global economy. The person affected by climatological disasters has increased over time, and the number is almost similar in economies irrespective of their income status. Among them, India's experience is unique in that its number is high compared to the rest of the

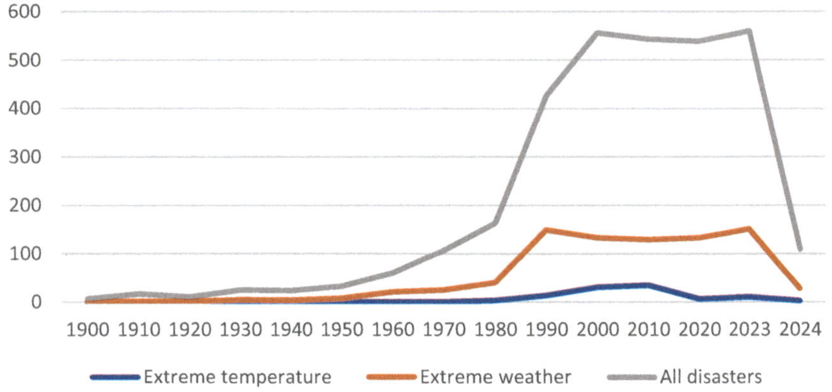

Fig. 5.10 Number of disaster events from 1900 to 2024 (*Source* EM-DAT, CRED)

countries. This simple mathematics indicates how vulnerable society is to climatological disasters and indicates institutional incapability to reduce climate-induced impacts.

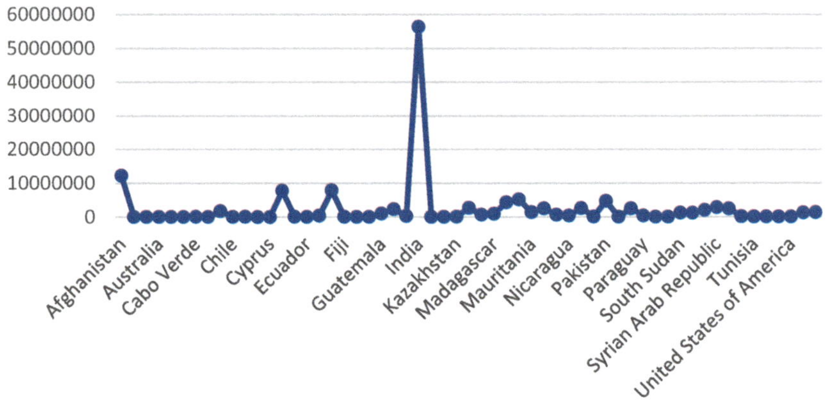

Fig. 5.11 People affected by every single climatological disaster event in the world 2012–2021 (*Source* www.emdat.be/data)

Mitigating climate risk is a global concern. However, it is practised at the local level. Scholars observe that countries that cannot afford preventive actions or where only a tiny portion of the population can access resources that provide resilience are more vulnerable to climatic disasters (Berlemann & Wenzel, 2018; Noy, 2009; Tol & Leek, 1999). Groups that experience adversities and are susceptible to prejudice, discrimination, and stigmatization because of their age, gender, race/ethnicity, socio-economic status, physical or cognitive abilities, etc., are known as vulnerable populations (Benevolenza & DeRigne, 2018).

In a country like India, many people are occupied in the geographical area that experiences climate risks. Asset vulnerability is a reality; hence, building climate resilience depends on the economic structure and capability of the economy. As said before, size and the economy's linkages matter in determining the financial resilience to climate risks. The climate risk score prepared by independent data sources supports the argument that higher risk results in higher-order GDP losses. See Fig. 5.12.

Figure 5.11 is a general observation of the interface between climate risk and GDP losses, and it is a fact that extreme climate risk has resulted

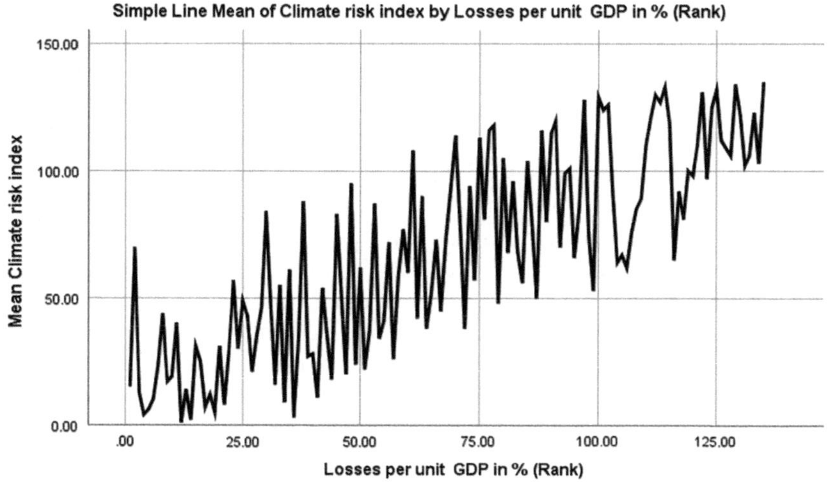

Fig. 5.12 Climate risk and GDP Losses

in loss of income. It could be interpreted as

$$\Delta GDP_t = \beta \times CR_t$$

ΔGDP_t is the GDP loss at the time t due to climate risk, β is a coefficient representing the sensitivity of the economy to climate risk, CR_t is the climate risk factor at a time t.

β is the critical point that explains how the climate risk pushes the value of economic resources down. The value of β is the decisive factor in determining climate change's impact on economic assets. Beta is highly influenced by capitalist market economies, in which the asset value is associated with positive economic externalities. It is also about economic resilience; extreme temperatures and emissions affect the economic resilience of assets. Poor resilience restricts the externalities of the economic process and results in inequalities. Studies show that an additional 1 degree Celsius increase in temperature results in an increment of 0.56 points of the GINI index with a standard error of 0.26. It is also assessed that temperature increases substantially reduce economic growth (Dell et al., 2012). A one-percent increase in temperature during the winter resulted in a 1.12% drop in agricultural production. It was also revealed that a 1% increase in temperature fluctuation during winter and spring resulted in a 0.09 and 0.14% drop in agricultural production in the Middle East and North Africa region (Alboghdady & El-Hendawy, 2016). Dang et al. (2023) in their study proved that one degree Celsius (i.e., 1 °C) an annual increase in temperature produces headcount poverty increases of 0.9, 1.8, and 2.3% points, respectively, using the daily poverty thresholds of \$1.90, \$3.20, and \$5.50. Azzurri and Signorelli (2020) demonstrate that a one-degree increase in long-term temperature is connected with a 2.8% point increase in poverty in 24 Sub-Saharan African nations. Also, Paglialunga et al. (2022), using panel data from 150 countries, argue that a one-percent temperature increase is associated with a 0.5% point increase in the Gini index. Dasgupta et al. (2023) further establish that income inequality increases with higher temperatures and low with decreasing temperatures. These facts proved that climate risk results in differential impact, and poor and backward economies are more exposed to climate change risks. The market economy and capitalist production are responsible for the massive impact apart from natural causes.

Furthermore, heat waves and droughts caused by temperature anomalies reduce agricultural productivity. Lesk et al. (2016) concluded that droughts and heat waves reduced worldwide grain productivity by 9–10% from 1964 to 2007. Furthermore, Li et al. (2009) found that primary grain yields are predicted to drop by more than 50% by 2050. This drop in yield and productivity upsets the equilibrium of food supply and demand, resulting in inflation (Odongo et al., 2022; Parker, 2018). Hristov et al. (2020) correlate global warming with a 49% loss in wheat production by 2050. However, Ciscar et al. (2011) predict that Northern Europe will see a 0.5–0.8% increase in agricultural welfare by 2080. In contrast, agriculture in Brazil is likely to be affected by global warming, with a 74% movement out of the "optimal climate space" by 2060 (Rattis et al., 2021). In one study, global hunger by 2050 has been expected to affect an additional 160 million people under strong mitigation policies relative to the no-climate policy baseline scenario. However, this is before the repercussions of climate damage are included (Fujimori et al., 2019). However, the market and capitalist model never wants to mitigate the risk at the cost of economic growth. These facts necessitate a critical inquiry into climate risk mitigation, adaptation, carbon trading, and alternatives.

5.5 Climate Finance

Climate finance is the term used to describe local, national, or international funding obtained from public, private, and alternative financial sources to assist climate change adaptation and mitigation initiatives. The Paris Agreement, the Kyoto Protocol, and the Convention all demand that Parties with more significant financial resources provide financial support to those who are less wealthy and more vulnerable. This acknowledges the wide variations in countries' contributions to climate change and their ability to prevent it and deal with its effects. The institution and capital for climate finance are in the neoclassical framework. As explained in the previous chapter, one of the essential contributions of the neoclassical production function is the law of diminishing marginal utility. This is a simple assumption. It explains that every additional input of factors of production increases the production, yet the output per factor input becomes lesser as the factor input goes up. This process is defined as the marginal productivity of the factor input. It is an essential aspect of risk-based investments in developing countries, wherein the marginal productivity of factor inputs fluctuates with the extent of risk. Another critical dimension of the neoclassical model is the importance of a return to scale. It assumes that a change in the factor inputs leads to a change in output. Risk governance is, in principle, based on the neoclassical theory. The central concern of neoclassical theory is the diminishing returns (Fingleton & Fischer, 2009). From a neoclassical point of view, consistent losses allude to the possibility that as extra units of variable info are added to a proper measure of different data sources, the negligible efficiency of the variable info will ultimately diminish. This is because of variables like restricted assets, fixed extents of sources of info, or the failure to use extra information sources completely. Diminishing returns or marginal return of value leads to risk returns. Climate risks and recurring disasters are risk returns due to diminishing capital returns. Chapter one of this book discusses sustainable development. Park (2015) calls it climate capitalism since capitalism cannot assess the value of natural resources.

The theory of climate financing needs to be studied in the neoclassical framework, primarily as a strategy to enhance the marginal productivity of capital assets, and decades of supernormal profit-oriented economic production resulted in a near-stationary stage in global capitalist production. Climate finance should be considered from this critical context in which it becomes an inevitable investment. Though the policymakers call it mitigation, the capital is still from the profit only, i.e., the source of profit should finance the risk mitigation. The 16th Conference of Parties to the United Framework Convention on Climate Change (UNFCCC) in Cancun 2010 pledged to raise USD 100 billion in international climate financing annually by 2020. Climate stabilization is a global public good that benefits everyone, regardless of a country's democratic standing or traditions. Climate finance decisions cannot and should not be made without norms. A vast array of binding agreements, treaties, resolutions, rules, and principles (Schalatek, 2012). It will also play an important role in widening our range of probable future outcomes by allowing us to predict the risk of conflict more correctly if mitigation measures fail and even more severe climate-related damages occur (Gilmore & Buhaug, 2021). Because of the financial challenges associated with global adaptation, specific individuals must be held accountable for prior climate change harms. More specifically, these people are "outcome responsible" (Miller, 2004, 2007), which means they bear the primary responsibility for their carbon-depleting actions because they purposefully constructed an adverse circumstance in a morally acceptable manner. The wider popularity of climate finance as a public good provided enough opportunities for the agents of risk to develop tools and methods to finance it. The international climate finance system exhibits a mitigation bias. Therefore, this bias needs to be addressed to achieve the Cancun Accord's goal of pursuing adaptation and mitigation with equal priority (Abadie et al., 2012); it is also about setting the right price for climate externalities (Nordhaus, 2013). The global negotiations and movement for climate justice have placed mitigation as a remedy, and financing is a collective responsibility. Country like India set up institutions at the public cost to mitigate climate risks, and agents of risk become one of the stakeholders of the risk and not the only source of risks. The most critical one is the carbon trade options.

5.6 Economic of Carbon and Climate Finance

The most significant contribution of global negotiations on climate change is the transformation of risk as a commodity, i.e., carbon trade. The emission has been demonstrated as a risk that pushes the marginal efficiency of capital assets and output value.

$$\text{Net Emissions} = \text{Total Emissions} - \text{Purchased Carbon Credits} \\ + \text{Sold Carbon Credits}$$

This simple logic enabled this trade in the profitability of high-income countries and production, which results in emissions. Emission trade is a dollar business, which could also be treated as an investment. This is an investment to protect the marginal productivity of capital assets and also to a global accord to ensure mitigation as a public good. New financial instruments are developed to trade the emission risks (Labatt & White, 2007). Emission trade is often treated as a strategy to practice sustainable development. However, it is a method to ensure profits and expansion of capital. As per the World Bank's State and Trend in Carbon Pricing, the revenue from carbon trading was 100 billion US dollars in the year 2023.

Developed and developing countries introduce institutions to trade carbon, otherwise called 'risk trading'. Figures 5.13 and 5.14 demonstrate that high-income countries are importers of carbon.

This consumption-induced emission impedes climate mitigation, and this consumption also influences climate mitigation policies. Shifting global manufacturing and hazardous industries to developing countries

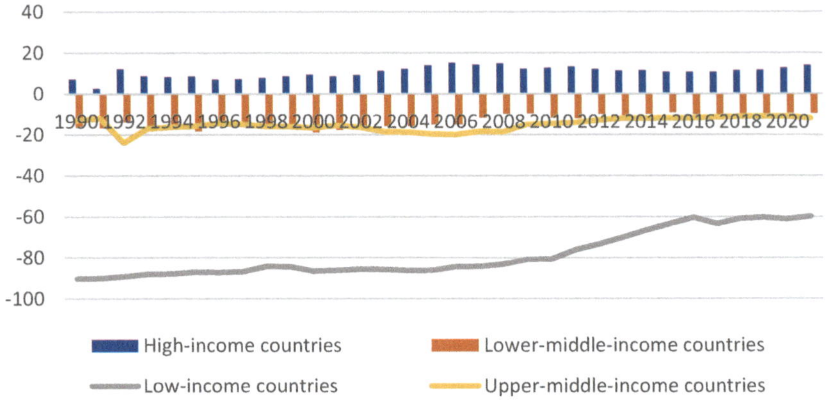

Fig. 5.13 Net export and import of carbon by income of the countries from 1990 to 2021 (*Source* ourworldindata)

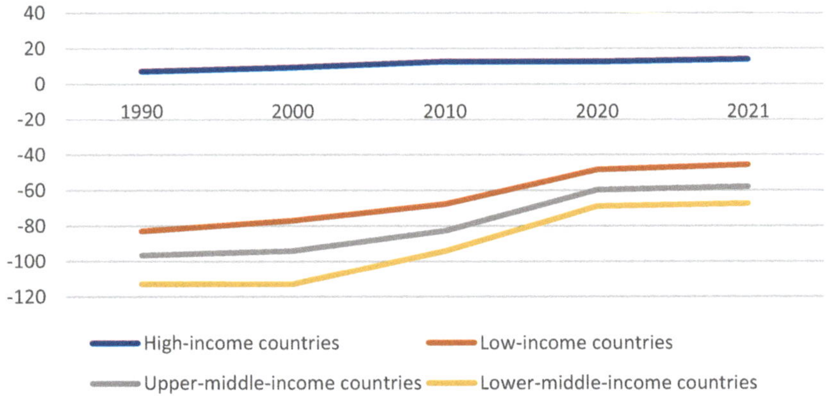

Fig. 5.14 Share of CO_2 emissions embedded in trade from 1990 to 2021 (*Source* https://ourworldindata.org/consumption-based-co2)

is also a triggering factor in deciding the unequal distribution of emission risks. Finance capitalism enabled this shift and created risk-induced industrial development in countries like China and India. Also, global and national capitalist sectors drive this high-risk-induced production. So, as mentioned above, emission trading becomes a mitigation option as studies show meeting national targets for greenhouse gas emissions is probably best achieved economically by using emissions trading to reduce greenhouse gas emissions into the environment (Stowell, 2005: 2). As part of these mitigation strategies, emissions in wealthier countries might be offset at a cheaper cost by acquiring "carbon credits" from developing countries. These financial flows may compensate for part of the foregone traditional economic progress in developing countries that may have sustained stability, especially in transition economies (Gartzke, 2012). Countries are struggling to strike a balance between capitalist profit and risks; for instance, recent data shows that in India, 2.1 million people died due to air pollution, and in China the number if 2.3 Million constituted 54% of the global disease burden in 2021 [State of Global Air (SoGA) 2024 report]. This figure explains the challenge of climate risk mitigation in the Global South and developing countries. Emissions and pollution are treated as the residual effect of economic development, employment generation, and economic competitiveness, so governments that promote capitalist industries are instrumentally weak in imposing effective mitigation policies.

The economic climate risk mitigation follows a neo-colonial approach in which global capitalism interfaces with local capitalist agencies to ensure unequal risk sharing.

Everyone is not equally accountable for climate change, and the repercussions are not dispersed evenly. Climate change is overwhelmingly caused by extractive and exploitative capitalist production (Omotayo Oladejo & Malherbe, 2023). Barnwell and Wood (2022) argue that carbon-fuelled colonial capitalism has thus been fundamental to the accumulation of riches in the Global North and the disenfranchisement of the Global South, which predates the Industrial Revolution. Over half of the worldwide industrial emissions since human-caused climate change was formally recognized may be traced back to just 25 corporate and state-producing entities that account for 51% of global industrial greenhouse gas emissions. Also, 100 producers account for 71% of global industrial greenhouse gas emissions (Griffin, 2017). It includes state-owned and private-sector companies. Some studies added that a single billionaire alone emits one million times more carbon than the wealthiest 10% of the world population (Maitland et al., 2022). Wealthy and capitalist class interests determine climate action, and it is evident in establishing institutions and tools to ease carbon trade rather than constitutions of local and country-level climate action policies.

5.7 Climate Action and Mitigation

Climate action is a multi-prong approach, not restricted to any single agency alone. It includes structural and non-structural measures; Goal 13 of the Sustainable Development Goals discusses climate action. It proposed a broader framework to engage with climate risk. See the Box 5.2.

Integrating climate action as part of sustainable development projects provides better visibility and institutional support for promoting climate action. SDG 13 is more popular among the SDGs since it encompasses a broader area of action and interventions. Also, SDG 13 influences institution-building to promote the goals; however, like other treaties, SDG does not come under any national priority; instead, it is treated under ad-hoc policy measures. Like other global treaties, SDG 13 is being given more comprehensive discussion, and unlike other climate actions, SDG 13 offers committed financial support. For instance, it promotes green climate fund-based adaption and mitigation strategies. The COP 16 held at Cancun decided to constitute the Green Climate Fund (GCF) to promote adaptation and mitigation among the member countries. Developed countries and public and non-public sources fund

Box 5.2 SDGs and Climate Action

The target of SDG 13

Target 13.1: Strengthen resilience and adaptive capacity to climate-related hazards and natural disasters in all countries

Target 13.2: Integrate climate change measures into national policies, strategies and planning

Target 13.3: Improve education, awareness-raising, and human and institutional capacity on climate change mitigation, adaptation, impact reduction, and early warning

Target 13.a: Implement the commitment undertaken by developed-country parties to the United Nations Framework Convention on Climate Change to a goal of mobilizing jointly $100 billion annually by 2020 from all sources to address the needs of developing countries in the context of meaningful mitigation actions and transparency on implementation and fully operationalize the Green Climate Fund through its capitalization as soon as possible

Target 13.b: Promote mechanisms for raising capacity for effective climate change-related planning and management in the least developed countries and small island developing States, including focusing on women, youth, and local and marginalized communities

Source www.unep.org

GCF. It is a collective financial support to promote climate adaptation and mitigation in developing and middle-income countries. It resembles the Marshal Aid Plan and Overseas Development Assistance programme. Unlike the above-mentioned financial assistance programme, GCF is directed towards short-term projects and has the element of building institutional capability to engage with climate risks. GCF is expected to create institutions to practice climate action through adaptation and mitigation. There is a considerable amount of money spent earmarked for this project. 13.9 Billion USD have been spent on 253 projects across the world, of which 129 are in developing countries (www.greenclimate.fund/projects/dashboard); of the total fund transfer, 40% is given as loans and 42% as grants. The loan needs to be repaid. It spends on both public and private projects. See Fig. 5.15.

Figure 5.16 shows that a significant share of the schemes are located in adaptation and crosscutting issues. This figure also tells how climate action operates and what the priorities are. See Table 5.1 for better clarity on the projects that GCF finances. These are mainly development-related projects that are connected with livelihood and ecological security. See Table 5.1.

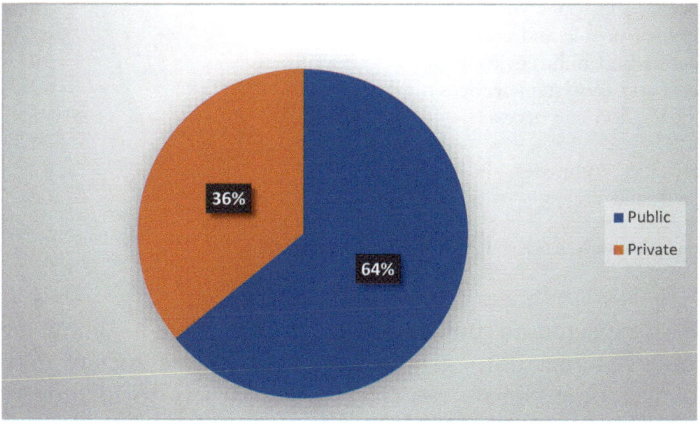

Fig. 5.15 Sectoral Allocation of GCF (*Source* https://www.greenclimate.fund/)

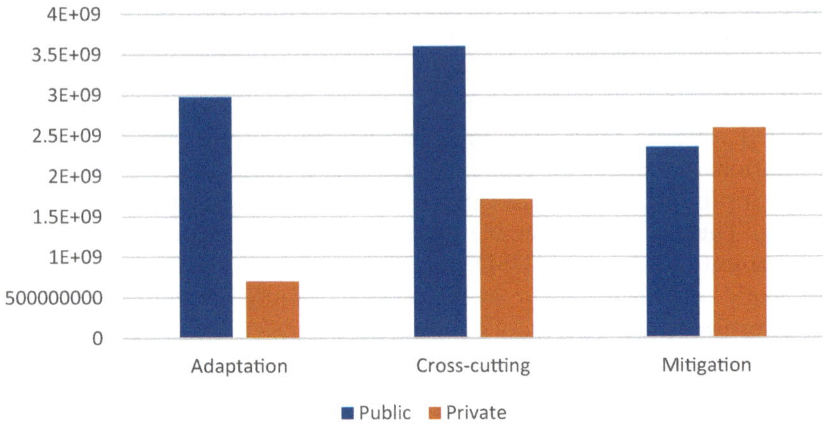

Fig. 5.16 Area of spending (*Source* https://www.greenclimate.fund/)

Table 5.1 Global climate fund spending and allocation

Projects	*Amount in billion US$*	*No of projects*
Health, food, and water security	1.6	128
Livelihoods of people and communities	1.9	167
Infrastructure and built environment	1.6	73
Ecosystems and ecosystem services	1.1	92
Energy generation and access	3.2	73
Transport	1.1	21
Buildings, cities, industries, and appliances	1.7	43
Forests and land use	1.7	68

Source https://www.greenclimate.fund/projects/dashboard#

GCF is expected to build resilience rather than promote emission reduction; it is meant to generate a system where society finds solutions to overcome climate risks. It enables society to identify risk and engage with it as an inevitable outcome of the development and flow of financial capitalism. GCF aims to address the developmental consequences of climate risk, including emissions. It enables an understanding that creates commitments among the countries and institutions to negotiate and make an acceptable level of risk. It is a global project to ease climate negotiations while keeping the economics of emissions at a higher rate. Climate risk adaptation and mitigation must be considered from this critical perspective in which vulnerable populations are at risk while institutions and the economy promote capital expansions. Also, one needs to see how climate risk impacts the population differently. Though international negotiations are active on emission reduction, climate risk pushes vulnerable populations into risk. A Word Bank (2020) study demonstrates that climate change will put 68 million to 135 million people into poverty by 2030. Climate change poses a grave threat to Sub-Saharan Africa and South Asia, where most impoverished people are concentrated. Also, the UNHCR report stated that 21.5 million people are displaced by climate change every year (McAllister, 2022). Mohanty and Wadhawan (2021), in their study on the district-level climate vulnerability in India, found that three in four districts of India are vulnerable to extreme climate risk. The unequal distribution of climate risk, though its impacts vary, results in devastating impacts on vulnerable populations. As mentioned before, asset inequality and vulnerability push people with low incomes into climate risk more than ever. The figure…explains that an additional number of people went into poverty from the baseline based on the method of US$1.90 per day. However, this US$1.90 per day is not the criteria accepted by a country like India. In India, per the Tendulkar committee's assessment of poverty, a person deemed poor spends Rs. 1000 per month, or Rs. 33 or less per day, in cities and Rs. 816 per month, or Rs. 27 or less per day in the countryside. In terms of dollars, it is US $ 0.40, so the number of poor added to the existing lists is higher than shown.

Figure 5.17 explains climate adaptation and mitigation as well. Diverse climate shocks and pressures have distinct effects on resources and tactics. The severity of climate change's effects varies and depends on the household and environmental factors (Matarira et al., 2013). Given the increasing impacts of climate variability and global ecological change, prioritizing adaptation strategies, adaptive capability, and risk reduction measures are necessary (Adger & Kelly, 1999). Because vulnerability depends on local features and varies over time, it is exceedingly challenging to assess the overall costs of adaptation (Bouwer & Aerts, 2006). The Intergovernmental Panel on Climate Change (IPCC) defines climate change adaptation '*as the adjustment process to actual or expected climate and its effects. In human systems, adaptation seeks to moderate or avoid harm or exploit beneficial opportunities. In some natural systems, human intervention may facilitate adjustment to the expected climate and its effects* (IPCC, 2014, p. 118).

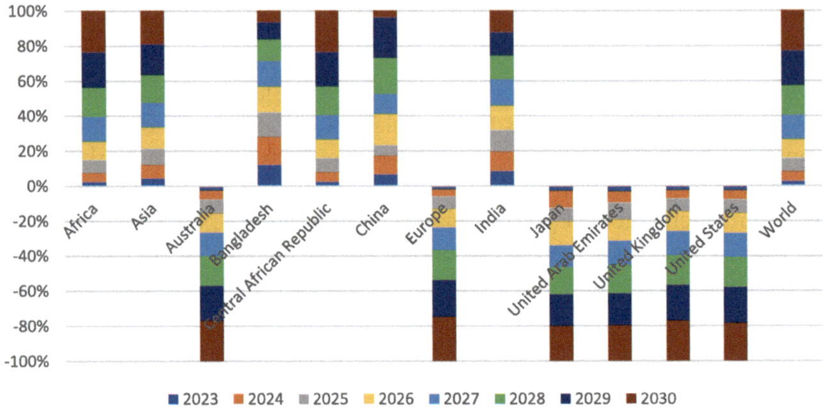

Fig. 5.17 Additional people at risk of extreme poverty with high climate adaptation challenges, 2015 to 2030 (*Source* https://ourworldindata.org/grapher/additional-extreme-poverty-climate-challenges?tab=chart)

Adaptation processes are not straightforward modifications in human behaviour and are substantially impacted by numerous contextual elements, such as dynamic power relations and the situatedness of social actors (Santha, 2020). The adaptive capacity of a social-ecological system could be understood as its ability to handle change and reconfigure itself without a significant decline in crucial functions (Folke, 2006). In economic terms, adaptation is any change in behaviour or capital that an actor (family, corporation, or government) makes to lessen the harm or boost the benefits of climate change (Mendelsohn, 2012). It is a process of investing in sustaining the marginal utility of the capital assets. Adaptation finance needs to be treated as capital investment; hence, the source and agent of investment are essential. Adaptation finance could be presented as

$$AF = \left(V \times E \times AC^{-1}\right) \times C$$

AF = adaptation finance requirement, V = vulnerability index, E = exposure index, AC^{-1} = adaptive capacity index, C = cost of adaptation.

The economics of adaptation is a specific target-oriented investment, and risk reduction is the return. In the business model, the cost of adaptation is capital, which is derived from either capitalist surplus or public finance as part of public good support. Finding capital for adaptation financing is often uneconomical in developing and underdeveloped countries like India. As the figure ... explains, developing and underdeveloped countries experience extreme inequality due to climate risks, and hence, adaptation finance does mean developmental interventions. It could be otherwise called building developmental institutions as well. This is the critical challenge as neoliberal economic policies dictate economic outcomes in developing and underdeveloped countries. The market requirement of adaptation determines the cost of the volume of adaptation investment. The value o n e d, cap A cap C to the minus one end superscript varies across economies and institutions. It is the decisive factor for developing and backward economies, and cap C and cap determine the resilience and adaptation of vulnerable populations. These parameters have a differential impact on developing countries' society and economy. Adaptive capacity is connected with the capability of institutions, economic agencies, and individuals. It is also associated with multiple institutional processes in developing countries; for instance, in India, adaption is possible through poverty reduction. Reducing poverty enables people to build economic resilience against climate risks; hence, it has long-term implications rather than short-term. In a country like India, adaptation finance is a project that builds the resilience of vulnerable populations. Resilience includes the reason and connection of people with one another and the struggle for land and livelihood access (Merilainen et al., 2021). One definition of resilience is a person's capability for adaptability (Butler et al., 2007), and it may be defined as the ability to adapt rather than stabilize (Handmer & Dovers, 1996; Waller, 2001). The ability of a system or individual to reduce direct and indirect risk by making tiny, incremental changes to the system is referred to as adaptive capacity (Kates, 2011). Community resilience relates also to the community's ability to adapt to the crises and losses caused by a natural disaster (Paton, 2006).

In countries like India, the exposure risk E is relatively high. The figure.... proves that an increase in climate risk pushes a large section of the population into poverty and danger. Reserve Bank of India's study also shows that the macro-economy is susceptible to climate risks. See Table 5.2, which explains that the Indian economy is more vulnerable to climate risk.

This analysis also poses critical questions about India's 3.3 trillion US Dollar economy, where the private sector significantly contributes to gross

Table 5.2 Impact on GDP due to climate change

Scenarios (deviations from baseline in percent)	*Impact on GDP (USA)*	*Impact on GDP (World)*	*Impact on GDP (India)*
Below 2 °C in 2030	– 1.93	– 1.67	– 1.91
Below 2 °C in 2050	– 2.29	– 3.02	– 3.8
NDC in 2030	– 2.59	– 2.14	– 3.16
NDC in 2050	– 5.56	– 5.74	– 9.08
Current policies in 2030	– 1.55	– 1.63	– 2.86
Current policies in 2050	– 5.09	– 6.05	– 9.87

Source RBI report on report on currency and finance 2022–23

capital formation. So, the climate change risk does affect the private sector as well. However, a study shows that the private sector contributes less than 0.1% of adaptation finance, while 53% of mitigation funds are from the private sector (Singh et al., 2021). Also, per the UN Adaptation Gap Report 2022, the estimated annual adaptation requirements are US$160 billion to US$340 billion by 2030 and US$315 billion to US$565 billion by 2050. The Report further assessed that low-income countries require an average of 3.09% of GDP (IQ range 1.18–4.96%), while lower-middle-income countries require 2.5% (IQ range 0.77–4.41%) and upper-middle-income countries require 1.43% (IQ range 0.14–3.20%). LDCs and SIDS require 2.67 and 3.39% of GDP, respectively (IQ range: 1.14–4.74% and 1.28–4.62%). This Gap indicates the need for replacement capital, income inequality, and adaptive capacity of people and institutions.

AC^{-1} is the factor determining the impact of adaptive capability, and it is an institution-driven programme. For instance, as per the IPCC Working Group (WG)-II (IPCC, 2012) report, the coastal population of India is one of the most vulnerable populations globally. It is assessed that by the middle of the present century, around 35 million people in India could face annual coastal flooding, with 45–50 million at risk by the end of the century (World Bank. 2021. Climate Risk Country Profile: India). Apart from flooding, studies also show that sea surface temperature due to climate risk affects livelihood and fish stock (Zacharia, 2016). The coastal communities, primarily fishing communities, are exposed mainly to climate change risk; for instance, in Kerala, one the coastal states in India, 18,685 coastal erosion-affected fisher families were identified as displaced from the coasts in 2012; later on, the number increased along with climate change induced coastal erosion (fisheries department, 2024). Climate-induced coastal erosion increases the number of families displaced in the state. The government of Kerala has proposed relocating those families as the solution, and it has become a kind of risk adaptation. The cost of relocation is comparatively less than the massive structural investment in risk reduction. The government of Kerala proposed a broader programme to deal with these risks; for instance, in Kerala, the Department of Fisheries has proposed a bureaucratic project called Punargeham (re-housing) (G.O (Rt) No. 1009/ 2019/F&PD dated 26.12.2019) funded by Chief Minister's Distress Relief Fund (CMDRF) and also with budget allocation of the department of fisheries of Kerala. Also, though the fishing communities are displaced, the government has proposed heavy development projects under blue economy initiatives in India. It is the issue of economies of climate risk sharing, in which the adaption or risk reduction seldom disturbs the heavy capital investment on coasts. For instance, the Sagarmala project of the Government of India aims to develop massive infrastructure on the Indian coast to tap deep sea fishing, harbors, and ports. The Sagamala project is a government programme spearheaded by Sagarmala Development Company Limited (SDCL) and implemented by Central Line Ministries, State Governments/State Maritime Boards, and Special Purpose Vehicles (SPVs) that can be established at the state or port level. SPV is the cornerstone of Sagarmala initiatives since it supports the private sector. It is a project idea that involves building, operating, and owning. Rs. 579,562 lakh core (69,460.79 Million US$) has been spent as of 24th April 2024 (https://sagarmala.gov.in/projects/projects-under-sagarmala).

This massive investment on coasts needs to be analyzed concerning the fact that about 90% of the heat emitted into the atmosphere due to global warming is deposited in the seas, and this heat storage contributes significantly to mean sea-level rise (Mimura, 2013). According to UN research, the ocean absorbs excess heat and energy from rising greenhouse gas emissions trapped in the Earth's system, making it the world's most spectacular carbon sink. Today, the ocean absorbs 90% of the heat generated by growing emissions. In the absence of any additional adaptation efforts, the risk associated with sea-level rise, including erosion, floods, and salinization—is expected to increase considerably along all low-lying coasts by the end of the century (very high confidence) (Oppenheimer et al., 2019). Hinkel et al. (2013) estimate that between 6000 and 17,000 km^2 of land will be lost in the twenty-first century due to increased coastal erosion caused by rising sea levels, among other things. The private sector is the primary beneficiary of the Sagarmala project, irrespective of its environmental costs. Climate change's impact on coasts and coastal communities is neglected in the project, and it prioritizes the blue economy. The expected capitalist benefits from the blue economy failed to establish an institutional structure for adaptation. This does not mean the governments have made no such attempt; the following case discusses this.

Institutional involvement in climate risk adaptation is a possibility of integrating multiple institutional rationalities into risk mitigation and risk reduction. Poverty and social inequality affect the adaptive ability of vulnerable populations. Public spending for adaptation and mitigation is a public institutional intervention in a country like India. The National Adaptation Fund for Climate Change by the National Bank for Agriculture and Rural Development (NABARD) of India shows both the success and limitations of adaptation finance in developing countries. NABARD's adaptation finance shows that adaptation financing is a bureaucracy-driven project in a country like India. Also, it needs state-planned developmental projects and institutions. See Fig. 5.18.

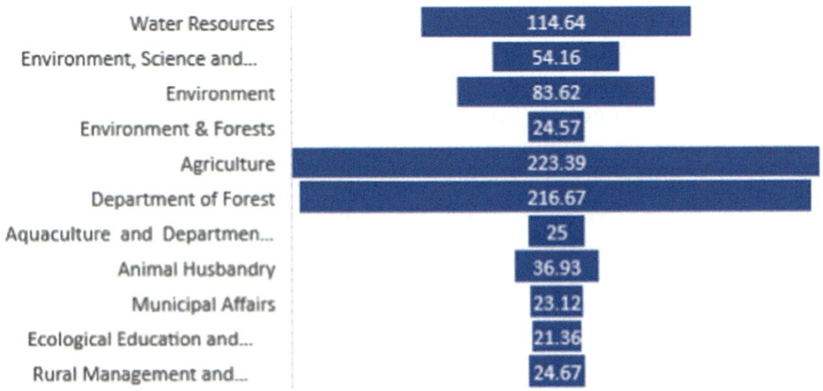

Fig. 5.18 NABARD's climate change adaption fund Rs. in crore (2015–2017) (*Source* https://www.nabard.org/content.aspx?id=585)

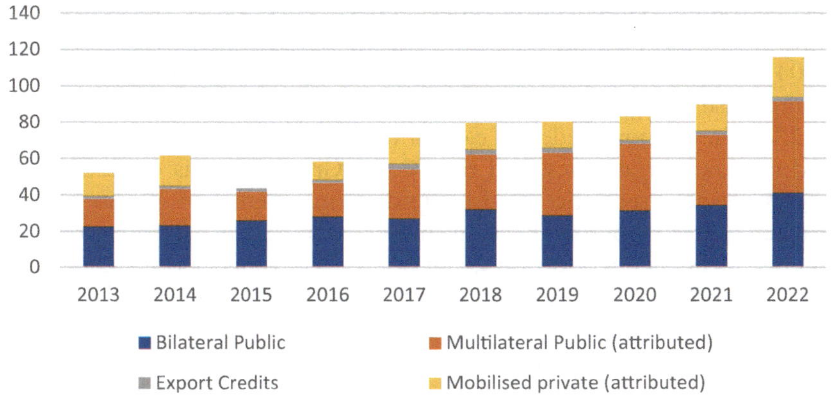

Fig. 5.19 Climate finance for developing countries in Billion US$ (*Source* OECD., 2024. Climate Finance Provided and Mobilized by Developed Countries in 2013–2022)

These are public initiatives; although the government favours scrapping the public institutions to promote the private sector, they still need to depend on public institutions to finance climate adaptation. It is evident in the mobilization of climate finance; see Fig. 5.19.

Figure 5.18 explains that the public sector adapts finance in developing economies like India. However, the benefits are not equally shared among the public. The two cases described above prove this; in the case of the Sagarmala project, the risk accumulates in the vulnerable fishing community, and economic benefits are concentrated among capitalist investors. In the NABARD project, public authority invests in adaptation. Compared to the Sagarmala project, NABARD's project cost is low and part of NABARD's institutional interventions. These cases represent the challenges of adaptation financing in a neoliberal economy.

5.8 Risk, Mitigation, and Finance

Carbon reduction is a business opportunity for financial institutions to find new sources for lending (Furrer et al., 2000). Most nations, including the United States, have various greenhouse gas mitigation policies that offer subsidies or limits, usually targeted at certain technologies or industries, rather than imposing a price on carbon across the economy (Gillingham & Stock, 2018). This pricing offers low-cost ways to cut carbon emissions and concrete financial incentives (Shogren, 2004). People have been concerned about the economic effects of climate change, particularly after the Kyoto Protocol was signed (Chen et al., 2023). The economic idea of carbon trading has initiated many business and risk transfer avenues, and the Global Green Bond is critical. Green bonds are debt securities used to fund environmental or climate-related projects. Green bonds, like conventional bonds, have fixed or variable interest rates. The worldwide green bond market has grown significantly over the last decade as investors prioritize sustainable and socially responsible investing. Green bonds are fixed-income instruments that raise financing for environmentally friendly projects such as renewable energy, energy efficiency, clean transportation, and sustainable water management. Following are the types of green bonds such as Climate Change Bonds, Renewable Energy Bonds, Energy Efficiency Bonds, Social or Sustainable Development Bonds, Green Infrastructure Bonds, Natural Resources Bonds, Project-linked bonds, Asset-linked bonds, Corporate green bonds, Sovereign Green bonds, and Green bond funds. Green Bond offers another source of raising capital for climate action by instituting sustainable development. It is an interest-bearing bond; hence, it could be read as a government-private intervention for climate action. The Paris Agreement emphasizes the need for green bonds to persuade the government and corporations to promote sustainable development goals. The world's largest economy and second-largest carbon emitter, the United States, vowed to withdraw from the Paris Agreement to restart its traditional and highly polluting sectors in 2020 (Schiermeier, 2020; Roelfsema et al., 2020). Alamgir and Cheng (2022) observed that green bonds reduce emissions and encourage renewable energy production. Still, they argue that the green bond market is not fully developed. It has also been found that firms that promote green bonds can increase their financial performance and brand value (Zhou & Cui, 2019; Flammer, 2020). One of the reasons for making green bonds popular is the big corporate interests, and the government also finds it easy to raise capital. It offers a win–win situation for both the investors and the government. Green bonds help pool investors to promote green development (Baulkaran, 2019). Also, some studies argue that the popularity of green bonds results from public acceptance of sustainable development (Tang & Zhang, 2020). About $2.5 trillion was raised globally to support green and sustainable projects by 2023 (World Bank, 2023). This green bond has become another financial instrument for generating capital investments. Figure…tells the amount of money collected through bonds and countries that issue bonds. There is an increasing trend. However, central issuance is in developed market economies, and low-income countries cannot issue vast volumes of green bonds. See Fig. 5.20.

One could see clear market preferences for green climate bonds, and developed countries are initiating this bond and taking the benefits. Countries that are creating risks generate bonds to reduce the risks. See Fig. 5.21.

There is a consistent increase in bonds, and developed countries' shares, as are the financial corporations and development banks, are increasing considerably. Issue green bonds as capital investments. See Fig. 5.22.

The Green bond is risk reduction and has become a source of green investments. The green bond market promotes the idea of green investments, green growth, and green capital. These are responsive capitalism, which invests while keeping the environment green and safe. Profit and conservation do not move together, and global climate risks proved that an increase in risk is the outcome of capital investment and attempts to make supernormal profits. The effectiveness of a Green Bond depends on

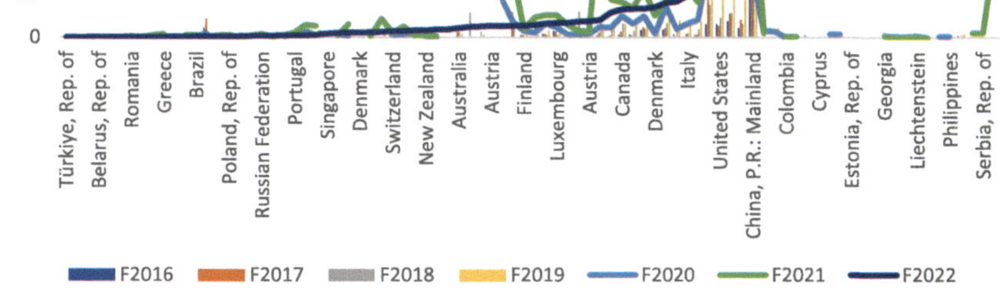

Fig. 5.20 Bond issued by countries million US$ (*Source* https://climatedata.imf.org/pages/climate-finance)

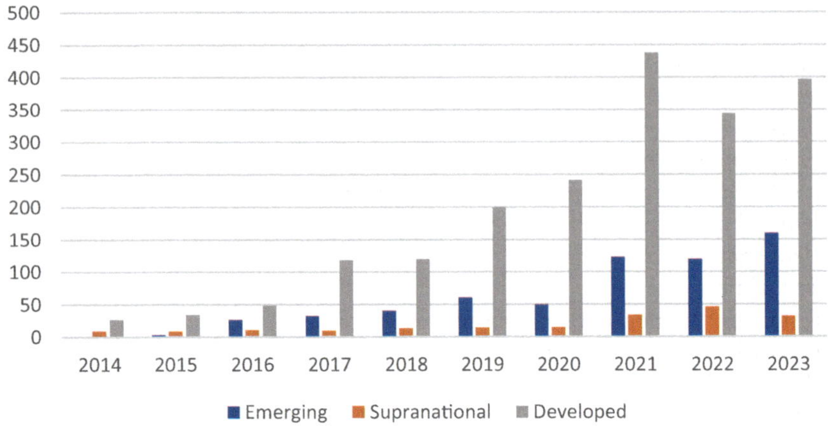

Fig. 5.21 Climate bonds initiative—market Type. b$ (*Source* https://www.climatebonds.net/market/data/)

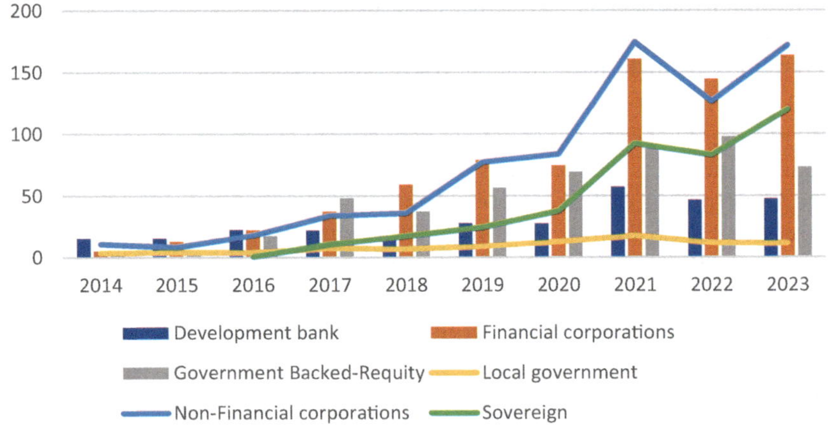

Fig. 5.22 Agencies issued Bon in b$ (*Source* https://www.climatebonds.net/market/data/)

the sector in which it is invested. Figure 5.23 shows the sectoral investment of Green Bond. The energy sector and buildings hold a significant share of green bonds, so the government and institutions must ensure this investment does not lead to emissions.

Green Bond is linked with sustainable development and has become a sustainable development source. The countries that issue bonds and invest have indeed agreed to promote sustainable or green development instead of emission-creating development. Pham (2021), in a study, observed that after changes in the general stock, energy, and fixed-income markets are considered, the reliance between green bonds and green equity is relatively minimal under typical market conditions. The evolution of new green investments across developed and emerging nations reveals a noteworthy intensity of new investments in renewables in developing economies (Mishra et al., 2023). The corporate sector's interest in Green Bond is closely associated with corporate sustainability-oriented strategy (Russo et al., 2020). The Government of India has proposed a broader framework to promote the sovereign green bond, which is a document to see the linkages of sustainable development and green bonds (India: Sovereign Green Bond Framework)—the Union Budget 2022–23 proposed to borrow sovereign green bonds to promote green infrastructure. The government of India proposed investing in green bonds in the following sectors: solar/wind/biomass/hydropower projects, public

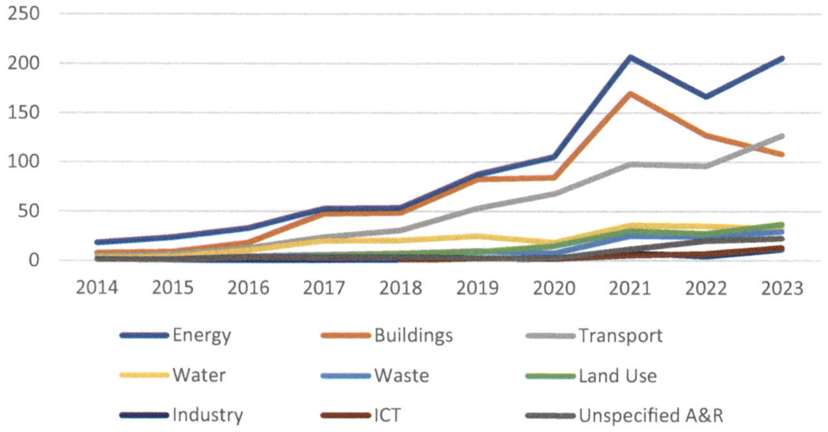

Fig. 5.23 Sectoral investment of green bond in B$ (*Source* https://www.climatebonds.net/market/data/)

lighting using light-emitting diode (LED), electrification of public transport, and afforestation/reforestation. These are public sector initiatives, and the fact is that the government should not pursue the private sector to follow these green developments. It is a risk transfer from the private to the public sector. Green bond is considered a global strategy to reduce the impact of climate risks. One needs to compare the volume of green bonds and GDP loss due to climate change, and one can see that the global bond value is less than the GDP losses. Green Bond enables the developed countries and corporate sectors to express their commitment to sustainable development and will allow them to reduce the risk at the cost of capital expansion.

5.9 Carbon Tax and Loss and Damage Fund

The carbon tax is again a popular risk transfer and a project of pricing risk. The internalizing externalities economic theory, which holds that those who cause carbon emissions do not bear the environmental consequences of such emissions, is where the idea of a carbon tax originated. Nordhaus (1977) proposes taxing emissions as a strategy to control pollution. A carbon tax could catalyze economies to reduce their carbon emissions in a way that yields financial benefits (Hecht et al., 2019). In energy-intensive sectors, a carbon tax levy may reduce carbon dioxide emissions. The primary purpose of carbon tax solutions is to reduce emissions at the expense of increased prices (Bai et al., 2020; Tan & Lin, 2020). The carbon tax follows the environmental tax proposed by Arthur Pigou (1920). It follows the framework of the Pigovian tax,

$$T = t^* \times Q$$

T = Pigovian tax imposed on the activity. t^* = optimal Pigovian tax rate, ideally equal to the external cost per unit of the harmful activity. Q = quantity of harmful activity.

Pigovian tax is considered an ideal method; however, finding an optimum tax rate under climate tax is challenging as the negative externalities of climate risks are complex.

To the asterisk operator, it co displacemen developd low—incomeuntries, its impact on income an social inequality has far-reaching implications in the long run. Figure 5.24 gives the names of countries that adopted carbon tax.

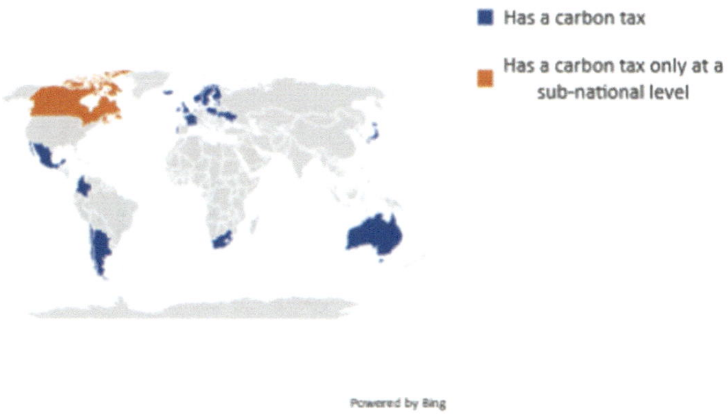

Fig. 5.24 Countries impose carbon tax (*Source* https://ourworldindata.org/carbon-pricing)

The emission trade is considered an option rather than putting a tax. See Fig. 5.25, which explains the economics of carbon tax. For instance, China and the United States carry zero carbon tax, making emission trade a significant option. Putting a carbon tax would affect low-cost manufacturing in China because China offers a competitive production cost to attract global commodity manufacturing. For the United States, both production and consumption-related emissions are higher; however, putting taxes on emissions affects the domestic economy. The economic impact of climate change is located in this critical context, in which capitalist production prefers to continue the method while exploring options to have preferable or acceptable risks. Also, look for options to capitalize on the vulnerabilities of the poor and marginal sections and economies.

A cap-and-trade system limits pollution and allows the market to operate in the buying and selling of rights to pollute (subject to the cap), determining a market clearing price. In contrast, a carbon tax places a price on CO_2 pollution and allows the market to determine the quantity of pollution (Metcalf, 2019). It is otherwise a method to put a price on risk and balance the costs and benefits. Also, a tax on pollution or emission is not a practical solution as the tax is often treated as compensation rather than reduction. Countries adopting carbon taxes follow a liberal capitalist economic policy and are low- or middle-income countries. High-income countries and countries that are emitting higher

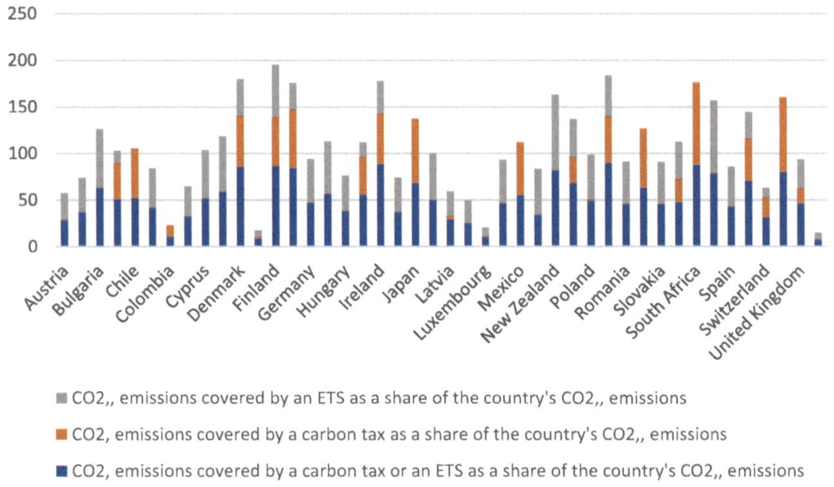

Fig. 5.25 Share of CO_2 emissions covered by a carbon price (*Source* https://ourworldindata.org/carbon-pricing)

amounts of carbon do not propose any such tax policies. Also, another fact is that tax and redistribution would operate in a welfare policy approach, and market-driven development cannot run the redistribution effects of taxation.

Climate action finance is an evolving project, and it moves along with financial capital and economic damage due to climate change. The COP 27 has decided to establish a loss and damage fund to mitigate climate-induced economic losses. The United Nations Environment Programme (UNEP) indicates that funding for adaptation is insufficient. Adaptation finance flows to developing countries are estimated to be less than the annual requirement of US$300 billion. The loss and damage fund is a capital pool to replace the economic loss and marginal utility reduction due to climate change. There are two broad options for financing loss and damage funds; one is to contribute to the public, including developed and developing countries, philanthropies, sovereign wealth funds, and the IMF and World Bank. Another option is to impose new taxes, such as levies on air travel, bunker fuel, fossil fuel extraction, greenhouse gas emissions, and financial transactions (Franczak, 2022); as of March 2024, USD 661 million had been pledged to the Loss and damage fund.

It is a contribution from countries that are at the top in emissions. The United Kingdom committed USD 50 million; France, Italy, Germany, and the United Arab Emirates, each of whom had committed USD 100 million or more; and other nations, such as the United States of America, which had pledged USD 17.5 million, and Japan, which had pledged USD 10 million (Schalatek & Richards, 2024). It primarily comes under the category of risk-bearing costs. This fund is for developing countries vulnerable to climate risk, and the World Bank is the nodal agency that implements the fund. The loss and damage fund needs to be assessed because climate-induced losses are increasing, and a vast adaptation gap exists in finance. Some studies show that lower- and lower-middle-income economies will lose 12% of their GDP due to extreme climate risk by 2050, and they have to invest 0.6–1% of GDP annually to prevent the losses (Amiot & Paul Munday, 2024). It is estimated that 3.2% and 5.1% of world GDP could be wiped out by climate hazards annually by 2050. Many independent assessments prove climate risk wipes out GDP and assets; for instance, one study assessed 38 trillion dollars in loss due to climate risk by 2049 (Potsdam Institute for Climate Impact Research, 2024). This loss pushes vulnerable people into risk and permanent loss of assets. The loss and damage fund is an option for vulnerable populations and countries affected by climate risks.

Loss and damage funds are treated as replacement capital for developing countries and could be another source of financing climate adaptation. The definition and impact of loss and damages vary across countries and economies. Macroeconomic conditions, stages of development, and resource dependency of vulnerable populations influence the economic loss due to climate change. So, the loss and damage fund is a big hope since it is a dedicated fund exclusively for replacing the capital loss or declining marginal utility of the resource and assets. However, the World Bank's governance of loss and damage funds does have the Bank's influence on the allocation and selection of projects.

Climate risk is an everyday reality, and the victims of this risk are primarily spread across the world's developing and poor countries and regions. Climate risk is an inevitable outcome of capitalism, and capitalism rules the global economy. So, a final resolution on emission reduction or reducing the impact of climate risk on large sections of vulnerable populations remains an 'unsettled issue'. There have been climate summits and international discussions to find a reasonable solution for risk mitigation. However, every such meeting ended up proposing policies to govern the impact of risk rather than risk reduction. There is a distinct neo-colonial approach to climate risk governance, which could be why the market determines climate economics. Capitalism continues to emit risk, and economics has evolved to search for an acceptable level of risk and provide capital to meet the risks. Climate risk economics primarily protects emitting capitalism and allows capital to regenerate the losses and replace the capital. A different type of economics proposes a theory of capital saving and risk transfer.

References

Abadie, L. M., Galarraga, I., & Rübbelke, D. (2012). An analysis of the causes of the mitigation bias in international climate finance. *Mitigation and Adaptation Strategies for Global Change, 18*(7), 943–955. https://doi.org/10.1007/s11027-012-9401-7

Acaravci, A., & Ozturk, I. (2010). On the relationship between energy consumption, CO_2 emissions and economic growth in Europe. *Energy, 35*(12), 5412–5420.

Ackerman, F., & Stanton, E. (2013). *Climate economics: The state of the art*. London: Routledge.

Al-Mulali, U., Saboori, B., & Ozturk, I. (2015). Investigating the environmental Kuznets curve hypothesis in Vietnam. *Energy Policy, 76*, 123–131.

Ang, J. B. (2007). CO_2 emissions, energy consumption, and output in France. *Energy Policy, 35*(10), 4772–4778.

Adger, W. M., & Kelly, P. M. (1999). Social vulnerability to climate change and the architecture of entitlements. *Mitigation and Adaptation Strategies for Global Change, 4*, 253–266.

Amiot, M., & Munday, P. (2024). *Investment in climate adaptation needs have high returns on growth*. https://www.spglobal.com/en/research-insights/special-reports/look-forward/investment-in-climate-adaptation-needs-have-high-returns-on-growth. Accessed on 29/06/2024.

Aichele, R., & Felbermayr, G. (2013). The effect of the Kyoto protocol on carbon emissions. *Journal of Policy Analysis and Management, 32*(4), 731–757.

Alamgir, M., & Cheng, M. (2022). Do green bonds play a role in achieving sustainability? *Sustainability, 15*(13), 10177. https://doi.org/10.3390/su151310177

Alboghdady, M., & El-Hendawy, S. E. (2016). Economic impacts of climate change and variability on agricultural production in the Middle East and

North Africa region. *International Journal of Climate Change Strategies and Management, 8*(3), 463–472. https://doi.org/10.1108/ijccsm-07-2015-0100

Azzarri, C., & Signorelli, S. (2020). Climate and poverty in Africa South of the Sahara. *World Development, 125*, 104691.

Bach, W., & Jain, A. K. (1990). The CFC greenhouse potential of scenarios possible under the Montreal protocol. *International Journal of Climatology, 10*(5), 439–450. https://doi.org/10.1002/joc.3370100502

Bansal, R., & Ochoa, M. (2011). *Temperature, aggregate risk, and expected returns*. NBER wp. 17575. https://www.nber.org/papers/w17575. Accessed on 18/06/2024.

Bai, Q., Xu, J., & Chauhan, S. S. (2020). Effects of sustainability investment and risk aversion on a two-stage supply chain coordination under a carbon tax policy. *Computers and Industrial Engineering, 142*, 106324.

Baulkaran, V. (2019). Stock market reaction to green bond issuance. *Journal of Asset Management, 2019*(20), 331–340.

Barnwell, G., & Wood, N. (2022). Climate justice is central to addressing the climate emergency's psychological consequences in the Global South: A narrative review. *South African Journal of Psychology, 52*(4), 486–497.

Benevolenza, M. A., & DeRigne, L. (2018). The impact of climate change and natural disasters on vulnerable populations: A systematic review of literature. *Journal of Human Behavior in the Social Environment*. https://doi.org/10.1080/10911359.2018.1527739

Berlemann, M., & Wenzel, D. (2018). Hurricanes, economic growth and transmission channels: Empirical evidence for countries on differing levels of development. *World Development, 105*(2018), 231–247.

Böhringer, C., & Löschel, A. (2002). Assessing the costs of compliance: The Kyoto Protocol. *European Environment, 12*(1), 1–16. https://doi.org/10.1002/eet.279

Bonanno, G. A. (2004). Loss, trauma, and human resilience: Have we underestimated the human capacity to thrive after extremely adverse events? *American Psychologist*, *59*, 20–28.

Bouwer, L. M., & Aerts, J. H. (2006). Financing climate change adaptation. *Disasters, 30*(1), 49–63. https://doi.org/10.1111/j.1467-9523.2006.00306.x

Bullard, R. D. (2007). *Growing smarter: Achieving liveable communities, environmental justice, and regional equity*. MIT Press.

Butler, L. D., Morland, L. A., & Leskin, G. A. (2007). Psychological resilience in the face of terrorism. In B. Bongar, L. M. Brown, L. E. Beutler, J. N. Breckenridge, & P. G. Zimbardo (Eds.), Psychology of terrorism (pp. 400–417). Oxford University Press.

Bilal, A., & Känzig, D. R. (2024). *The macroeconomic impact of climate change: global vs. local temperature*. Working paper 32450 http://www.nber.org/papers/w32450 National Bureau of Economic Research. 1050 Massachusetts Avenue Cambridge, MA 02138 May 2024.

Burke, M., Hsiang, S. M., & Miguel, E. (2015). Global non-linear effect of temperature on economic production. *Nature, 527*, 235–239.

Bodansky, D. (2001). The history of the global climate change regime. In U. Luterbacher & D. F. Sprinz (Eds.), *International relations and global climate change*. London: MIT Press.

Cappelli, F., Costantini, V., & Consoli, D. (2021). The trap of climate change-induced "natural" disasters and inequality. *Global Environmental Change, 70*, 102329. https://doi.org/10.1016/j.gloenvcha.2021.102329

Chen, M., Yao, T., & Wang, K. (2023). The economic impact of climate change: A bibliometric analysis of research hotspots and trends. *Environmental Science and Pollution Research, 30*, 47935–47955. https://doi.org/10.1007/s11356-023-25721-2

Ciscar, J.-C., Iglesias, A., Luc Feyen, L. S., Regemorter, D. V., Amelung, B., & Nicholls, R. M. A. (2011). Physical and economic consequences of climate change in Europe. *PNAS, 108*, 2678–2683.

Choudhury, T., Kayani, U. N., Gul, A., Haider, S. A., & Ahmad, S. (2023). Carbon emissions, environmental distortions, and impact on growth. *Energy Economics, 126*, 107040. https://doi.org/10.1016/j.eneco.2023.107040

Cao, G., Xu, W., & Guo, Y. (2015). Effects of climatic events on the Chinese stock market: Applying event analysis. *Natural Hazards, 77*(3), 1979–1992. https://doi.org/10.1007/s11069-015-1687-9

Dang, H.-A. H., Nguyen, M. C., & Trinh, T.-A. (2023). *Does hotter temperature increase poverty and inequality? Global evidence from subnational data analysis*. Policy research working paper 10466. World Bank, US.

Dasgupta, S., & Shayegh, J. E. S. (2023). Inequality and growth impacts of climate change—Insights from South Africa. *Environmental Research Letters, 18*(12), 1.

Deryugina, T., & Hsiang, S. M. (2014). *Does the environment still matter? Daily temperature and income in the United States*. NBER working paper no. 20750.

DuPuis, E. M., & Gareau, B. J. (2008). Neoliberal knowledge: The decline of technocracy and the weakening of the montreal protocol*. *Social Science Quarterly, 89*(5), 1212–1229. https://doi.org/10.1111/j.1540-6237.2008.00576.x

Durney, J. (2017). Defining the Paris agreement: A study of executive power and political commitments. *Carbon and Climate Law Review, 11*(3), 234–242.

Dell, M., Jones, B. F., & Olken, B. A. (2012b). Temperature shocks and economic growth: Evidence from the last half century. *American Economic Journal: Macroeconomics, 4*(3), 66–95.

Epstein, G., Pérez, I., Schoon, M., & Meek, C. L. (2014). Governing the invisible commons: Ozone regulation and the Montreal Protocol. *International Journal of the Commons, 8*(2), 337–360.

Falkowski, P., Scholes, R. J., Boyle, E., Canadell, J., Canfield, D., Elser, J., Gruber, N., Hibbard, K., Högberg, P., Linder, S., Mackenzie, F. T., Moore, B., III., Pedersen, T., Rosenthal, Y., Seitzinger, S., Smetacek, V., & Steffen, W. (2000). The global carbon cycle: A test of our knowledge of earth as a system. *Science, 290*(5490), 291–296.

Farhani, S., & Tiwari, A. K. (2019). Co2 emissions, industrial production, and coal consumption in the U.S. Industrial sector. *The Journal of Energy and Development, 45*(1/2), 33–50.

Folke, C., Carpenter, S. R., Walker, B., Scheffer, M., Chapin, T., & Rockström, J. (2010). Resilience thinking: integrating resilience, adaptability and transformability. *Ecology and Society, 15*(4), 1.

Foxon, T. J. (2011). A coevolutionary framework for analysing a transition to a sustainable low carbon economy. *Ecological Economics, 70*(12), 2258–2267.

Fourier, J. B. J. (1827). Memoire sur les temperatures du globe terrestre et des espaces planetaires. *Memoir De L'academie Royale Des Sueries De L'institute De France, 1*, 569–604.

Fortems-Cheiney, A., Saunois, M., Pison, I., Chevallier, F., Bousquet, P., Cressot, C., Montzka, S. A., Fraser, P. J., Vollmer, M. K., Simmonds, P. G., Young, D., O'Doherty, S., Weiss, R. F., Artuso, F., Barletta, B., Blake, D. R., Li, S., Lunder, C., Miller, B. R., … Yokouchi, Y. (2015). Increase in HFC-134a emissions in response to the success of the Montreal Protocol. *Journal of Geophysical Research: Atmospheres, 120*, 11728–11742. https://doi.org/10.1002/2015JD023741

Franczak, M. (2022). *Options for a loss and damage financial mechanism*. International Peace Institute. http://www.jstor.org/stable/resrep43844

Furrer, B., Hugenschmidt, H., & Koncz, P. (2000). Climate change and finance: New business opportunities. *Corporate Environmental Strategy, 7*(2), 137–145. https://doi.org/10.1016/s1066-7938(00)00050-6

Folke, C. (2006). Resilience: The emergence of a perspective for social–ecological systems analyses. *Global Environmental Change, 16*, 253–267.

Fujimori, S., Hasegawa, T., Krey, V., Riahi, K., Bertram, C., Bodirsky, B. L., Bosetti, V., Callen, J., Després, J., Doelman, J., Drouet, L., Emmerling, J., Frank, S., Fricko, O., Havlik, P., Humpenöder, F., Koopman, J. F. L., van Meijl, H., Ochi, Y., & van Vuuren, D. (2019). A multi-model assessment of food security implications of climate change mitigation. *Nature Sustainability, 2*, 386–396. https://doi.org/10.1038/s41893-019-0286-2

Flammer, C. (2020). Green bonds: Effectiveness and implications for public policy. *Environment and Energy Policy Economics, 2020*(1), 95–128.

Fingleton, B., & Fischer, M. M. (2009). Neoclassical theory versus new economic geography: Competing explanations of cross-regional variation in economic development. *The Annals of Regional Science, 44*(3), 467–491. https://doi.org/10.1007/s00168-008-0278

Gartzke, E. (2012). Could climate change precipitate peace? *Journal of Peace Research, 49*(1), 177–192. https://doi.org/10.1177/0022343311427342

Gignac, R., & Matthews, H. D. (2015). Allocating a 2 °C carbon budget to countries. *Environmental Research Letters, 10*(7), 075004.

Gilmore, E. A., & Buhaug, H. (2021). Climate mitigation policies and the potential pathways to conflict: Outlining a research agenda. *Wiley Interdisciplinary Reviews. Climate Change*. https://doi.org/10.1002/wcc.722

Griffin, P. (2017). *The carbon majors database: CDP carbon majors report 2017*. https://www.cdn.cdp.net/cdp-production/cms/reports/documents/000/002/327/original/Carbon-Majors-Report-2017.pdf

Gupta, J., Olsthoorn, X., & Rotenberg, E. (2003). The role of scientific uncertainty in compliance with the Kyoto Protocol to the Climate Change Convention. *Environmental Science and Policy, 6*(6), 475–486. https://doi.org/10.1016/j.envsci.2003.09.001

Gillingham, K., & Stock, J. H. (2018). The cost of reducing greenhouse gas emissions. *The Journal of Economic Perspectives, 32*(4), 53–72.

Hallegatte, S., Bangalore, M., Bonzanigo, L., Fay, M., Kane, T., Narloch, U., Rozenberg, J., Treguer, D., & Vogt-Schilb, A. (2016). *Shock waves: Managing the impacts of climate change on poverty*. Climate Change and Development Series. Washington, DC: World Bank. https://doi.org/10.1596/978-1-4648-0673-5

Hepburn, C., (2007). Carbon trading: a review of the Kyoto mechanisms. Annu. Rev. Environ. Resour., *32*(1), pp.375–393.

Hosseinzadehtalaei, P., Tabari, H., & Willems, P. (2020). Satellite-based data driven quantification of pluvial floods over Europe under future climatic and socioeconomic changes. *Science of the Total Environment, 721*, 137688.

Heal, G. (2017). The economics of the climate. *Journal of Economic Literature, 55*(3), 1046–1063.

Hristov, J., Toreti, A., Dominguez, I. P., Dentener, F., Fellmann, T., Elleby, C., & Bratu, M. (2020). *Analysis of climate change impacts on EU agriculture by 2050*. Seville: European Commission.

Huang, W. M., Lee, G. W., & Wu, C. C. (2008). GHG emissions, GDP growth and the Kyoto Protocol: A revisit of Environmental Kuznets Curve hypothesis. *Energy Policy, 36*(1), 239–247. https://doi.org/10.1016/j.enpol.2007.08.035

Henseler, M., & Schumacher, I. (2019). The impact of weather on economic growth and its production factors. *Climatic Change, 154*, 417–433.
Hecht, B., Valaskova, K., Kral, P., & Rowland, Z. (2019). The digital governance of smart city networks: Information technology-driven economy, citizencentered big data, and sustainable urban development. *Geopolitics, History, and International Relations, 11*(1), 128–133.
Hinkel, J., Vuuren, D., Nicholls, R., & Klein, R. T. (2013). The effects of adaptation and mitigation on coastal flood impacts during the 21st century. An application of the DIVA and IMAGE models. *Climate Change, 117*, 783–794.
Lin, B., & Huang, C. (2022). Analysis of emission reduction effects of carbon trading: Market mechanism or government intervention? *Sustainable Production and Consumption, 33*, 28–37. https://doi.org/10.1016/j.spc.2022.06.016
IPCC. (2018). *Global warming of 15 °C*. https://www.ipcc.ch/sr15/
IPCC. (2012). *Managing the risks of extreme events and disasters to advance climate change adaptation*. IPCC.
IPCC. (2014). *Climate change 2014: Mitigation of climate change*. https://www.ipcc.ch/report/ar5/wg3/
Jaccard, M. (2014). The climate casino risk, uncertainty, and economics for a warming world. *Science, 343*(6169), 371–372.
Jeff, P., & Owen, A. D. (2009). Emission trading schemes: Potential revenue effects, compliance costs and overall tax policy issues. *Energy Policy, 37*(1), 4595–4603.
Joseph, C., Pellerin, M., & Rodriguez, J. (2020). The economics of climate change. *Social Science Research Network*. https://doi.org/10.2139/ssrn.3715848
Handmer, J., & Dovers, S. (1996). A typology of resilience: Rethinking institutions for sustainable development. *Industrial and Environmental Crisis Quarterly, 9*, 482–511.
Kartha, S., Kemp-Benedict, E., Ghosh, E., & Nazareth, A. (2020). *The carbon inequality era: An assessment of the global distribution of consumption emissions among individuals from 1990 to 2015 and beyond*. Stockholm Environment Institute, And Tim Gore, Oxfam.
Liu, X., Leung, Y., Xu, Y., & Yung, L. C. W. (2017). The effect of carbon tax on carbon emission abatement and GDP: A case study. *Journal of Geographical Systems, 19*(4), 399–414. https://doi.org/10.1007/s10109-017-0254-1
Kates, R. W. (2011). What kind of a science is sustainability science? *Proceedings of the National Academy of Sciences of the United States of America., 108*(49), 19449–19450.
Kahn, M. E., Mohaddes, K., Ng, R. N. C., Pesaran, M. H., Raissi, M., & Yang, J.-C. (2019). *Long-term macroeconomic effects of climate change: A*

cross-country analysis. IMF working paper. Fiscal Affairs Department. October 2019.

Kompas, T., Pham, V. H., & Che, T. N. (2018). The effects of climate change on GDP by country and the global economic gains from complying 71REPORT ON CURRENCY AND FINANCE with the Paris climate accord. *Earth's Future, 6*(8), 1153–1173.

Labatt, S., & White, R. R. (2007). *Carbon finance: The financial implications of climate change*. Wiley.

Lesk, C., Rowhani, P., & Ramankutty, N. (2016). Influence of extreme weather disasters on global crop production. *Nature, 529*, 84–87.

Li, Y., Chiu, Y., & Lin, T. (2019). The impact of economic growth and air pollution on public health in 31 Chinese cities. *International Journal of Environmental Research and Public Health, 16*, 393.

Li, Y., Ye, W., Wang, M., & Yan, X. (2009). Climate change and drought: A risk assessment of crop-yield impacts. *Climate Research, 39*, 31–46.

Maréchal, K. (2007). The economics of climate change and the change of climate in economics. *Energy Policy, 35*(10), 5181–5194. https://doi.org/10.1016/j.enpol.2007.05.009

Mitić, P., Fedajev, A., Radulescu, M., & Rehman, A. (2023). The relationship between CO_2 emissions, economic growth, available energy, and employment in SEE countries. *Environmental Science and Pollution Research, 30*, 16140–16155. https://doi.org/10.1007/s11356-022-23356-3

Matarira, C. H., Pullanikkatil, D., Kaseke, T., Shava, E., & Manatsa, D. (2013). Socio-economic impacts of climate change on subsistence communities. *International Journal of Climate Change Strategies and Management, 5*(4), 404–417. https://doi.org/10.1108/ijccsm-06-2012-0034

Mani, M., Bandyopadhyay, S., Chonabayashi, S., & Markandya, A. (2018). *South Asia's hotspots: The impact of temperature and precipitation changes on living standards*. London: World Bank Publications.

Meckling, J., (2011). Carbon coalitions: Business, climate politics, and the rise of emissions trading. MIT Press.

Mendelsohn, R. (2012). The economics of adaptation to climate change in developing countries. *Climate Change Economics, 3*(2), 1250006.

Merilainen, E., Joseph, J., Jauhola, M., Yadav, P., Romo-Murphy, E., Marin, J., & Gadhavi, S. (2021). Examining relational social ontologies of disaster resilience: Lived experiences from India, Indonesia, Nepal, Chile and Andean territories. *Disaster Prevention and Management: an International Journal, 3*, 2. https://doi.org/10.1108/DPM-02-2021-0057

Moffatt, I. (2004). Global warming: Scientific modelling and its relationship to the economic dimensions of policy. In A. D. Owen & N. Hanley (Eds.), *The economics of climate change*. London: Routledge.

Morin, J.-F., & Bialais, C. (2018). *Strengthening multilateral environmental governance through bilateral trade deals*. Centre for International Governance Innovation. http://www.jstor.org/stable/resrep17319

Miller, D. (2004). Holding nations responsible. *Ethics, 114*, 240–268.

Miller, D. (2007). *National responsibility and global justice*. Oxford University Press.

Maitland, A., Lawson, M., Stroot, H., Poidatz, A., Khalfan, A., & Dabi, N. (2022). *Carbon billionaires: The investment emissions of the world's richest people*. London: Oxfam International.

Metcalf, G. E. (2019). On the economics of a carbon tax for the United States. *Brookings Papers on Economic Activity, 2019*, 405–458.

Mishra, T., Park, D., Parhi, M., Uddin, G. S., & Tian, S. (2023). A memory in the bond: Green bond and sectoral investment interdependence in a fractionally cointegrated VAR framework. *Energy Economics, 121*, 106652. https://doi.org/10.1016/j.eneco.2023.106652

Mohanty, A., & Wadhawan, S. (2021). Mapping India's climate vulnerability: A district-level assessment. New Delhi: Council on Energy, Environment and Water.

Moellendorf, D. (2015). Climate change justice. *Philosophy Compass, 10*(3), 173–186.

Naimoli, S. (2021). Carbon dioxide removal solutions. Center for Strategic and International Studies (CSIS). www.csis.org. Accessed on 18th June, 2024.

Noy, I. (2009). The macroeconomic consequences of disasters. *Journal of Development Economics, 88*(2), 221–231.

Odongo, M. T., Misati, R. N., Kamau, A. W., & Kisingu, K. N. (2022). Climate change and inflation in Eastern and Southern Africa. *Sustainability, 12*(22), 1–17.

OECD. (2024). *Fostering catastrophe bond markets in Asia and the Pacific, the development dimension*. OECD Publishing.

Oppenheimer, M., Glavovic, B. C., Hinkel, J., van de Wal, R., Magnan, A. K., Abd-Elgawad, A., Cai, R., Cifuentes-Jara, M., DeConto, R. M., Ghosh, T., Hay, J., Isla, F., Marzeion, B., Meyssignac, B., & Sebesvari, Z. (2019). Sea level rise and implications for low-lying islands, coasts and communities. In H.-O. Pörtner, D. C. Roberts, V. Masson-Delmotte, P. Zhai, M. Tignor, E. Poloczanska, K. Mintenbeck, A. Alegría, M. Nicolai, A. Okem, J. Petzold, B. Rama, & N. M. Weyer (Eds.), *IPCC special report on the ocean and cryosphere in a changing climate* (pp. 321–445). Cambridge: Cambridge University Press. https://doi.org/10.1017/9781009157964.006

Pan, J. (2022). *Climate change economics*. Springer Books.

Pereira, A. M., Rui, M. P., & Rodrigues, P. G. (2016). A new carbon tax in Portugal: A missed opportunity to achieve the triple dividend? *Energy Policy, 93*, 110–118.

Paton, D. (2006). Disaster resilience: Integrating individual, community, institutional, and environmental perspectives. In D. Paton & D. Johnston (Eds.), *Disaster resilience: An integrated approach* (pp. 305–318). Springfield: Charles C. Thomas.

Paglialunga, E., Coveri, A., & Zanfei, A. (2022). Climate change and within-country inequality: New evidence from a global perspective. *World Development, 159*, 106030.

Pigou, A. C. (1920). *The economics of welfare.* Macmillian.

Pham, L. (2021). Frequency connectedness and cross-quantile dependence between green bond and green equity markets. *Energy Economics, 98*(2021), 105257.

Park, J. (2015b). Climate change and capitalism. *Consilience: the Journal of Sustainable Development, 14*(2), 189–206.

Parker, M. (2018). The impact of disasters on inflation. *Economics of Disasters and Climate Change, 2*, 21–48.

Parikh, J., & Shukla, V. (1995). Urbanization, energy use and greenhouse effects in economic development: Results from a cross-national study of developing countries. *Global Environmental Change, 5*(1995), 87–103.

Philibert, CeHdric. (1999). The economics of climate change and the theory of discounting. *Energy Policy, 27*(1999), 913–927.

Plass, G. N. (1956). The carbon dioxide theory of climate change. *Tellus, 8*, 140–154.

Posner, E. A., & Weisbach, D. (2010). *Climate change justice.* Princeton University Press.

Rabe, B.G., (2007). Beyond Kyoto: Climate change policy in multilevel governance systems. Governance, *20*(3), pp.423–444.

Ramananthan, V., Cicerone, R. J., Singh, H. B., & Kiehl, J. T. (1985). Trace gas trends and their potential role in climatic change. *Journal of Geophysical Research, 90*, 5547–5566.

Rattis, L., Brando, P. M., Macedo, M. N., Spera, S. A., Castanho, A. D., Marques, E. Q., & Coe, M. T. (2021). Climatic limit for agriculture in Brazil. *Nature Climate Change, 2021*, 1098–1104.

Riahi, K., Van Vuuren, D. P., Kriegler, E., Edmonds, J., Brian, C., O'neill, Fujimori, S., Bauer, N., Calvin, K., Dellink, R., & Fricko, O. (2017). The shared socioeconomic pathways and their energy, land use, and greenhouse gas emissions implications: an overview. *Global Environmental Change, 42*(2017), 153–168.

Rising, J. (2023). *Loss and damage today: How climate change is impacting output and capital.* Gerard J. Mangone Climate Change Science and Policy Hub Report. University of Delaware.

Reid, H., Huq, S., & Murray, L. (2003). *Mainstreaming adaptation to climate change in least developed countries*. International Institute for Environment and Development. London.

Roca, J., & Padilla, E. (2023). Conventional climate change economics: A way to define the optimal policy? In S. Villamayor-Tomas & R. Muradian (Eds.), *The Barcelona school of ecological economics and political ecology: A companion in Honour of Joan Martinez-Alier* (pp. 327–334). Cham: Springer.

Roos, M., & Hoffart, F. M. (2021). What's problematic about mainstream climate economics? In M. Roos & F. M. Hoffart (Eds.), *Climate economics: A call for more pluralism and responsibility* (pp. 57–96). Springer Nature.

Roelfsema, M., van Soest, H. L., Harmsen, M., van Vuuren, D. P., Bertram, C., den Elzen, M., Höhne, N., Iacobuta, G., Krey, V., Kriegler, E., Luderer, G., Riahi, K., Ueckerdt, F., Després, J., Drouet, L., Emmerling, J., Frank, S., Fricko, O., Gidden, M., ... Vishwanathan, S. S. (2020). Taking stock of national climate policies to evaluate implementation of the Paris Agreement. *Nature Communications, 11*(1), 2096.

Russo, A., Mariani, M., & Caragnano, A. (2020). Exploring the determinants of green bond issuance: Going beyond the long-lasting debate on performance consequences. *Business Strategy and the Environment, 30*(1), 38–59.

Saha, D. (2024). Green climate economy. In D. J. Fiorino, T. A. Eisenstadt, & M. K. Ahluwalia (Eds.), *Elgar encyclopedia of climate policy*. London: Edward Elgar Publisher.

Shahbaz, M., Solarin, S. A., Mahmood, H., & Arouri, M. (2013). Does financial development reduce CO_2 emissions in Malaysian economy? A time series analysis. *Economic Modelling, 35*, 145–152.

Silvi, M. (2024). Behavioral economics and climate policy. In D. J. Fiorino, T. A. Eisenstadt, & M. K. Ahluwalia (Eds.), *Elgar encyclopedia of climate policy*. London: Edward Elgar Publisher.

Singla, A. (2024). The economics of climate change: Assessing the costs and benefits of mitigation and adaptation strategies. *SS Journal of Climate Economics, 1*(1), 18–23.

Schalatek, L., & Richards, J.-A. (2024). *The loss and damage fund board: Getting it right from the start*. https://us.boell.org/en/2024/03/18/loss-and-damage-fund-board-getting-it-right-start. Accessed on 29/06/2024.

Santha, S. D. (2020). *Climate change and adaptive innovation a model for social work practice*. London: Routledge.

Schalatek, L. (2012). Democratizing climate finance governance and the public funding of climate action. *Democratization, 19*(5), 951–973. https://doi.org/10.1080/13510347.2012.709690

Stowell, D. (2005). *Climate trading: Development of greenhouse gas markets*. London: Palgrave Macmillan.

Smith, K. (2013). *Environmental hazards: Assessing risk and reducing disaster* (6th ed.). London: Routledge.

Smith, P., Davis, S., Creutzig, F., Sabine, F., Jan, M., Benoit, G., Etsushi, K., Jackson, R. B., Cowie, A., Kriegler, E., van Vuuren, D. P., Rogelj, J., Ciais, P., Milne, J., Canadell, J. G., McCollum, D., Peters, G., Andrew, R., Krey, V., ... Yongsung, C. (2016). Biophysical and economic limits to negative CO_2 emissions. *Nature Climate Change, 6*, 42–50. https://doi.org/10.1038/nclimate2870

Sadorsky, P. (2010). The impact of financial development on energy consumption in emerging economies. *Energy Policy, 38*(5), 2528–2535.

Shogren, J. (2004). Climate protection: What insight can economics offer? In A. D. Owen & H. Nick (Eds.), *The economics of climate change*. London: Routledge.

Singh, T., Ahuja, R., & Malhotra, S. (2021). *Mobilizing the private sector for developing resilient infrastructure in India*. SNAPF. https://www.diw.de/documents/dokumentenarchiv/17/diw_01.c.821399.de/snapfi_developing_resilient_infrastructure_india_12072021.pdf. Accessed on 26/06/2024.

Schiermeier, Q. (2020). *The US has left the Paris climate deal—What's next?* https://doi.org/10.1038/d41586-020-03066-x. Accessed on 3/7/2024.

Song, Y., Pan, Z., Lun, F., Long, B., Liu, S., Han, G., Wang, J., Huang, N., Zhang, Z., Ma, S., Sun, G., & Liu, C. (2023). Temperature impact on the economic growth effect: Method development and model performance evaluation with subnational data in China. *EPJ Data Science, 12*(1), 1–24. https://doi.org/10.1140/epjds/s13688-023-00425-2

Tang, D. Y., & Zhang, Y. (2020). Do shareholders benefit from green bonds? *Journal of Corporate Finance, 2020*(61), 101427.

Tyndall, J. (1861). On the absorption and radiation of heat by gases and vapours, on the physical connections of radiation, absorption and conduction. *Philosophical Magazine (4th Series), 22*, 169–194.

Tan, R., & Lin, B. (2020). The influence of carbon tax on the ecological efficiency of China's energy intensive industries—A inter-fuel and inter-factor substitution perspective. *Journal of Environmental Management, 261*, 110252.

Tucker, M. (1995). Carbon dioxide emissions and global GDP. *Ecological Economics, 15*(3), 215–223. https://doi.org/10.1016/0921-8009(95)00045-3

Tol, R., & Leek, F. (1999). Economic analysis of natural disasters. In T. Downing, A. Olsthorm, & R. Tol (Eds.), *Climate change and risk*. London: Routledge.

McAllister, S. (2022). *There could be 1.2 billion climate refugees by 2050. Here's what you need to know*. https://www.zurich.com/en/media/magazine/

2022/there-could-be-1-2-billion-climate-refugees-by-2050-here-s-what-you-need-to-know. Accessed on 24/06/2024.
Mankiw, N. G. (2020). *Principles of economics* (9th ed.). Cengage Learning.
Mimura, N. (2013). Sea-level rise caused by climate change and its implications for society. *Proceedings of the Japan Academy Series B, Physical and Biological Sciences, 89*(7), 281–301. https://doi.org/10.2183/pjab.89.281
Nordhaus, W. (2013b). *The climate casino risk, uncertainty, and economics for a warming world*. Yale University Press.
Nordhaus, W. D. (1992). An optimal transition path for controlling greenhouse gases. *Science, 258*, 1315–1319.
Nordhaus, W. D. (1977). Economic growth and climate: The carbon dioxide problem. *The American Economic Review, 67*(1), 341–346.
Omotayo Oladejo, A., & Malherbe, N. (2023). Climate justice, capitalism, and the political role of the psychological professions. *Review of General Psychology*. https://doi.org/10.1177/10892680231175394
Pindyck, R. S., & Rubinfeld, D. L. (2018). *Microeconomics* (9th ed.). London: Pearson.
Unruh, G. C. (2000). Understanding carbon lock-in. *Energy Policy, 28*(12), 817–830.
Varian, H. R. (2014). *Intermediate microeconomics: A modern approach* (9th ed.). London: W.W. Norton & Company.
Van Aalst, M. K. (2006). The impacts of climate change on the risk of natural disasters. *Disasters, 30*(1), 5–18. https://doi.org/10.1111/j.1467-9523.2006.00303.x
Velders, G. J. M., Fahey, D. W., & Daniel, J. S. (2009). The large contribution of projected HFC emissions to future climate forcing. *Proceedings of the National Academy of Sciences of the United States of America, 106*, 10949–10954. https://doi.org/10.1073/pnas.0902817106
van den Bergh, J., Faber, A., Idenburg, A., & Oosterhuis, F. (2006). Survival of the greenest: Evolutionary economics and policies for energy innovation. *Environmental Sciences, 3*(1), 57–71.
Wang, W. J., Xie, P. C., Hu, J. L., & Zhao, D. Q. (2016). Analysis of relative mitigation cost advantages of carbon tax and ETS for the cement industry. *Climate Change Research, 12*(1), 53–60.
Watkiss, P. (2011). Aggregate economic measures of climate change damages: Explaining the differences and implications. *Wiley Interdisciplinary Reviews: Climate Change, 2*(3), 356–372. https://doi.org/10.1002/wcc.111
Whiteman, G. (2013). The climate casino: Risk, uncertainty, and economics for a warming world. *Nature, 502*(7472), 444–444.
Waller, M. (2001). Resilience in ecosystemic context: Evolution of the concept. *American Journal of Orthopsychiatry, 71*, 290–297.

World Bank. (2020). *Global action urgently needed to halt historic threats to poverty reduction*. https://www.worldbank.org/en/news/feature/2020/10/07/global-action-urgently-needed-to-halt-historic-threats-to-poverty-reduction. Accessed on 24/06/2024.

World Bank. (2023). *From India to Indonesia, green bonds help countries move toward sustainability*. https://www.worldbank.org/en/news/feature/2023/04/10/from-india-to-indonesia-green-bonds-help-countries-move-toward-sustainability. Access on 28/06/202.)

Yang, H., Huang, J., & Liu, D. (2020). Linking climate change and socioeconomic development to urban land use simulation: Analysis of their concurrent effects on carbon storage. *Applied Geography, 115*, 102–135.

Yang, S., Yang, J., Shi, S., Song, S., Luo, Y., & Du, L. (2023). The rising impact of urbanization-caused CO_2 emissions on terrestrial vegetation. *Ecological Indicators, 148*, 110079. https://doi.org/10.1016/j.ecolind.2023.110079

Zhang, X. P., & Cheng, X. M. (2009). Energy consumption, carbon emissions, and economic growth in China. *Ecological Economics, 68*(10), 2706–2712.

Zhang, Y., & Zhang, S. (2018). The impacts of GDP, trade structure, exchange rate and FDI inflows on China's carbon emissions. *Energy Policy, 120*, 347–353. https://doi.org/10.1016/j.enpol.2018.05.056

Zhuang, Y., & Zhang, J. (2020). Diurnal asymmetry in future temperature changes over the main Belt and Road regions. *Ecosystem Health Sustain, 61*, 1–10.

Zacharia, P. U., Gopalakrishnan, A., George, G., Muralidhar, M., & Vijayan, K. K. (2016). Climate change impact on coastal fisheries and aquaculture in the SAARC region: a country paper-Indi. In S. S. Giri (Ed.), *Climate change impact on coastal Fiaheries and aquaculture in South Asia*. Dhaka: Dhaka, Bangladesh SAARC Agriculture Centre.

Zhou, X., & Cui, Y. (2019). Green bonds, corporate performance, and corporate social responsibility. *Sustainability, 2019*(11), 6881.

CHAPTER 6

Concluding Observations

Theorizing economic risk with reference to climate change and disaster is the process of engaging the theory of utility, risk return, and capitalist economic policies. This book intends to theorize risk from an economic perspective, and it is a challenging process since economists perceive disaster and climate risk as events that displace the value of assets and capital. Scholars defined risk as how modern development and capitalists approach resources and assets. Risk is the outcome of the project of supernormal profits, and supernormal profit is the norm of modern-day capitalism. Supernormal profit is possible through the appropriation of resources and production systems. The appropriation is otherwise called monopolizing the economic process, and such a massive appropriation project challenges the economic system's resilience. The capitalist system, which generates value and controls resources, is not equipped to promote a resilient economic system. The global economy witnessed that powerful economies and Multinational and transnational corporations are institutionally incapable of dealing with the risk of climate change and disasters. However, these agencies can price the risk and transfer it. There is a normative expectation of utility from every economic decision-making, and hence, every agent prefers to keep the maximum expected utility from every economic decision.

S. M. Irshad, *Economics of Disasters and Climate Change*, Sustainable Development Goals Series,
https://doi.org/10.1007/978-981-97-9415-7_6

A market agent prefers maximizing expected utilities while keeping low transaction costs, and a welfare state agency looks for the maximum possible utility expectations from each intervention or investment. Climate and disaster risks influence the expected utility of an investment and an economic decision. Increasing emissions and the number of disaster events are pushing the expected utilities of capital investments, which is why disaster-prone areas are excluded from investments. It does not mean that these areas are totally excluded; however, for instance, the coastal regions of India wherein investments to extract resources are happening and those investments are not for promoting marginal utilities of the resources. Theoretically, risk reduces the marginal utility of resources and relates to the environmental Kuznets curve theory. The relationship between several measures of environmental deterioration and per capita income is theorized to be represented by the environmental Kuznets curve (EKC). Pollution emissions rise and environmental quality fall during the early phases of economic expansion, but the pattern reverses at high-income levels when per capita income reaches a certain threshold (which will vary depending on many factors). This suggests that the relationship between per capita income and environmental effects or emissions is an inverted U (Stern, 2017). Theoretically, EKC is a reality in the present context of extreme weather and climate risks. Higher-order environmental degradation due to extreme weather and climate risk persuade the schools to engage with the EKC theory in detail. U-shaped SKC is subject to multiple academic inquiries in the context of rising environmental risks and capitalist investment; Lorente and Álvarez-Herranz (2016), in their study, observed that an economy grows at a higher state without innovation would enable environmental risk to reappear. They proposed an N-shaped Kuznet Curve, and Wang et al. (2024), in their study, further support this argument and observe that per capita carbon emissions are positively impacted by geopolitical risk, ICT, and food security; however, the effects of composite risk, institutional quality, digital economy, energy transition, and population ageing are notably unfavourable. The shift from a U-shared to an N-shaped Kuznet curve makes it challenging to assess expected utilities. So, the negative externalities of investments could manifest in the form of risk, which further affects utility expectations. The theoretical foundation of risk economics is located in this critical context in which the risks are an everyday reality, and it moves along with the capital. So, it is true that the capital movement and its manifestation influence the economics of risks.

The rising number of disaster events and extreme climate change-induced risks are another critical challenge in perceiving the economics of risks. Anthropogenic and Anthropocene factors influence the risks and push the large geographical areas into risk, and hence sharing risks is the responsibility of the agencies. Risk sharing in economics is the sharing of profit and loss; this economic model was traced back to the early Islamic model. Such risk sharing never matches with modern capitalism. It wants to shift the risk rather than share it. The increasing disaster and climate risk-induced events make risk sharing a complex process, resulting in a differential and unequal impact of risks. Risk sharing is an economic project that needs capital support, so volume capital support influences risk sharing. In a country like India, public finance shares the risk between the affected agent and the state, so risk sharing in India is essentially a risk transfer from an agent of risk to the state—such publicly funded risk transfer and sharing results in a transformation of risk perception. The idea of state support for sharing risk means reducing the implication of risks in various aspects of life and livelihood. Risk sharing is a process of governing institutions that engage with risk reduction and mitigation. Insurance and reinsurance companies broadly capture risk sharing as financial cost sharing, enabling market-driven economies to take control of economic decisions in their favour. Risk sharing becomes a business of its own; the exponential growth of insurance companies' assets demonstrates the capitalization of risks and wealth accumulation through risk sharing. Profit accumulation of insurance companies could be read as controlled risk mitigation and risk reduction. The higher rate of profit of insurance firms means these firms have greater control over the economic cost of risk and sectoral impacts. It seems that the profit of insurance firms moves along with disaster and extreme weather risks. It excludes economically vulnerable sections from being included in the risk sharing and mitigation process; for them, public-funded risk sharing is the only option. Also, the extensive vulnerability and risk exposure levels hardly encourage insurance firms to sell risk insurance products. Disasters and climate risks increasingly affect huge populations and push many of them into poverty risk, so expecting them to buy risk insurance is impossible. Developed market economies can sell risk insurance products as risk mitigation instruments, and economies like India are struggling to finance risk sharing costs. The impact of risk on assets varies across economies; developing countries have huge, vulnerable assets on which many depend. Its use value rather than market value is essential for risk recovery; pricing those assets never ensures better economic returns to firms, and insurance becomes a loss-making business.

Risk sharing is indeed a manifestation of risk governance, and it's an institutional process driven by specific objectives and expectations. Risk governance has emerged as a discipline and an institution over a period of time. Theoretically, it is the process of controlling the agent of risk, uncertainty, and hazards. Governing risk is an institutional process that needs continuous engagement with policies and programmes for governance. It is possible through building institutions and consensus among the actors. Risk governance has multiple perspectives associated with the micro and macroeconomic structure of the economy. It also depends on the level of risk exposure and vulnerability. A market economy perceives risk governance as a project securing asset price and a structural process to protect the marginal efficiency of capital and assets. An economy in which unequal distribution of wealth and people with deprivation look for democratic and welfare-oriented risk governance. It is a process of creating institutions and also makes institutions adapt themselves to the needs of the society and economy, which look for institutional interventions. Governing the risk of climate change and disaster is possible through institution-building, and hence, it is part of the democratic process of the state. Institutions for disaster and climate risk governance are indeed the reflection of the democratization of decision-making. It is primarily because a large number of people are exposed to risk every year and hence look for risk reduction interventions that are not based on economic returns. International treaties and commitments are part of this governance. However, these global treaties are in tandem with the interests of the market economies. Evidently, developing economies hardly benefit from international treaties and rather govern the risk through domestic policies and projects. The Disaster Management Act of India 2005 is an example of a national risk governance treaty that enables the local self-government to join the government to govern the disaster risk and finance relief and response expenditures. The institutional sustainability of risk governance is entirely dependent on how the institutions are able to move along with the changing perception of risks and the everyday implications of risks. Capitalism kept the policy of adaptation and planning strategies to survive even at the cost of the environment; this also impacts risk governance. The influence of the market is visible in risk governance in terms of negotiant and searching for acceptable and tolerable risks.

Understating the economics of disaster is one of the critical inquiries that this book proposes. It never intends to approach disaster as an event in itself; instead, it is a result of the historical process and manifests in the critical context in which it affects the epistemology and institutions of governance. The economy of disaster is about how the economy is resilient to disaster risks and uncertainties. The chapter on disaster economics proposes to see it from a neoclassical and Keynesian approach, which enables a government, society, and individuals to see disaster as declining marginal efficiency of the nation and household economy. Asset vulnerability and income disparities exist in economically backward regions, and countries are subject to massive economic loss due to disasters. Still, this risk does not often manifest in all aspects of the economy; instead, it is located among the vulnerable assets and communities. It is evident in the case of India, a country in which larger geographical areas are prone to disaster, and disasters manifest recurring events. Still, India's GDP measurement has never been impacted by disasters. This is not mere negligence alone. Instead, it is a fact that the assets that are affected or destroyed by disasters never come under the market price. These are 'poor assets' with high dependencies, so the livelihood matters; however, these livelihoods are for the mere sustenance of the poor households. On the contrary, developed market economies are more susceptible to disaster risk as the cost of mitigation and relief is from market sources, and it could be the reason why academic studies on the economics of disasters are mainly from developed market economies rather than third-world economies. Treating disaster as a humanitarian crisis is dominant in countries like India; hence, relief and response expenditures are treated as a financial burden in India. The government of India is active in proposing reforms in centralizing disaster management finance and looking for options to introduce public–private partnerships in disaster finance. Apart from that Word Bank is emerging as a lead lending agency in India's disaster rehabilitation programmes. It does not mean that the World Bank gives liberal financial support. Instead, this is sectoral support and not substantial financial support. For instance, the World Bank estimated that the Uttarakhand flood in India in 2013 cost 3.8 Billion US$ (Agrawal & Chauhan, 2023); however, the total World Bank lending for the Uttarakhand flood rehabilitation project by World Bank is 346.00 Million US (World Bank, 2019). This gap explains how the World Bank assesses losses and capital to replace the losses. Almost all World Bank-funded projects follow this method because the Bank could find that sector that generates capital and positive externalities. It prioritizes economic infrastructures rather than focuses on vulnerable assets. The gap also shows the financial burden each disaster event poses to governments. Though both the union and state governments in India favour neoliberal policies, states have to promote a welfare state approach when it comes to disaster rehabilitation. This economic dilemma makes disaster economics a theoretical and policy challenge in India. Supernormal profits of the private sector are the cause of disasters in general, and the state takes to bear the cost of capital replacement.

Climate change and its implication on the economy is a matter of series academic debate, and the climate negotiation otherwise shows how powerful countries dominate the global economy. Climate change-induced risks are increasingly posing a threat to the capital value of natural capital, and as in the case of disasters, degrading the value of this natural capital further pushes a section of the population into extreme poverty and risks. Climate risks create differential impacts on society and the economy, and countries that cause emissions are indeed ruling the climate negotiations. The emission is rising, and the pricing of emissions is the agenda of climate change economics. High-income countries' economic growth depends on creating risks such as carbon emissions, and low-income and developing countries often restrict even capitalist development as a commitment to emission reduction. The economics of climate change is about emission trade and managing climate finance. The global debate and negotiation on climate change remind us of colonial economic policies. Climate finance, green climate funds, green tax, etc., are part of a more significant economic policy to ensure the financial interest of advanced capitalist industries. These facts need to be studied in the context of the fact that poor and vulnerable economies are subject to climate-induced risk a lot. Economics of climate change proposed risk as a tradable commodity. Carbon trade is otherwise a risk trade for profiteering. It is also a fact that developing and vulnerable economies do not have their climate policies, including climate action and promoting climate justice. Climate justice is possible through promoting economic justice in terms of livelihood and income security against climate risks of poor and marginal communities. Climate action and negotiations are part of the global capitalist business plan model rather than any locally specific models. One can see the apparent success of global industrial capitalist countries and firms dictating climate policies, resulting in risk accumulation and trade-offs.

Climate and disaster risks have become an integral part of the economic decision-making of both the Global South and the Global North. Still, the poor and vulnerable in the Global South are indeed more affected than the Global North. Risk is an outcome of the capitalization of resources and extensive and rapid growth paradigm. One could argue that over the past three decades, "*grow first, clean later*" has frequently been used as a standard for national programmes and as a comparison for various climate models (Kaika & Zervas, 2013; Koondhar et al., 2021). Growth is unequal, however, the climate action is to manage the unequal growth with commodifying risks. The success of climate economics is that it instituted a solution to continue capital accumulation and growth. This economy is beyond the neoclassical framework; however, the carbon trade could be read as an intervention in maintaining capital good demand.

Disaster and climate risks have increasingly become inseparable from contemporary economic and social life, and nobody is exempted from these risks. Regulating risk within the existing financial system is prioritized rather than promoting a risk-free environment. Increasing risk exposure and a higher rate of profits are indeed putting every risk reduction at stake. This book is an attempt to see disaster and climate risk economics from a critical perspective, and this inquiry needs to continue.

References

Agrawal, S., & Chauhan, A. S. (2023). *A decade after the floods, is Kedarnath safer*? https://dialogue.earth

Kaika, D., & Zervas, E. (2013). The environmental Kuznets curve (EKC) theory—Part A: Concept, causes and the CO_2 emissions case. *Energy Policy, 62*, 1392–1402.

Koondhar, M. A., Shahbaz, M., Memon, K. A., Ozturk, I., & Kong, R. (2021). A visualization review analysis of the last two decades for environmental Kuznets curve "EKC" based on co-citation analysis theory and pathfinder network scaling algorithms. *Environmental Science and Pollution Research, 28*, 16690–16706.

Lorente, D. B., & Álvarez-Herranz, A. (2016). Economic growth and energy regulation in the environmental Kuznets curve. *Environmental Science and Pollution Research, 23*, 16478–16494.

Stern, D. I. (2017). The environmental Kuznets curve. *Reference Module in Earth Systems and Environmental Sciences*. https://doi.org/10.1016/B978-0-12-409548-9.09278-2

Wang, Q., Li, Y., & Li, R. (2024). Rethinking the environmental Kuznets curve hypothesis across 214 countries: The impacts of 12 economic, institutional, technological, resource, and social factors. *Humanities and Social Sciences Communications, 11*(1), 1–19. https://doi.org/10.1057/s41599-024-02736-9

World Bank. (2019). *India–Uttarakhand disaster recovery project: Restructuring and additional financing (English)*. Washington, DC: World Bank Group. http://documents.worldbank.org/curated/en/318001551063686694/India-Uttarakhand-Disaster-Recovery-Project-Restructuring-and-Additional-Financing

Index

S. M. Irshad, *Economics of Disasters and Climate Change*, Sustainable Development Goals Series,
https://doi.org/10.1007/978-981-97-9415-7

GPSR Compliance

The European Union's (EU) General Product Safety Regulation (GPSR) is a set of rules that requires consumer products to be safe and our obligations to ensure this.

If you have any concerns about our products, you can contact us on ProductSafety@springernature.com

In case Publisher is established outside the EU, the EU authorized representative is:

Springer Nature Customer Service Center GmbH
Europaplatz 3
69115 Heidelberg, Germany

Batch number: 10703845

Printed by Printforce, the Netherlands